Children's Literature: Approaches and Territories

This volume is designed to be of use to today's teachers and students of children's literature by bringing together a collection of lively and accessible scholarly essays, which provide a social and literary perspective on the field of children's literature: its history and genres, its current concerns and its possible future directions. A companion volume, *Children's Literature: Classic Texts and Contemporary Trends* (ed. Montgomery and Watson, 2009), provides a complementary set of essays combining case studies of important classic texts with a survey of contemporary trends in children's fiction. These two volumes can be used separately or together as the basis for study in this field.

Both Readers are part of the Open University course Children's Literature (EA300), a level 3 undergraduate course which can count towards many Open University degrees at Bachelor's level, and specifically the BAs in Humanities, Literature (and Humanities with Literature), English Language and Literature and Childhood and Youth Studies. The course is also part of the Diplomas in Literature and in Literature and Creative Writing.

Details of these and other Open University courses can be obtained from the Student Registration and Enquiry Service, The Open University, PO Box 197, Milton Keynes MK7 6BJ, UK: telephone +44 (0) 845 300 6090, e-mail general-enquiries@open.ac.uk.

Alternatively, you may wish to visit the Open University website at www.open.ac.uk, where you can learn more about the wide range of courses and packs offered at all levels by The Open University.

Children's Literature: Approaches and Territories

Edited by

Janet Maybin and Nicola J. Watson

palgrave
macmillan

The Open
University

First published 2009 by
PALGRAVE MACMILLAN in association with THE OPEN UNIVERSITY.

The Open University, Walton Hall, Milton Keynes, MK7 6AA

Palgrave Macmillan in the UK is an imprint of Macmillan Publishers Limited, registered in England, company number 785998, of Houndmills, Basingstoke, Hampshire RG21 6XS.

Palgrave Macmillan in the US is a division of St Martin's Press LLC, 175 Fifth Avenue, New York, NY 10010.

Palgrave Macmillan is the global academic imprint of the above companies and has companies and representatives throughout the world.

Palgrave® and Macmillan® are registered trademarks in the United States, the United Kingdom, Europe and other countries

ISBN 978–0–230–22713–2   paperback

This book is printed on paper suitable for recycling and made from fully managed and sustained forest sources. Logging, pulping and manufacturing processes are expected to conform to the environmental regulations of the country of origin.

A catalogue record for this book is available from the British Library.

A catalog record for this book is available from the Library of Congress.

10   9   8   7   6   5   4   3   2   1
18   17   16   15   14   13   12   11   10   09

Printed and bound in Great Britain by
CPI Antony Rowe, Chippenham and Eastbourne

Contents

Figures

Plates

(between pp. 176 and 177)

1 'Shock-headed Peter', from Heinrich Hoffmann, *The English Struwwelpeter* (1845), Dragon's World Ltd, 1996

2 Edward Viles, 'Black Bess, or 'The Knight of the Road', cover of a 'penny dreadful' magazine (1866)

3 'Alice and the Duchess', from Lewis Carroll, *Alice's Adventures in Wonderland*, illus. John Tenniel (1865), London: Macmillan & Co. Ltd, 1962

4 'The Queen of Hearts', from the series *R. D. Caldecott's Collection of Pictures and Songs*, London: Routledge, 1881

5 'Sleeping Beauty', from *The Sleeping Beauty Picture Book*, illus. Walter Crane, London: Routledge and New York: Dodd Mead & Co., 1911

6 'Biggles', from Captain W.E. Johns, *Biggles in the Jungle*, London: Oxford University Press and Geoffrey Cumberlege, 1949

7 Front cover, *Beano* magazine (no. 367, 30 July 1949), illus. Dudley D. Watkins, Dundee: D.C. Thomson

8 Front cover, Enid Blyton, *First Term at Malory Towers*, first edition, illus. Stanley Lloyd, London: Methuen & Co. Ltd, 1946

9 Front cover, Jacqueline Wilson, *Girls in Tears*, London: Doubleday, 2002

10 Front cover, Bertha Upton, *The Adventures of Two Dutch Dolls*, illus. Florence K. Upton, London & New York: Longmans Green & Co., 1895

11 From Julius Lester, *Sam and the Tigers*, illus. Jerry Pinkney, Dial Books for Young Readers, 1996; Puffin Books, 2000

12 Front cover, Kate Greenaway, *Under the Window*, London: G. Routledge & Sons, 1879

13 Front cover, Roald Dahl, *Revolting Rhymes*, illus. Quentin Blake, London: Puffin Books, [1984] 2001

14 From Jan Pieńkowski and Helen Nicoll, *Meg and Mog*, London: Puffin Books, 1972

15 Front cover, Alan Garner, *Elidor*, illus. Charles Keeping, London: Collins, 1965; Puffin Books, 1967

16 Title-page verso, David Macaulay, *Black and White*, Boston: Houghton Mifflin, 1990

17 'I think ... someone's out there', from David Wiesner, *The Three Pigs*, New York: Clarion Books, 2001

Acknowledgements

This volume was produced by the team responsible for preparing the Open University course in Children's Literature (EA300) and was a collaboration between the Faculties of Education and Arts. Course team members are credited as the authors of the Introductions for each section. In the preparation of this course we consulted widely, and are grateful for advice provided by Peter Barnes, Peter Hunt, Kim Reynolds, Kay Sambell, Philip Seargeant, Nigel Thomas and other critical readers of the material in draft.

The editors would also like to acknowledge the many people who worked behind the scenes to produce this book. At the Open University, we would like to thank Liz Camp, course manager, and Christine Hardwick, course secretary, for all their help with the preparation of this manuscript and for making sure deadlines were met. Gill Gowans and Gary Nelmes also worked tirelessly to ensure that the book came together on schedule.

At Palgrave we would like to thank Senior Editor Kate Haines, Production Editor Sarah Fry, Administrative Secretary Felicity Noble and Senior Marketing Executive Abigail Coften.

For copyright text

The editor and publishers wish to thank the following for permission to use copyright material:

Ashgate Publishing Group for material from Nicholas Tucker, 'Setting the Scene' from *Children's Book Publishing in Britain Since 1945*, ed. K. Reynolds and N. Tucker, Scolar Press (1998) pp. 1–19;

Joseph Bristow for material from his book, *Empire Boys: Adventures in a Man's World*, HarperCollins Academic (1991) pp. 4–52;

Felicity Bryan Literary Agency on behalf of the Estate of the author for material from Humphrey Carpenter, *Secret Gardens: The Golden Age of Children's Literature*, Allen and Unwin (1985) pp. 1–19. Copyright © Humphrey Carpenter 1985;

Cambridge University Press for material from Deborah Cartmell, 'Adapting Children's Literature' from *The Cambridge Companion to Literature on Screen*, ed. Deborah Cartmell and Imelda Whelehan (2007) pp. 167–80;

Continuum Publishing Group for material from Morag Styles, *From the Garden to the Street* (1998) pp. 186–96;

Copyright Clearance Center on behalf of Taylor & Francis for material from Bette Goldstone, 'The Paradox of Space in Postmodernism Picturebooks' in *Postmodernism Picturebooks: Play, Paraody and Self-referentiality*, ed. L. Sipe and S. Pantaleo, Routledge (2008) pp. 117–29, and L. Hutcheon, *A Theory of Adaptation*, Routledge (2006) pp. 8–9, 176–7;

The Johns Hopkins University Press for material from Kenneth Kidd, 'Prizing Children's Literature: The Case of Newbery Gold', *Children's Literature*, 35 (2007) pp. 166–190, Copyright © The Hollins University Corporation; and L. Hutcheon, 'Harry Potter and the novice's confession', *The Lion and the Unicorn*, 32:2 (2008) pp. 169–79, Copyright © The Johns Hopkins University Press;

Oxford University Press for Jack Zipes, 'Fairy Tales and Folk Tales' from *Oxford Encyclopedia of Children's Literature*, ed. Jack Zipes (2006);

The Society of Authors on behalf of the Literary Trustees of the author for extracts from Walter de la Mare, 'The Listeners' from *The Complete Poems of Walter de la Mare* (1975 reprint);

Taylor & Francis Books UK for material from W Moebius, 'Introduction to picturebook codes', *Word and Image*, 2:2 (1986) pp. 141–58; Susanne Greenhalgh, 'Drama' from *International Companion Encyclopedia of Children's Literature*, ed. Peter Hunt, Routledge (1996) pp. 599–613, and J. Whalley, 'The Development of Illustrated Texts and Picture Books' from *International Companion Encyclopedia of Children's Literature*, ed Peter Hunt, 2nd edn, Routledge (2004) pp. 220–30.

For copyright images

The editors and publishers wish to thank the following for permission to reproduce copyright material:

Alamy Ltd for Plate 6 © Antiques & Collectables/Alamy and Figure 17 © The Print Collector/Alamy;

Bridgeman Art Library for Figure 2 © Norwich Castle Museum and Art Gallery/The Bridgeman Art Library;

British Library for Plate 2 © British Library Board. All Rights Reserved, shelfmark: C.140.a.15, cover, Figure 1 © British Library Board. All Rights Reserved, shelfmark: ch.760/6, Figure 5 © British Library Board. All Rights

Reserved, shelfmark: C.117.d.5 and Figure 11 © British Library Board. All Rights Reserved, shelfmark: C.59.a.19;

Catherine Ashmore for Plate 20;

Curtis Brown Group Ltd for Figure 6, illustration from *The Wind in the Willows* by Kenneth Grahame, illus. E.H. Shepard (1930), Methuen & Co. Ltd, 1949. Copyright © The Estate of E.H. Shepard, reproduced with permission of Curtis Brown Group Ltd, London;

Curtis Brown Group Ltd for Figure 20, illustration from *Stories of Winnie-the-Pooh* by A.A. Milne, illus. E.H. Shepard, Methuen & Co. Ltd, 1989. Copyright © The Estate of E.H. Shepard, reproduced with permission of Curtis Brown Group Ltd, London;

D.C. Thomson & Co. Ltd for Plate 7, from the *Beano*, Issue No. 367, 30 July 1949;

Dial Books for Young Readers, A Division of Penguin Young Readers Group, A Member of Penguin Group (USA) Inc., 345 Hudson Street, New York, NY 10014, and Sheldon Fogelman Agency, Inc. for Plate 11, an illustration from *Sam and the Tigers* by Julius Lester, illustration copyright © 1996 by Jerry Pinkney. First published in the United States by Dial Books for Young Readers. All Rights Reserved. Used with permission;

HarperCollins Publishers for Plate 18, screenshot from www.thenightmare room.com by R.L. Stine;

Houghton Mifflin Harcourt Publishing Company for Plate 16, illustration from *Black and White* by David Macaulay. Copyright © 1990 by David Macaulay. Reprinted by permission of Houghton Mifflin Harcourt Publishing Company. All rights reserved;

Houghton Mifflin Harcourt Publishing Company for Plate 17, Figures 22, 23, and 24, illustrations from *The Three Pigs* by David Wiesner. Copyright © 2001 by David Wiesner. Reprinted by permission of Clarion Books, an imprint of Houghton Mifflin Harcourt Publishing Company. All rights reserved;

Houghton Mifflin Harcourt Publishing Company for Figure 21, from *Curious George* by H.A. Rey. Copyright © 1941, and renewed 1969 by Margret E. Rey. Curious George is a registered trademark of Houghton Mifflin Harcourt Publishing Company. Reprinted by permission of Houghton Mifflin Harcourt Publishing Company. All rights reserved;

Macmillan Children's Books for Plate 3, 'Alice and the Duchess', from *Alice's Adventures in Wonderland* by Lewis Carroll, illus. John Tenniel (1865), Copyright © 1962 by Macmillan & Co. Ltd;

Macmillan Children's Books for Figure 8, frontispiece from *William the Conqueror* by Richmal Crompton, illus. 'Thomas Henry' (Thomas Henry Fisher) (1926), George Newnes Ltd, 1931. Copyright © Macmillan Children's Books 1947;

Mary Evans Picture Library for Figure 4;

Pavilion Children's Books, Anova Books Ltd for Plate 1, from *The English Struwwelpeter* by Dr Heinrich Hoffmann, © Pavilion Children's Books 1996;

Penguin Books Ltd for Plate 15, front cover of *Elidor* by Alan Garner, Collins, 1965; Puffin Books, 1967. Copyright Alan Garner, 1965. Reproduced by permission of Penguin Books Ltd;

Penguin Books Ltd and Jan Pieńkowski for Plate 14, from 'Meg and Mog' by Helen Nicoll and Jan Pieńkowski, Puffin Books, 2004. Reproduced by permission of Jan Pieńkowski and Penguin Books Ltd;

Penguin Books Ltd for Plate 13, front cover of *Revolting Rhymes* by Roald Dahl, illus. Quentin Blake, Puffin Books, 1984, 2001. Text copyright © Roald Dahl Nominee Ltd, 1982. Illustrations copyright © Quentin Blake, 1982, 1984, 2001. Reproduced by permission of Penguin Books Ltd;

Princeton University Library for Plate 4, 'The Queen of Hearts' by Randolph Caldecott, Cotsen Children's Library, Department of Rare Books and Special Collections, Princeton University Library;

Princeton University Library for Figure 3, from *The Holiday Spy*, Cotsen Children's Library, Princeton University Library, Department of Rare Books and Special Collections, Call no.: Eng 18/Newbery 6771;

Project Gutenberg for Plate 12, front cover of *Under the Window* by Kate Greenaway, G. Routledge & Sons, 1879;

Simon & Schuster for Plate 19, from *Alice's Adventures in Wonderland*, a pop-up adaptation of Lewis Carroll's original tale, by Robert Sabuda. Copyright © 2003 Robert Sabuda, reprinted with the permission of Little Simon, an imprint of Simon & Schuster Children's Publishing Division;

The New York Public Library for Plate 5, from *The Sleeping Beauty Picture Book* by Walter Crane, Dodd Mead & Co., 1911, Children's Center, The New York Public Library, Astor, Lenox and Tilden Foundations;

The Random House Group Ltd for Plate 9, from *Girls in Tears* by Jacqueline Wilson, Doubleday, 2002. Reprinted by permission of The Random House Group Ltd;

Tony Summerfield, The Enid Blyton Society for Plate 8, from *First Term at Malory Towers*, by Enid Blyton, illus. Stanley Lloyd, first published Methuen & Co. Ltd, 1946;

V&A Images, Victoria and Albert Museum for Plate 10, from *The Adventures of Two Dutch Dolls* by Florence K. Upton, words by Bertha Upton, Longman's Green & Co., 1895, Renier Collection, Image no.: 2006AN2215 and Figure 19, from *The Children in the Wood*, Image no.: 2007BM3039;

Warner Bros Entertainment, Inc. for Figure 18, from *Little Women*, © Turner Entertainment Co. A Warner Bros. Entertainment Company. All Rights Reserved.

Introduction

Janet Maybin and Nicola J. Watson

Children's literature is, as Peter Hunt has argued, a 'remarkable area of writing: it is one of the roots of western culture, it is enjoyed passionately by adults as well as children, and it has exercised huge talents over hundreds of years' (1994: 1). The enjoyment brought by children's literature is generally taken for granted – as it relates to child-readers. Less evident, less confessed, but deeply seated, is the continuing foundational investment of adult readers in their childhood reading. As a field of academic study rather than a source of private pleasures, children's literature has not always been accorded the status that Hunt gives it. The academic study of children's literature has only become firmly established relatively recently; until the 1970s, it tended to be dismissed as trivial, easy, often ephemeral and fundamentally 'childish'. While adults might recall with pleasure the books they read as children, the idea that children's books could be studied seriously, for what they said about literature or, indeed, about childhood, was a radical one, which has taken time to gain ground. Yet it is arguably the case that children's literature is not merely one of the roots of Western literature and culture, but a foundation of shared intergenerational national and international culture, a barometer of beliefs and anxieties about children and childhood and a body of literature with its own genres, classic texts and avant-garde experiments. These features recommend it as an important area of interest for scholars, whether of literature, or of childhood, or of culture more generally.

These are exciting times for children's literature. The turn of the millennium has been a golden time for children's book publishing and associated art forms and industries. Arguably, children's books have achieved unprecedented public visibility, sales and popularity. A market which has traditionally been seen as mostly a matter of maintaining and republishing past established titles suddenly expanded into publishing new titles at an unprecedented rate. The 1990s were characterised by huge market excitement about best-selling series fiction, and especially by the astonishing global phenomenon of Harry Potter, which suggested an unsuspected appetite in the modern child for reading at epic length. A children's author, Jacqueline Wilson, was hailed as the most borrowed author from British libraries and an International Library of Children's Literature opened in Tokyo. Another children's author, Philip Pullman, became the first winner of the Whitbread Prize with a children's book. The British post of Children's Laureate was inaugurated in 1999, filled initially by Quentin Blake, and in 2008 Jon Scieszka became the first Children's Laureate in the USA. Children's literature became a major category at literary festivals, with sell-out readings by famous authors. Book prizes for children's literature proliferated and children's authors were showered with honours, including honorary degrees from many universities. There was a renaissance in storytelling performances for children (and adults) in school and elsewhere, despite and alongside a proliferation of other media directed to children: television, film, DVDs, computer games and the internet, all of which presented fundamental challenges to traditional conceptions of reading, together with new narrative possibilities. The remit of children's literature extended into a burgeoning list of titles for young adults, and the success of crossover fiction, and picture books for older readers (most notably manga) suggested that there was a profound sea change taking place in the sense of what differentiated literature for the young from that for grown-ups.

Many books, old and new, were adapted to both stage and screen, in the aggregate enjoying phenomenal financial success (e.g. *Harry Potter and the Philosopher's Stone* was directed by Chris Columbus and released by Warner Brothers in 2001, with films of the sequels appearing every one or two years. Nicholas Hytner directed a two-part, six-hour performance of Pullman's trilogy *His Dark Materials* at London's Royal National Theatre, 2003–4 (see Plate 20), the theatre adaptation of Jamila Gavin's *Coram Boy* transferred successfully from London to Broadway, New York in 2007 and the National Theatre's production of Michael Morpurgo's *War Horse* enjoyed two sell-out seasons in 2007–8, transferring to the West End in 2009.) Places associated with classic children's writing boomed; there were unprecedented numbers of visitors to Beatrix Potter's house in the Lake District, to original sites for the film version of Hogwarts Academy, including Christ Church, Oxford, and to sites in Kent associated with Milne's Winnie-the-Pooh. The house on Prince Edward Island, Canada, which commemorates L.M. Montgomery's *Anne of Green Gables*, draws 350,000 visitors each year. In 2005 the Roald Dahl Museum and Story Centre was opened in Buckinghamshire, and Newcastle opened an archive and visitors' centre,

'Seven Stories', devoted to the manuscripts of children's authors. The British Library in London had a major exhibition devoted to children's books in 2002, and one on children's poetry in 2009. In this context, it was not surprising that suggestions were made that this was a Third Golden Age of children's literature, rivalling the glories of the First Golden Age (late Victorian and Edwardian) and the Second Golden Age (in the 1960s and 1970s). Alongside this euphoria ran perennial anxieties that children (especially boys) were not reading, or were only reading rubbish, or watching screen adaptations, that picture books were in decline, and that the imaginative and literary quality of writing for children (and so of childhood) would be engulfed by increasing commercialisation and merchandising.

In tandem with the unprecedented visibility and popularity of children's books and associated cultural activity, in many ways children's literature has come of age as an academic field of study: universities in both North America and Britain boast not only postgraduate but undergraduate courses, prestigious professorships, and funded centres of research excellence. Scholarly journals such as *The Lion and the Unicorn, Children's Literature in Education* and *Children's Literature Quarterly*, all launched in the 1970s, have continued to thrive. The growing body of criticism and numbers of international conferences and associations are reflected on the bookshelves of major academic bookshops. Blackwell's in Oxford, for instance, now devotes an entire section to children's literature, stocked with encyclopedias, anthologies, readers and companions. The field, in short, has come a long way from its roots in early twentieth-century bibliophilia. Rising above early anxieties that children's literature was easy, trivial and, above all, 'childish', it has now become firmly established, with a growing body of well-respected international scholars conducting lively theoretical and critical debates which are showing signs of obtaining an increasing purchase on the older studies of literature and childhood, amongst others.

All this said, there are some serious general difficulties in conceptualising and studying children's literature. What children's literature *is* remains an area for continuing debate, centred on the conception of children's literature itself. It is an oddity in being a category defined by its putative and implied consumers. The term itself appears to be an oxymoron: how can books which are written by adults, published and disseminated by adults, and largely bought by adults be appropriately called 'children's literature'? Jacqueline Rose's seminal study *The Case of Peter Pan; or, the Impossibility of Children's Literature* (1984) remains the foundational statement of this paradox, arguing that children's literature has nothing much to do with real children and their reading experience, but everything to do (at any rate in the twentieth century) with how adults view childhood. Rose, followed, qualified and contested by others, finds in this a rationale for viewing so-called children's literature as symptomatic of the entire culture, a body of work which is just as much about what it means to be 'grown-up', arguably the subject matter of all literature, as about what it might mean to be a child.

There are affiliated difficulties to do with the project of literary and cultural criticism as it operates in relation to children's literature. One relates to the diverse nature of the genres involved and associated questions about their appropriate critical treatment. For example, can the sorts of literary criteria by which adult literature is judged be usefully applied to picture books such as Beatrix Potter's *The Tale of Peter Rabbit* or Anthony Browne's *Voices in the Park?* Another is to do with audience. What is to be done when adult evaluation of children's books diverges from child enthusiasm, as in the notorious and well-documented struggle over the presence on children's bookshelves of Enid Blyton's output? Is what a real child-reader thinks about a book (given that they are its presumed and implied audience) more valid than what an adult literary critic might think? This raises yet another problem, to do with the purposes of such criticism. How are children's books to be evaluated – by adult literary and aesthetic criteria? As documents in a cultural history of childhood? Or are they essentially to be viewed as a didactic and pedagogic literature, and, if so, is the function of criticism to focus on endorsing or condemning the conceptions of the child embodied by various texts and the theories of learning with which they are underpinned?

These difficulties are compounded by the sheer range of material that has at different times and places counted as children's literature. In addition to fiction, 'children's literature' might well encompass picture books, storytelling, drama, television, ballet and film and the wide variety of nursery rhymes, ballads and limericks typically found in poetry anthologies for children. It might include popular fiction by Enid Blyton and Jacqueline Wilson alongside prestigious classics, extend to magazines, manga and other comics, and expand to take in pop-up books, toy theatres, hybrid picture-book toys and Japanese mobile-phone novels. Where might computer gaming and theme-park rides, both often derived from familiar literary narratives (think of Disneyworld's rides themed to *Peter Pan* and *The Wind in the Willows*), fall in relation to children's 'literature'? Are books for young adults also 'children's literature'? What about non-fiction, which comprises a substantial amount of the material generated for children?

Faced with this wealth of possibilities, and acknowledging both the impossibility and inadvisability of trying to be comprehensive in such a volume, we have adopted a fairly broad and inclusive concept of children's literature, in terms of mode, genre, popularity and target age. Our focus has been on the anglophone tradition, with some reference to materials that have fed into it in translation. This decision has been strategic, in that it allows for an adequately thorough exploration of one tradition amongst the many that we might have featured (see e.g. Beckett and Nikolajeva, 2006). But it has also been driven by a sense that the anglophone tradition of children's literature has historically had a disproportionate and avant-garde influence upon the development of the *idea* of a children's literature. Inevitably, this influential body of work reflects the particular sociohistorical context in which it developed and the essays in this volume include consideration of how children's books, and their reception and critique, have been shaped by social processes and historical circumstance. We have chosen, too, to foreground the changing materiality of the children's book within this tradition, by providing both extensive illustration throughout the text, and a section devoted entirely to colour plates, designed to serve as a free-standing picture-essay upon the look of the child's book from the early nineteenth century through to the early twenty-first.

Each section in the volume focuses on a topic which has preoccupied recent scholarship in the field. Sections are prefaced by short introductions which explain the significance of the area of work presented, introduce the individual essays and offer suggestions for further reading. This framework may be used as the basis for a series of seminars organised around key questions, as suggested below.

The opening section, 'Purposes and histories', focuses on some of the most basic questions in the field. What counts as children's literature? What is its purpose and why is it important? How has it changed over time and does it display enduring themes? Is children's literature essentially conservative or radical? The essays in this section (Hunt, Zipes, Grenby, Carpenter, Paul and Reynolds) address debates about the nature and significance of children's literature, trace its early history and discuss its ideological content and impact. Together, they provide an introduction to important issues which underpin current work in the field.

The essays in the second section, 'Publishing, Prizes and Popularity', explore questions connected with the valuing and consumption of children's literature. Who decides what counts as prestigious or 'popular' literature for children and what kind of criteria do they use? In what ways do judgements about books reflect different social and commercial investments, and differing conceptions of childhood? How are recent changes in publishing and marketing affecting the nature of children's literature and the ways in which individual books are valued? Starting with a famous essay about teenagers' personal reading preferences in the late nineteenth century (Salmon), the section includes discussion of Victorian penny dreadfuls and the shaping of colonial masculinity (Bristow), the appeal of Enid Blyton (Rudd), changing publishing practices over the course of the twentieth century and into the twenty-first (Tucker, Squires) and the role of literary prizes in the marketing and promotion of particular kinds of children's books (Kidd).

The section on 'Poetry' pays an unusual amount of attention to what has been a neglected area in children's literature studies. Questions addressed here include: How have particular poems, songs, rhymes and various oral forms come to be regarded as 'children's poetry'? What criteria have underpinned the choice of poems in the anthologies which introduce most children to the genre? Does poetry for children have its own distinctive forms and styles? The three essays trace the history of poems and verse written for children or assigned to them (Styles), examine the purposes and nature of anthologies from different periods (Styles) and suggest an approach to the critical analysis of children's poetry informed by stylistics (Jeffries).

Making space for another relatively neglected area by comparison to fiction, the fourth section, 'Story-telling, Stage and Screen', provides three essays designed to serve as starting-points for the study of different types of dramatic entertainment for children: from story-telling (Swann) and live theatre (Greenhalgh) to screen entertainment derived from children's fiction (Cartmell). Questions addressed by this section include: What different kinds of stories in performance might be included in 'children's literature' and how have their distinctive features changed over time? What kinds of transformation, technical, political and cultural, are involved in translating a children's book onto the screen?

The fifth section, 'Words and Pictures', foregrounds the importance of pictures in children's books whether as a form of text for the very young, decoration or illustration. It includes an historical account of the development of illustration and the picture book (Whalley), a seminal essay analysing the relationship of words and pictures in such texts (Moebius) and a consideration of postmodern explorations of space in more recent picture books (Goldstone). Questions related to this section include: How have the features of children's book illustration and picture books changed over time? How do words combine with pictures and the material features of the book to produce different meanings and aesthetic effects? What kinds of ideas are explored in postmodern picture books?

The concluding section, 'Contemporary Transformations', takes as its subject the transformation of old traditions and reading practices in the twenty-first century. Questions addressed here include: How is literature transformed across different media and what is the value of adaptation? What different processes are involved in translation? How are digital media changing children's literature and their reading practices? How are current changes in the conceptualisation of childhood affecting the nature of children's literature and its readership? Thus Hutcheon examines the migration of story across media and the proliferation of new modes, Gupta considers cross-cultural adaptation with special reference to Harry Potter, and Flewitt explores the generic possibilities of new technologies. Lastly, Falconer speculates on the emergence of crossover fiction, and what it might tell us about modern conceptions and valuations of childhood and adulthood.

The colour-plate insert offers a chance to readers to examine how the look of children's books has changed over time. It allows comparison between the earliest colour lithography in the 1840s exemplified by *Struwwelpeter*, the woodblock printing of the late nineteenth century of which Crane, Caldecott and Greenaway made such good use, and modern four-colour offset lithography which heralded what many regard as the Golden Age of the picture book in the 1960s. Together, these plates raise a number of questions: What is the relation through the history of children's literature between the luxury illustrated hardback and the popular magazine, flimsy penny dreadful and ephemeral paperback? What might these various visual depictions of children (and adults) in fiction, stage or film suggest about changing versions of childhood? How have they imagined the private and the public, the rural and the urban? How are girls depicted by comparison to boys? What, finally, can they tell us about what has 'sold' children's literature to both children and adults?

References

Beckett, S.L. and Nikolajeva, M. (eds) 2006. *Beyond Babar: The European Tradition of Children's Literature*. Langham, MD, Scarecrow.

Hunt, P. 1994. *An Introduction to Children's Literature*. Oxford, Oxford University Press.

Rose, J. 1984. *The Case of Peter Pan; or, the Impossibility of Children's Literature*. London, Macmillan.

1
Purposes and Histories

Introduction
Heather Montgomery

The scholarly study of children's literature is a relatively new endeavour and it is only recently that a large body of critical literature has grown up around children's books. The folklorists Peter and Iona Opie laid important groundwork for the study of children's cultural worlds in producing compilations of nursery rhymes (1951) and fairy tales (1974), and Harvey Darton's early study *Children's Books in England* (1932) remains an important authoritative point of reference on children's literature. *The Cool Web: The Pattern of Children's Reading* edited by Margaret Meek and colleagues (1977) provided a further landmark but, on the whole, children's books were long excluded from more general literary criticism. One of the earliest works of criticism, John Rowe Townsend's *Written for Children*, was first published in 1965, has gone through six editions since then, and stands out as a pioneering volume. Similarly Humphrey Carpenter's landmark *Secret Gardens* (1985), which came out of Carpenter and Prichard's work on writing *The Oxford Companion to Children's Literature* (1984), a project they took over from the Opies, is another important achievement in the field. Despite this slow start, the study of children's literature is now a thriving and dynamic field and, as the essays below will show, children's books are much theorised and analysed.

The first section of this reader contains seven essays which raise questions about the nature, significance and purposes of children's literature and the import of it as a field of academic study, as well as supplying its history in outline. Taken together, they make claims for the importance of children's literature. They challenge the notion that children's literature is simplistic or marginal, show how children's literature is shaped by wider sociocultural changes and indeed contributes to those changes, and examine how the study of children's books can reveal the way they reflect and construct social attitudes towards children as well as pointing to adult anxieties about contemporary childhoods.

The essays

Peter Hunt's 'Instruction and Delight' provides a starting point for the study of children's literature, challenging typical assumptions made about writing for children: that it is trivial, easy, often ephemeral and fundamentally 'childish'; that it is marginal to literature for adults; that it is intrinsically conservative and that reading it constitutes merely an escape from the harsh realities of adult life. He tackles the specific question of what children's literature is for, what its appropriate subject matter is, and discusses the perennial question of whether its role is primarily to entertain or to instruct. Hunt additionally asks whether children's literature is inevitably something imposed on children by adults to reflect their own politicised conceptualisations of childhood.

The next three essays together supply the outline of a history of British children's literature from its origins in oral culture to the publication of *Alice's Adventures in Wonderland* in 1865 and the inauguration of the so-called First Golden Age. Jack Zipes's 'Fairy Tales and Folktales' explores how fairy tales became associated with literature specified to children. Fairy tales are often seen as the epitome of stories for children in that they are simple and repetitive, based on standard characters and stock phrases. Andrew Lang's series of coloured fairy-story books, starting with *The Blue Fairy Book* (1889), introduced many children to the formula in the late nineteenth and early twentieth century, while in the later twentieth century, it was Walt Disney's film interpretations on film that were most influential. Disney adapted many fairy tales for the cinema specifically as wholesome family entertainment, with the result that in the twentieth century the fairy tale became firmly identified with both children and childishness. From a historical perspective, however, fairy tales have not always been identified with children; as Zipes argues, fairy tales were oral tales told by adults, which children may have heard but which were not designed for them. Zipes goes on to discuss the longevity of fairy tales within print culture.

Matthew Grenby's essay, 'Children's Literature: Birth, Infancy, Maturity' analyses the rise of children's literature in the eighteenth century through to the great explosion of British children's literature in the second half of the nineteenth century, and provides a revisionary take on received histories.

Grenby agrees with the customary location of the beginnings of anglophone children's literature proper in the eighteenth century, with the first publication of novels and books written especially for children in which other children were the heroes and heroines. He warns, however, against espousing too uncritically a comfortable and teleological narrative in which children's literature has got better, less moralistic, and increasingly child-focused. He writes of the wide variety of literature for children in the eighteenth and nineteenth centuries, discussing the ways that both child-readers and the authors who wrote for them subverted and resisted didacticism.

Humphrey Carpenter's landmark essay, extracted from *Secret Gardens* (Carpenter, 1985), picks up the historical narrative from Grenby and focuses on the nineteenth century in more detail, examining in particular a rise in the quality and quantity of children's literature from the 1860s onwards. He discusses how the changing roles of children, the expansion of empire and the demographics of the period all had an impact on imaginative writing for children. He analyses how changing constructions of the child, inspired by Romantic sensibilities, led to new ideas about both what they should read and how they should be portrayed in literature.

Kim Reynolds's 'Transformative Energies' picks up from Hunt's meditations upon the ideological leanings of children's literature and makes the case for regarding it as 'radical'. She refutes the claim that children's literature is innately conservative in terms of style, content and in the way it frames the adult–child relationship. Some commentators, such as Jacqueline Rose (1984), have argued that children's literature is reactionary and nostalgic, inventing a culture of childhood which has no true relation to the lives of real children but which is calculated instead to provide comfort and reassurance to adults. Reynolds disputes this, arguing that the children's books of one generation prepare the way for adult books of the next, and, further, that children's literature is both a 'safe house' for literary modes temporarily out of fashion and a breeding ground and incubator for future innovation. She argues that children's literature has had a direct, significant and measurable influence on adult writing, and that some of the most innovative children's writers of recent years, such as Philip Pullman, have had important and far-reaching effects on all literature, not simply that for children. Reynolds argues that children's literature does not simply reflect cultural change, but prefigures and sets this change in motion and therefore properly lies at the vanguard of social and literary study.

Reynolds's sense of children's literature as formally avant-garde is tested and contested in Hunt's second essay for this volume, 'The Same but Different: Conservation and Revolution in Children's Fiction'. In it he extends the historical narrative, analysing the two acknowledged Golden Ages of children's literature, the late nineteenth century and the 1960s–1970s, and speculating about whether the 1990s, when books by authors such as J.K. Rowling, Jacqueline Wilson and Philip Pullman were selling in their millions to adults and children alike, ushered in a Third Golden Age. He also discusses how many of the themes and concerns of children's literature have not changed fundamentally over the last 150 years, despite superficial differences, and how even the multimedia world of the early twenty-first century displays continuities with this recognisable tradition.

Finally, Lissa Paul's 'Multicultural Agendas' shifts the focus away from the UK to her native Canada, and back to didacticism in the shape of multiculturalism. By tracing the social history of the concept and explaining in detail the historical, social and cultural context in which it developed, she shows the impact that changing ideas about gender, ethnicity and disability have had on the development of children's literature, both in Canada and elsewhere. This, she argues, was not simply a one-way process; as well as reflecting these changes, children's literature also contributed to the cultural shift towards inclusion and diversity. Like Reynolds, Paul argues that children's literature both reflects social change and helps to shape it.

References

Carpenter, H. 1985. *Secret Gardens: A Study of the Golden Age of Children's Literature*. London, Allen & Unwin.

Carpenter, H. and Prichard, M. 1984. *The Oxford Companion to Children's Literature*. Oxford, Oxford University Press.

Darton, H. 1932. *Children's Books in England: Five Centuries of Social Life*. Cambridge, Cambridge University Press.

Meek, M., Warlow, A. and Barton, G. (eds) 1977. *The Cool Web: The Pattern of Children's Reading*. London, Bodley Head.

Opie, P. and Opie, I. 1951. *The Oxford Dictionary of Nursery Rhymes*. Oxford, Oxford University Press.

Opie, P. and Opie, I. 1974. *The Classic Fairy Tales*. Oxford, Oxford University Press.

Reynolds, K. 2007. *Radical Children's Literature: Future Visions and Aesthetic Transformations in Juvenile Fiction*. London, Palgrave Macmillan.

Rose, J. 1984. *The Case of Peter Pan, or, the Impossibility of Children's Fiction*. London, Macmillan.

Townsend, J.R. 1965. *Written for children: An Outline of English Children's Literature*. London, Garnet Miller.

Zipes, J. (ed.) 2006. *Oxford Encyclopaedia of Children's Literature*. Oxford, Oxford University Press.

Further reading

Avery, G. 1975. *A Study of the Heroes and Heroines of Children's Fiction 1770–1950*. London, Hodder & Stoughton.

Avery, G. 1994. *Behold the Child: American Children and Their Books, 1621–1922*. London, Bodley Head.

Briggs, J., Butts, D. and Grenby, M. 2008. *Popular Children's Literature in Britain*. Aldershot, Ashgate.

Hunt, P. 1994. *An Introduction to Children's Literature*. Oxford, Oxford University Press.

Lesnik-Oberstein, K. (ed.) 2004. *Children's Literature: New Approaches*. Basingstoke, Palgrave Macmillan.

Reynolds, K. (ed.) 2005. *Modern Children's Literature: An Introduction*. Basingstoke, Palgrave Macmillan.

Townsend, J.R. 2003. *Written for Children: An Outline of English-language Children's Literature,* 6th edn. London, Bodley Head.

Tucker, N. 1990. *The Child and the Book: A Psychological and Literary Exploration*. Cambridge, Cambridge University Press.

Instruction and Delight
Peter Hunt

The key questions

Children's literature is probably the most exciting and vibrant of all literary studies, and its wide range of texts, from novels to picture books, and from oral forms to multimedia and the internet, presents a huge challenge. Not only is there a vast range of material – texts for children have been around, abundantly, in one form or another for at least 250 years – but that material has many different purposes and can be studied for many reasons. It is important because it is embedded in our cultural, educational and social thinking central to the success of publishing and media, and crucial to our understanding of literacy and personal development. As a result we need to engage with a perhaps startling and unexpected array of fundamental issues before we can ask and answer what might seem to be obvious questions.

Words that might seem to have straightforward meanings, such as *quality, value, literature* and *children* need to be looked at closely. Things that might at first seem simple, such as how children understand texts, what meanings they make from them, how these differ from the meanings that adults make, and how children are affected, suddenly become problematical. The role of adults in reading and mediating children's books has to be examined in terms of motivation, ideology (all the attitudes that constitute a culture) and the manipulation or idealising or commodification of childhood. Should children's books be for instruction or delight?

The subject is 'children's *literature*', but can the same types and scales of judgement be used as are used for adult literature – and if they are, does that mean that 'children's literature' is inevitably an oxymoron? And can all children be lumped together as one species – and if they are, does that imply wishful thinking or disrespect? And what does that awkward little possessive''s' in 'children's' actually mean? Do these texts really *belong to* children, or are they simply *aimed at* them? Are the texts we are talking about *of* childhood, *for* childhood, *about* childhood, or *by* children? As A.A. Milne admitted about the verses in *When We Were Very Young*: 'They are a curious collection; some *for* children, some *about* children, some by with or from children' (Thwaite, 1992: 53).

However we answer these questions, our subject has one inescapable feature: some idea of a child or childhood motivates writers and determines both the form and the content of what they write; some idea of a child or childhood influences how we interpret, judge, analyse and use texts, whether we are interested primarily in texts, or primarily in children, or primarily in both children and texts. Beyond that, we need to tailor our definitions to suit our purposes.

If children's literature is beginning to look like something rather different from what might have been expected, it is worth asking: why are we interested? What led us here?

Many people come to children's literature as a relief, as a rest from the rigours of 'adult' studies, and their image of the texts is often based on nostalgia or wishful thinking. Children's books are *nice*; they take us back to a golden world, one which we might also want to share with our children or grandchildren. Books that people enjoyed when they were children have a special, and often very personal, value and meaning (which is not surprising, considering the change that a single book may make to an inexperienced reader), and there is a perfectly natural urge to revisit them. But if we look a little more closely, problems arise. It might be that the books read as a child were actually an escape, and that it is the escape, not the childhood, that the reader wishes to relive: far from being a happy, lost state, many (perhaps most) childhoods are difficult, and many adults (and adult writers) have an ambivalent relationship with their own childhood. To reread a children's book from childhood, perhaps as an escape from the stresses of adulthood, evades both the real now and the real then. Is childhood innocent? Are the books innocent?

As Judy Blume, who wrote some of the most controversial children's/teenage books of the late twentieth century, including *Forever* (the first 'full-frontal' children's book (1975)) wrote:

> I don't know what childhood innocence is supposed to mean. Children are inexperienced, but they are not innocent. Childhood can be a terrible time of life.

No kid wants to stay a kid. It is only adults who have forgotten who say, 'If only I could be a kid again.' The fantasy of childhood is to *be* an adult.

West, 1988: 11–12

And so it soon becomes clear that the relationship between children's books and childhood is far from simple; even the bright world of *Winnie-the-Pooh* carries within it echoes of Milne's traumatic experiences in the First World War – the need to create a retreatist, idyllic world – and his ambivalence towards real childhood, shown in the oversentimentalised image of Christopher Robin. The filmed versions, of course, are notable (or notorious) for their commodification of childhood.

Of course, it may be that children's literature is being studied out of general cultural-literary, aesthetic interest, or as part of literacy studies, but even then, the need for a sharp, unsentimental eye remains. Similarly, if the focus of interest is in history or the history of childhood, it is as well to remember that texts for children do not portray childhood as it was or is, but portray childhood as the writers wished it to be seen for political, sociological or dramatic reasons. Fiction is fiction, and children's books say a great deal to adults about the relationships of adults to childhood, or about the concept of childhood at a particular period, rather than portraying *actual* childhoods.

Children's books, adults and children

Questions such as those raised in the paragraph above are vital because, unlike other forms of literature, children's literature is at root about power – about a power struggle. Adults write, children read, and this means that, like it or not, adults are exercising power, and children are either being manipulated, or resisting manipulation: there is a tension between the reader *implied* by the writer, and the real readers. Children's books are thus *inevitably* didactic in some way: even the most child-friendly is adopting some implicit attitudes. It is generally assumed that those who write for children will, naturally, be persons of goodwill, wishing to do 'good' in some form, for their readers. The difficulty with that, of course, is establishing the nature of 'good' – are we here for entertainment or instruction, and just what should those two things mean? In a book that is still controversial after over twenty years, *The Case of Peter Pan, or the Impossibility of Children's Literature* (1984), Jacqueline Rose proposed that because of the gulf between adults and children, a genuine, 100 per cent children-owned-and-operated book is an impossibility, and what is lurking behind the apparently innocent children's book is in fact something very intrusive, controlling, and often downright sinister. Critics following Rose's lead, notably

Karín Lesnik-Oberstein, have suggested that any comments made by critics must inevitably serve adults first – because it is they who are deciding what the text means and what childhood should be (Lesnik-Oberstein 2004). To some this has seemed a step too far into theory, leaving behind the pragmatic world occupied by parents and teachers interested in the interaction between texts and children. However, it cannot be denied that 99.9 per cent of children's books are written by adults, nor that all those writers will, necessarily, have an agenda. Even those writers who claim to be nothing but entertainers have their own ideological stance, their own ideas of what is right and wrong, their own way of seeing the world, and it is impossible that they should not in some way convey this in their writing, manipulatively or not. Equally, however childhood is defined, adult writers cannot think their way into it: there is inevitably some gap. Some writers, such as Enid Blyton, or Arthur Ransome or J.K. Rowling, seem to have a close empathy with their audience; some books, such as Pat Hutchins's *Rosie's Walk* or Shirley Hughes's *Dogger* seem, from all visible signs, to bridge the gap. But however sensitive the mediator – the parent or the teacher – they are working with imperfect instruments. The very nature of the relationship between adulthood and childhood precludes the existence of a 'true' children's book. The surprising difficulty of this area demonstrates how carefully we have to step in what looks at first to be a sunny, carefree world!

Children's books are *not* innocent or simple; Ursula Le Guin once observed sardonically: 'Sure it's simple, writing for kids. Just as simple as bringing them up' (Le Guin, 1992: 49), and involving ourselves with children's literature means involving ourselves in a complex, active literary–social system. As the Professor of Children's Literature at Newcastle University, Kim Reynolds, has written:

> If children's literature fails to offer young people ways of thinking about themselves and their world that suggest that they can make a difference and help them construct a discourse of their own to empower them as political subjects, it cannot be excluded from the other social forces implicated in the gelding of youth and youth culture.
>
> Keenan and Thompson, 2004: 147

This means that dealing with children's literature involves responsibility, because what may at first sight seem like trivial or ephemeral texts are in fact immensely powerful. They have been read by millions upon millions of people at the period in their lives when they are most susceptible to new ideas. It is inconceivable that these texts have not shaped society in fundamental and lasting ways. More people, probably, have read the books of Enid Blyton, more often and more repetitively, than those of any other author *ever*. Is it possible to imagine that her middle-class, middle-England, rather racist and sexist attitudes and values, and her patterns of narrative pass through the minds of her child-readers without, as it were, touching the sides?

The question is: if we, as adult readers, see horror and incest and murder in fairy tales, or male exploitation and female repression in *Little Women*, or sexism and class distinctions in *Thomas the Tank Engine* (the carriages are female, the trucks working-class), do we not have a duty to do something about it? What goes into children's minds is our responsibility, just as much as what goes into their stomachs.

At this point, I suspect that we should confront perhaps the most common objection to this kind of approach: 'but surely the children won't *see* that!' All this interpretation, this detection of hidden meanings and subtexts is what *adults* do, not children. I'm afraid that the simplest answer is that the assumption that children somehow, like shellfish, live among unsavoury things, but filter them out, and subsist in a pure, innocent state, is wishful thinking. We can, perhaps, make pragmatic guesses about what a child *can* understand, or what is irrelevant to the child and might thus be ignored – but these are only guesses. And if one is prepared simply to *believe* that books do not have the potential to pass on subliminal messages, then why are we as a culture so concerned with the influence of advertising or propaganda on the young? Is it because with children's literature we are dealing with stories, and that stories are, by definition, fiction, untrue and therefore not influential? Surely not, when we acknowledge that stories are so powerful throughout the culture.

On top of that is the whole question of literacy and understanding. How we measure who understands what is endlessly difficult: as Michael Benton, a distinguished educationalist, has observed: 'There are ... few of us who have not felt unnerved at some time by the fact that when children read stories there is no observable outcome ... The story has happened inside the child's head' (in Fox, 1983: 19). The awesome complexity of how children learn to read, and then how they negotiate longer texts – denotation, connotation, genre, intertextual meanings and all the rest – should make us extremely careful about applying the curious formulae that occur so often in literary criticism: 'the reader sees', 'we see', and so on (or the equivalent phrases of children's-book reviewing: 'children will like', 'girls will love'). The most common, and commonly unchallenged, oddity about all literary criticism is the assumption that all readers will 'read' the same thing from a text: the same images, the same emotions, the same allusions. This is difficult enough to imagine among adults even of the same class and same generation in the same country: to imagine that it is possible with inexperienced readers is absurd. If we are engaging with texts for children we need to see that our motivation does not entitle us to make assumptions about what any reader but ourselves perceives.

Even if we leave aside for a moment what the child-reader might make of a text, we have to accept that, for adults, reading a text produced for children is at least twice as complicated as reading a text written for our peers (a fact that provides good ammunition should we ever be criticised of dealing with an *easy* subject). When we read a peer text, we usually read in two ways: first for ourselves (normally adopting the role of the implied reader), and secondly more analytically, in order to discuss it with others. With children's books, we read the text for ourselves, but we read it in two ways – as an adult (ignoring the implied readership) and as a child (accepting the implied readership) – and this is further complicated by whether the child we become as we read is the remembered or a constructed child. Thirdly, we read analytically, in order to discuss the book with others (further complicated by the discipline – education, history, criticism – that we are concerned with). Then, fourthly, very often we are reading *for* or *on behalf of* the child, to decide whether this book is suitable for a specific child or group of children.

One consequence of this is that when reading books for children, adults commonly make many local judgements – they think for themselves, rather than relying on existing opinions. Perry Nodelman, one of the most prolific critics and theorists in the field, was teaching literature in a university in Canada when he was asked to run a children's book course. And he made a remarkable discovery:

> [Guides to children's literature] all made judgements of excellence in terms of the effects of books on their audience – and that astonished me, for in the ivory tower of literary study I had hitherto inhabited, one certainly did not judge books by how they affected audiences; in fact, one often judged audiences by the extent to which they were affected by books, so that, for instance, anyone who wasn't overwhelmed by Shakespeare was simply assumed to be an intransigent dummy.
>
> Nodelman, 1985: 4

If, as students of children's literature, we are empowered to make our own judgements about texts, then it follows that we must make our own judgements about what constitutes our subject. If we can do that, then it will be much easier to deal with the questions with which we began.

The problem of 'literature': quality and value, 'good' and 'good for'

Although 'children's literature' is a useful enough – and universally recognised – shorthand title for our subject, the use of the word 'literature' tends to cause confusion. To many critics 'children's literature' is a contradiction in terms. As Henry James wrote in an essay in 1899, 'The Future of the Novel':

> The literature, as it may be called for convenience, of children is an industry that occupies by itself a very considerable quarter of the scene. Great fortunes, if not great reputations, are made we learn, by writing for schoolboys ... The published statistics are extraordinary and of a sort to engender many kinds of uneasiness. The sort of taste that used to be called 'good' has nothing to do with the matter: we are so demonstrably in the presence of millions for whom taste is but an obscure, confused, immediate instinct.
>
> quoted in Hughes, [1978] 1990: 75

In discussing literature, there are, fundamentally, two views. The first is that there are absolute standards of quality or goodness; these are generally undefined (and undefinable), but may be perceived by the cultured, the elite, or the gifted: whether you regard the priesthood who elect themselves to make these decisions as part of the divine order, or as the preservers of cultural continuity, or as oppressive egomaniacs (canonising the dead white males) is, of course, up to you. The alternative view (oddly called 'relativist' by the first group – to whom everything is relative to their own standards) is to value everything as *fit for purpose*; thus you can't compare, say, apples and oranges, because although they are both fruits, what is good about either is intrinsic to the species. Mozart wrote good music of its kind, the Beatles wrote good music of its kind; *War and Peace* is good of its kind, *We're Going on a Bear Hunt* is good of its kind.

Therefore, to say that one form (children's books) is, by definition, inferior to another (adults' books) may be an interesting philosophical discussion, but it is a dangerous one in the context of children and their books. The 'inferior' form will not be taught or taken or analysed seriously (as was the case not so long ago with 'women's writing'), and that can cause serious multiple confusions in the education system. Shakespeare at school and Jackie Wilson at home should be seen as doing different things, rather than one being 'superior' to the other. Both are leading their readers into different aspects of the culture, and to compare them directly is not a useful exercise.

When *Harry Potter and the Prisoner of Azkaban* came up against Seamus Heaney's translation of the Old English poem *Beowulf* for the 2000 Whitbread literary award, the critic Antony Holden wrote that it would be a 'national disgrace' if Harry won. (*Beowulf* won.) Much of the hot air generated in that discussion came from a confusion of what is meant by *good* in the abstract (undefinable except by assertion) as opposed to good *for* (demonstrable empirically), and from not comparing like with like. Children's books are most usefully seen as part of their own separate literary system, which has its own special qualities and values and techniques, and which relates primarily to children. As the *New York Times* commented:

> Whereas adults see in Harry Potter a fairly conventional supernatural adventure story – one not nearly as brilliant or literary as, say, *The Hobbit* or the *Alice in Wonderland* books [sic] – something more fundamental evidently reverberates in the minds of children, something as powerful as the witch of 'Hansel and Gretel'.
>
> quoted in Zipes, 2001: 184

The problem is that – with a few exceptions – children's books are equated with 'popular' texts in the adult system, and are therefore, by definition, inferior. Any teachers or parents who have at the back of their mind the idea that the majority of what they are giving their children – and what they and their children enjoy – is inescapably inferior, has an unnecessary problem. Thus the *Harry Potter* books are most usefully seen from the point of view of children.

Defining children's literature: some case studies

Having said that, how do we define this body of texts that we are going to look at? At this point, the pragmatist will say: surely, it is obvious what a book is, from its cover and layout (the peritext). There might be some marginal cases, books that cross over between children and adults, such as the work of Philip Pullman, or J.R.R. Tolkien, or Mark Hadden's *The Curious Incident of the Dog in the Night Time*. And there seems to be some sliding around over time – so that fairy tales and Sherlock Holmes, both originally for adults, are now commonly marketed for children, while *The Water-Babies* finds itself in the annotated Oxford 'Worlds' Classics'. But most children's books are *obviously* children's books, for example Roger Hargreaves's 'Mr Men' and 'Little Miss' books, Jill Murphy's *Five Minutes' Peace*, A.A. Milne's *Winnie-the-Pooh*, or anything by J.K. Rowling or Enid Blyton. What else can they be?

Answering that question leads into more interesting waters than one might expect. Take Roger Hargreaves's immensely successful series: small books with short stories, illustrated with bold, even crude, drawings. *Obviously* for the small child, the very inexperienced reader. *Obviously* they are simple! And yet ... Look at any of those Hargreaves drawings: the figure on the cover of *Little Miss Splendid* (Hargreaves, 1981) for example. How much symbolic interpretation is required to interpret two pale green circles and a small u shape as being a woman? How much cultural knowledge is required to understand that, once we have decided that the blobs of red are meant to represent hat, bag and shoes, they are pretentiously, risibly unfashionable? Or that the upturned nose and the closed eyes are symbolic (in one particular culture) of snobbery? And how much technical knowledge is needed to realise that the small lines beside the shoes are the graphic cartoon code for movement? This may seem laborious, let alone fatuous in the face of 100 million copies sold – but if the (very) young readers *do* take the intended meaning, then it is at least worth considering how it is done, and what sophisticated cognitive processes are at work. If these are children's books, is that because adults make them so, rather than because they are designed for the needs and abilities of the child-readers?

And many children's books might not actually be for children. Jill Murphy's *Five Minutes' Peace* is one of a very successful series featuring anthropomorphised elephants, the Large family. It begins with Mrs Large regarding her family (off-page) with the verbal text: 'The children were having breakfast. This was not a pleasant sight.' The question is – whose point of view is this? The rest of the book, for all the 'obvious' trappings of the children's book, deals with adult preoccupations entirely from an adult viewpoint: the implied reader is *not* the child. What, then, does the child-reader, or the child-read-to make of this? Is he/she learning a lesson in empathy? Perhaps, but this may not be what one naturally assumes to be a *children's* book.

Other books, like *Winnie-the-Pooh*, which has been a children's classic for generations, are in fact books aimed at two audiences. Barbara Wall, in her analysis of how authors address their narratee (the reader), *The Narrator's Voice* (1991: 35), suggests that there are many books marketed for children where writers actually write for adults and children separately:

> their narrators will address child narratees overtly and self-consciously, and will also address adults, either overtly, as the implied author's attention shifts away from the implied child reader to a different older audience, or covertly, as the narrator deliberately exploits the ignorance of the implied child reader and attempts to entertain an implied adult reader by making jokes that are funny primarily because children will not understand them.

This is the mark of the author who is not comfortable with writing for children, and who winks at the adults. Until A.A. Milne got into his stride, he was rather inclined to do this:

> Once upon a time, a very long time ago now, about last Friday, Winnie-the-Pooh lived in a forest all by himself under the name of Sanders.
> ('What does "under the name" mean?' asked Christopher Robin. 'It means he had the name over the door in gold letters and lived under it.')
>
> Milne, [1926] 1965: 2

This approach can be seen either as disrespectful to the reading child, or as reflecting a relationship between writer and child that was more common a hundred years ago than it is today. Thus that great, if eccentric, classic,

The Water-Babies (1865) begins, notoriously: 'Once upon a time there was a little chimney-sweep, and his name was Tom. That is a short name, and you have heard it before, so you will not have much trouble in remembering it.' J.M. Barrie's second prose version of 'Peter Pan', *Peter and Wendy* (1911) ends, 'and thus it will go on, so long as children are gay and innocent and heartless'. It can be argued that such books *were* for children, but now embody undesirable ideas or implied relationships that are now not relevant or appropriate.

Generally speaking, this patronising attitude has died out, although it survives in much-vaunted authors such as E. Nesbit and Roald Dahl. Arthur Ransome, author of *Swallows and Amazons,* avoided the trap, by treating his readers as his equals:

> I do not know how to write for children and have the gravest doubts as to whether anybody should try to do any such thing. To write a book *for* children seems to me to be a sure way of writing what is called a 'juvenile', a horrid, artificial thing, a patronising thing, a thing that betrays in every line that an author and his intended victims are millions of miles apart, and that the author is enjoying not the stuff of the book, but a looking-glass picture of himself or herself 'being so good with children' ... a most unpleasant spectacle.
>
> Ransome, [1937] 1977: 6

In contrast, C.S. Lewis, in a statement very often quoted with approval, when it is in fact denigrating children's literature, wrote: 'I am almost inclined to set it up as a canon that a children's story which is enjoyed only by children is a bad children's story' (Lewis, 1966: 24). We might well argue the exact opposite: the *real* children's books are the ones read *only* by children – ones that do *not* have anything to say to adults, and which are not, therefore, subject to adult judgements. This is a radical thought, that places, say, Enid Blyton in the forefront of children's literature (rather than more respectable, adult-like writers such as Kenneth Grahame or Philip Pullman). For Barbara Wall (1991: 35), these *genuine* children's books are marked by writers who talk directly to the child reader, 'showing no consciousness that adults too might read the work'. Interestingly, as David Rudd has pointed out in *Enid Blyton and the Mystery of Children's Literature* (2000), these kinds of books are not usually approved of by adults:

> There is a fear of children being controlled, becoming mindless beings, slaves to the .... text ... Blyton is thus a modern Pied Piper ... There is no room for children to have their own pleasures in the text: celebrating having tales told about themselves at the centre. The other point ... is that this celebration of the in-group – the children – must be at the expense of the out-group: the adults whom the piper leaves out in the cold.
>
> Rudd, 2000: 169

The fact that J.K. Rowling's books are widely read by adults says more about adult attitudes to fantasy than it does about J.K. Rowling, whose focus, like that of Blyton, is her developing audience, not other adults. To criticise her books *as if they were written for adults* is to miss the point, and to misdirect the criticism.

A working definition of 'children's literature', or, perhaps better, 'literature for children', then, might be arrived at by choosing your own interpretation of the three elements, the literature, the children and the 'for-ness'.

The word 'literature' is a spectrum: at one end is the small handful of 'canonical' texts 'generally' agreed to have some kind of eternal value; at the other is the vast range of 'texts' routinely and traditionally absorbed by the category: myth, legend and folk tale, verse, picture books, 'chapter books', novels, cartoons, films, video games, websites, merchandise, and so on. You may feel that the oral tale or seventeenth-century chapbooks are no longer for children, and therefore do not fit into your idea of children's literature, or you may feel that the study of electronic media is different from the study of printed texts, or you may feel that the printed book is really of little relevance to the modern child and that what we should be looking at is the mediation of story through electronic and multimedia channels. Or, perhaps, that there are many *kinds* of children's literature, and that only certain ones are within your field of interest.

When we describe literature as being *'for'* children, do we exclude those texts which, as we have seen, address adults over the heads of children? If so, do we exclude the huge industry of 'children's' films, such as *Shrek,* or *Toy Story*, which are clearly for a mixed audience, or, indeed, any of the classic Walt Disney feature-cartoons, almost all of which are concerned with courtship and marriage? Or do we include or exclude books according to whether they are designed to instruct or to amuse their audience? Most histories of children's literature suggest that children's books were initially entirely designed for educational purposes, with 'delight', if any, an incidental sugar-ing of the pill. In the course of the nineteenth century, instruction gave way to entertainment, religion to fantasy – with *Alice's Adventures in Wonderland* seen as a kind of anarchic, liberating turning-point. One problem here is that childhood was very different 200 years ago, especially in terms of what we would now call media input; children had fewer things to entertain them, and different mindsets. Therefore it is too easy to suggest that, say, the pious and severe discourses on virtue by evangelistic writers such as Mrs Trimmer (in *The History of The Fairchild Family* (1818) disobedient children are burned to death or whipped or made to reflect on rotting corpses at a gibbet) were not entertaining to their recipients, or that they were popular only because they were imposed on their audience.

Which leaves us with deciding what we mean by 'children'. Childhood is generally defined either by physical and mental characteristics – size, development or immaturity, and so on – which are common to all children, or by local, cultural decisions. This second idea of childhood changes with time, place, commercialism, politics, and even with individuals; in the West, it has been commonly associated with lack of responsibility. Consequently, how do we categorise children's books – as suitable for children of certain ages, or certain developmental levels, or for children in certain social or geographical areas? Are we happy to accept such generalisations, or would we prefer to think about individual children? And even if we are happy to accept such generalisations, is it practical to do so?

Rousseau put the problem succinctly in *Emile* (1762):

> We know nothing of childhood: and with our mistaken notions the further we advance the further we go astray ... Nature wants children to be children before they are men ... Childhood has ways of seeing, thinking, and feeling peculiar to itself; nothing can be more foolish than to substitute our ways for them
> quoted in Jenks, 1996: 2, 3

Equally, it is important to realise that it is the concepts of childhood held by writers and publishers, rather than 'real' childhoods, which determine what appears in texts. What is important for children's literature is that the inevitable variety of childhood and childhoods is acknowledged in its real readers, and its variability as a social and commercial construction is acknowledged in the texts.

Content, censorship and understanding

A more obvious way of deciding what constitutes a children's text might seem to be by looking at the contents. Are there certain things that, in our view, should not appear in children's books – things, perhaps, that are solely adult concerns (such as sexuality) or which society tends to shy away from (such as death)? There are those who cannot understand what the savage and brutal myths and folk tales, concerned with murder, rape, incest and other horrors, have to do with children at all: as J.R.R. Tolkien observed,

> the association of children and fairy-stories is an accident of our domestic history. Children as a class – except in a common lack of experience they are not one – neither like fairy-stories more, nor understand them better than adults do.
> Tolkien, 1964: 34

Melvin Burgess's *Junk* is about drugs; Pullman's *His Dark Materials* trilogy is about the death of God – and there is even a death joke on the second page of Beatrix Potter's *The Tale of Peter Rabbit*. Should some books – such as picture-books depicting the bombing of Hiroshima – only be given to children under adult supervision? Both fantasy and realism have been frowned on: fantasy as providing easy, impractical answers, and realism as raising more problems than it can solve. As Ursula Le Guin notes:

> But what, then, is the naturalistic writer for children to do? Can he present the child with evil as an *insoluble* problem ... To give the child a picture of ... gas chambers ... or famines or the cruelties of a psychotic patient, and say, 'Well, baby, this is how it is, what are you going to make of it' – that is surely unethical. If you suggest that there is a 'solution' to these monstrous facts, you are lying to the child. If you insist that there isn't, you are overwhelming him with a load he's not strong enough yet to carry.
>
> Le Guin, 1992: 64–5

But we still have the problem of what the child-reader understands. As Joan Aiken said: 'What terrifies one child may seem merely comic to another, or may be completely ignored; one can't legislate for fear' (Haviland, 1980: 63). Therefore, she goes on: 'Exercising any degree of control over the kind of books written for or read by children is a highly doubtful policy.'

That may be so in principle, but in practice, children's books are relatively vulnerable to acts of censorship because people in general feel confident of their authority to intervene. In the UK, unlike the USA, direct acts of censorship are rare: control is built into the children's book 'system' by publishers and book-sellers. Generally, however, the logic of censorship is often unclear. Does reading about, teenage sexual activity for example, encourage such activity, or is ignorance of such activity actually more dangerous? Very often, it seems that it is the adults who are protecting themselves, or their idea of childhood.

What we think of as *suitable* for children is part of a complex network of social values, and there are many interesting historical examples. In 1782, Sarah Trimmer produced *Sacred History* (1782), a heavily edited version of the Bible for children; Beatrix Potter was asked to remove a picture of a rat drinking alcohol in *The Tailor of Gloucester*, Jan Ormerod was asked to not to show a small girl naked in her wordless picture-book *Sunshine*; in Roald Dahl's *Charlie and the Chocolate Factory*, the Oompa Loopas were originally black pygmies. What is acceptable changes with time: Hugh Lofting's *The Story of Dr Dolittle* (1922) originally featured Prince Bumpo of the Jolliginki tribe, who wished to be white, while Helen Bannerman's *Little Black Sambo* (1899) and Bertha and Florence Upton's Golliwog (from *The Adventures of Two Dutch Dolls – and a Golliwogg* (1895) were both sympathetic, even heroic figures before they became racist symbols (see Plate 10).

As Roald Dahl proved, adults can use children's books to share a pleasure in anarchy or vulgarity that they might not otherwise be able to express.

The limits of what can be published in this direction 'for children' have been pushed a long way, with, for example, William Kotzwinkle and Glenn Murray's '#1 *New York Times Bestseller*', *Walter, the Farting Dog* (2001) and Werner Holzwarth and Wolf Erlbruch's excremental *The Story of the Little Mole Who Knew it was None of his Business* (1989, UK 1994). (It is instructive to read the opposing views about these books on the Amazon USA website.)

The study of children's literature, then, is often hampered by unclear thinking – as when the second and third editions of Enid Blyton's 'Noddy' series were *simplified* to match the reputation that Noddy has for being simple. It is a complex field, traversed by literary idealists and commercial marketers, literacy experts and committed parents, and graced by some of the most innovative talents at work in the arts. Far from being a marginalised study, it is central to the way culture develops – but to negotiate its many delights, we need to realise that, perhaps more than in any study in the humanities, we have a duty to make our own decisions and to realise our responsibilities. The study of children's texts is technically *more* complex than the study of adult books, partly because the audience is different, and their responses more obviously unknowable, and partly because of the *range* of texts and the *range* of purposes. With the rapid growth of electronic texts, we are at a turning point, or a new starting point, in literacy and narrative, and children's literature is in a key position. To understand what is happening to narrative and our children we need to understand the processes of decoding texts, as well as their history and their contemporary forms: the study of children's literature can provide us with this understanding.

References

Fox, G. (ed.) 1983. *Responses to Children's Literature*. Munich, K.G. Saur.

Hargreaves, R. 1981. *Little Miss Splendid*. London, Egmont.

Haviland, V. 1980. *The Openhearted Audience: Ten Authors Talk About Writing for Children*. Washington, DC, Library of Congress.

Hughes, F. [1978] 1990. 'Children's Literature, Theory and Practice' (*English Literary History*, 45, 1978: 542–61), in P. Hunt (ed.) *Children's Literature: The Development of Criticism*. London, Routledge.

Jenks, C. 1996. *Childhood*. London, Routledge.

Keenan, C. and Thompson, M.S. (eds) 2004. *Studies in Children's Literature 1500–2000*. Dublin, Four Courts Press.

Le Guin, U.K. 1992. *The Language of the Night*. New York, HarperCollins.

Lesnik-Oberstein, K. (ed.) 2004. *Children's Literature: New Approaches*. Basingstoke, Palgrave Macmillan.

Lewis, C.S. 1966. 'On Three Ways of Writing for Children', in C.S. Lewis, *Of Other Worlds*. London, Geoffrey Bles.

Milne, A.A. [1926] 1965. *Winnie-the-Pooh*. London, Methuen.

Nodelman, P. (ed.) 1985. *Touchstones: Reflections on the Best in Children's Literature,* Vol. 1. West Lafayette, IN: Children's Literature Association.

Ransome, A. [1937] 1977. 'A Letter to the Editor' (*Junior Bookshelf*, 1, 4), in M. Crouch and A. Ellis (eds) *Chosen for Children*, 3rd edn. London, Library Association.

Rose, J. 1984. *The Case of Peter Pan, or the Impossibility of Children's Literature.* Basingstoke, Macmillan.

Rudd, D. 2000. *Enid Blyton and the Mystery of Children's Literature*. Basingstoke, Macmillan.

Thwaite, A. 1992. *The Brilliant Career of Winnie-the-Pooh*. London, Methuen.

Tolkien, J.R.R. 1964. *Tree and Leaf*. London, Allen & Unwin.

Wall, B. 1991. *The Narrator's Voice*. Basingstoke, Macmillan.

West, M. 1988. *Trust Your Children: Voices Against Censorship in Children's Literature*. New York, Neal-Schuman.

Zipes, J. 2001. *Sticks and Stones. The Troublesome Success of Children's Literature from Slovenly Peter to Harry Potter.* New York and London, Routledge.

Origins: Fairy Tales and Folk Tales
Jack Zipes

Each region of the world has a different and distinctive fairy tale tradition, and since it is difficult to summarize the history of the fairy tale for children throughout the world, this article will focus largely on the development of the fairy tale for children in the West. Many fascinating commonalities are present between the cultivation of the fairy tale in the West and in other areas of the world, and parallels can be drawn to show similar characteristics – especially in recent years, during the period of so-called globalization.

Beginnings

As with most *literary* genres of children's literature, the fairy tale was never told or written explicitly for children, nor is this the case today. During its conception a few hundred years ago the fairy tale distinguished itself as a genre when storytellers began appropriating different kinds of magical folk tales, transforming them and conventionalizing them, for it became gradually necessary in the modern world to adapt the oral tales to standards of morality, literacy, and aesthetics of a particular society and to make them acceptable for diffusion in the public sphere.

Originally published as 'Fairy Tales and Folk Tales' in J. Zipes (ed.), *The Oxford Encyclopedia of Children's Literature* (Oxford: Oxford University Press, 2006).

The fairy tale is only one type of appropriation of a particular oral storytelling tradition – the wonder folk tale, often called the magic tale which generally focuses on miraculous transformations that enable disadvantaged protagonists to gain advantages and succeed in life. In Europe and North America many tales recount the adventures of banished heroes and heroines, youngest sons and daughters, impoverished and abused characters, and people who have been cursed. The introduction of the printing press in the 15th century brought about a revolutionary change in the way these tales were transmitted. As more and more wonder tales were written down in the 15th, 16th, and 17th centuries, they began to constitute the genre of the *literary* fairy tale that began forming its own conventions, motifs, topoi, characters, and plots, based to a large extent on those developed in the oral tradition but altered to address a reading public formed by the aristocracy and the middle classes. Although the peasants were excluded in the formation of this literary tradition, it was their material, tone, style, and beliefs that were incorporated into the new genre in the 15th, 16th, and 17th centuries.

Although storytelling was cultivated largely by the peasantry, wonder tales were told in Europe by all social classes of people for various purposes: wish fulfillment, improvement of social status, compensation for misery, preservation and celebration of rituals within a community, and the celebration of power. Some were stories of warning, while others were didactic and moral and absorbed motifs from the Greek and Roman myths and the Judeo-Christian sacred writings. For the most part the wonder tales were secular and included pagan beliefs and superstitions. The tales were told in the fields, at the hearth, and in the spinning rooms by the peasants. Not only were they the common people's mode of entertainment, but storytelling was common at the courts and in middle-class societies. Peasant women and men also transmitted these tales to the upper classes when they worked for them as wet nurses, maids, servants, and day laborers.

These tales were considered trite and irrelevant, more suited for children and peasants than for polite society. However, priests began to incorporate them into their sermons in the vernacular as exempla and parables to illustrate a moral message. While the priests "Christianized" certain folk tales, they also created new ones that were in turn appropriated by the peasants and often changed and spread without the Christian elements. Aside from the peasants and the priests, there were travelers such as merchants, journeymen, soldiers, and sailors, who told tales in fields, taverns, inns, and hostels and during voyages and campaigns. There were also professional storytellers or troubadours. These tales were generally told to startle, delight, and impress the listeners. They were also taken over by peasants and became part of their repertoire. There is no evidence that there were special tales cultivated just for children. Some so-called warning tales dealing with dangerous animals were apparently directed at children, but they were not considered "children's tales." The fact is, children were not excluded from the audience when tales were told, no matter how frank, bawdy, erotic, or scatological they might have been. It was through the tales that one gained a sense of values and one's place within the community. The oral tradition was in the hands of the peasantry for hundreds of years, and each peasant community made its mark on tales that circulated beyond its borders.

The oral tradition of the wonder tale was maintained throughout the late Middle Ages. If there were changes in the social function of the tales, they were brought about as the communities themselves changed. For instance, the growth of towns, the religious conflicts, and the peasant uprisings had an effect on both the subject matter of the tales and the way they were used. Most important during this period was the rise of the literary fairy tale. The influence of the oral tradition was clear in Boccaccio's *Decameron* (1348–53) and Chaucer's *Canterbury Tales* (1387) in the 14th century, but their collections made very little use of the wonder tale. It was first in Giovan Francesco Straparola's *Piacevoli notti* (translated as *The Facetious Nights* and *The Delectable Nights*, 1550–3) and then in Giambattista Basile's *Lo cunto de li cunti* (better known as the *Pentamerone*, in 1634–6) that wonder tales were fully adapted and transcribed to amuse courtly and educated middle-class readers. The social function of representation and entertainment was the dominant one in these collections, although the stories also contained a good deal of social commentary about love, marriage, and power. Essentially, however, the authors altered the motifs and topoi of the oral tradition to represent upper-class interests.

The 17th century

Since the authors of fairy tales in Italy did not consciously seek to create a new mode of writing, and since they did not form a social network in which the tales could become instituted, the literary genre did not take a firm hold. However, in France, which, for all intents and purposes, gave "birth" to the literary fairy tale, the situation was different. By the mid-17th century, there were literary salons established by aristocratic women, who organized types of parlor games that incorporated the use of folk motifs and narrative conventions. The participants were expected to show their wit and eloquence by inventing wondrous tales, and they were the first to coin the term *conte de fées*, or fairy tale. By 1690, various authors such as Madame d'Aulnoy and Mademoiselle Bernard began to incorporate fairy tales into their novels and then publish entire collections of fairy tales. A veritable vogue if not a deluge of fairy tales appeared from 1696 to 1704 in France. Madame d'Aulnoy, Mademoiselle L'Héritier, Charles Perrault, Madame de la Force, Madame Durand, Mademoiselle Lubert, Madame de Murat, Chevalier de Mailly, Mademoiselle Bernard, and other gifted writers published remarkable collections of fairy tales. The most famous writer from this era is Charles Perrault, who published his collection *Histoires ou contes du temps passé* (Stories or Tales of Past Times, often mistakenly referred to as "Tales of Mother Goose") in 1697.

Aristocratic and bourgeois women and men performed their tales in the salons and also published them to demonstrate their unique personalities, their command of eloquent conversation, and their wit or esprit. The tales were intended to amuse the listeners but also to establish conventions pertaining to a discourse on manners and *civilité*. Implicit was a code that corresponded to the ideals and standards of propriety. Therefore, the oral tales, which most of the tellers had learned from their nurses, governesses, or servants, or which were based on tales they had read, such as those by Straporola, Basile, and other Italian writers, were radically changed in content and style.

All these fairy tales were written explicitly for adults, even those by Perrault; although it is generally supposed that the fairy tale for children originated during this time, there is actually no evidence documenting that these complex and subtle tales were read to children or that children read them. Of course, these "adult" fairy tales did influence the tales that were developed for children. For instance, soon after their publication, the tales of d'Aulnoy, Perrault, and others were printed in a series of chapbooks called the *Bibliothèque bleue* distributed by peddlers called *colporteurs* throughout France, central Europe, and England to members of the middle and lower classes. The tales were often translated and shortened; the language was changed and made simpler; and there were multiple versions, which were read to children.

The 18th and 19th centuries

As early as 1729 Perrault's tales had been translated into English, and these works and some of the other tales by French authors like d'Aulnoy that had also been translated were circulated as chapbooks in England. Despite the hostility of the Puritan censors in England, it gradually became acceptable to incorporate some fairy tales in volumes intended for children. The most notable examples here are The *Governess; or, Little Female Academy* (1749) by Sarah Fielding and *Magasin des enfants* (English trans., *The Young Misses' Magazine*, 1757) by Madame Leprince de Beaumont.

Both Fielding and Leprince de Beaumont used a frame setting to transmit different kinds of didactic tales in which a governess engages several young girls in discussions about morals, manners, ethics, and gender roles; the stories illustrate her lessons of morals and manners. Often particular tales such as "The Cruel Giant Barbarico, the Good Giant Benefico, and the Pretty Dwarf' and "Beauty and the Beast" were published separately. These works along with other publications such as chapbooks, memoirs, social histories, and biographies indicate that most adults among the educated classes in Great Britain had a familiarity with classical French fairy tales, that English folk tales still circulated among lower and upper classes in the oral tradition, and that chapbooks included fairy tales, legends, fables, and other popular literature. Although there was not really a children's literature publishing industry until the end of the 18th century, children by that time had clearly been exposed to the fairy tale as genre. And, indeed, by the end of the 18th century, several generations of aristocratic and bourgeois children had been introduced to the literary fairy tale in Great Britain.

At the beginning of the 19th century the function of the fairy tale for adults underwent a major shift throughout Europe, thanks to the German Romantic movement and tales by Novalis, Ludwig Tieck, Adelbert von Chamisso, and E.T.A. Hoffmann, among others, that made it an appropriate medium to carry on a sophisticated dialogue about social and political issues within the bourgeois public sphere. However, the fairy tale for children remained more traditional and was also rejected by many educators and the clergy because of its lack of explicit morals until the 1820s. This suspicion did not prevent fairy tales from being published and circulated. There were, in fact, various collections of fairy tales published for children in England by John Harris (*Mother Bunch's Fairy Tales*, 1802) and Benjamin Tabart (*Popular Fairy Tales*, 1804–8) along with illustrated chapbooks containing "Little Red Riding Hood," "Cinderella," "Sleeping Beauty," "Jack the Giant-Killer," "Beauty and the Beast," and so on. These collections flourished throughout Europe and were read by children and adults, but they were not considered the prime reading material for children, nor were they considered to be "healthy" for the development of children's minds. The majority of the tales and stories for children were sentimental, moralistic, realistic, and didactic, intended to demonstrate manners and morals. Even the Brothers Grimm, in particular Wilhelm, began in 1819 to revise their collected tales, *Kinder-und Hausmärchen* (English trans., *Children's and Household Tales*), first published in 1812 and 1815, for children, adding Christian sentiments and cleansing narratives of their erotic, cruel, or bawdy passages. However, the fantastic and wondrous elements were kept, so they were not fully accepted by the bourgeois reading public. Nevertheless, it was during the 1820s that a change in attitude toward the fairy tale for children was signaled in England by the publication of Edgar Taylor's translation of the Grimms' tales under the title of *German Popular Stories* (1823).

Educators and parents began to realize, probably due to their own reading experiences, that fantasy literature and amusement would not necessarily destroy or pervert children's minds. On the contrary, children needed amusement so they could relax and recharge themselves after the effort of a rigid day. Whether the children were of the middle classes and attended school or were of the lower classes and worked on the farm or in a factory, they needed a recreation period – the time and space to reinvigorate themselves without having morals and ethics imposed on them, without having the feeling that their reading or listening had to involve indoctrination.

Significantly, it was from 1830 to 1900, during the rise of the middle classes, that the fairy tale came into its own for children. It was exactly during this time, from 1835 onward, to be precise, that Hans Christian Andersen began publishing his tales, which became extremely popular throughout Europe and America. Almost all his tales were immediately translated and published in England and America. Andersen brilliantly combined humor, Christian sentiments, and fantastic plots to form tales that amused and instructed young and old readers at the same time.

Old tales and new tales: from conventional tellings to radical retellings

Up until the 1850s, the majority of fairy tale writers for children – including Catherine Sinclair, George Cruikshank, and Alfred Crowquill in England; Carlo Collodi in Italy; Comtesse Sophie de Ségur in France; and Ludwig Bechstein in Germany – emphasized the lessons to be learned in keeping with the principles of the Protestant ethic. This ethic highlighted the values of industriousness, honesty, cleanliness, diligence, virtuousness – and male supremacy. The fairy tale was intended to play a major role in the socialization process. However, just as the "conventional" fairy tales for adults had become subverted at the end of the 18th century, there was at the same time a major movement to write parodies of fairy tales for children, to turn them upside down and inside out, to question the traditional value system and suggest alternatives to the endings that appeared to contradict the notion of wonder and transformation that had been so dominant in the wonder folk tale. Writers such as William Makepeace Thackeray (*The Rose and the Ring*, 1855), George MacDonald ("The Light Princess," 1863), Lewis Carroll (*Alice in Wonderland*, 1865), Charles Dickens ("The Magic

Fishbone," 1868), Jean Ingelow (*Mopsa the Fairy*, 1869), Juliana Ewing (*Old-Fashioned Fairy Tales*, 1882), Andrew Lang (*Princess Nobody*, 1884), Mary Louisa Molesworth ("The Story of a King's Daughter," 1884), Oscar Wilde (*The Happy Prince, and Other Tales*, 1888), Kenneth Grahame (*The Reluctant Dragon*, 1898), Edith Nesbit (*The Last of the Dragons*, 1900), and many others began to experiment with the fairy tale in a manner that would make young readers question the world around them. The British writers had a great impact on Americans, who began to develop their culturally specific fairy tale tradition toward the middle and end of the 19th century. The firm of John McLoughlin began publishing numerous fairy tale toy books at midcentury, Writers such as Nathaniel Hawthorne, James Kirke Paulding, Christopher Pearse Cranch, Horace Scudder, Louisa May Alcott, Frank Stockton, Howard Pyle, Catherine Pyle, and others contributed fairy tales to magazines like *St. Nicholas* in the 1870s and 1880s or published their own collections of tales. There was even a collection of Native American fairy tales, *The Indian Fairy Book* (1869). The major writer of this time was Frank Stockton, who published some unusual tales such as *Ting-a-Ling* (1871), *The Floating Prince, and Other Fairy Tales* (1881), and *The Bee-Man of Orn*, and *Other Fanciful Fairy Tales* (1887). While the European fairy tales served as models for the American writers, there was clearly a movement to "Americanize" that was part of a movement to establish a genuine American literature.

It is not by chance that the most notable and memorable American fairy tale was produced right at the end of the 19th century: L. Frank Baum's *The Wizard of Oz* (1900), clearly based on the structure of the European fairy tale, depicts Dorothy's great desire and need to break out of the gray bleakness of Kansas. Her imagination and initiative are awakened so that she can ultimately determine her destiny with the assistance of three helpers. Though Dorothy returns to America, she realizes in the sixth Oz book, *The Emerald City of Oz* (1910), that she cannot stay in a country where farmers are driven to ruin by bankers and exploitation is accepted as the "American way of life." Baum's creation of fourteen *Oz* books, considered as an American fairy tale saga, is a political and cultural commentary with profound ramifications for the eventual development of the fairy tale as genre. In fact, Baum set the stage for other fairy tale novels and series such as those by J.R.R. Tolkien, C.S. Lewis, T.H, White, and Michael Ende. Salman Rushdie, author of *Haroun and the Sea of Stories* (1990), has often paid a tribute to *The Wizard of Oz*, and numerous books and films continue the *Oz* tradition through the 21st century.

At the same time that Baum made history in America, J.M. Barrie contributed to the imaginative radicalization of the fairy tale with his drama

Peter Pan; or, The Boy Who Wouldn't Grow Up (1904), based on tales he first published in *The Little White Bird*. Barrie's fairy tale drama, later adapted as a novel, *Peter and Wendy*, in 1911, is a play about the resistance to conformity and convention, indicating just how important the fairy tale had become for adult and young readers and spectators.

From the beginning of the 20th century up through the 1940s the dominant trend tended to consist of the re-publication of illustrated collections of fairy tales by Perrault, the Grimms, and Andersen by such notable artists as Arthur Rackham, Charles Robinson, Charles Folkard, Harry Clarke, Margaret Tarrant, Mabel Lucy Atwell, F.D. Bedford, Edmund Dulac, W.W. Denslow, John R. Neill, Johnny Gruelle, and others, as well as individual picture books in all sorts of formats, not to mention comic books and cartoons. The illustrations have ranged from hackwork to brilliant interpretations of the stories. Many other collections of fairy tales appeared that were sanitized or dumbed down for children, with the fairies depicted as ephemeral tenderhearted creatures. Among the better writers and illustrators of this time were Walter de La Mare in England and Johnny Gruelle and Wanda Gág in America. Walter de La Mare published *Told Again: Old Tales Told Again* (1927), and his work is characterized by gentle irony, careful exploration of character motivation, and original plots. Johnny Gruelle's *Raggedy Ann and Andy* books of the 1920s and 1930s incorporated whimsical fairy tales with unusual plots. His stories continued Baum's tradition of nonviolence and emphasis on the importance of imaginative play for children. Wanda Gág, who made her mark with *Millions of Cats* in 1928, published her adaptations of *Tales from Grimm* (1936), *Snow White and the Seven Dwarfs* (1938), and *Three Gáy Tales* (1943). Illustrated with unusual ink drawings, Gág altered the plots in an endeavor to endow her tales with the authentic tone of the traditional storytellers.

Although one might expect many fairy tale writers to have written "political" stories about the Depression and World War II during the 1930s and 1940s, there were few who did. The notable exception was J.R.R. Tolkien's *The Hobbit* (1937), written with World War I in mind and with the intention of warning against a second world war. Whether Tolkien's fairy tale novel was written for children or for adults is a moot point. Indeed, during the first part of the 20th century it became increasingly difficult to draw boundaries between fairy tales for children and adults. Yet one thing is clear and has always been true: adults have always read, censored, approved, and distributed the so-called fairy tales for children. On the other hand, as more and more children have become functionally and culturally literate, and as they have become more worldly, they have either sought the reading material of adults or been exposed to this reading material. In fact, part of children's schooling – and this is a major functional shift in the 20th century – was to train children to become adept in recognizing, appreciating, and learning from fairy tales. As a result of this schooling, the social function of the fairy tale for children has undergone two major changes, pedagogical and political.

Pedagogy and psychology

The fairy tale had been introduced into the school curriculum and published in primers in Great Britain and the United States at the end of the 19th century. This pedagogical trend continued and was reinforced in the 20th century, so much so that children were encouraged to act out and create fairy tale plays. With the help of teachers and librarians, the fairy tale became a staple of education throughout the West, leading to the establishment of a canon of "classical" fairy tales for children: "Cinderella," "Little Red Riding Hood," "The Frog Prince," "Jack and the Beanstalk," "The Ugly Duckling," "Beauty and the Beast," "Rumpelstiltskin," "Sleeping Beauty," "Bluebeard," "Hansel and Gretel," "Rapunzel," and so on. The full-scale introduction of the fairy tale into schools, libraries, and households along with fairy tale plays, radio productions, and fairy tale cinematic animation (beginning in the 1930s) led to a complementary production of theoretical works with a psychological bent that established the "proper" age group (five to ten) for introducing fairy tales to children and expounded on the spiritual and psychological value of the tales. This development was in stark contrast to the heated controversy about the fairy tale in the early part of the 19th century, when educators and clergy tried to prevent the fairy tale from entering the nursery.

Of course, there was still a residual distrust of the fairy tale: many parents and educators believed and continue to believe that fairy tales have such a powerful effect on children that any violence and cruelty should be eliminated. In the United States there was a general tendency after 1945 to "clean up" or sanitize the classical fairy tales so that children did not have nightmares or imbibe weird ideas. Religious groups have always objected to the presence of witches and magic in fairy tales and led campaigns to ban fairy tales from schools and libraries. (This trend continues into the 21st century, for example in the way that the popular *Harry Potter* novels by J.K. Rowling are considered by some to be pernicious.) It was, to a great extent, in opposition to the "puritan" censors of fairy tales that Bruno Bettelheim wrote his significant though questionable study *The Uses of Enchantment* (1976), which is unfortunately marred by his plagiarism and false claims about the therapeutic effects of the fairy tale. Despite the defects in his analysis, Bettelheim's work has stimulated educators, psychologists, social workers, parents, and critics to explore the beneficial aspects of all kinds of fairy tales. In fact, fairy tales are now widely used in therapy, particularly with disturbed or abused children, because they enable a child to gain distance from trauma and deal with it on a symbolical level that enables the therapist to understand and work with the child.

The 20th century's comprehensive embrace of the fairy tale may in hindsight be inseparable from the timely entry and enormous impact of the filmmaker Walt Disney and the Disney Corporation in the field of fairy tales, with correspondingly enormous commercial success. During his lifetime, Disney produced six major animated fairy tale films: *Snow White and the Seven Dwarfs* (1937), *Pinocchio* (1940), *Cinderella* (1950), *Peter Pan* (1953), *Sleeping Beauty* (1959), and *Mary Poppins* (1963). After his death, his corporation continued this work with films such as *The Little Mermaid* (1989), *Beauty and the Beast* (1991), and *Aladdin* (1992). Along with the production of these films, the Disney Corporation has published thousands of fairy tale books worldwide, so that it is not an exaggeration to say that most children, if not adults, learn about the classical fairy tale as well as the classics in children's literature through Disney films, books, videos, and other ephemera. Whether this is negative or positive – the Disney adaptations have been criticized for being sexist, racist, and imperialist – is open to debate. What is clear is that most children throughout the world have a conventionalized notion – that is, a "Disneyfied" notion – of what a fairy tale is and should be. Even the work of the highly original writer Lloyd Alexander, who published *The Truthful Harp* in 1967 to complement his *Prydain Chronicles*, could not escape being absorbed by the Disney empire. His *Prydain Chronicles* consist of five novels: *The Book of Three* (1964), *The Black Cauldron* (1965), The *Castle of Llyr* (1966), *Taran Wanderer* (1967), and *The High King* (1968). Based on the Mabinogion, a collection of Welsh tales, Alexander's chronicles form a delightfully ironic and intricate fairy tale about a young assistant pig-keeper who performs valorous deeds to become a High King. While the original books competently transformed this ancient legend into a unique fairy tale opus that subverts many of the conventional motifs of the genre, the Disney film, a shortened, animated version entitled *The Black Cauldron* (1985), reduced an epic story to a simple rite-of-passage tale.

Politics and parodies

Working well outside the influence of the "new canon" of Disney adaptations in the aftermath of World War II, and especially since the late 1960s, have been gifted writers whose politicization of the fairy tale for children has produced some interesting experiments. The Anglo-American writer Joan Aiken published a series of fascinating and original fairy tales such as *All You Ever Wanted* (1953), *A Necklace of Raindrops* (1968), and *The Faithless Lollybird, and Other Stories* (1977). Her work challenges conventional notions of fairy tales, and she has consistently parodied and satirized the genre while creating new possibilities for its development. Other innovators include Lloyd Alexander, Catherine Storr, Nicholas Stuart Gray, and Dr. Seuss. *The Iron Man* (1968), by the British poet Ted Hughes, radically combines elements of the fairy tale and science fiction to comment on ecological problems.

Perhaps the most significant development in the field up through the 21st century, however, has been the evolution of feminist fairy tales for children and adults. Feminist fairy tale anthologies such as Rosemary Minard's *Womenfolk and Fairy Tales* (1975), Ethel Johnson Phelps's *Tatterhood, and Other Tales* (1978), *Alison Lurie's Clever Gretchen, and Other Tales* (1980), Letty Cottin Pogrebin's *Stories for Free Children* (1982), Jack Zipes's *Don't Bet on the Prince*: *Contemporary Feminist Fairy Tales in North America and England* (1986), and Jane Yolen's *Not One Damsel in Distress* (2000) have been particularly important. In fact, there have been well over a hundred or more writers and illustrators who have rearranged familiar motifs and characters and reversed plot lines to provoke readers to rethink conservative views of gender and power. The aesthetics of these tales are ideological, for the structural reformation depends on a nonsexist world view that calls for a dramatic change in practice. Among the more significant works produced for young readers since the 1970s are Tanith Lee's *Princess Hynchatti, and Some Other Surprises* (1978), Joanna Russ's *Kittatinny* (1978), Jay Williams's *The Practical Princess, and Other Liberating Fairy Tales* (1979), Jane Yolen's *The Moon, The Hundreth Dove, and Other Tales* (1979), Robert Munsch's *The Paper Bag Princess* (1980), Robin McKinley's *The Door in the Hedge* (1981), Babette Cole's *Princess Smartypants* (1986), Judy Corbalis's *The Wrestling Princess, and Other Stories* (1986), Katharine Paterson's *The King's Equal* (1992), Priscilla Galloway's *Truly Grim Tales* (1995), Vivian Vande Velde's *Tales from the Brothers Grimm and the Sisters Weird* (1995), Emma Donoghue's *Kissing the Witch*: *Old Tales in New Skins* (1997), Francesca Lia Block's *The Rose and the Beast* (2000), and Katrin Tchana's *The Serpent Slayer, and Other Stories of Strong Women* (2000).

Along with the feminist tales, there has been a resurgence of ethnic and multicultural tales. Many of the writers of these tales seek to preserve native traditions and to revise misconceptions about ethnic identity and history. Julius Lester was one of the pioneers in this endeavor with the publication of *Black Folk Tales* in 1969, and other writers such as Virginia Hamilton (*The People Could Fly: American Black Folktales*, 1985) have continued his efforts, as has the talented illustrator Robert Pinkney. Among the pioneers in Asian and multicultural tales, Laurence Yep has produced *The Rainbow People* (1990) and *Tongues of Jade* (1991), two collections of folk tales told by Chinese American immigrants, as well as several picture books such as *The Man Who Tricked a Ghost* (1993) and *Tiger Woman* (1996). In the Native American tradition, Michael Lacapa has written and illustrated Apache folk tales such as *Antelope Woman* (1995) and *Flute Player* (1995).

Experimentation with the fairy tale has been done not only from a sociopolitical perspective but also from a psychological one. For example, Donna Jo Napoli has produced a series of intriguing fairy tale novellas such as *The Prince of the Pond* (1992), *The Magic Circle* (1993), *Zel* (1996), *Spinners* (written with Richard Tchen; 1999), and *Beast* (2000), all of which are unusually deep explorations of classical tales such as "The Frog King," "Hansel and Gretel," "Rapunzel," "Rumpelstiltskin," and "Beauty and the Beast." Robin McKinley and Gregory Maguire have also produced noteworthy fairy tale novels. McKinley's *Beast* (1978) and *Rose Daughter* (1997) depict the heroine of "Beauty and the Beast" as a strong, independent young woman, while his *Deerskin* (1993) deals delicately with the theme of incest in "Donkey-Skin," and *Spindle's End* (2000) is an original revision of "Sleeping Beauty" as a tale of rebellion. Maguire's *Wicked: The Life and Times of the Wicked Witch of the West* (1997) is a heretical version of *The Wizard of Oz*, which recounts the life of a little green girl who grows up to become the Wicked Witch of the West. His *Confessions of an Ugly Stepsister* (1999), made into a television film, is a masterly historical fairy tale that focuses on an obsessive stepmother in 17th-century Holland.

Most modern-day revisions of the classical fairy tales are serious discourses about contemporary mores and values, but there are also remarkable fairy tale parodies such as Jon Scieszka's *The Frog Prince Continued* (1991) and *The Stinky Cheese Man and Other Fairly Stupid Tales* (1992), with brilliant surrealistic illustrations by Lane Smith. Perhaps the most important series of humorous fairy tales were the TV-animated *Fractured Fairy Tales* produced by Jay Ward for *Rocky and His Friends* (1959–61) and *The Bullwinkle Show* (1961–4). Highly irreverent, these TV parodies influenced the work of Jim Henson's Muppet fairy tales and some of the productions in Shelly Duvall's *Faerie Tale Theatre*.

An ever-growing reach

The enormous production of fairy tale films for the theater and television and the steady growth of multimedia versions of fairy tales for the Internet have not diminished the effect of the fairy tale as an oral and literary genre that can be regarded as the most dominant in the field of children's literature. If anything, the new media have provided new possibilities for the fairy tale's development as literature and as image. Today thousands of parents buy and read fairy tales to their children during the day and before the children go to bed in the evening. Thousands of teachers and librarians read fairy tales to children and stimulate children to write or tell their own fairy tales. In some cases, fairy tales have become part of a school's curriculum, and Waldorf schools, for instance, have also incorporated a particular philosophy (that of Rudolf Steiner) with regard to the telling of fairy tales. Numerous schools and libraries invite storytellers of all types and beliefs to come and tell or read fairy tales to children. Children watch television and cinematic versions of fairy tales and then play and create their own versions to enact their own family dramas or ontological struggles. Or, they bring home the tales they have heard or created in school and continue to play with them and improvise at home. Therapists, social workers, and psychiatrists rely on fairy tales to analyze psychic problems of both children and adults, and they have devised different methods of tale-telling to bring about revelations on the part of their patients. Commensurate with new devices of tale-telling are new methods of tale-listening, which is in itself an art.

Advertisers base many of their commercials on fairy tale plots and motifs. In fact, most commercials on television exploit the resources of fairy tales to create a sense of wonder and induce viewers to believe that there is something magical in the product that they are offering. Professional writers and artists create fairy tale versions for the public through which they make statements about themselves, society, and the fairy tale tradition itself. Their products include classical remakes, innovative tales with multiple perspectives, commercial products, novels, poems, plays, cartoons, paintings, records, tapes, films, and hypertexts on the Internet.

In short, the fairy tale has become totally institutionalized in Western society, part of the public sphere, with its own specific code and forms through which we communicate about social and psychic phenomena. Children are initiated and expected to learn the fairy tale code that has its keywords, icons, and metaphors, but it is not a static code. As long as the fairy tale continues to awaken the wonderment of the young and to project counterworlds to our present society – where children's yearnings and wishes may find fulfillment – it will serve a meaningful social function not just for compensation but for revelation.

Further reading

Avery, Gillian. *Behold the Child: American Children and Their Books, 1621–1922*. London: Bodley Head, 1994.

Bettelheim, Bruno. *The Uses of Enchantment: The Meaning and Importance of Fairy Tales*. New York: Knopf, 1976.

Jones, Steven Swann. *The Fairy Tale: The Magic Mirror of Imagination*. New York: Twayne, 1995.

Lieberman, Marcia. "Some Day My Prince Will Come: Female Acculturation through the Fairy Tale." *College English* 34 (1972): pp. 383–95.

Sale, Roger. *Fairy Tales and After: From Snow White to E.B. White*. Cambridge, Mass.: Harvard University Press, 1978.

Tatar, Maria M. *Off with Their Heads: Fairy Tales and the Culture of Childhood*. Princeton, N.J.: Princeton University Press, 1992.

Warner, Marina. *From the Beast to the Blonde: On Fairytales and Their Tellers*. London: Chatto and Windus, 1995.

Zipes, Jack. *Fairy Tales and the Art of Subversion: The Classical Genre for Children and the Process of Civilization*. 2d rev. ed. New York: Routledge, 2006.

Zipes, Jack. *When Dreams Came True: Classical Fairy Tales and Their Tradition*. New York: Routledge, 1999.

Children's Literature: Birth, Infancy, Maturity
Matthew Grenby

It is difficult to resist the temptation to identify precisely when children's literature began. The majority of scholars have placed the start line in London in the early 1740s. This was when Thomas Boreman began publishing his 'Gigantick Histories' (1740–43) – tiny books chummily describing the sights of London – and when *A Child's New Play-Thing* (1742) – a spelling book that ended with engaging stories like 'Guy of Warwick' and 'St. George' – and *Tom Thumb's Song Book* (1744) – the earliest known collection of nursery rhymes – were issued by Thomas and Mary Cooper. Even more famous, and often seen as the first modern children's book, is *A Little Pretty Pocket-Book* published by John Newbery in 1744 (see Figure 1). Although one critic sees it as 'the work of a thoroughly trivial, commercial, and disinherited mind', and seethes that 'its continuing *succès d'estime* is something of a mystery', Newbery's book is important simply because his firm endured while Boreman's and Cooper's did not: Newbery and his various heirs continued producing books for children for the rest of the century.[1] These anonymous, almost ephemeral publications of the 1740s – what one critic has called the 'incunabula of children's literature' – looked like nothing that had been published before.[2] They may have been fundamentally didactic, teaching the alphabet, civic history and good behaviour, but the instruction was being contained within a framework of pictures, rhymes, riddles, jokes and stories designed to amuse children.

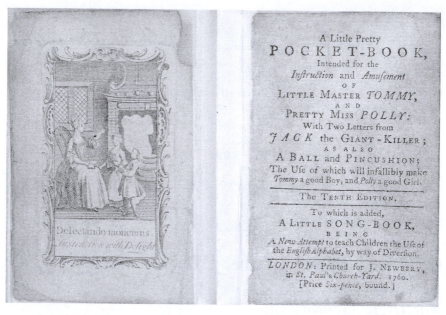

Figure 1   Frontispiece and title-page, *A Little Pretty Pocket Book*, London: John Newbery, [1744] 1760. By kind permission of the British Library. © British Library Board. All Rights Reserved, shelfmark: ch.760/6.

But saying that children's literature began in the mid-eighteenth century, and in Britain, immediately invites dissension. A case could be made for the primacy of French children's literature, for example, although a lack of copyright laws, a more rigidly hierarchical society and the Jesuit domination of schools (and the chaos caused by its sudden end) inhibited its development, and it was only after Newbery that French producers made a determined effort to combine instruction and delight.[3] But even if we take the 'delightfulness' of Newbery's books as the basis for their significance, we should remember that about eighty per cent of his list comprised straightforwardly educational books (not to mention his larger range of books for adults). His *Circle of the Sciences* series (1745–48), for example, taught grammar, geography, arithmetic and so on without much to captivate the child-reader. However celebrated and influential the 'delightful' books subsequently became – books like *The History of Little Goody Two-Shoes* (1765) or his short-lived children's periodical, *The Lilliputian Magazine* (1751–52) – Newbery's business probably relied much more on the educational titles. In this sense, he was less a pioneer than another contributor to a long tradition, for instructive material for children had been published throughout the seventeenth and eighteenth centuries. Even after the 1740s, successive editions of George Fisher's *The Instructor; or, the Young Man's Best Companion* (1727), say, or Daniel Fenning's *British Youth's Instructor* (1754?), easily outsold anything that Newbery or his competitors were offering. Moreover, the line between instruction and delight in the newer type of book is often very blurred. Thomas Boreman's first venture into the children's book market was *A Description of Three Hundred Animals* in 1730. Even if its preface presented the book as 'for the Entertainment of Children', it was primarily a work of natural history (though including such fabulous beasts as the manticora and cockatrice) and offered a part anecdotal and part technical 'Particular Account of the Whale-Fishery'.

In any case, the argument that books designed to entertain children appeared only with Newbery and his competitors in the mid-eighteenth century is pretty easy to undermine – especially if we are open-minded about exactly what child readers would find fun. François Fénelon's *Les Avantures de Télémaque fils d'Ulysse* (1699), almost instantly translated into English, provided a popular mix of Homeric adventure and moral instruction. Isaac Watts's *Divine Songs* (1715) was a collection of deeply religious poems, enforcing theological orthodoxy, but was couched in such amiable and sometimes whimsical verse that it would surely have been attractive to children. It is no surprise that it stayed in print throughout the eighteenth century and beyond. The same might be said for John Bunyan's *A Book for Boys and Girls, or, Country Rhimes for Children* (1686), later known as *Divine Emblems*. It comprised a series of spiritual lessons cleverly derived from 74 short poems on familiar subjects (bees, butterflies, beggars, 'the Boy dull at his Book'). That these emblematical poems function almost as riddles was acknowledged by Bunyan when he said that he aimed to 'entice' children,

> To mount their Thoughts from what are childish Toys,
> To Heav'n, for that's prepar'd for Girls and Boys.[4]

It is even possible to argue that some of the less obviously playful Puritanical children's books of the later seventeenth century would, in their way, have delighted children. James Janeway's *A Token for Children* (1671–72), which (as its subtitle spells out) provides 'an Exact Account of the Conversion,

Holy and Exemplary Lives, and Joyful Deaths of several young Children',
may seem brutally disciplinary to modern eyes, but in some ways it is
empowering literature, allowing boys and girls to read about people their
own age, showing children in full control of their lives, and even lecturing
their elders. The children may be dying, but, as Gillian Avery points out,
'they are 'enjoying the sort of dignity and esteem that few of their contemporaries could have experienced and all must envy'.[5]

Why stop here? There is plenty of evidence that children were reading,
and delighting in, all sorts of material long before Janeway and Bunyan, let
alone Newbery, were writing for them. Journals, memoirs, spiritual autobi-
ographies and other such sources reveal that, throughout the early modern
period, children were reading fables, courtesy books, the *Gesta Romano-
rum* (a collection of legends, lives of saints and heroes and stories), chapbooks (short, cheap popular stories often sold by peddlers), even chivalric
romances and novels. Francis Kirkman (born in 1632) reminisced about his
early devotion to chapbooks, then romances:

> once I happened upon a Six Pence & having lately read that famous Book of the
> *Fryar and the Boy*, and being hugely pleased with that, as also the excellent His-
> tory of the *Seven Wise Masters of Room* [i.e. Rome], and heard great Commen-
> dation of *Fortunatus*, I laid out all my money for that, and thought I had a great
> bargain ...; now having read this Book and being desirous of reading more of
> that nature; one of my School-fellows lent me *Doctor Faustus*, which also pleased
> me, especially when he travelled in the Air, saw all the world and did what he
> listed ... The next book I met with was *Fryar Bacon*, whose pleasant Stories
> much delighted me: But when I came to Knight Errantry, and reading *Montelion
> Knight of the Oracle*, and *Ornatus* and *Artesia*, and the Famous *Parismus*; I was
> contented beyond measure.[6]

None of these titles were intended especially for children, but clearly this
did not stop children reading and enjoying them. Indeed, the first of Kirkman's books, *The Friar and the Boy*, telling of a boy's use of a magic
charm to make his stepmother fart uncontrollably, has been called (surely
too emphatically) 'perhaps the first story appealing directly to children'.[7]
It was first printed by Wynkyn de Worde in about 1510, but had been
circulating in manuscript for much of the fifteenth century. For that matter, Chaucer's *Canterbury Tales* were probably read and enjoyed by children, the evidence for which is the existence of various abridgements,
as well as the apparently juvenile marginalia that sometimes covers the
manuscripts. Some medievalists now argue that, as Nicolas Orme puts it,
'Children's literature in England, in terms of both content and readership,
began in the middle ages', meaning by 1400 at the latest.[8] Going further

back still, others have written about children's reading in classical Rome and Greece, ancient Egypt and, most fascinatingly, in the earliest of all recognised civilisations, ancient Sumer (located in what is now Iraq and Iran).[9]

This gallop back through the early history of children's literature shows two things. First, we find that there is no simple way to define children's literature. When we use the term, do we mean books read only by children? Or only books that children would have enjoyed? Or only those that were deliberately intended for their amusement? Second, whichever definition we use, we find that children's literature has no easily discernible starting point. For as long as books (or manuscripts, or clay tablets) have been read, children have been reading them too, and their reading has throughout all these centuries often been entertaining as well as instructive. Whichever text we identify as the first 'proper' children's book, an earlier example can almost always be found to fit whatever criteria we are using.

Yet surely something did change in the mid-eighteenth century in Britain. What Newbery and his competitors and successors did was to establish children's literature as a distinct branch of print culture. They were the first to market a product which was exclusively for children (or at least putatively so, for the producers of these books also had to convince the adults who would actually be buying most of them that this was a new product worth investing in). And they were the first to try ostentatiously to offer both amusement and instruction, whether religious or secular, moral or commercial. Bunyan and Janeway may have written children's *books*, but, simply because no such thing yet existed, they were not producing children's *literature*. By the same token perhaps the first books produced by Newbery, Boreman, Cooper and others were not children's literature either, but as this kind of commodity gained a foothold in the market, the idea of children's literature was born in the minds of their contemporaries.

Purchasers were certainly plentiful enough to keep Newbery and his rivals publishing this kind of product, all the while steadily refining it. Indeed, by the end of the century publishing houses specialising in children's literature had sprung up, and even some of the most august mainstream publishers had been drawn into the market. There were specialist children's bookshops. Children's books began to be stocked in circulating libraries. Reviews of children's books began to appear in the main literary journals, and in 1802 Sarah Trimmer established the *Guardian of Education* as a periodical dedicated to the subject. By the close of the century it had become possible for a few men and women to carve out careers for themselves as writers for children – Richard Johnson, for instance, who wrote many books for

Newbery, or Trimmer, whose death after a long career in children's literature prompted letters to the *Gentleman's Magazine* demanding a 'national
monument' in St Paul's Cathedral. Such was the growing status of children's
literature, and its remunerative possibilities, that a number of successful
writers for adults were drawn to attempt children's books. When, in 1749,
Sarah Fielding turned from novels for adults to write a girls' school story,
The Governess, her claim that she wrote only 'to cultivate an early Inclination to Benevolence, and a Love of Virtue, in the Minds of young Women'
is credible (although she apparently made the very large sum of £256 from
the book).[10] But fifty years later, the letters of the celebrated if penurious
poet and novelist Charlotte Smith make it clear that she turned to children's literature because it paid well and was (she thought) easier to write.
She hoped for £50 per volume, the same as for her novels for adults. Even
William Godwin, the philosopher and successful novelist, turned his hand
to children's literature, as both author and publisher, 'to establish a more
secure income' (as his entry in the *Oxford Dictionary of National Biography* puts it).

This was still the infancy of children's literature though, not its full
maturity. Certainly, even at the end of the eighteenth century, the new
kind of children's literature was not reaching all of the nation's youth.
For one thing, not all children were literate, limiting the maximum constituency for children's literature to a few tens of thousands. For another,
even the most successful children's books had small print runs, seldom
more than 1000. And although many chapbook-style children's books
were available for as little as a penny, the more respectable books generally cost between one and two shillings for each volume, effectively pric-
ing readers from outside the middle and upper classes out of the market.
What this meant was that many children, even after the arrival of a new
children's literature, were still reading the same kinds of texts that their
predecessors had made do with, whether bibles and psalters, primers and
textbooks, fables, chapbooks or romances. A second important point is
that the growth of children's literature was a symptom of wider social,
economic and cultural changes rather than the result of the sudden creation of instantly appealing texts by a circle of brilliant authors and daring
publishers. The 'causes' of children's literature are too various, and too
little researched, to be dealt with in detail here. Demographic change is
clearly one important factor, for a diminishing childhood mortality rate
resulted in a larger market for children's books and a greater willingness to invest in children. Economic changes were crucial too, not only
because increased affluence and the 'consumer revolution' brought more
commodities, of which literature was one, into homes, but because of the

greater possibility, in the increasingly capitalistic eighteenth century, of socio-economic advancement. Children's books not only celebrated this possibility, describing how poor children could become rich (Newbery's Goody Two-Shoes, for instance, who starts off so poor that she has only one shoe, but ends as the Lady of the Manor), but were also marketed to parents as the very instruments by which children could acquire a more prosperous future. This promise is neatly encapsulated in the title of a later work, *The Alphabet of Goody Two Shoes; By Learning Which, She Soon Got Rich* (1808).

Just as important in the development of children's literature was a growing emphasis on the importance of education, and particularly maternal education. Mothers' education of their children was represented throughout eighteenth-century culture not only as a personal responsibility but as a national, some critics say imperial, duty. Hannah More, for example, was in no doubt about how crucial it was: 'The great object to which YOU, who are or may be mothers, are more especially called, is the education of your children', she wrote in 1799; this was no small thing, she insisted, but 'a power wide in its extent, indefinite in its effects, and inestimable in its importance'.[11] This argument had been made since the reign of Queen Anne at the start of the century, not only in conduct books and educational treatises, but across a full range of media, from poetry to portraiture to children's books. Well before the advent of a commercial children's literature, mothers had been devising their own educational techniques. Many accounts describe mothers using pictorial ceramic tiles, for instance, to teach the alphabet or the Bible. Others painstakingly manufactured their own educational tools, most famously Jane Johnson who, in the 1740s, wrote out and beautifully decorated hundreds of cards, toys and homemade books to teach her children how to read and what to think (miraculously, these artefacts still survive, though many others, no doubt, have been destroyed).[12] The precise link between these home-made texts and the subsequent wave of commercial children's books is obscure, but the continuities are obvious. To put it bluntly, Newbery and his competitors commercialised a process that already existed (although to commercialise was not necessarily always to supersede, for handmade books and teaching aids continued to be made). Many later eighteenth-century children's books were explicitly designed to be used by mothers teaching their children. They often represented exactly this process in both text and image, perhaps especially in the dedications and frontispieces, two parts of the 'peritext' designed to persuade consumers to buy the books and use them in the 'proper' manner (see Figure 2).[13]

Figure 2   Henry Walton (1746–1813), *Sir Robert and Lady Buxton and their daughter Anne*, *c*.1786 (oil on canvas). © Norwich Castle Museum and Art Gallery/The Bridgeman Art Library.

Accounts of eighteenth-century children's actual reading experiences – diaries, letters, memoirs – confirm that children's books were sometimes used under close supervision, as stringently recommended by most educationalists and in the books themselves. Henry Walton's portrait of *Sir Robert and Lady Buxton and their daughter Anne* (*c*.1786) shows just such a reading context. But other accounts – the more candid of the memoirs and, occasionally, marginalia – reveal children's sometimes solitary, secretive, promiscuous and even subversive reading habits. Often, it seems, the chief pleasure children derived from their books was not from the lessons, nor even from the stories, but from the book as a physical object – its illustrations, its feel in their hands, and the satisfaction of the simple fact of ownership. Certainly many books tried desperately to instil in children a textual rather than material appreciation of their books, and warned parents that close supervision was the only way to ensure that children benefited from their books. But even if Walton's portrait is not necessarily an accurate depiction of children's reading it remains interesting for what it tells us about the centrality that children and their books had achieved in the middle-class family. The parents' devotion to their child is emphasised, and represented in terms of their interest in her education. Sir Robert has even interrupted his own reading to register what is perhaps a crucial stage in his daughter's development as she reads with her mother. Just as important is that Anne is shown as a consumer, with her own toys (the miniature basket), her own furniture (the low chair) and her own books (one has been casually dropped on the floor, for books were clearly no longer quite so valuable as they had once been). It was in this changed economic, pedagogic and emotional context that children's literature was able to become established as a separate part of print culture.

So, what kinds of books were produced for children in the second half of the eighteenth century? Probably the dominant genre was the moral tale, at least in terms of influence if not of numbers (purely instructional and devotional books remained the best-sellers). Among the most celebrated are Sarah Fielding's school story *The Governess* (1749) and Anna Laetitia Barbauld's deftly pedagogic four-volume *Lessons for Children* (1778: small books printed with much white space to enhance readability, the content becoming progressively more sophisticated as the putative reader grew), Thomas Day's Rousseauvian *Sandford and Merton* (1783–89) and Sarah Trimmer's animal story *Fabulous Histories* (1786), later known as *The History of the Robins*. Others were set out as a series of linked shorter stories, notably the six-volume *Evenings at Home* by John Aikin (1792–96), with additions by Barbauld, and Maria Edgeworth's tales of Rosamond and Frank, Harry and Lucy, the first of which appeared in 1796 in *The Parent's Assistant* with many others added in an array of different titles over the course of the next quarter-century. Many of these moral tales were written by the 'Impeccable Governesses, Rational Dames, and Moral Mothers' – astute and quietly pioneering women whom Mitzi Myers collectively named the 'mentorias'.[14] But some hack writers also turned their hand to this newer kind of respectable, not to say earnest, publication – Richard Johnson, for example – and they often succeeded admirably. If Barbauld, Trimmer, Edgeworth and others were writing for more affluent readers – their child protagonists often had servants, spare cash and parents with private incomes – their works were imitated and made cheaper to suit less affluent markets. *The Governess* and *Evenings at Home* cost one shilling and sixpence per volume. Works by Johnson such as *The History of Tommy Careless or the Misfortunes of a Week* (1787), published by Elizabeth Newbery (wife of John Newbery's nephew), could cost as little as one penny.

There were many varieties of moral tale, increasingly directed at discrete sub-sections of the market (older or younger, girls or boys, more or less affluent), but in general they can be characterised as novels in miniature, succinct narratives set out over fifty or a hundred pages, or sometimes divided into a series of linked shorter stories. They usually took children as their lead characters, and the text always advanced one or more easily comprehensible behavioural lesson. What was left out of them is in a way more important that what was put in. They were not overtly pious and they included little that was fanciful or fantastic and redolent of popular literature. (Some of Newbery's early publications were unusual in this regard: *A Little Pretty Pocket-Book* began with a letter from Jack the Giant-Killer, and Goody Two-Shoes teaches a raven to read and write.) Samuel Johnson's somewhat confused reactions to this new kind of product highlights this shift away from popular culture. According to his friend Hester Lynch Piozzi, Johnson's own childhood delight (like Francis Kirkman a century before) had been chapbooks tales such as 'St. George and the Dragon', and he claimed that 'it was the only reading which could please an infant'. Indeed, continued Piozzi (who might be expected to know something about children's tastes, being the mother of twelve children), 'he used to condemn me for putting Newbery's books into their hands, as too trifling to engage their attention. "Babies do not want," said he, "to hear about babies; they like to be told of giants and castles, and of somewhat which can stretch and stimulate their little minds." '[15] Yet in a 1750 number of *The Rambler* Johnson was more perceptive: 'The works of fiction, with which the present generation seems more particularly delighted', he wrote, 'are such as exhibit life in its true state, diversified only by accidents that daily happen in the world, and influenced by passions and qualities which are really to be found in conversing with mankind.' If this was happening in literature for adults, in the novels of Samuel Richardson, Henry Fielding, Tobias Smollett and others, it was the policy of writers for children too. The underlying principle, as spelled out by Johnson, was straightforward:

> when an adventurer is levelled with the rest of the world, and acts in such scenes of the universal drama, as may be the lot of any other man; young spectators fix their eyes upon him with closer attention, and hope by observing his behaviour and success to regulate their own practices, when they shall be engaged in the like part.[16]

The Holiday Spy, probably by Richard Johnson and published by Elizabeth Newbery in around 1780 (price one penny), perfectly embodies this rationale (see Figure 3). It begins with Tommy Thoughtful coming home to London from school for the Whitsuntide holidays. He is taken by his father to 'the great warehouse for little books at the corner of St. Paul's Church-Yard' – Newbery's shop – where he is noticed by a kind lady – presumably

Figure 3 Frontispiece and title-page, *The Holiday Spy; Being the Observations of Little Tommy Thoughtful*, London: printed for E. Newbery, at the Corner of St. Paul's Church Yard, *c*.1800. By kind permission of Cotsen Children's Library, Princeton University Library, Department of Rare Books and Special Collections. Call number: Eng 18/Newbery 6771.

meant to be Elizabeth Newbery herself. She is so impressed at the very correct selection of books that Tommy makes that she offers him the chance to turn author himself and to write an account of all his friends. Having gained his father's permission, Tommy accepts the offer with alacrity. After all, the lady has promised him payment of 'the best cake my pastry-cook can make, and likewise of a complete set of Mr. Newbery's little gilt books'. What follows, as the book's full title puts it, are *The Observations of Little Tommy Thoughtful, on the Different Tempers, Genius, and Manners, of the Young Masters and Misses, in the Several Families which he visited, during his last Breaking-up, to be continued occasionally for the Entertainment of his School Fellows*. When he visits Peter Playful's house, for instance, Tommy is impressed by Peter's skill at marbles, whipping tops, making kites and so on, and his all-round jollity. But, says Tommy, because he is encouraged by his lax father, Peter 'spends too much of his time in acquiring these useless perfections, while the ... solid advantages he would derive from his books are little thought of'. Miss Betsy Goodchild, by contrast, 'read to admiration, and showed me some of her needle-work, which almost equalled painting'. Tommy is particularly impressed by the harmony reigning in her home:

> I did not observe in this house, what I have too often see in many others, violent disputes between mothers and daughters. I have seen many a pretty little Miss crying for half an hour together, and her Mamma talking to her in high words, threatening to whip her, or put her in the coal-hole, if she was not quiet, and at the last let the little Miss have what she wanted. No, it was very different in this house; for if Miss Betsy had a particular mind to any thing, she would ask for it in the most humble and submissive manner. If her Mamma smiled, it meant *Yes*; if she frowned or shook her head, it was as good a *No* as if she had said a thousand words: for Miss Betsy never asked for one thing twice, nor ever entered into any altercation, in hopes of getting what she wanted, as she had always been taught to consider, that nothing would be denied her which was proper for her, and she had too much good sense to persist in endeavouring to obtain what might be hurtful to her.[17]

There is perhaps no such thing as the 'typical' moral tale, but many of the form's characteristics are visible here. This is a thoroughly secular text, and deeply quotidian: deliberately, even overstatedly, rooted in what are supposed to be children's ordinary lives. Equally characteristic is the unvarnished presentation of models for readers either to emulate or execrate, their virtues or failings clearly signalled in their names. It is important to notice, though, that parents are very thoroughly implicated in the behaviour of their children, good or bad. This attempt to lecture both children and adults is another frequent feature of such moral tales. Also familiar is the way in which attitudes to books provide an index of children's moral worth. So many of these early moral tales are metafictive in this way, books depicting their own use (proper and improper), and publishers using their products to endorse their own products. Embedded in *The Holiday Spy* we can also find what might be regarded as the overriding ethos of the moral tales, namely the control of childhood. This text is very nakedly about the surveillance of children, the book attempting to ensure that readers internalise the monitoring gaze of the lady in the shop. In the fictional world Tommy is her hired 'spy'. But in the readers' real world it is the books that are her agents, coming into children's homes as the rewards of virtue but also to expose their vices, and even those of their parents. A moral tale like this is about espionage, but it is also itself the instrument of inspection and regulation. And in

The Holiday Spy, as throughout the genre, what is being controlled is the child's desire. What most impresses Tommy about Betsy Goodchild is that she conquers her own yearnings, not asking for anything twice, nor entering into any debate, but wholly submitting to her mother's judgement. The good children of the moral tales do not simply do what they are told, but, like Winston Smith in George Orwell's *1984*, learn not to want anything other than their supervisors, or think anything different.

If this sounds oppressive we should remember that books like *The Holiday Spy* were, in another way, liberating. They pointedly provided children with a literature of their own, a literature that was pitched at children and designed to entertain them. The same might be said of the very much more religious works that started to appear as one manifestation of a pervasive evangelical revival at the very end of the eighteenth century. The Religious Tract Society (RTS) was founded in 1799 with the specific aim of commissioning and distributing cheap, pious publications; within a few years some of these were being written exclusively for children. The tracts may have been strict but they were carefully designed to appeal to children through eye-catching illustrations, engaging narratives and the sheer pleasure for children of owning a product designed especially for them. They also effectively spread children's literature to much less affluent sections of society. The RTS's *Interesting History and Pleasing Adventures or Tommy Trip*, published in about 1830, is a good example. It loses no opportunity to explain that 'the Saviour ... came down from Heaven to die for poor sinners, that being cleansed from their sins by His precious blood they may have their hearts changed', or, in more secular but no less stern terms, that 'A kite flies best when you hold it tight, so when children are kept in the right way they will be happiest.' Yet, while kept short and cheap, the tract was made to resemble an enjoyable children's book of the sort Newbery and his successors might have published. Tommy Trip was a familiar name (he had made his first appearance, accompanied by his dog Jouler and Woglog the Giant, in Newbery's 1752 *A Pretty Book of Pictures*) and his story in the RTS appropriation parallels the worldly advancement of a Goody Two-Shoes. She had become the Lady of the Manor; Tommy, through his pious and kind behaviour, rises to become 'head ploughman, and has the highest wages of any body on the farm' (although it is noticeable that Tommy stays firmly within his class while Goody had joined the squirearchy). The RTS tract also offers an attractive woodcut on each page and, alongside the piety, includes several scenes of games-playing and Guy Fawkes Night effigy-making (for Tommy 'recollected the minister said that this day was kept as a holiday to remind us of the designs of the papists against the protestant religion, and that where the papists had power they would not let people have Bibles or Testaments').[18]

Other evangelical authors, outwith the auspices of the RTS, produced similar works but at greater length and for more affluent readers. The most enduring of these texts was Mary Martha Sherwood's *The History of the Fairchild Family* (1818, with further parts in 1842 and 1847). It is renowned as a severe book, even cruel, reprising the seventeenth-century Puritan conviction that humans are born sinful and need to be strongly disciplined in this world, especially in their youth, if they are to avoid eternal punishment in the next. In accordance with this doctrine, Lucy, Henry and Emily are variously harangued, shamed, ostracised, beaten, starved, incarcerated and, most notoriously, taken to see the rotting corpse while it hangs in a gibbet. Yet nineteenth-century memoirs time and again record a childhood fondness for the book. The children's author Mary Louisa Molesworth (born 1839) insisted that '*The Fairchild Family* was my favourite by far', although she disliked the prayers that closed each chapter. Revealing how children's reading strategies can subvert authorial intentions, she recalled that 'These I was too conscientious to "skip", but they were a sore trial, till at last I hit upon the plan of *reading forward* a certain number of them, so that I could then go back and enjoy the story straight on without the uncongenial break!'[19]

But not all nineteenth-century children were reading such evangelical works. Many of their accounts resemble those of Francis Kirkman and Samuel Johnson in their description of a fascination with chapbooks tales that were not especially intended for children. While we should not discount them entirely, these claims may be a little tendentious. The reasons why William Wordsworth, John Clare and Charles Dickens, all of whom offer this kind of testimony, admired chapbooks was because (they said) they were somehow 'of the people' and fuelled the imagination in a way that modern children's books did not. They were resentful that didactic and religious texts, intended solely for children, had supposedly supplanted folk literature, and were stultifying the rising generations. 'Think what you would have been now', Charles Lamb wrote to Samuel Taylor Coleridge, 'if instead of being fed with Tales and old wives' fables in childhood, you had been crammed with geography and natural history?'[20] In reality, the divide between chapbooks and children's literature was much less pronounced that the Romantics' nostalgia made it seem. The increasingly dynamic publishing industry was developing a new product around 1800, a sort of fusion of the traditional chapbook and the moral tale: what might be called the 'children's chapbook'. A typical title, giving an indication of its hybrid nature, is *The House that Jack Built, To which is added Some Account of Jack Jingle, Showing by what Means he acquired his Learning and in consequence thereof got rich, and built himself a House.* These children's

chapbooks were cheap and often printed outside London. They were probably designed to reach consumers who had become aware of the attractions
of the new children's literature, but who could not either access or afford
more expensive and metropolitan children's books.

The proliferation of these children's chapbooks demonstrates that the rise
of the moral tale and religious tract had not quelled the appetite for the
fanciful and fantastic. In fact, though some authors might have rejoiced –
or complained – that 'dragons and fairies, giants and witches, have van-
ished from our nurseries before the wand of reason', the supernatural
had never really been absent from children's literature.[21] The classic fairy
tales of Charles Perrault, Madame d'Aulnoy and others were published
throughout the later eighteenth century. Even some of the most respectable children's writers – Fielding, Fenn, Sherwood (not to mention the New-
berys) – employed fairy-tale characters, motifs and narratives to advance
their rational or spiritual agendas, developing a new sub-genre, the 'moral
fairy tale'. But in the first decades of the nineteenth century the fantastical became more central to children's literature. William Roscoe's *The
Butterfly's Ball and the Grasshopper's Feast* (1806), charming engraved
images and text giving a whimsical account of the social lives of insects,
inspired a welter of imitations. Benjamin Tabart began publishing book-
length fairy tales and individual stories from the *Arabian Nights* and the
chapbook traditions from 1804. And John Harris, who had taken over the
Newbery firm in 1801, quickly began to issue delightfully illustrated titles
like *The Comic Adventures of Old Mother Hubbard* (1805). Even his more
didactic titles, published in 'Harris's Cabinet of Amusement and Instruction', showed the influence of this new emphasis on the fanciful: *Peter Piper's Practical Principles of Plain and Perfect Pronunciation* was published in
1813 and *Marmaduke Multiply's Merry Method of Making Minor Mathe-
maticians* in around 1816. By the time the fairy tales of the Brothers Grimm
were published in Britain in 1823 they were appealing to a taste that was
already firmly established.

It might be said, then, that by the accession of Victoria in 1837 children's
literature was approaching maturity. Some critics have argued that Lewis
Carroll's *Alice's Adventures in Wonderland*, published in 1865, is the first
truly modern children's book, for it offered a full-length narrative designed
solely for children's pleasure. But rather than seeing it as something entirely
new, it is probably more accurate to regard *Alice* as the zenith of a taste
for the whimsical and marvellous that had been established in the early
nineteenth century. It certainly has much in common with books that came
before: outright whimsy like Edward Lear's *A Book of Nonsense* (1846), and
extended fairy tales like John Ruskin's *The King of the Golden River* (1851),

William Makepeace Thackeray's *The Rose and the Ring* (1854) and Charles Kingsley's *The Water-Babies* (1863). And it is not so far removed from some of the more light-hearted evangelical novels, such as Catherine Sinclair's *Holiday House* (1839). This was ultimately a religious book, with a pious deathbed scene as a conclusion, but it also celebrated the exploits of its mischievous child protagonists in a manner not wholly dissimilar to modern accounts of acceptable transgression like Dorothy Edwards's *My Naughty Little Sister* or Richmal Crompton's *Just William* stories. Lewis Carroll gave a copy of *Holiday House* to the Liddell sisters shortly before he told them the first version of the Alice story.

This 'genealogical' approach to children's literature – to establish *Alice's* literary lineage – is not always helpful. It is too teleological, and the artificial narratives that are imposed on the history of children's literature can distort our readings of individual texts. In any case, by the middle of the nineteenth century, children's literature had become too diverse to be easily organised into one, or even several, lines of descent. Children's literature had become so securely established that it ranged across markets and genres. Different books were being published for rich and poor, for girls and boys, for Anglicans and dissenters, for metropolitan, provincial and colonial readers, for infants, children and young adults. As well as fables, fairy stories and moral tales, children were reading adventure novels like Frederick Marryat's *Children of the New Forest* (1847), family stories like Charlotte Yonge's *The Daisy Chain* (1856), school stories like Thomas Hughes's *Tom Brown's Schooldays* (1857), and this is not to mention poetry, picture books, moveable and doll books, devotional works and all sorts of non-fiction. Dozens of publishers had entered the market, some enduring but most going to the wall after a brief burst of productivity. New technologies (especially for illustration) and more sophisticated promotional and distribution strategies transformed the market. Books became larger, and more colourful. They become more cheaply and widely available – and often, as a result, since they were no longer the treasured luxuries they had once been, more ephemeral. At the other end of the market, *Alice's Adventures in Wonderland* sold for the exorbitant price of seven shillings and sixpence. That it was an immediate success (in terms of sales even if not with its first reviewers) is testimony to the maturity of the market. Consumers, it is clear, no longer had to be persuaded that children's books were a worthwhile purchase, as had been the case when Newbery began his operation. Rather, publishers, authors and illustrators were competing against each other for their share of the profits that were evidently to be made. It was this competition that triggered what has been called the Golden Age of children's literature from the 1860s to the 1920s, just as, a century before, it had been the struggle to establish the appeal and utility of children's literature that had led to its first blossoming.

Notes and references

1. Geoffrey Summerfield, 1984. *Fantasy and Reason*. London, Methuen: 86.
2. Brian Alderson, 1999. 'New Playthings and Gigantick Histories: The Nonage of English Children's Books', *Princeton University Library Chronicle*, 60: 178–95.
3. See Penny Brown, 2008. *A Critical History of French Children's Literature* (2 vols). London, Routledge, vol. 1: 7 and 128.
4. John Bunyan, 1686. *A Book for Boys and Girls, or, Country Rhimes for Children*. London: n.p. [ii].
5. Gillian Avery, 1989. 'The Puritans and their Heirs', in Gillian Avery and Julia Briggs (eds) *Children and their Books. A Celebration of the Work of Iona and Peter Opie*. Oxford, Clarendon Press: 95–118 (112).
6. Francis Kirkman, 1673. *The Unlucky Citizen. Experimentally Described in the Various Misfortunes of an Unlucky Londoner*. London: 10–12.
7. Hugh Cunningham, 2006. *The Invention of Childhood*. London. BBC Books: 58.
8. Nicholas Orme, 2001. *Medieval Children*. New Haven, Yale University Press: 271.
9. See Seth Lerer, 2008. *Children's Literature. A Reader's History from Aesop to Harry Potter*. Chicago and London, University of Chicago Press: 17–56, and Gillian Adams, 'Ancient and Medieval Children's Texts', in Peter Hunt (ed.) *The Routledge International Encyclopedia of Children's Literature*, 2nd edn (2 vols). London, Routledge, vol. 1: 225–38.
10. 'To the Honourable Mrs. Poyntz', Sarah Fielding, *The Governess; or, The Little Female Academy*, ed. Candace Ward, 2005. Peterborough, ON, Broadview: 45; *The Correspondence of Henry and Sarah Fielding*, 1993. ed. M.C. Battestin and C.T. Probyn, 1993. Oxford, Clarendon Press: xxxviii.
11. Hannah More, 1799. *Strictures on the Modern System of Female Education* (2 vols). London, Cadell and Davies, vol. 1: 59.
12. For digital images, see *A Guide to the Jane Johnson Manuscript Nursery Library, ca. 1740–1759*, online at www.dlib.indiana.edu/collections/janejohnson, accessed 29 August 2008.
13. 'Peritext' is a term, originally used by Gérard Genette, describing those elements of the book that mediate the relations between the text and reader but are not part of the actual text. Together with 'epitext' (mediating elements 'outside' the physical book, such as reviews or advertisements), the peritext constitutes the 'paratext'.
14. Mitzi Myers, 1986. 'Impeccable Governesses, Rational Dames, and Moral Mothers: Mary Wollstonecraft and the Female Tradition in Georgian Children's Books', *Children's Literature*, 14: 31–59.
15. Hester Lynch Piozzi, 1786. *Anecdotes of the Late Samuel Johnson, LL.D. During the Last Twenty Years of His Life*. London, T. Cadell: 16.
16. *The Rambler*, no. 4 (Saturday 31 March 1750), *The Yale Edition of the Works of Samuel Johnson*, vol. III: *The Rambler*, eds. W.J. Bate and Albrecht B. Strauss. New Haven, CT, Yale University Press, 1969: 19–25 (19 and 21).
17. Richard Johnson, *c*. 1780. *The Holiday Spy; Being the Observations of Little Tommy Thoughtful*. London, E. Newbery: 7, 12, 25, 26–7.
18. Anon., *c*. 1830. *The Interesting History and Pleasing Adventures or Tommy Trip*. London, Religious Tract Society: 4, 10 and 13.
19. Quoted in Jane Cooper, 2002. *Mrs Molesworth. A Biography*. Crowborough, East Sussex, Pratts Folly Press: 48.

20. Charles Lamb to Samuel Taylor Coleridge, 23 October, 1802. *Letters of Charles and Mary Lamb*, ed. E.V. Lucas. London, J.M. Dent: 326.
21. Lucy Aikin, 1801. *Poetry for Children. Consisting of Short Pieces, to be Committed to Memory*. London, R. Phillips: iii.

The First Golden Age
Humphrey Carpenter

When Wordsworth published his 'Ode: Intimations of Immortality' in 1807 he was issuing a call to revolution against the view of childhood which had persisted throughout the eighteenth century, a view which had dominated both education and the writing of children's books. To the typical writer of the Enlightenment, a child was simply a miniature adult, a chrysalis from which a fully rational and moral being would duly emerge, providing parents and educators did their job properly. There was no question of children having an independent imaginative life of any importance, or of their being able to perceive anything that was invisible to adults. The only necessity was for instruction to be poured into their ears, and the only argument was about what sort of instruction it should be.

The mainstream of English child-rearing in the eighteenth century worked along lines laid down by Locke, practised moderation in all things, and gave children virtually nothing to stimulate their imaginations. Had not Locke inveighed against such 'perfectly useless trumpery' as fairy stories? *Aesop and Reynard the Fox* were the only imaginative works he thought fit for the nursery. Then there was the Rousseau school of child nurture, which had pockets of following in England in the late eighteenth century. Rousseau's *Émile* was to have the noble savage in him cultivated more subtly than by Locke's methods. Yet Rousseau had just as narrow a view as Locke of what children should be allowed to read. According to *Émile*, just about the only tolerable book was *Robinson Crusoe*. And alongside the Locke and Rousseau factions was a third group of educationalists, typified by Mrs Sarah Trimmer – the indomitable lady who delivered the tirade against *Cinderella*. Severe piety was their characteristic; they were concerned that children should be taught the true principles of religion, and they deplored both Locke's emphasis on the child's unaided use of his reason and Rousseau's concept of the noble (and potentially

---

Extracted from 'Prologue: The Road to Arcadia', in H. Carpenter, *Secret Gardens: A Study of the Golden Age of Children's Literature* (London and Boston: Allen & Unwin, 1985), pp. 1–19.

God-less) savage. Yet they too agreed with Locke and Rousseau about not giving children reading matter that would merely excite the imagination.

The Romantics' view of childhood turned this upside down. In England the first stirrings of change came in 1789 with Blake's *Songs of Innocence*. Though they were in no way polemic, and made no statement about the nature of the child's imagination, the *Songs* were nevertheless an ardent affirmation that children have access to a kind of visionary simplicity that is denied to adults. Blake's introductory poem describes his 'happy songs' as those which 'Every child may joy to hear'. Adults, it is implied, will not have the same instinctive understanding of their visions. Nine years later came *Lyrical Ballads*, to which Wordsworth contributed several poems describing the child's view of the world. One of them, 'Anecdote for Fathers', celebrates a child's simple directness of thought, and concludes:

> Oh dearest, dearest boy! my heart
> For better lore would seldom yearn,
> Could I but teach the hundredth part
> Of what from thee I learn.

One imagines that Locke, if not Rousseau, might have scratched his head and wondered precisely what it was that Wordsworth claimed to be learning from the child. But such poems in *Lyrical Ballads* contained only a hint, the first approaches to a thesis. That thesis was worked out more fully in Wordsworth's 'Intimations of Immortality from Recollections of Early Childhood', to give the poem its full title:

> There was a time when meadow, grove, and stream,
> The earth, and every common sight,
>   To me did seem
>   Apparelled in celestial light,
> The glory and the freshness of a dream.
> It is not now as it hath been of yore; –
>   Turn wheresoe'er I may,
>   By night or day,
> The things which I have seen I now can see no more.
>
>   Not in entire forgetfulness,
>   And not in utter nakedness,
> But trailing clouds of glory do we come
>   From God, who is our home:
> Heaven lies about us in our infancy!
> Shades of the prison-house begin to close
>   Upon the growing Boy ...

The notion that children are in a higher state of spiritual perception than adults, because of their nearness to their birth and so to a pre-existence in Heaven, was not a new one in English poetry. The metaphysical poet Henry Vaughan expressed it in much the same terms in the mid-seventeenth century in 'The Retreate', which looks back nostalgically to 'those early dayes! when I / Shin'd in my Angell-infancy', and speaks of early childhood as a time when God's face was still visible; growing up, says Vaughan, consists of putting on a 'fleshly dress' over this angel-innocence. The poem concludes:

> O how I long to travell back
> And tread again that ancient track!

Vaughan's contemporary Thomas Traherne shared this view; in 'The Approach' he writes of the child's nearness to God:

> He in our childhood with us walks,
> And with our thoughts mysteriously he talks ...
> O Lord, I wonder at thy love
> Why did my infancy so early move ...

And he speaks of childhood itself as being 'My tutor, teacher, guide'.

In all these poems there is surely a hint of Eden. Certainly it is not a far step from the Genesis story to the notion that, to children, the earth appears as beautiful and numinous as it did to Adam and Eve. Growing up becomes synonymous with the loss of Paradise. Does this perhaps have a little to do with the Victorian and Edwardian children's writers' fondness for the symbol of a garden or Enchanted Place, in which all shall be well once more?

Wordsworth's Ode was perhaps not as directly influential on attitudes to children as the writings of Locke and Rousseau had been in their time. But by the mid-nineteenth century there had been a discernible alteration. The old view of the child as miniature adult, as moral chrysalis, had largely receded. On a purely practical level there were suggestions that children might simply be allowed to be themselves. *Holiday House* (1839), a novel for children by a Scottish writer named Catherine Sinclair, has some claim to attention as the first work of fiction in which children's propensity towards naughtiness is actually enjoyed by the author, even praised. The book describes the pranks of young Laura and Harry Graham, left in the charge of a rod-of-iron housekeeper called Mrs Crabtree, and a jolly, tolerant uncle. At every turn of the story Mrs Crabtree is mocked for her severity, and the uncle delights in the children's high spirits, even when they nearly burn the house down. (Harry is given a shilling for helping to put out the fire which he himself started.) *Holiday House* was too revolutionary to inspire imitations – its own author was sufficiently unsure about it to write some rather lugubrious closing chapters in which a dying brother exhorts Harry and Laura to reform themselves – but it is an indication of the reaction that was going on against the old view of childhood. It proved popular enough to be reprinted several times, and C.L. Dodgson ('Lewis Carroll') gave a copy to Alice Liddell and her sisters at Christmas 1861, a few months before he told them the story of *Alice's Adventures*.

Around the middle of the nineteenth century the change of attitude towards children became visible in adult novels. *Jane Eyre* and *Wuthering Heights*, both published in 1847, accept that children have a clear, even heightened, vision of the world. The child Jane's imprisonment in Lowood School is narrated exactly as she herself sees it, and Emily Brontë's melodrama is largely an instance of childhood passions being carried forward into adult life. Something of the same understanding of childhood may be found in George Eliot's *The Mill on the Floss* (1860) and *Silas Marner* (1861), and, more than any other novelist of this period, Dickens fully perceived the value of the child's-eye-view. One notes how the Oliver Twist type of hero was also taken up and used for their own purposes by many evangelical writers in England and America, so that by the 1860s and 1870s the market was being flooded by novels in which orphan waifs were leading their elders spiritually by the hand and inculcating in them a true love of God. Gillian Avery writes of such books:

> Children are not only shown as better than their parents, but are frequently the instruments of their parents' salvation. It is not, however, Blake's Innocent Child that we are shown. The tract book writers gave us a child who although appearing sinless to our eyes, knew he was sinful but was conscious that he had turned to Christ and Christ had saved him, and now urgently wished to pass on the message.[1]

Wordsworth's child, trailing clouds of glory, had been put to a use that Wordsworth himself certainly did not have in mind.

By the second half of the nineteenth century, then, the child had become an important figure in the English literary imagination. The detritus of the moralists had not been entirely cleared away: alongside *Holiday House* on the bookshelves of Alice Liddell and her sisters, in the deanery of Christ Church, Oxford, seems to have stood a recent reprint of Isaac Watts's *Divine Songs*, first published in 1715 and still going strong in the 1860s. These little verses, with their pious injunctions ('Satan finds some mischief still / For idle hands to do'), were to be parodied wickedly in *Alice's Adventures in Wonderland* – a sure indication that they were still being read in nurseries. Copies of the old moral tales were still lying around too, and, despite the fact that fairy stories were no longer dismissed as useless trash, there was little imaginative fiction for children appearing from the presses. The typical mid-Victorian nursery would have its Grimm and Andersen alongside its Perrault, and a book of nursery rhymes too (these had been collected by scholars since the late eighteenth century), but as late as 1860 there was scarcely anything in the way of full-length imaginative children's novels. Ruskin and Thackeray had attempted to provide something to fill this gap, but Ruskin's *The King of the Golden River* (1851) was really only a Grimm-type story on a larger scale, with the moral all too clearly pointed, while Thackeray's *The Rose and the Ring* (1855), though witty and deservedly popular, scarcely extended the bounds of imaginative writing for children, being a comic squib chiefly intended as a parody of the then fashionable style of London pantomime.

A few other British writers had produced a little of what might be called 'fantasy'. A Staffordshire clergyman named F.E. Paget, calling himself 'William Churne', wrote *The Hope of the Katzekopfs* (1844), which is strictly speaking the first original full-length English fantasy for children; but with its mixture of unimaginative fairy-tale narrative and heavy moralising it soon passed into oblivion. One or two other writers, such as the humorists Mark Lemon and Tom Hood, turned out original fairy tales, but nothing made a deep impression. Typical of the time was the *Home Treasury* series of traditional fairy stories, issued (under the pseudonym 'Felix Summerly') by Sir Henry Cole, mid-Victorian public servant and a founding father of the Great Exhibition, the Albert Hall, and the South Kensington Museum. Cole engaged 'eminent modern artists' to illustrate his *Little Red Riding-Hood, Jack and the Beanstalk*, and the rest; but the results', published during the 1840s, were heavyweight and reminiscent of a Royal Academy exhibition rather than exciting.

In fact, though in many respects the soil had been ready as early as 1830 for the development of imaginative writing for children, nothing could really happen in Britain during the first half of the nineteenth century. It was not enough for writers in general to perceive the qualities of a child's mind and imagination: before anything of value for children could come out of this, individual authors would have to feel themselves driven away from an adult audience towards a child readership. That apparently could not really happen before the 1860s, because up to then the adult world seems to have been (despite its political and social troubles) too hopeful, too inviting, for men and women of literary genius to reject it and seek a private, childlike voice for themselves. The Great Exhibition of 1851 was a celebration of Britain's position as a leader of industrial society, a leadership established painfully but in the end peacefully, for by 1851 even the working-class ferment visible during the previous decade in the Chartist marches, the Peterloo massacre, and the Bristol riots, had died down. Britain was indeed almost the only nation in Europe to have escaped the 1848 revolutions, and an enormous growth in the national economy was under way by the time of the Great Exhibition. The middle-class Englishman of 1851, like his counterpart a century later, had never had it so good.

Figure 4   Front cover, Edward Lear, *A Book of Nonsense*, London: Frederick Warne & Co., 1846; Boston: Robert Brothers, 1894. By kind permission of the Mary Evans Picture Library.

Yet in the middle of this complacency a lone voice was beginning to mutter, chiefly into the ears of children. Its message was that the public world was vindictive and intolerant, and that the man of vision, the true artist, must alienate himself from society and pursue a private dream. Edward Lear's *Book of Nonsense*, a collection of limericks, first appeared pseudonymously in 1846, five years before the Great Exhibition, and slowly established itself as the common property of English nurseries. The dedication of the 1861 reprint, to the great-grandchildren, grand-nephews, and grand-nieces of the thirteenth Earl of Derby, for whose parents 'the greater part of ... this book of drawings and verses ... were originally made and composed', might suggest that Lear had a comfortable niche in society. But by 1861 Lear had long ago abandoned his job as resident water-colourist to the Earl, and had exiled himself to the Mediterranean, where he scraped a living as an itinerant 'dirty landscape painter' – words which a passing English traveller once used of him. He was homosexual, depressive, and suffered from epileptic fits. Not surprisingly he felt himself to be an outcast. He lived his Mediterranean life largely in a state of deep unhappiness, but usually became cheerful when chance threw him into the company of children, whom he could reduce to helpless laughter with his comic drawings, funny alphabets, and rhymes. His alienation from society is the real subject of his Book of *Nonsense*, with its catalogue of eccentric individuals, many of whom suffer the contempt, hostility, and often violent reactions of the public world – which is always labelled as 'They':

> There was an Old Person of Buda,
> Whose conduct grew ruder and ruder;
>   Till at last, with a hammer,
>   They silenced his clamour,
> By smashing that Person of Buda.

After the Book of *Nonsense* was published, Lear was able to turn his mind to more positive things, and his later verses for children consist largely of explorations of the possibilities of Escape:

> They went to sea in a Sieve, they did,
>   In a Sieve they went to sea:
> In spite of all their friends could say,
> On a winter's morn, on a stormy day,
>   In a Sieve they went to sea!

The purpose of such strange journeys is stated bluntly enough. As the Duck observes to the Kangaroo,

> 'My life is a bore in this nasty pond,
> And I long to go out in the world beyond!'

The Nutcracker remarks much the same thing to the Sugar-Tongs: ' "Don't you wish we were able / Along the blue hills and green meadows to ride? / Must we drag on this stupid existence for ever?" ' And Lear's strange travellers, despite their often perilous means of journeying, usually get to their destinations. The Jumblies cross the Western Sea in their leaky craft and come to an earthly paradise where 'they bought an Owl, and a useful Cart, / And a pound of Rice, and a Cranberry Tart.' The Yonghy-Bonghy-Bò is borne away from a broken love affair on the back of a turtle, who carries him 'Towards the sunset isles of Boshen', and even the Pobble Who Has No Toes lands up in comfort at his Aunt Jobiska's Park, while of course the Owl and the Pussycat come to the Land where the Bong-Tree grows. In these and other rhymes, published from the 1870s to the 1890s, Lear is stating a theme that becomes central to the great children's writers: the search for a mysterious, elusive Good Place.

Such a place had in a sense been the goal of the religious writers for children from John Bunyan to Mrs Sherwood. But Lear rejected their view of the universe. He could not accept any form of hellfire teaching. The notion that, as he put it, 'the Almighty damns the greater part of His creatures' seemed ridiculous to him. He described himself as one of those 'who believe that God the Creator is greater than a Book, and that millions unborn are to look up to higher thoughts than those stereotyped by ancient legends, gross ignorance, and hideous bigotry'.

These sentiments are extraordinarily close to those expressed in 1939 by A.A. Milne. In his autobiography, *It's Too Late Now*, Milne condemned organised religion for its narrowness of view, and pleaded for the recognition of 'God' as something far huger and more mysterious than the deity of Christian doctrine. A thread of connection runs here between Lear and Milne; for, almost without exception, the authors of the outstanding English children's books that appeared between 1860 and 1930 rejected, or had doubts about, conventional religious teaching. The doubts, as we shall see, are less visible in the writers who operated earlier in this period. Charles Kingsley, Lewis Carroll, and George MacDonald were all three clergymen, and their religious uncertainties can only be detected beneath the surface of their writings for children, though they were a very strong motive behind them. The group of writers who followed later – Kenneth Grahame, Beatrix Potter, J.M. Barrie, and A.A. Milne – were more conscious of their rejection of conventional Christianity. Their search for an Arcadia, a Good Place, a Secret Garden, was to a very large extent an attempt to find something to replace it.[2]

By the time that Edward Lear published his *Nonsense Songs* (1871), the book which contained 'The Owl and the Pussy-Cat', his urge to comment sardonically on the public world was beginning to be shared by writers of a very different kind. The mid-Victorian belief in progress, which had steered Britain to her recent economic successes and had motivated the Great Exhibition, was starting to be shaken. The realisation had dawned that the apparent triumphs of the Industrial Revolution had produced widespread misery for the working classes. First Dickens in fiction, then Henry Mayhew in his documentary survey of London poverty (concluded in 1862), revealed this truth. Many writers tried to find some solution to the dilemma. Among them were Ruskin, whose *Fors Clavigera* (1871–84) inveighed against working-class poverty (and incidentally attacked complacent Sunday School teachers for showering the children of the poor with useless little moral tracts), and Charles Kingsley, who before turning to a child readership with *The Water-Babies* wrote adult novels about the insanitary lives of the poor. The Pre-Raphaelites, and William Morris in particular, started to preach that the route back to a healthy society lay through a flight from industrialisation, a return to medievalism, and the revival of the old methods of craft. Morris's ideals led him to write *The Earthly Paradise* (1868–70), a narrative poem which describes the search for a land 'across the western sea where none grow old'. George Borrow went searching for earthly paradises on the real map, escaping from industrial England to Europe and the East; in such books as *Lavengro* (1851) he created his own literature of Escape, which was to influence Kenneth Grahame. And in 1871, the year of 'The Owl and the Pussycat', Matthew Arnold, whose voice was among the loudest being lifted against industrial society, had this to say in *Friendship's Garland* on the subject of urban life:

> Your middle-class man thinks it the highest pitch of development and civilisation when his letters are carried twelve times a day from Camberwell to Islington, and if railway-trains run to and fro between them every quarter of an hour. He thinks it is nothing that the trains only carry him from an illiberal, dismal life at Islington to an illiberal, dismal life at Camberwell; and the letters only tell him that such is the life there.

This growing vein of scepticism about the quality of contemporary life was accompanied, during the final quarter of the nineteenth century, by a certain faltering in Britain's fortunes in the public world. The prosperity of the 1850s and 1860s gave way to a period of economic uncertainty and even depression. François Bédarida, in his *Social History of England, 1851–1975* (1979), observes that during this period the economic health of Britain 'was not so radiant as it had been in the past', and describes a crisis of confidence which 'shattered all the old certainties', so that 'pessimism and anxiety became the rule'. For contemporary confirmation of this, one need turn no further than to the private journal of Beatrix Potter, compiled in code during the 1880s and 1890s. Potter draws a picture of the English middle class (to which her family belonged) deeply worried by workers' protest marches, by explosions set off by Irish Home Rulers, and by the supposedly incompetent and wrong-headed Prime Ministerial behaviour of Gladstone. 'I am terribly afraid of the future,' Beatrix Potter wrote in 1885. No wonder that she turned away, in her Journal, from the contemplation of public affairs to a meditation about her own happiness in early childhood, and eventually began to create a series of books set in a world which, though far from safe and untroubled, was not touched on by politics or other overtly adult concerns.

This widespread uncertainty, from the 1870s onwards, came despite the great expansion of the British Empire, just then taking place. The imperial spirit (certainly to be found alongside the pessimism) did not go unnoticed by writers for children, but the books it inspired were ephemeral. During the 1880s such writers as G. A. Henty turned out sheaves of stories about brave British lads abroad; but this optimistic school of fiction was to produce no classic, no narrative of more than trivial interest. Probably the nearest that one can find to an 'Empire' classic for children is Kipling's *Stalky and Co* (1899), an apparently amoral book which is in fact subtly organised to demonstrate that boyish anti-authoritarian pranks at school are a good training for manly service in the cause of one's nation. In the final chapter Stalky is seen putting into good effect as an officer on the North-West Frontier the lessons in cunning he learnt from his pranks at the College, with Beetle and M'Turk. But almost no other children's book of note reflected the imperial spirit, while Kipling's own children's writings spread into an area not far from that occupied by Kenneth Grahame and A.A. Milne; their stories have certain affinities with his *Jungle Books* (1894 and 1895) and his *Just So Stories* (1902). Moreover, *Kim* (1901), Kipling's brilliant study of a white child adrift in the Indian underworld, has something of the Arcadian yearnings of the great introspective children's authors, with its account of the old lama's search for a sacred River, an Enchanted Place where he can find peace.

Kipling was almost the only writer who straddled the two streams of children's literature, which divided in about 1860 and never really came together again until the 1950s. On the one hand was the breezy, optimistic adventure story, set firmly in the real world (though greatly exaggerating certain characteristics of that world). Stories of school life, pioneered by Thomas Hughes and then mass produced by hack writers from the 1880s, belonged in this category, as did the girls' stories by L.T. Meade, Angela Brazil, and other popular novelists of the same sort. 'Realistic' fiction of this

Figure 5   Mowgli mourns Akela', from Rudyard Kipling, 'Red Dog', in *The Second Jungle Book*, illus. J. Lockwood Kipling, London: Macmillan & Co., 1895. By kind permission of the British Library. © British Library Board. All Rights Reserved. Shelfmark: C.117.d.5.

kind attracted few writers of any quality – besides Kipling, Robert Louis Stevenson was almost the only outstanding author to involve himself with it, in *Treasure Island* (1883) and *Kidnapped* (1886) – and it was not, of course, 'realistic' in any deep sense. Except in the hands of a Kipling or a Stevenson it dealt in stereotyped characters and ideas and presented a thoroughly rose-coloured view of the world. Its ideals were a *reductio ad absurdum* for children of the notion of 'chivalry' which dominated Victorian society and was derived from a spurious Arthurian-style medievalism.[3] The ethic of this strand of children's fiction – a belief in heroism for its own sake, a condemnation of the coward or 'muff', and a conviction that the English were the best race in the world – may have contributed to the causes of the First World War.

The other strand of writing for children, the one with which this present book is chiefly concerned, was introspective, and is generally described as 'fantasy' in that its stories, more often than not, involve some impossible thing, such as talking animals or toys, or inexplicable or magical events.[4] To this strand belong most of the great names of the late Victorian and Edwardian nursery: Kingsley, Carroll, MacDonald, Grahame, Potter, Nesbit, Barrie, with Milne as a latecomer. While it was not overtly 'realistic' and purported to have nothing to say about the 'real' world, in this fantastic strain of writing may be found some profound observations about human character and contemporary society, and (strikingly often) about religion. It dealt largely with utopias, and posited the existence of Arcadian societies remote from the nature and concerns of the everyday world; yet in doing this it was commenting, often satirically and critically, on real life.

It is notable that this fantasy writing took root most quickly and deeply in England. Other European countries produced only a tiny handful of memorable children's fantasies before 1914: Carlo Collodi's chaotic but charming *Pinocchio* (1883) and *The Wonderful Adventures of Nils* (1906–7) by the Swedish writer Selma Lagerlöf are really the only examples of note. America was almost equally unproductive before 1900, and most fantasies that did appear there were imitative of British writers. Only with *The Wonderful Wizard of Oz*, published in the first year of the new century, did the United States produce a fantasy which, like its great British counterparts, examined society critically in fairy story terms. Baum's was an isolated voice (and a rather shaky one: he wrote sloppily and scarcely bothered to work out the implications of his subversive tale); no one managed to equal his achievement for more than half a century after the first appearance in print of Dorothy, the Tin Man, the Scarecrow, and the Cowardly Lion. America was still possessed with the kind of optimism that had infected British society around the time of the Great Exhibition; and optimistic societies do not, apparently, produce great fantasies. It was to take the Vietnam War and the general loss of national confidence during that period before fantasy could flower in America to the extent that it had in England. J.R.R. Tolkien produced the seeds: his English-made *The Lord of the Rings* (1954–5), with its lyrically melancholic portrait of a society in decline and threatened with total destruction, became the subject of a 'campus cult' just after the assassination of John F. Kennedy, and during the time when the international arms race was building up. The eventual consequence of this was the creation of a whole breed of native American fantasy novels, some of them of high quality.[5]

All books, of course, require readers, and the upsurge of introspective, non-realistic writing for children in Britain during the late nineteenth century suggests that a new audience had arisen. The general market for children's books had been active for a century before this; the business of being a 'juvenile bookseller' really became economically viable in the 1740s, concurrent with the rise of a middle class sufficiently leisured to undertake the 'instruction and amusement' of its children's minds, and sufficiently affluent to pay for the books that this required. The audience for the books of Lewis Carroll and his successors, more than a century later, was in a sense

unchanged: almost entirely middle class and affluent. Comfortably off parents bought *Alice* and *The Water-Babies* for their children, while the children of the poorer classes had to make do with the pious trash that the
Sunday Schools handed out as 'reward books'. But there was a certain difference between the middle-class child readership of the mid-eighteenth century and that which greeted the works of Carroll and Kingsley in the 1860s.

During the second half of the nineteenth century small families were
coming into fashion among the middle classes in England, America, and
Western Europe. Until the middle of the century it was perfectly acceptable
socially, indeed almost the norm, to produce large families. One only has
to look at the authors themselves to see this. Edward Lear, born in 1812,
was the youngest of twenty children. Charles Kingsley (born in 1819) and
George MacDonald (1824) were each one of six; C.L. Dodgson ('Lewis
Carroll'), born in 1832, was one of eleven. Then around the 1850s the birth
rate fell, at times steeply. Rosalind Mitchison writes, in *British Population
Changes since* 1880 (1977):

> The birth rate in Britain began to decline in the last quarter of the nineteenth cen-
> tury. The decline was not uniform: it was faster in times of economic recession
> and slower in booms, but on the whole it became progressively steeper until [it]
> reached a low point in 1933 ... This decline in fertility has its parallels in other
> European countries and in other developed parts of the world. Most such coun-
> tries maintained a high birth rate until the 1870s, then experienced a fall, and the
> fall continued until the 1930s.

The reasons for the decline have never been entirely explained. Mitchison
observes that 'similar changes took place in countries at very different stages
of their economic development', and it appears that factors other than the
purely economic were in operation. The middle classes, themselves still a
comparatively new element in society, seem to have experienced a vague but
widespread feeling that their children could 'do better' if there were fewer
of them to feed, clothe, and educate. And certainly increasing knowledge of
birth control was a factor; in the words of François Bédarida it led to 'the
fading of that age-old fatalism, which meant that all children were accepted
passively as "sent by God"'. In particular, the trial in 1877 of Charles Brad-
laugh and Annie Besant, accused of obscenity because they had reprinted
an old pamphlet about contraception, helped to publicise birth control
methods, judging by the marked fall in the birth rate in many countries
(including Britain) from that date onwards. Quite apart from this, the medical profession was by this time stressing the debilitating effects of too many
children on a woman's health. One writer[6] stated that 'it is looked upon
as supremely ridiculous to have a great many [children]', and Dr Elizabeth

Blackwell, in *How to Keep a Household in Health* (1870), went so far as to say: 'I do not consider, as it is so often stated, that the great object of marriage is to produce children; marriage has higher humanitarian objects.'

The numbers of children dropped perceptibly. Again we may see this from the children's writers themselves. Beatrix Potter, born in 1866, was one of two siblings. Kenneth Grahame, though he came from a large family, and A. A. Milne, though he had two brothers, were each to produce only one child when they married. They were not untypical. And the beginning and end of the period of the falling birth rate coincide almost to the years with the time during which the outstanding English children's books were being written.

Parents with small families inevitably tend to lavish closer attention on their offspring than do those with large broods,[7] and it is scarcely surprising that one literary result of the falling birth rate should be a sentimental idealisation of childhood, the creation (chiefly by lady writers) of such beings as Little Lord Fauntleroy (Frances Hodgson Burnett's novel was published in 1886). Any tendency towards a tougher attitude to children must moreover have been modified by the fact that there was no corresponding decline in the death rate of children before the beginning of the twentieth century. Despite a general increase in hygiene and continuing improvements in medicine, the young frequently fell victim to scarlet fever (the children's writer Mrs Molesworth lost a daughter because of it), or tuberculosis (Frances Hodgson Burnett lost a son through it), while others were sent to their grave by the continuing fondness of the medical profession for over-administering semi-poisonous medicines such as calomel (Charles Kingsley and Louisa Alcott were among those overdosed with this).

One suspects too that the late Victorians tended to lavish more attention on their children because of the uncertainty of the adult, public world. It was a climate which must have encouraged people to turn inward to their own families, to obtain from their children the sense of security and stability which the outside world was not providing. In such conditions, the work of the great introspective children's writers was especially likely to be appreciated.

Notes and references

1. Gillian Avery, with Angela Bull, *Nineteenth Century Children* (1965). The evangelical writers undoubtedly developed this notion of child-as-spiritual-guide partly from James Janeway's celebrated Puritan tract, *A Token for Children* (1672), which is a collection of accounts of the pious deaths of children; it was read in evangelical circles well into the nineteenth century. However, the type of evangelical book in which a poor slum child helps to convert his or her elders did not appear in any quantity until Dickens's fiction was well known. The best known examples of this type of book are

Jessica's First Prayer (1867) by 'Hesba Stretton' (Sarah Smith), in which a poor waif brings about the repentance of a chapel attendant, and Mrs O.F. Walton's *Christie's Old Organ* (1875), in which a street-arab arranges for the religious education of a dying organ grinder.

2. One might suppose that the atmosphere of religious uncertainty in which the great children's books were written was a direct consequence of the Darwin controversy (*The Origin of Species* was published in 1859, three years before the upsurge of imaginative children's writing in England). Undoubtedly there is a connection. Yet Charles Kingsley was the only outstanding children's author who seems to have taken any direct interest in Darwin, and he fully supported the theory of evolution and adapted it into his own imaginative scheme in *The Water-Babies*. It appears that the religious doubts suffered by him and his fellow authors were more a consequence of the doctrinal liberalism purveyed by F.D. Maurice and his supporters than of Darwin's shaking of the foundations.

3. See, on this, Mark Girouard, *The Return to Camelot: chivalry and the English gentleman* (1981).

4. My definition of 'fantasy' does not precisely agree with that of C.M. Manlove, in *The Impulse of Fantasy Literature* (1983), where he defines it as 'A fiction evoking wonder and containing a substantial and irreducible element of supernatural or impossible worlds, beings or objects with which the mortal characters in the story or the readers become on at least partly familiar terms'. While this serves adequately as a definition of the fantasy element in, say, Kingsley, Carroll, MacDonald, Nesbit, and Barrie, it does not properly describe the stories of Beatrix Potter, Kenneth Grahame, or A.A. Milne. Perhaps these should properly be classed as 'fable', in that their use of animals as human types is ultimately descended from Aesop; but they seem to me to demand consideration as part of the late Victorian and Edwardian genre of fantasy writing for children, sharing as they do so many of its motives.

5. I am thinking particularly of the 'Earthsea' trilogy by Ursula le Guin (1967–72). Most other American fantasies of the 1960s and 1970s are too plainly an attempt to scramble on the Tolkien bandwagon.

6. Quoted by Patricia Branca in *Silent Sisterhood: middle-class women in the Victorian home* (1975).

7. Philippe Ariès virtually says this in *Centuries of Childhood* (English translation, 1962, p. 404) when he observes that in the modern family 'all the energy ... is expended on helping the children to rise in the world, individually and without any collective ambition: the children rather than the family'.

The Same but Different: Conservatism and Revolution in Children's Fiction
Peter Hunt

Reading the history of children's books, and looking at the children's fiction on the bookshop shelves, it is tempting to think that children's books, despite all the different titles and colourful packaging, are all rather similar. The same sorts of things happen to the same sorts of people in the same sorts of situations and, especially, the endings are all much the same.

Look at these examples:

- A vulnerable character sets out on a quest with some supportive friends (bumbling anti-hero, strong but sensitive leader, solid sergeant, weak-but-brave sacrificial figure, comic foil); he/she has adventures in strange places, makes sacrifices, and returns home to security. Am I describing *The Hobbit, Winnie-the-Pooh, The Lion, the Witch and the Wardrobe*, any of the Harry Potter books – or even *Saving Private Ryan*?
- Times are changing; adults are unreliable; what is best – the comfortable past, or the uncertain future – the safe countryside or the dangerous town? Are we reading *The Borrowers? Tom's Midnight Garden? The Wind in the Willows? The Secret Garden?*
- The world is a jungle: you're growing up, for all intents and purposes, on your own – how do you become part of the life around you? Can you realistically expect a happy ending? Does this describe *The Other Side of Truth? Junk? The Jungle Book? Girls in Tears?* (see Plate 9) *The Tale of Peter Rabbit?*

Sameness and difference is the essence of children's books; they have many recurrent ideas. As Perry Nodelman (1985: 20) says, 'perhaps that's not surprising; [some] themes are central issues in our conceptions of childhood and the process of maturing ... they combine what one wishes for with what one must accept, [and] deal with freedom and constriction, home and exile, escape and acceptance, and all create balances'.

And so stories *for* children usually have happy endings: things often happen in safe spaces – idyllic rural settings or symbolic gardens, schools and families. Quest and adventure stories are produced for boys, involving initiation, toughness, even sacrifice – and then a return to the safety of home. Romances are produced for girls, involving families, finding identity, and, at extremes, finding partners or finding self-determination. The characters are familiar: the 'feisty' girl who overcomes adult prejudices, the 'manly' boy who helps conquer the empire – even the 'weedy' boy who comes good. And we know where we are with *genres*: in school stories we will find initiation rituals and insider/outsider relationships; in a pony book we will find class conflict and goodness rewarded, in 'other-world' fantasies there is a catalogue of wizards, monsters, strange companions, and desperate battles. And how many stories are 'Cinderella' all over again – from Frances Hodgson Burnett's *A Little Princess* (1905), to Meg Cabot's *The Princess Diaries* (2000)?

Different kinds of stories are popular at different times, and this tells us a lot about what a society thinks about childhood at any given moment. It also tells us a lot about what adults need: are male heroics and female subservience (or invisibility), fairy-tale happy endings, religious moralising, or fantasy and escapism really what children need or want? And what about the thousands of children's books featuring talking animals, or animals behaving like humans – like Judith Kerr's 'Mog' series, or Tove Jansson's 'Moomin' series, or Jill Murphy's 'Large Family'? Do they really cater for an innocence that doesn't distinguish animals from humans, or are they actually indulging adult whimsy – which makes adults comfortable or nostalgic? Or are they convenient vehicles for satire or allegory? And when the anthropomorphised animals come up against themes such as political awareness or rejection or 'the other' – as in Kipling's *The Jungle Book* (1920) – is it then that they make a real impact? If we look at contemporary science fiction – are the stories of the evils of technology actually an expression of the fears of technophobic adults, and not actually helpful for a generation of children for whom technology is a given?

Because the same sorts of patterns in the texts and (the often questionable) attitudes of the writers are repeated, it is possible to construct a history of ideas about childhood by looking at the sameness or difference of children's books across time.

What emerges is that while the books reflect the underlying preoccupations of a culture, the most notable ones also challenge and subvert. Take Robert Louis Stevenson's *Treasure Island* ([1883] 1985), which looks at first sight very much like a conventional nineteenth-century boys' adventure story. It seems to be about adventure and conquest, good versus evil, and growth and initiation; its setting is exotic, its characters conventional (the noble boy-hero, the evil pirates and the honest doctor and squire), and its shape is reassuring (as the 'good' characters return home at the end). Stevenson's master-stroke was to subvert all of these conventions: the adventure is uncomfortable, the conquest inherently destructive; the villain is seductive, the Doctor and Squire are at best greedy; and the 'hero' betrays his comrades and returns home frightened and dissatisfied. The book is actually about corruption and moral ambiguity: it may be an exciting page-turner, but it is also a critique of the approved social order, and of the books with which Victorian children were so familiar.

This is how children's literature progresses: at its best, it is always at once conservative and revolutionary, pushing at the boundaries imposed upon it. In the first Golden Age of British children's literature, conventionally from *Alice's Adventures in Wonderland* (Carroll, 1865) to the beginning of the First World War, the distinction between books for adults and books for children became more distinct (it had often been fuzzy before, rather as it is now). Childhood came into its own and, most importantly, 'Lewis Carroll' found a new way of writing for children: the implied child reader was treated as an equal rather than as a subordinate. As a result it was possible to explore more complex themes – and in a period of increasing instability, when British power and established religion were being challenged, and women and the working classes were demanding representation, there were plenty of issues upon which to reflect.

Between the world wars, children's books were about protection – ostensibly protecting the child, actually protecting the adult. Out there was civil war in Spain, the Wall Street crash, the rise of Nazism. In children's-book land there were worried stuffed toys, a mystic nanny, and a Hobbit trying not to be a hero: a garden, a fantasy, a quest.

In the second Golden Age, between the mid-1950s and the 1970s, the production of 'quality' children's books expanded rapidly, and children's writers grappled with another huge social change: the rejection of generations that had failed. This was the age of the 'angry young men' – of adult novels such as *Saturday Night and Sunday Morning* (Sillitoe, 1958), of socialist governments, neo-realism, the Cold War, experimental theatre with Joan Littlewood, the surreal humour of Spike Milligan, and, into the 1960s, youth and pop culture. How did the old patterns of children's books, the rural idyll, the family, heroic boys and domestic girls, negotiate this new age?

And, in the twenty-first century, when we have the makings, perhaps, of a Third Golden Age, with unprecedented numbers of children's books being produced, what has happened in terms of sameness and difference, conservativeness and revolution? Now that childhood and children's books have been efficiently commodified, are we seeing a homogenised product, with little contrast or variation, and a reinforcing of the oldest, safely marketable patterns? Or does new technology and the internet mean that completely new types of narrative are taking over?

The First Golden Age

At the beginning of *Alice's Adventures in Wonderland*, Alice finds a little bottle with the label 'DRINK ME':

> but the wise little Alice was not going to do *that* in a hurry ... for she had read several nice little stories about children who had got burnt, and eaten up by wild beasts, and other unpleasant things, all because they *would* not remember the simple rules their friends had taught them: such as, that a red-hot poker will burn you if you hold it too long; and that, if you cut your finger *very* deeply with a knife, it usually bleeds; and she had never forgotten that, if you drink much from a bottle marked 'poison', it is almost certain to disagree with you, sooner or later.
>
> Carroll, [1865] 2009: 13–14

And with that masterpiece of irony, and with the parodies of pious verses that are scattered through the book, Carroll went some way to demolishing nearly a century of children's books designed to keep children in their place. The exemplar of this kind of book was Mary Martha Sherwood's bestselling *The History of the Fairchild Family; or, The Child's Manual* (1818), each episode graphically showing the punishment meted out to children who disobey the word of God (or of their father, which is much the same thing). Despite its rather severe reputation, this book, like many others of its kind, portrayed a close-knit and loving family; the father is ever-present, and 'stands in place of God' at the head of the family, while the mother represents the church, and the children the obedient congregation. This image of the family is one that carries on through major novels such as *Little Women* (Alcott, 1868) and *Swallows and Amazons* (Ransome, 1930) where the fathers, though absent, still have a God-like authority, and it reflects a desire for stability in childhood and society in general. (The yearning for a coherent family life can still be found throughout modern children's fiction, from *The Other Side of Truth* (Naidoo, 2000) to *Junk* (Burgess, 1997).)

In the nineteenth century the gender divide was clear: the 'waif' novels of writers like Hesba Stretton (*Jessica's First Prayer*, 1867) or Mary Louisa Charlesworth (*Ministering Children*, 1867) featured charitable children, poverty-stricken families, and pious deaths, and were, broadly, aimed at girls. For boys there were 'empire-building' novels, epitomised by the work of G.A. Henty, most of which had the same circular pattern of home – foreign conquest – home, and, from R.M. Ballantyne's *The Coral Island* (1857) onwards, a sense of British superiority. Females were marginalised, codes of behaviour were everything, and there were no ambiguities. The same conventions infused thousands of school stories (initially for boys), epitomised by Thomas Hughes's *Tom Brown's Schooldays* (1857). The patterns and shapes of children's books were clearly established and clearly recognisable: the adult voice addressed an inferior child-narratee, morality and religion were certain, and endings were resolved and (for the virtuous) happy.

In the context of a stable, self-confident society, there were gradual changes. Attitudes to children and books became more liberal – landmark texts were Catherine Sinclair's *Holiday House* (1839), Heinrich Hoffmann's *Struwwelpeter* (translated 1848) and Edward Lear's *A Book of Nonsense* (1846), and fantasy and folk tales challenged the religious morale. But in the years of the First Golden Age, society began to change rapidly. Issues of religious faith and doubt preoccupied intellectuals; Britain's military might was challenged in the Crimean War (1854–56) and the Boer War (1899–1902); Marx published *Das Kapital* in 1867; the 1870 Education Act, the secret ballot (1872), the Trade Union Amendment Act (1876) which gave protection to the trade unions, the founding of the National Union of Women's Suffrage Societies in 1897 – even the invention of the motor car – all challenged the way Britain saw itself.

Naturally enough, children's literature reacted. There were the same sorts of stories, with the same sorts of heroes and female heroes, and the same sorts of endings – but children's books now began to reflect society's doubts and ambiguities – especially about the concept of childhood (and the value placed on children). Beneath the surface of fairy fantasies, family stories and books about manly boys, there was subversion, individuality and a new empowerment of the child.

Three books changed the face of children's fiction. *Treasure Island*, as we have seen, introduced ambiguity into all the major features of the boy's story: it looked like one thing while being quite another.

Alice's Adventures in Wonderland, equally, did two startling things: it changed the idea of what children were allowed to think and, as a corollary, it changed the tone of voice of children's books. Its reputation is that it introduced 'liberty of thought in children's books' (Darton, 1982: 268). Darton's famous judgement is usually taken to mean that the book was *fun* and light-hearted, and did not preach the usual morals about religion, punishment, death, and so on. In fact, *Alice* is far from light-hearted: death, for example, is no longer something controlled by doctrine, it is uncertain, difficult, challenging; adults are no longer reliable, they live in a frustrating, solipsistic, nonsensical, and aggressive world. The book places itself squarely on the side of an intelligent child-reader; it is *focalised* almost entirely through Alice, and the controlling adult narrator – the norm in the nineteenth century – fades away. The result is a book that places a rational and rebellious child at the centre, exposing an adult world that is mad, arbitrary, evasive and threatening. Carroll's influence was over the long, rather than the short term (his immediate imitators copied his comic elements and missed his innovations): writers such as Beatrix Potter, Frances Hodgson Burnett, E. Nesbit (sporadically) and Rudyard Kipling picked up both the tone of voice and the attitude of mind which produced books addressed without condescension or control to children, and which made complex themes accessible to them.

Both *Treasure Island* and *Alice's Adventures in Wonderland* were subversive because they appeared to be conventional, and the same is true of the third of these influential books, Louisa May Alcott's *Little Women* (1868) – the product of a USA that was also passing through a period of rapid change (the Civil War was fought between 1861 and 1865). It has a reputation for being a picture of happy domesticity – it is even modelled on *The Pilgrim's*

Progress (Bunyan, 1874) – but not far beneath the surface is frustration with the old patterns. The father still dominates, 'Marmee' is an intermediary, and pride ('Meg Goes to Vanity Fair') and other sins are duly punished. But there is an implicit assertion of female independence: the family *does* survive without the male; Jo does *not* marry the 'right' man. Similarly, in *What Katy Did*, by Susan Coolidge (1872), Katy is punished for her disobedience in playing on a broken swing against the orders of her Aunt Izzie, but, as Shirley Foster and Judy Simons (1995: 119) point out, '*What Katy Did* is not an evangelical tract, for all its recall of the type ... it enacts fantasies of female power and heroism; it formulates a Utopia of childhood autonomy'.

What followed shows how rapidly things were changing. The 'feisty' heroine, challenging, and often subduing, adult authority, became a new convention in Eleanor Porter's *Pollyanna* (1913), Kate Douglas Wiggin's *Rebecca of Sunnybrook Farm* (1903), L.M. Montgomery's Canadian *Anne of Green Gables* (1908), Ethel M. Turner's *Seven Little Australians* (1894), and Johanna Spyri's *Heidi's Early Experiences* (trans. 1909) and *Heidi's Further Experiences* (trans. 1884). And the endings change, too: whereas Alice, and the March girls, are disempowered by the strong 'closure' of their books – the return to the constricting status quo – many of their successors have more open endings, looking to the future. Frances Hodgson Burnett's *A Little Princess* (1905), which epitomises the familiar Cinderella story, and the sentimental attitude that appeared in hundreds of 'waif' novels, avoids (unlike the latest film version) the totally happy ending.

It is far from incidental that all the female heroes of these books (except the fatherless Rebecca) are motherless, and this is also true of Mary Lennox in Burnett's *The Secret Garden* (1911). In this book Hodgson Burnett blends the newly recurring story of the orphan who takes on the world (as opposed to the dutiful, subservient motherless girls of the nineteenth century, such as M. Finley's *Elsie Dinsmore* (1867)) with one of the oldest ideas in literature and children's literature, the garden. The garden, a secure mini-Arcadia, was particularly attractive in the context of a threatening, changing society. The garden at Misslethwaite Manor is secure space between the gloomy, adult-dominated house, and the rather wilder freedom of the moor, where Dickon's mother runs an elemental family. Unlike the gardens in the 'Alice' books, which are full of madness, this garden is a place where the children can grow safely, but Burnett adds the positive (for children) idea that the children must achieve growth through their own efforts. Colin's father is a self-indulgent romantic, who has left the children to fend for themselves, an emblem perhaps of the way in which fathers became progressively less admirable as the century progressed.

Beyond the garden is the countryside, seen since before Shakespeare as redemptive and pure: what more natural, then, than for adult writers to use it in children's books to preserve a wholesome, conservative idea of childhood? Rudyard Kipling's animated history lesson, *Puck of Pook's Hill* (1906), shows this at its most positive (and political) in the lush descriptions of the idyllic Sussex countryside. At its most idealistic we find it in the pictures of children by Kate Greenaway. At its most regressive and questionable, we find it in Kenneth Grahame's *The Wind in the Willows* (1908), where the countryside becomes a place of retreat, rather than freedom or renewal, where gender is rejected, rather than encountered, and where food is more for comfort than for growth (see Figure 6).

Figure 6 'Mole and Rat by the fireside', from Kenneth Grahame, *The Wind in the Willows* (1908), illus. E.H. Shepard (1930), London: Methuen & Co. Ltd, 1949. Copyright © The Estate of E.H. Shepard, reproduced with permission of Curtis Brown Group Ltd, London.

Perhaps the novel that best sums up the books of the First Golden Age is E. Nesbit's *The Railway Children* (1906). The father is absent, and the family is held together by the independent mother and the strong female hero, Bobbie (although she has a male name!). Then there is the binary opposition of countryside and town (or the wide world), a genuine attempt to broaden what children can think about by taking on political ideas and class conflict, and an attempt to shake off the old nineteenth-century storyteller's tone. *The Railway Children* seems at first sight to be less radical than it is – the males, after all, are still dominant, and its shape is comfortingly circular, and yet the child characters' experiences set them squarely in an essentially troublesome world.

Of course, thousands of largely forgotten books carried on the old certainties – such as the school stories of Frank Richards and Angel Brazil – but the books that have become classics are the ones that transform the old formulae. Beneath their conventional surfaces, they are about empowerment, subversion, growth, liberation, finding a voice, finding *depth*. Perhaps the most well-camouflaged are the ironic and unflinching books by Beatrix Potter, whose subtlety and acerbity are belied by their delicate watercolours and rural settings.

And there was one other feature of this period's children's books which has been carried forward: the use of the children's book as a place for the exploration of the writers' own psyche – and especially of the relationship between adulthood and childhood. As Victor Watson (1992: 18) put it, Carroll, especially, showed how children's books 'could be made into an imaginative space for writing about the dynamics that exist when adults and children engage with one another – dynamics that might be complex, loving, intimate or problematical, but were no longer just authoritarian'. Occasionally, these 'dynamics' could become the raison d'être of the text, with extremely ambiguous results, notably in J.M. Barrie's *Peter Pan and Wendy* (1939).

Rustic playgrounds: 1918–1939

Between the two world wars was a period that is sometimes seen as the 'doldrums' of children's literature, when the market was dominated by the 'reward' books. These were anthologies or annuals which were bulked out by being printed on thick paper and which harked back to all the clichés of the previous generation: boys' school stories and war stories with stiff-upper-lipped heroes; girls' school stories populated by madcaps and anti-soppists and featuring crushes, campfires and hockey sticks.

But there was much more to it than this. The First World War had deeply scarred those who survived it, and Hugh Lofting's 'Dr Dolittle' series (1920—), and A.A. Milne's 'Pooh' books (1926, 1928) are set in quiet, redemptive rural retreats, where the talking animals or the idealised child – and the adult writers and readers, too – can be safe. Some other survivors, such as Joyce Lankester Brisley's 'Milly-Molly-Mandy' books (1928–48), emphasise this unworldliness – and even the antidote to the sentimental-child fashion (seen, not at its worst, in Christopher Robin), Richmal Crompton's William Brown, conducts his campaigns against adults in a country village.

The William books, then, are the same, but different. And so are John Masefield's fantasies, *The Midnight Folk* (1927) and *The Box of Delights* (1935), or P. L. Travers's 'Mary Poppins' books (1934—), which seem to celebrate an essentially backward-looking Englishness, but which contain an outrageous, surreal inventiveness. Arthur Ransome is more subtle: his books look back to settled family values and the behavioural codes of the previous century, and have secure, rural settings. *Swallows and Amazons* (1930) – and vast numbers of its successors – has a traditionally circular, resolved plot shape, and not only ends where it began but has the same characters 'on stage'. And yet the book contains one of the purest examples of 'single-address' narrative in the whole of children's literature – the narrator writing to his child-audience as though he were one of their peers. To Ransome, it didn't matter who you were: what was important was what you did, and as a result he goes a long way towards circumventing class and gender conventions.

Even more misleading in its appearance, and just as influential, was J.R. R. Tolkien's *The Hobbit* (1937): the Shire epitomises an Arcadian (and garden-centred) England; as its subtitle, *There and Back Again*, emphasises, it has a secure, closed-circle shape. But our hero is an anti-hero: Bilbo is a lucky pragmatist, while almost everyone around him is motivated by pride or greed; the circle is not secure – Bilbo has brought the One Ring back with him; and the wild lands are genuinely comfortless. For all Tolkien's 'cordial dislike' of allegory, here is a book that reflects the Europe of the late 1930s, and the vulnerability of the small: Hobbit or child, there is nowhere that is safe any more.

The Second Golden Age

At the end of the Second World War, in Britain, 'the bulk of children's fiction was still located in a dream world of boarding schools, ponies, the prevention of crime, impossible reversals of fortune and holiday high-jinks' (Cadogan and Craig 1978: 238). But not for long: within twenty years almost every British publishing house had developed a children's book department, a whole new category of book – teenage or 'young adult' – had appeared, and a remarkable number of new 'quality' authors. Fantasy, especially, flourished, with C.S. Lewis, Mary Norton and Lucy Boston; the local, English, family themes were explored by William Mayne, Philippa Pearce and Shirley Hughes; and fantasy and history came together with Susan Cooper's 'The Dark is Rising' sequence (1965—), Patricia Wrightson's 'The Ice Is Coming' sequence (1977—) and the work of Alan Garner (see Plate 15). Later there was the anarchic humour of Roald Dahl and

Raymond Briggs, and into the 1970s the neo-realism of Judy Blume, Louise Fitzhugh and many others. Some of these, such as Lewis, Cooper and Hughes, used traditional forms to say traditional things, albeit in forceful and striking ways; others, like Mayne and Garner, made radical advances in style and thought; and some, like Norton and Pearce, encapsulated the tension present in very many of the authors: the tension between the authors' personal preference for the past, and the child characters' (and readers') preference and aspirations for the future.

Thus *The Borrowers* (Norton, 1952) and *Tom's Midnight Garden* (Pearce, 1958) pit the conservative values of (adult) tradition – and countryside and the garden – against the corruptions of the modern world, and yet it is the modern world which the child characters have to live in, and look forward to. The degeneration of Tom's garden, the polluted river, the helpless substitution of food for affection by Tom's aunt, look forward to the grim spaces of Burgess, Blackman and Naidoo. Mary Norton's Borrowers are displaced people, the parents looking backwards, and the children looking forwards. Alan Garner's *The Stone Book* quartet (1978–79) laments the steady loss of craftsmanship in successive generations, but recognises the need of the modern child to find a unique identity. These books are essentially rural and nostalgic, but they acknowledge, if reluctantly, a change to a new kind of world.

And it is acknowledged, perhaps for the first time, that the new world belongs to the children reading more than to the children's writers. The endings of books become more open and ambiguous: Louise Fitzhugh's *Harriet the Spy* (1964) is a devastating tragi-comedy about childhood neurosis and parental irresponsibility. Child-characters now experience a more savage *angst* than the female heroes of the First Golden Age, where readers of *A Little Princess* could anticipate a happy ending. The scene was set for wholesale revisionism, as in Judy Blume's sexually revolutionary *Forever* (1975), or Robert Cormier's demolition of the traditional school story in *The Chocolate War* (1974). An idea that would have been shocking forty years before, that childhood is not necessarily, or even commonly, a nice place to be, is reflected in the work of Ann Fine, Margaret Mahy and Jan Mark.

It is hardly surprising, then, that father figures in the late twentieth-century children's book are not figures that bear any relation to God or family stability. Even where they are sympathetic – as in Mildred D. Taylor's *Roll of Thunder, Hear My Cry* (1976) – they are often ineffectual. At worst, as in Melvin Burgess's *Junk* (1996) or Gillian Cross's *Wolf* (1990), they are violent or even homicidal towards their children. Endings are more likely to be unresolved – for example, on the last page of *Roll of Thunder Hear My*

Cry, Cassie is in bed: 'both Mama and papa came to tuck me in ... Their presence softened the hurt, and I did not cry.' But after they have left, she does cry: nothing has been resolved. This is a book about growth and good versus evil, and, as much as anything, the open-ended 'shape' of the story classifies it and gives us a way of interpreting it.

However, it is some indication of the continuing need to preserve at least the semblance of innocent childhood in society that in books for young children in recent years, it has been quite hard to find endings that are not reassuring. The vast majority have a 'circular' shape, beginning and ending with home and/or security. Of the 100-plus books in Nicholas Tucker's *Rough Guide to Children's Books 0–5 Years* (2002), only two (Raymond Briggs's *The Snowman* (1978) and David McKee's *Not Now Bernard* (1980)) do *not* have resolved endings – and even then it can be argued that the melting of the snowman is a condition of the boy's return to his family. *Not Now Bernard* (in which Bernard, eaten by a monster, does *not* return to his own shape at the end) has been seen as controversial, and unsuitable for a young age group.

The twenty-first century: a Third Golden Age?

Today, more children's books are being published than ever before, they have a higher media profile than ever before and some are selling in huge numbers. One might be forgiven for thinking that we are in another Golden Age.

The primary difference, however, between the Second Golden Age and today is one of commercial logic: then, there were relatively small publishers who could nurture talent and maintain a 'backlist' that kept good but not blockbusting books in print for many years. The twenty-first century has become the age of the 'bottom line': the bulk of children's book publishing is in the hands of a small number of large companies, and even those who maintain smaller publishing units within them are driven by the demands of mass-marketing. Whereas, forty years ago, children's books had a 'sameness' rooted in tradition, but the potential for originality, today the big sellers – with one or two (perhaps) encouraging exceptions – are carefully planned, designed and marketed, almost (and sometimes literally) before they are written. The percentage of books that are *not* commissioned is tiny and the 'sameness' is now quite deliberate: the cart of marketing is driving the horse of creativity.

And so, for all the goodwill of the individuals within the publishing system, does this mean that we are seeing a bland, safe, neo-conservatism in children's books, with even the 'different' books being carefully calculated?

Are the majority now 'play-safe' books which reinforce the sorts of stories that we have seen a million times before? Is the child positioned subserviently in an adult-conceived childhood, just as manipulated and controlled as children were two hundred years ago?

Of course, some ideas have been used so often that they have long since evolved into clichés – the stuff of mass-market texts that make few demands on readers, and are essentially 'comfort reading'. Some have become so well-worn that they satirise and (perhaps) reinvigorate themselves, as has happened to stories containing quests and the polarisation of good and evil. Intertextuality – making the meaning of one text rely on knowledge of another – is now commonplace, and allows texts to look like one thing but to be another. Examples are the films *Shrek* (2001) or *Hoodwinked* (2005), and for young children, books by Tony Ross (*The Three Pigs*, 1983), Babette Cole (*Princess Smartypants*, 1986) or Lauren Child (*Beware of the Storybook Wolves*, 2000).

There are many intriguing questions here: have the unresolved endings, or the reversals of gender roles that once marked the *difference* of a book, now become conventions? Is the adoption of current adult fantasies – such as the desire to be a WAG or a princess or a secret agent – by children's writers destroying a certain kind of childhood? And do the stories for younger children which promote what might look like a stable, comfortable, family-oriented lifestyle actually take all the edge and danger out of childhood?

Fortunately, publishing is not an exact science. Philip Pullman, a master of 'conventional' storytelling, has productively used the new conventions of the 'open' ending: in *Northern Lights* (1995) Lyra doesn't get back even to her quasi-home; the *difference* of his books is the radical content. Even in the twenty-first century, to write, literally, about the death of God has proved to be, if not shocking, then controversial. J.K. Rowling, a rather less intellectually acclaimed bestseller, has also used an interesting mixture of traditional and radical. The 'Harry Potter' series, most ingeniously, has an ironically inverted pattern: the first books *are* circular, and Harry comes from and returns to the 'family'. But, of course, Harry is actually returning *from* his ambiguous comfort zone of Hogwarts into the dysfunctional 'normality' of Muggle-land. Progressively, the books become more and more open-ended; even the coda of the final book, which appears to resolve matters, holds the seeds of an uncertain future. Rowling, using an array of 'sameness', from the conventions of the school story to the single-address mode pioneered by Lewis Carroll, has produced a work both singular and singularly successful.

The ambiguous world of writing for the twenty-first century child is admirably summed up in Jacqueline Wilson's books. The latest available

UK government statistics (National Statistics Online, 2001) point out that 23 per cent of all children live in lone-parent families (91 per cent of those householders being women) or, to put it another way, 16 per cent of all households are lone parents with children, while 65 per cent of children live with their natural parents (or 59 per cent of households with children have married couples, and 11 per cent cohabitees) and 17 per cent of children live in a 'no-work' family. And yet the dysfunctional families of Jacqueline Wilson yearn to be complete: Nick Sharratt's illustrations of family groups and (sometimes) their settings in her books are remarkably similar to those in the 'Milly-Molly-Mandy' stories. Wilson manipulates the shape of her books to subvert their appearance as comic: she seems at first to be writing 'comfort-books', where the resolution does not reflect what might have happened in reality (as Oscar Wilde said, 'The good ended happily, the bad unhappily. That is what fiction means'). However, in several of her books the circle is – at the last possible minute – not quite closed: *Girls in Tears* (2002) ends reassuringly, but also implies a gentle open-endedness ('We'll have to wait and see') – and *Lola Rose* (2003) ends: 'We're going to live happily ever after ... Fingers crossed.' These books are books for their times, reassuring, yet inviting their readers to face the uncertain world: the ideas of home and exile and so on are still there, but they are challenged by darker ones of displacement and uncertainty, and these are reflected in the structures.

The books that represent a dark present and a dark future may, then, reflect a world that publishers think appropriate to current childhood. But is this a world of dysfunction that has some hope (*Junk, The Other Side of Truth*), or an urban nightmare, with little hope (*Noughts and Crosses* (Blackman, 2001)), or an urban nightmare taken to its fantastic conclusion, as London rolls its way across a devastated Europe in *Mortal Engines* (Reeve, 2001)? *Mortal Engines* owes something to both the echo of the idyllic garden and the successful quest resolved by returning home. Do 'happy' endings persist in the face of horror (*Coram Boy* (Gavin, 2000), *Junk*) because, in the calculation of what childhood should be, they *must*?

And the future

If the children of the twenty-first century, steeped in multimedia and the internet, think differently to their parents, and process narrative differently, what does this mean for the way stories are told? The book is still alive and well, but it exists in a context that marks it off as requiring different skills – sustained linear concentration, rather than holistic hypertext-linked association. At present we have the book at one extreme, and the computer game and the virtual life sites at the other. For the first, the plot is fixed but the images are generated by the reader; in the second, the images are fixed and the plot is generated by the 'reader'; in the third the distinction between author and reader virtually disappears. The rules of the game have changed.

Somewhere between these extremes are the graphic novels and comics, fixed by their physical form but borrowing from the structures of the new media. The questions that need to be answered at this most exciting point in the history of narrative are: how far can we move from the old patterns to the new, and will the new patterns continue to relate to the old? Will the characters, situations and plots that we have seen being repeated over the centuries survive this radical change in mode of thought? Are they intrinsic to the mode of the book, or are they intrinsic to the human psyche?

Either way, the new media offer the opportunity to subvert the grinding of the mass-cultural machine, and the commercialism of childhood, and to reassert difference, perhaps in the context of a new sameness.

References

Cadogan, H. and Craig, P. 1978. *Women and Children First*. London, Gollancz.

Carroll, L. [1865] 2009. *Alice's Adventures in Wonderland and through the Looking Glass*, ed. Peter Hunt. Oxford, Oxford University Press.

Foster, S. and Simons, J. 1995. *What Katy Read: Feminist Re-Readings of 'Classic' Stories for Girls*. Basingstoke, Macmillan.

Darton, F.J. Harvey, 1982. *Children's Books in England. Five Centuries of Social Life*, 3rd edn, revised by B. Alderson. Cambridge, Cambridge University Press.

Tolkien, J.R.R. 1964. *Tree and Leaf*. London, Allen & Unwin.

Tucker, N. 2002. *The Rough Guide to Children's Books 0–5 years*. London, Rough Guides.

National Statistics Online: Focus on Families, www.statistics.gov.uk (/cci/nuqqet.asp?id=1865), accessed 18 March 2009.

Nodelman, P. 1985. 'Interpretation and the Apparent Sameness of Children's Novels', *Studies in the Literary Imagination*, XVIII, 2, 5–20.

Watson, V. 1992 'The Possibilities of Children's Fiction', in M. Styles, E. Bearne and V. Watson (eds) *After Alice*. London, Cassell.

Multicultural Agendas
Lissa Paul

Imagine a boardroom in the Disney marketing offices prior to the release of the animated feature film *Pocahontas* in 1995. The promotable qualities of the title character must have been on the table: brown-skinned and articulate, a free-spirited heroine who communes with trees and animals, has brand-name recognition in American history and Barbie Doll good looks. Multiculturalism, feminism and environmentalism all wrapped up in one character. Pocahontas presented a sporty new image (running, paddling her own canoe) while maintaining a family likeness to her successful (white-skinned) animated princess predecessors, Snow White and Cinderella, who also talked to small animals though they patiently did the housework while waiting for their respective princes to come.

The brand of multiculturalism promoted in *Pocahontas* makes everyone feel good about themselves and the world. It is also exactly the message promoted in one of Disney's oldest and most popular theme-park rides, 'It's a Small World After All', in which racially diverse dolls costumed in clothes from around the world parade by as the song plays on. That sunny Disney multiculturalism reads with the superficiality of greeting-card cheeriness. It's a commercial version of multiculturalism, the most generally familiar and easily recognised form, and used, for instance, in the Coca-Cola song: 'I'd like to teach the world to sing / in perfect harmon-y, / I'd like to hold it in my arms / and keep it company'.[1] The commercial feel-good version of multiculturalism sells, and it is the one that dominates children's literature. That's why I've chosen to start with it before addressing the uses and abuses of multiculturalism that mark the history of the idea from its inception in Canada in the 1960s through to its incarnations over time and around the globe in the twenty-first century.

Multiculturalism: the biography of an idea

Multiculturalism has become so much a part of our workaday vocabulary that we've lost the miracle – both the joy and the suffering – of its birth. In the second edition of the *International Companion Encyclopedia of Children's Literature*, Lisa Rowe Fraustino (2004), in her entry on publishing, describes multiculturalism only as a 'buzzword of the late 1980s to mid-1990s' – that is, as something so much part of the ordinary cultural scenery that it is taken for granted as just being there. Even the *Oxford English Dictionary* defines multiculturalism in flatly neutral terms as 'the policy or process whereby the distinctive identities of the cultural groups within such a society are maintained or supported'. Neither description even hints at how radical an idea multiculturalism was when it was invented, or how much its presence in the cultural landscape influenced our views of who we are and how we see each other.

Multiculturalism was born in Canada – in Book 4 of the *Report of the Royal Commission on Bilingualism and Biculturalism*, published in 1970. In the relevant passage the authors conclude that people of 'non-British

[and] non-French origin' consider Canada 'to be a country that is officially bilingual but fundamentally multicultural'. That was the first use of the term in the way the *OED* defines it. The Commission's conclusion came as a surprise – as their mandate was to explore only French/English biculturalism. They had no precedent. What the commission found, however, was that people living in Canada who were not of English or French origin (including everyone who had emigrated from other countries around the globe, but excluding Indigenous people) repeatedly identified themselves as 'hyphenated' Canadians: Icelandic-Canadians, Polish-Canadians, Lithuanian-Canadians – and so on. Those hyphenated terms of identification became hallmarks of multiculturalism – though it is unlikely anyone in the 1960s could have envisioned such a possibility. Across the world, however, traditionally disenfranchised groups quickly began adopting those hyphenated forms of self-identification. By the 1980s, 'African-American' (a term popularized by Jesse Jackson) had become the preferred term in the USA for people who had been identified as 'black' in the 1970s, or, prior to that, as 'Negro'. In Canada, the Indigenous people who had been excluded from the Royal Commission's mandate began to call themselves Native Canadians – though they avoided the hyphen.

When the Royal Commission on Bilingualism and Biculturalism was founded in 1963, it had no idea that multiculturalism would be its greatest accomplishment. From a twenty-first century perspective it is impossible not to understand that the Anglo-French relations that prompted the formation of the Commission in the first place only arose because Canada (as it came to be in 1867) had been among the spoils of the early nineteenth-century wars between France and England. From the late sixteenth century European colonial powers had started claiming squatter's rights to rather large tracts of Africa, Australia, New Zealand, and North and South America – though in the 1960s, no one gave much (if any) thought to the illegality of colonising other people's land. The colonial encounter was a fact of life. Only decades later, in the 1980s, when postcolonial discourses (to which I'll return later) began to reshape the idea of multiculturalism did anyone pay attention to the way the Indigenous people of those colonised countries had been treated. It wasn't until 2008 that both Canada and Australia made formal apologies to their Indigenous populations. Nevertheless, despite what we now know as sins of omission, in the 1960s, multiculturalism was a thrilling, radical new idea. Multiculturalism took off like a virus, or wildfire – inevitable and dangerous, spreading with relentless speed and in need of control.

As a child of the 'baby-boom' generation, I grew up in the Canada that gave rise to multiculturalism. I was the only dark-haired Jewish child in a

Toronto elementary school classroom dominated by the blond children of parents who had left Latvia or Estonia or Poland, countries that had, at the time, been swallowed up by the USSR. Although there were Chinese greengrocers and Italian construction workers in our neighbourhood, our school world was white, Christian and deeply connected to England. We sang 'God Save the Queen' and the Queen's portrait was part of every class-room's décor. We said the Lord's Prayer every morning. Our history lessons on the Indigenous populations of Canada were about environmentally sen-sitive, historically remote (read dead) Indians. We were routinely exposed to 'Indian folk tales', refracted largely by white folklorists. To my acute embar-rassment, I remember vividly participating in the construction and decora-tion of a brown-paper tepee one fall, and, in the winter, an igloo, made out of stacks of white tissue paper-covered shoeboxes. We went on field trips to reconstructions of Indian villages. No one even hinted to us at the time that there were real, live Native Canadians living on reserves just minutes away from the fake tourist attraction villages we were taken to see. The Indians and Eskimos of our school lessons were generic, not distinguished by tribe or date or place or history, and not related to the apparently home-less Indigenous people occasionally glimpsed covertly in the city. We had no idea that while we were living at home with our families in Toronto and walking to our local school each day, Native children were, by order of the federal government, forcibly removed from their homes and families, sent to remote Christian-run residential schools and forbidden to speak their own languages.

The reason I've exposed my experience of elementary school in Toronto is that it shows, by way of contrast, how miraculous the idea of multi-culturalism must have been at the time. It is often difficult to remember how Anglo-American, middle-class, implicitly Christian and lily-white the worlds of school and of mainstream children's books had been until the mid-twen-tieth century. The Golden Age of children's literature, in the late nineteenth and early twentieth centuries, consisted of books almost entirely populated by upper-class, white, Christian children: think of John Tenniel's illustra-tions of Lewis Carroll's blonde, upper-class Alice, Kate Greenaway's ele-gantly dressed pretty children, and Ernest Shepard's drawings of Christopher Robin.[2] By the mid-twentieth century, the children in picture books were still predominantly white and Christian, but they tended to be middle-rather than upper-class. By that time, Anglo-American children were being inducted into literacy via mass-market readers: British schoolchildren from Janet and John reading schemes; North American children from Dick and Jane basal readers. The only characters of colour in mainstream children's books were depicted as either inferior or comic: *Little Black Sambo*, for example, as drawn by Helen Bannerman, Florence Upton's illustrations of Bertha Upton's golliwogs (see Plate 10), and the hugely popular illustrated 'Ten Little Niggers' nursery verse. In retrospect all scream 'racist', and many have been banned from schools and children's libraries for decades.[3]

Growing pains

In the 1970s and 1980s, the anglophone children's book-publishing industry had a growth spurt: buoyed by the potential audience of Anglo-American baby-boom children, political mandates encouraged the spread of multiculturalism. Issues of race and gender had moved from the margins to the mainstream, though the battles to get them there had been painfully fought. The linguistic and cultural efforts of the civil rights movement in the USA in the 1960s had galvanised political change, as did the 'second wave' (as it was known) of feminism in the 1970s. Both brought new attention to issues of legal, economic and social equity for people (not just women and people of colour) who had traditionally been disadvantaged by the privilege implicitly afforded to white, Christian men. The idea of multiculturalism flourished because feminism and the civil rights movement had prepared the ground. Children's books, remember, reflect and are reflected by social conditions, and multiculturalism and feminism were glimpsed as ways of correcting systemic social injustices.

Retrospectively it is easy to mock the apparently crude way in which multiculturalism entered mainstream children's books. When the white American author, Ezra Jack Keats, published *The Snowy Day* in 1962 it was regarded as daring and innovative in its depiction of a little black boy in a red snowsuit playing, as children do, in the snow. Yet even at the time the book was criticised for its assumption that because the child was black he must be poor and urban, and because his mother, no matter how sympathetic, was shown as a 'fat black' mamma in the Aunt Jemima style. Keats had constructed what we'd now call a 'trope' (a metaphor that has slipped from its status as metaphorical and has come to mean something that is true) of a lower-class black family: poor, urban, with a fat mother. A fat white mother would have been unthinkable. Picture-book mothers at the time were suburban, middle-class, white and thin. Yet race and gender diversity in children's books publishing in the USA were made possible partly by the success of Keats's book, so the contribution should be acknowledged – despite the fact that the attempts which followed were largely cosmetic.

Feminism, like multiculturalism, was a hot topic in the 1970s and 1980s. Revisionist feminist fairy tales were popular. *The Paperbag Princess* (1980) for example, by Robert Munsch, was regarded as feminist because it ostensibly promoted a positive (read active) female role model. The idea that activity was preferable to passivity was reinforced. But because activity is generally understood as a masculine characteristic and passivity as feminine, the status quo was still maintained: it was better to be a boy. Until about the late 1980s, the presence of a child of colour was enough to classify a book as multicultural and the presence of an active female character was enough to classify a book as feminist. Both kinds of books were often put on recommended lists used by schools and libraries. As a result, those books that found their way into schools tended to be the feel-good commercial kind of the sort produced by Disney and Coca-Cola. 'Boutique multiculturalism', a term coined by literary critic Stanley Fish, describes the kind of books which dominated the scene. As Fish (1997: 378) explains, boutique multiculturalism is 'characterized by its superficial or cosmetic relationships to the objects of its affection'. It is the multiculturalism of costume and food, what one of my former students used to call 'Taco Tuesday' multiculturalism. Think about it as a façade, a fake front disguising a multitude of inequities, injustices and outrageous historical property thefts and other sins. Let me show you the kind of books I mean – and explain how difficult they are to spot.

The most successful boutique multicultural books were those that seemed comfortably familiar to Anglo-American readers while still appearing to include outsiders. The reinterpreted folk tale was a perfect vehicle. *Sootface: An Ojibwa Cinderella Story* (1994) by Robert San Souci, with illustrations by Daniel San Souci, looks like, and is marketed as, a Cinderella story – so it is familiar to Anglo-European audiences. Its relationship to Ojibwa culture is, at best, tangential. But in the feel-good spirit of multiculturalism, only image matters. The cover of *Sootface*, for instance, perfectly reinscribes the Anglo-American trope of the environmentally sensitive Native: a green giant of a ghostly translucent warrior, both superimposed on the leaves and branches of a tree and hidden by them, looks down with god-like equanimity on the solid 'sootfaced' girl in the corner of the frame. He is meant to be interpreted as the equivalent of Cinderella's fairy godmother. What the cover image and title communicate, glaringly, is that the Ojibwa story is worth reading because it is going to be just like the Cinderella stories we know, except in fancy dress. There is not even a suggestion that Ojibwa stories might have something different to tell us, something we don't know and might want to learn. Instead, because the story is set in a Native context it counts as multicultural. The form is familiar. *Arrow to the Sun* (1973) is described as a Pueblo story. It is a highly praised, widely known picture book by the celebrated (white) author and illustrator Gerald McDermott. But the emphasis is not on what we can learn about Pueblo culture, but rather on how the story is a variant of something familiar. As Pueblo native and scholar Debbie Reese (2006) informs us, the quest pattern of McDermott's *Arrow to the Sun* – in which a young boy's mettle is tested by having to pass through four ritual huts called kivas, each containing something dangerous (respectively lions, serpents, bees and lightning) – is Eurocentric. '[K]ivas', explains Reese, 'are places of instruction and ceremony, not places of trial.' Yet without access to that specialized knowledge, no non-Pueblo teacher or librarian or parent would be likely to recognize the fake multiculturalism of McDermott's story. Multiply the problem by all the cultures in the world and it becomes instantly apparent that offering children access to genuine multicultural exchange is extremely difficult if not impossible.

As the twentieth century drew to a close, it became clear that multiculturalism wasn't going to make it possible for 'the world to sing in perfect harm-o-ny', so attention turned to attempts to identify the sources of dissonance. The most influential idea came from the Palestinian-American scholar, Edward Said, in *Orientalism*, published in 1978. Basically, Said describes the ways in which colonising European cultures demonised the people of the countries they invaded, and constructed the inhabitants as primitive 'others' in need of 'civilising'. In colonial terms, to be white, European and Christian was defined as good and normal – and to be anything else was to be primitive, bad and in need of correction. By drawing attention to what had been an implicit assumption about a normal (colonial) world order, Said provided authors with a language for reimagining alternatives. By the 1970s and 1980s, children's books in which the dominant characters were not white, middle-class boys did begin to change the contours of the literary landscape.

Reimagining the colonial adventure

Increasingly, as the political landscape of the twenty-first century began to take shape, it became obvious that many of the world's conflicts had arisen because of the colonial encounter. Europeans had treated Africa as a source of free labour and so built a profitable slave trade. The Indigenous populations of the Americas and Australia had been unceremoniously wiped out or marginalised. Europeans simply exploited, settled on and otherwise took over land they had regarded as uninhabited. In the 1960s, the Royal Commission on Bilingualism and Biculturalism accepted the status quo: 'Canada,' they explained blithely, 'a vast territory inhabited in the beginning by Indians and Eskimos, was first colonized by the French, beginning in the early 17th century, and then by the British.' Readers were then directed to a footnote: 'Since the terms of reference contain no mention of Indians and Eskimos, we have not studied the question of Canada's native population' (1970: 4). That was easy. Keep Indigenous 'others' on the margins and there is no need to worry about them too much – except as they figure in narratives about the colonial encounter.

Historically, Natives did have parts to play in children's books – either as enemies or as foils or sidekicks to the brave adventurers who had gone out from the old world to conquer the new. The adventure story is an archetypical genre of children's literature, constructed, as critic Clare Bradford points out in *Unsettling Narratives*, as 'colonial narratives of settlement and adventure' (Bradford, 2007: 148), and following the model of the original story of the genre, *The Life and Strange Surprizing Adventures of Robinson Crusoe of York, Mariner*. First published in 1719 by Daniel Defoe (1660–1731), Crusoe's fiction has been the paradigmatic adventure story for almost three hundred years. The word 'adventure' itself derives from the idea of 'venture' capital: people setting off on adventures – commercial, profitable enterprises, including, for example, the slave trade. Crusoe himself becomes rich while he is stranded on his island because of his investments in slave-run plantations. That story is usually glossed over in favour of one of the most famous episodes of the novel – the one in which Crusoe witnesses the remains of a cannibal feast and rescues an intended victim (Friday) who then, in eternal gratitude, promises to be a slave to his rescuer forever. The trope of the white saviour to the grateful Native then became a staple of the genre.

By the nineteenth century there were reams of adventure stories marketed especially for boys, by authors such as Captain Frederick Maryatt (1792–1848), R.M. Ballantyne (1825–94) and Talbot Baines Reed (1852–93), all of whom were popular in their own time, though their names are unlikely to be familiar to twenty-first-century children. The focus was on rugged, brave British adventurers who re-enacted the colonial encounter by conquering wild landscapes and wilder Natives. These were masculine stories about active heroes travelling outside domestic space into dangerous territories. Stories with female focalisers, on the other hand, tended to be about passive girls who were happy to stay at home. Action was driven by what is called the 'marriage' plot. So, in the history of American children's literature, for instance, Mark Twain's *Tom Sawyer* (1876) and *Huckleberry Finn* (1884) were traditionally regarded as models of great American boys' adventure stories, while their near contemporary, *Little Women* ([1868] 1989) by Louisa May Alcott, was regarded as a girls' book – and so of a lower order. It wasn't until the 1970s and 1980s, with the rise of critical attention to issues of feminism and postcolonial discourse that it became possible to imagine new ways of reading classic girls' books such as *Little Women* and reimagining adventure. Although enduring as a heartwarming example of domestic fiction, of motherhood and sisterhood, remember that *Little Women* is deliberately set during the American Civil War (1861–65) when the Southern States were battling the North – at least partly over the legality of slavery. Most of the war action occurs off-stage, filtering through only in the character of Mr March, who is carefully kept at war for the most part, away from home and in the margins of the story. Jo's struggle for the right to freedom of expression is constructed, seamlessly, as a counterpoint to the war about freedom, which occupies the background of the story.

For twenty-first-century readers, *Little Women*, almost a hundred and fifty years after its publication, still offers new insights on issues of gender, race, class, nationhood – and adventure. Adventures rooted in colonial encounters no longer had to involve travel away from home to wild and dangerous places. Instead, as Alcott demonstrates in *Little Women*, colonial encounters could be domesticated, without losing the inspiring thrill of traditional adventures. Women too, as Alcott shows, could exhibit all the desirable characteristics of the male adventure hero. If, for example, I turn to the croquet game in *Little Women*, played between the American characters and their British opponents (Laurie's guests), I see that Alcott has stitched issues of gender and national identity into the game: 'the Englishers played well', comments the narrator, 'but the Americans played better and contested every inch of the ground as strongly as the spirit of '76 [1776 was the date Americans claimed independence from England] that inspired them' (Alcott, 1989: 124). Jo wins the game 'by a clever stroke' against her male, English opponents, even though one of them, Fred, had cheated (Alcott, 1989: 124–5). In asserting American independence, honesty and strength against British power and, implicitly, corruption, Jo demonstrates that she can beat boys and beat the English. The winning move on her part seems of particular importance, especially when read as a sly counterpoint to a scene not much later in the story when Jo loses a foot race against Laurie – indicating that she still acquiesces to masculine domination even if she triumphs over colonial domination. It has always pleased me to know that as an adolescent, tall and strong, Alcott had said, 'no boy could be my friend until I had beaten him in a race' (Showalter, 1988: xiii). In the croquet game episode, Alcott manages to appear to satisfy the cultural assumptions of her time (girls are weaker and slower than boys), while still arranging a scene in which she wins against an English boy – who would have embodied, in her time, a cluster of associations related to the American War of Independence (so the spirit of '76).

For Alcott in the nineteenth century, the USA was a breakaway demo-cratic republic bravely asserting independence from tyrannical, exploitative imperialist England. In the twenty-first century, the principles have remained the same, though the players have changed. As the USA has become the dan-gerous superpower, critical attention has shifted back to the colonial encoun-ter as the source of so many of the world's twenty-first-century inequities and displacements – from African-Americans in the USA to Palestinian Arabs in the Middle East. The feel-good, sunny version of multiculturalism that heralded its discovery in the 1960s has given way to something more disturbing. It's tempting to call it a feel-bad version, as it involves uncov-ering and articulating the harm done by the original colonial encounter. If Edward Said's 1978 *Orientalism* drew attention to the exotic other as both an attractive and threatening construct, the 1989 publication of *The Empire Writes Back: Theory and Practice in Post-Colonial Literatures* by Bill Ash-croft, Garth Griffiths and Helen Tiffin opened the possibilities of colonised people writing back to the colonisers. Their title is taken from Salman Rush-die, who coined the phrase 'the empire writes back'. The term has sticking power (see, for example, Plate 11 from Julius Lester's 'Sam and the Tigers', a retelling and reclaiming of Helen Bannerman's *Little Black Sambo*). In children's book history, I'll show that the narrative arc can be tracked in the shift from the coloniser's poems to those of the colonised.

Disenchanting verse

Let me begin with two poets writing at the zenith of the British Empire, Robert Louis Stevenson (1850–94) and A.A. Milne (1882–1956) – both identified as quintessential children's poets. Stevenson's *A Child's Garden of Verses* ([1885] 1975) and Milne's *When We Were Very Young* ([1924] 1946) and *Now We are Six* ([1926] 1946) have never been out of print and have been recited and loved by generations of children. Their lyrical virtuos-ity and playful intelligence never goes out of fashion. And both poets gave fresh individual voices to children as the narrative focalisers of the poems. With Stevenson, young readers still play with the magic of their shadows: 'I have a little shadow that goes in and out with me, / And what can be the use of him is more than I can see'. And children being pushed on swings in the playground may hear 'The Swing' being recited in time to the actions: 'How do you like to go up in a swing, Up in the air so blue? / Oh I do think it the pleasantest thing / Ever a child can do'. And children turning 6 in anglophone countries can mark the occasion with lines from Milne's poem: 'But now I am six, / I'm as clever as clever, / So I think I'll be six now for ever and ever' (Milne, [1926] 1946: 102). I hope my selections of poems by

Milne and Stevenson evoke pleasant memories. Both poets are still charmingly, disarmingly wedded to ideals of perfect, sunny childhoods.

As the twentieth century drew to a close and the twenty-first century began, aspects of the verse of Milne and Stevenson began to look less enchanting. Like a relentlessly pulsing, ugly sore thumb, something naggingly irritating was asserting itself. It's not that the poems had changed, only the readers. The implicit ideological assumptions (to use Peter Hollindale's phrase) of the late nineteenth and early twentieth centuries had changed. The social, cultural and political damage from the colonial encounter began to insinuate itself into discussions of children's poetry and, as I'll show, poets from formerly colonised communities were finding alternative voices with which to talk back to Stevenson and Milne.

Stevenson's poems in *A Child's Garden of Verses* are often filled with imagined travel to exotic locations, though the focalising narrator is usually safely at home, often in bed while projecting his journeys elsewhere. To a twenty-first-century reader raised on Edward Said's explanation of how people from colonised countries were characterised as dangerous and exotic by the colonisers, the word 'racist' comes to mind almost immediately on reading many of Stevenson's poems. In 'Travels', for instance, the narrator imagines forests, 'Full of apes and cocoa-nuts / And the Negro hunters' huts'. Stevenson's forests are inevitably primitive, threatening and wild – the colonizer's version of the wildness of the Americas and Africa.

For the colonised to write back to the coloniser, however, it is necessary to invert the terms of 'wild' and 'cultivated'. That's exactly what Caribbean-British poet Grace Nichols does in 'My Gran Visits England' from *Give Yourself a Hug* (1994). She takes a gardening Caribbean grandmother, a (black) foreigner, and metaphorically inverts the colonial paradigm. The grandmother becomes the civilised, cultivated person, which is signalled in her cultivation of the land. Nichols also includes another subtle inversion of the colonial encounter: 'Gran' stakes a claim in the 'old' world of England – a parody of the white men driving flags into the sand as they claimed a 'new' world. At the very end of the poem, Gran says, 'Boy, come and take my photo – the place cold – But wherever there's God's Earth, I'm at home' (Nichols, 1994: 16–17). 'Gran' becomes a brilliant, wonderfully economical postcolonial inversion of the male coloniser who stakes a claim, cultivates what he perceives as a wild landscape and superimposes his old world on the new one, which that doesn't belong to him. In Nichols's poem, the new-world woman conquers the old world, stakes a claim and cultivates its foreignness and wildness. Home and away are successfully inverted, the colonised character effectively writes back to the coloniser. If I take another of Stevenson's poems, 'Foreign Children', and set it against

Benjamin Zephaniah's 'Neighbours', I'll demonstrate another take on the destabilisation of home and away, self and other.

Stevenson's 'Foreign Children' has become the poem most likely to be censored in schools. To twenty-first-century eyes, the poem appears blatantly racist. Stevenson sets the child narrator's English home ('But I am safe and live and home') against the exotic, threatening lives of the 'foreign' children, the 'little Indian, Sioux or Crow', the 'Little frosty Eskimo' and the 'Little Turk or Japanee'. All have 'curious things to eat', including 'ostrich eggs', and have cruelly 'turned the turtles off their legs'. Smugly, safely 'at home', the narrator assumes that those 'foreign children' envy him and want his life. The last line in both the first and last stanza reads: 'O! don't you wish that you were me?' There feels something tainted now about 'Foreign Children' and other poems written at the height of the British Empire. Zephaniah writes back, addressing directly the colonisers' fear of the colonised. 'I am the type you are supposed to fear', he says in 'Neighbours', 'Black and foreign / Big and dreadlocks / An uneducated grass eater' – a reference to the poet's vegetarianism and a sly dig at uncivilised British carnivores. The narrator of Zephaniah's poem challenges the reader to consider the response to having a black man move next door:

> You should feel good
> You have been chosen
> I am the type you are supposed to love
> Dark and mysterious
> Tall and natural
> Thinking, tea total.
> I talk in schools
> I sing on TV
> I am in the papers
> I keep cool cats
> And when the sun is shining
> I go Carnival
>
> (1996: 163)

Here Zephaniah brilliantly trades on both his 'exotic' otherness and his celebrity status, flaunting his dangerousness on the one hand and his attractive media personality. He is both grey, conventional, English conservative ('tea total') and 'when the sun is shining', its antithesis ('Carnival'). The repeated 'I' forms the refrain that speaks back to the imagined (white) neighbour of the poem and also inverts the traditional colonial encounter in which the European explorer lands unannounced on African or American shores and expects the people already living there to welcome him into the neighbourhood.

The upper-class arrogance of many of Milne's poems, like Stevenson's, tends to irritate twenty-first-century readers. 'Nursery Chairs', for instance, assumes British power over foreigners as the narrator takes a series of imaginary adventures out of England. Each chair becomes the symbolic means of transportation to a new world. The section called 'First Chair' begins:

> When I go up the Amazon
> I stop at night and fire a gun
> To call my faithful band.
> And Indians in twos and threes,
> Come silently between the trees,
> And wait for me to land.
> And if I do not want to play
> With Indians to-day,
> I simply wave my hand.
> And they turn and go away –
> They always understand.
>   Milne, [1924] 1946: 16

It is impossible not to cringe now at the calm assertion of the right to command Indians at will. The entire 'Nursery Chairs' sequence, in fact, seems jarringly arrogant. 'The Island' ends with the line, 'There's nobody else in the world, and the world was made for me'. That sense of completely assured entitlement, so natural in the 1920s, has become utterly unimaginable in a world transformed by the multicultural agenda.

The darkest side

My critical trajectory of the story of multiculturalism in children's literature began with the bright, sunny, commercial versions of the idea and tracked attempts to capture something about the original conception that was missing. The terms 'inclusion', 'diversity', 'internationalism' and 'pluralism' all found their moments of favour, especially in the policies that Anglo-American educational authorities tried to put into place to accommodate their increasingly multicultural (or diverse or international) populations. I regret that I do not have the space to include a discussion of gender politics here or to demonstrate the inclusion of gay and lesbian issues in children's books, nor can I do more than mention that the crude 'just like us' versions in a picture book such as Leslea Newman's *Heather Has Two Mommies* (1989) evolved into more subtly expressed configurations of gender and family in something like Laurel Lee Gugler's *Little Wynne's Giggly Thing* (1995).

Children's book publishers tried to meet the demand for more diverse representation, though until the twenty-first century the books that tended to circulate were of the boutique multicultural kind. The general thrust was to capture an idea Paul Hazard (a French comparative literature scholar) had presciently imagined in 1944 as the possibility of a 'universal republic of childhood'.

What the idealised versions of multiculturalism (as I'll continue to call it, despite its various incarnations) tended to omit were the ugly stories, the ones from which children were typically shielded because they were categorised, ironically, with other formerly marginalised groups (servants, people of colour, and, until well into the twentieth century, women). As post-colonial discourses have penetrated into mainstream publishing, formerly marginalised people have been able to tell their own stories of the colonial encounter. Imagine these as origin myths told by the colonised to the colonisers. These are not brave, heroic adventure stories; they are often terrifying stories of dislocation, gross inhumanity and suffering. In *Fortune's Bones* (2004), African-American poet Marilyn Nelson, with measured calm, graphically tells the story of a nineteenth-century American physician needing a skeleton for instructional purposes. So when his slave, Fortune, dies, the physician – in a macabre inversion of the trope of the African cannibal boiling up missionaries – cooks up Fortune's body in order to hang the bones in his offices. Nelson then imagines the thoughts of Fortune's wife as she dusts her husband's skeleton in the doctor's office. In the early days of multiculturalism, Fortune's story would have been too impossibly painful to tell. Only once the sunny ideals had been secured was it possible to explore the dark side.

In the globalised world of the twenty-first century, stories of dislocation abound. British poet Jackie Kay (1992) expresses her disorientation at growing up black in Scotland. And Beverley Naidoo (2000), in the fittingly titled *The Other Side of Truth*, explores the jarring class and race divides that set Sade's comfortable, middle-class experience of home in Nigeria apart from her uncomfortable experience of exile in England. The hyphenated forms of self-identification that looked so promising in the 1970s now look shabby and superficial, yet 'home' and 'away' are losing their oppositional meanings – as Mavis Reimer (2008) demonstrates in *Home Words*, a collection of essays about children's literature discourse in Canada.

As the new millennium begins to define itself separately from the old, the hopeful feature is that it is possible to tell the difficult and painful stories. The past can't be changed, but a recognition and acknowledgement of what went wrong offers a sense of where to go from here. Access to books originating in other cultures and then translated into English are still woefully few and far between so it remains difficult to understand how other people perceive the English-speaking world – and why they feel as they do.

Increasingly, however, publishers of children's books are trying to make previously silent voices audible. With each new voice, maybe, we'll all be able to look tentatively towards a more tolerant future. We'll see.

Notes

1. Originally composed as an advertising jingle for Coca-Cola by Roger Cook and Roger Greenaway and released in 1971, at about the same time as the idea of multiculturalism became established internationally.
2. See John Tenniel's illustrations for Lewis Carroll's *Alice in Wonderland* (1865), Kate Greenaway's *Under the Window* (1879) and Ernest Shepard's illustrations for A. A. Milne's *Winnie-the-Pooh* (1926).
3. Helen Bannerman, *The Story of Little Black Sambo* (1899), Bertha Upton, *The Adventures of Two Dutch Dolls and a Golliwog*, illus. Florence Upton (1895) and *Ten Little Nigger Boys* (1869) by Frank Green.

References

Alcott, L.M. [1868] 1989. *Little Women*. Ed. Elaine Showalter. Harmondsworth, Penguin.

Ashcroft, W., Griffiths, G. and Tiffin, H. 1989. *The Empire Writes Back: Theory and Practice in Post-Colonial Literature*. London, Routledge.

Bradford, C. 2007. *Unsettling Narratives: Postcolonial Readings in Children's Literature*. Waterloo ON, Wilfrid Laurier University Press.

Defoe, D. [1719] 1998.*The Life and Surprizing Adventures of Robinson Crusoe of York, Mariner*. Ed. J. Donald Crowley. Oxford, Oxford University Press.

Fish, S. 1997. 'Boutique Multiculturalism, or Why Liberals are Incapable of Thinking about Hate Speech', *Critical Inquiry*, Vol. 23, No. 2 (Winter): 378–95.

Fraustino, L.R. 2004. 'Children's Book Publishing', in *International Encyclopedia of Children's Literature*, 2nd edn. Ed. Peter Hunt. London, Routledge: 647–50.

Gugler, L.L. 1995. *Little Wynne's Giggly Thing*. Illus. Russ Wilms. Toronto, Annick Press.

Kay, J. 1992. *Two's Company*. London, Puffin.

Keats, E.J. 1962. *The Snowy Day*. New York, Viking.

McDermott, G. 1973. *Arrow to the Sun: A Pueblo Indian Tale*. New York, Viking.

Milne, A.A. [1924] 1946. *When We Were Very Young*. Illus. Ernest Shepard, 43rd edn. London, Methuen.

Milne, A.A. [1926] 1946. *Now We Are Six*. Illus. Ernest Shepard, 26th edn. London, Methuen.

Munsch, R. 1980. *The Paper Bag Princess*. Toronto, Annick Press.

Naidoo, B. 2000. *The Other Side of Truth*. London, Puffin.

Nelson, M. 2004. *Fortune's Bones: The Manumission Requiem*. Honesdale, Front Street.

Newman, L. 1989. *Heather Has Two Mommies*. New York, Alyson Books.

Nichols, G. 1994. *Give Yourself a Hug*. London, A&C Black.

Pocahontas. 1995. Directed by Mike Gabriel and Eric Goldberg. Disney.

Reese, D. 2006. Blog on *Arrow to the Sun* by Gerald McDermott, www.americanindiansinchildrensliterature.blogspot.com/2006/10/gerald-mcdermotts-arrow-to-sun-gerald.html.

Reimer, M. 2008. *Home Words: Discourses of Children's Literature in Canada*. Waterloo, ON, Wilfrid Laurier University Press.

Royal Commission on Bilingualism and Biculturalism. 1970. *Report of the Royal Commission on Bilingualism and Biculturalism*. Book 4. *The Cultural Contribution of the Other Ethnic Groups*.

Said, E. 1978. *Orientalism*, 25th anniversary edn. New York, Vintage.

San Souci, R. 1994. *Sootface: An Ojibwa Cinderella Story*. New York, Delacorte.

Showalter, E. (ed.) 1988. *Alternative Alcott*. New Brunswick, NJ, Rutgers University Press.

Stevenson, R.L. [1885] 1975. *A Child's Garden of Verses*. Illus. Charles Robinson, 1896. La Jolla, Green Tiger.

Zephaniah, B. 1996. *Propa Propaganda*. Highgreen, Bloodaxe Books.

Transformative Energies
Kimberley Reynolds

G.K. Chesterton once observed, 'in everything that matters, the inside is much larger than the outside' (1959: 41). Whether you are thinking about individual children's books or the whole domain of children's literature, the inside often turns out to be surprisingly larger than the outside might suggest – sometimes literally so as when material pops out and unfolds from apparently flat pages. Usually, however, it is the words and images of often physically small texts that turn out to be capable of filling the minds of generations of young readers with experiences, emotions, and the mental furniture and tools necessary for thinking about themselves and the world they inhabit.

This surprising quality can be hard to detect in studies of children's literature. As the field has developed, these have tended to take five forms, often in combination: those that trace the history of children's book; attempts to define children's literature and identify its characteristics; works that consider the relationship between children's literature and critical theory; studies that explore what children's literature does to its readers by, for instance, encoding ideological assumptions or disseminating strategies for resisting them; and analyses focussing on the ideas of the child and childhood inscribed in children's texts and critical works about them. My own project owes something to all of these approaches, but is rather different: it attempts to map the way that children's literature contributes to the social and aesthetic transformation of culture by, for instance, encouraging readers to approach ideas, issues, and objects from new perspectives and so prepare the way for change. This is the sense in which I see writing for the young as replete with radical potential.

Jack Zipes has pointed to the way that fairy tales, and by extension children's literature, are implicated in acculturation – in transmitting cultural values and 'civilizing' children (1991: 9), a view elaborated by Robyn

Extracted from 'Breakings Bounds: The Transformative Energy of Children's Literature', in K. Reynolds, *Radical Children's Literature: Future Visions and Aesthetic Transformations in Juvenile Fiction* (Basingstoke: Palgrave Macmillan, 2007), pp. 1–23.

McCallum (1999), who sees much of children's literature as part of an ideological trap that seduces readers into accepting a liberal humanist world view. While children's literature is undeniably implicated in cultural integration, such explanations overlook an important and contrary impulse in many of the fictions we give to and make for the young. Childhood is certainly a time for learning to negotiate and find a place in society, but it is also about developing individual potential suited to a future in which societies could be different in some significant ways – for instance, in the organisation of families, the distribution of resources, or the circulation of power. It is not accidental that at decisive moments in social history children have been at the centre of ideological activity or that writing for children has been put into the service of those who are trying to disseminate new world views, values, and social models. The influence of Puritan beliefs and values extended far beyond the relatively small number of Puritans, and one means by which this came about was through their efforts to address the young on the page. In the same way, children's literature was used in the eighteenth century to help establish and promulgate the thinking and behaviour of the rising middle class in England (O'Malley, 2003).

Growing up involves making choices and shaping an identity. As a general rule, choosing one path, whether this is educational, cultural or social, closes down options. Much of the symbolic potential of childhood in culture derives from the fact that children have most of their choices before them; they represent potential. As a group, the fictions of childhood emphasise this view of childhood because they tend to be narratives in which the future is still an unknown and the self is in formation though, as I have argued elsewhere (Reynolds, 1994), the realistic 'problem novels' that started to appear in the 1960s have a tendency to foreclose on childhood, requiring readers to engage with events such as rape, death, and family breakdown. By the end of such novels, characters are shown to have matured, and by implication, readers too will have moved a step closer to adult knowledge and experience.

Children's literature provides a curious and paradoxical cultural space: a space that is simultaneously highly regulated and overlooked, orthodox and radical, didactic and subversive. It is a space ostensibly for children – and certainly in the fictions created for them, children encounter ideas, images and vocabularies that help them think and ask questions about the world – but children's literature has also provided a space in which writers, illustrators, printers, and publishers have piloted ideas, experimented with voices, formats and media, played with conventions, and contested thinking about cultural norms (including those surrounding childhood) and how societies should be organised. Because writing for the young has a future orientation, there is often a freshness and urgency to the storylines of children's fictions that correspond to the fact that their target readers are generally encountering ideas and experiences for the first time. Many children's books offer quirky or critical or alternative visions of the world designed to provoke that ultimate response of childhood, 'Why?' 'Why are things as they are?' 'Why can't they be different?' With this in mind, children's literature can be equated with the 'monster child' that Jean-François Lyotard associated with creativity and the potential for change: 'The monster child is not the father of the man; it is what, in the midst of man, throws him off course [*son décours*]; it is the possibility or risk of being set adrift' (in Burman, 1998: 72).

The aesthetic of childhood innocence

This study is in many ways a response to two very different accounts of writing for children that have done much to encourage scrutiny of children's literature as an area of cultural and aesthetic activity. The first and more influential of these is Jacqueline Rose's *The Case of Peter Pan, or, The Impossibility of Children's Fiction* (1984). Despite the fact that it was written nearly a quarter of a century ago and has been discussed often and at length (see, for instance, Lesnik-Oberstein, 1994 and Rudd, 2004, 2006), its centrality to this study makes a brief recapitulation of Rose's central arguments as I read them helpful. Many of her insights into the forces at work in children's literature are valuable. However, there are also aspects of her thesis with which I cannot agree and which I feel distort the way children's literature is received in culture. Of particular concern to me is the fact that Rose sees the child in children's literature (and by extension, children's literature itself) not as embodying the disruptive and creative force of Lyotard's monster-child, but as having an innately conservative effect on what can be written for children.

One of Rose's central activities in *The Case of Peter Pan* is the identification and interrogation of the impulse to set boundaries around what children's literature 'should' do and be. Since the beginnings of commercial publishing for children in the eighteenth century, she says, there has been 'a set of barriers constructed which assign the limits to how far children's literature is allowed to go in upsetting a specific register of representation – one which ... is historically delimited and formally constrained' (139). Rose's formulation implies that the barriers she identifies are agreed and stable. In fact, although since at least the seventeenth century, religious thinkers, parents, philosophers, educationalists, and critics have attempted to define what kind of writing is suitable for children (for an overview and indicative sample of such critical material, see Tucker, 1976) and to make informed choices about what constitutes 'good' children's literature (see, for instance, Hunt, 1991: 7), the boundaries around children's literature have always been in dispute. Often these disputes arise from different understandings of what children are like and what children's literature is and does, differences at work at particular historical moments and arising from changing attitudes over time.

Ted Hughes's initial attempts to become known as a children's writer provide a useful illustration of such differences and changes and their potential consequences for children's literature. In the 1950s, when publishers of children's books were increasingly turning to formulaic, 'I Can Read' series, with their emphasis on the acquisition of reading skills and vocabulary, Hughes was producing short fables and creation stories which were then deemed to be 'too sophisticated' (Paul, 2005) for children. Subsequently they were published as *How the Whale Became* (1963) and accorded high status in the field of children's literature. So, while at one point Hughes's work fell outside the boundaries of what was deemed suitable for children, later it was so firmly inside and reflected so strongly the aspirations of those involved in the production of children's books for children's literature that his writing became a benchmark against which much other work for the young was measured.

As the case of Ted Hughes shows, the boundaries around children's literature are neither rigid nor agreed; nevertheless, those involved in creating, producing, and studying children's fiction have for long acknowledged that they exist. For much of the twentieth century, a combination of received wisdom and a strong sense of what the main purchasers of children's fiction (librarians, parents, and teachers) wanted to see in the books they gave to children resulted in an unwritten code of practice: no sex, no violence, and no 'bad' language (meaning that the writing should refrain from swearing, slang, and most aspects of colloquial or idiomatic use, and be grammatically correct). In *The Case of Peter Pan*, Rose argues that the purpose of these boundaries has much less to do with children's tastes and development than with adult needs, and specifically the desire for an image of childhood based on children's relationship with language that, she claims, results in children's literature being arrested as a literary form.

For Rose (who in 1984 was herself pushing at the boundaries of academic criticism as they were then set with her interest in Lacanian psychoanalysis and poststructuralist critical theories), writing for children is committed to taking its readers (and writers and critics) back to a mythical time when the world was knowable and could be expressed in language (9). As she sees it, children's fiction has tended to be regarded as a cultural safe-house which preserves an ideal of the innocent child dating back to Locke and Rousseau.

Rose maintains that adults need this image of the child – she pointedly does not claim that this is how children are or how they read – to keep a sense of themselves intact. According to *The Case of Peter Pan*, children's literature reassures and stabilises adults by refusing to disturb their views of childhood at the levels of language, content (specifically content that could disturb at psychic and sexual levels) and form (20; 142): these comprise the barriers around children's literature to which she refers and result, she claims, in an aesthetic of childhood innocence that she feels dictates what children's literature is and does.

But Rose's argument sits uneasily with evidence both from within children's literature and from other aspects of Western culture. As art historian Anne Higonnet demonstrates in *Pictures of Innocence* (1998), images of children and childhood have become deeply conflicted, with the entrenched but essentially residual allegiance to the innocent child (Higonnet, like Rose, associates this image with Locke, Rousseau, and the Romantics) giving way to what she terms the 'knowing' child in the course of the twentieth century. Rose overlooks the ambivalent nature of many images of childhood, including in children's literature, past and present. On the basis of a very limited sample of material she comes to the conclusion that because it is specifically addressed to and works to secure an audience of children, the child in children's literature (by which she means both the idea of childhood it contains and the implied notion of the child reader outside the book) plays a central role in an 'impossible' collective fantasy about childhood. Moreover, because this image is imbibed by children during the primary stages of language acquisition, with all that entails for the development of self and social understanding, it persists into adulthood, informing and shaping subjectivity, responses, and decision-making at a number of levels.

According to *The Case of Peter Pan*, this cycle stifles innovation. However, many writers – and particularly writers for children – have specifically acknowledged the way fictions encountered in childhood inspired them to think in new ways and to break free from prevailing views of childhood.

Rose's argument is that the primary function of children's literature is to secure the child in culture: it is coercively normalising. To show how it does this, she identifies a number of demands that shape what writing for children's literature should and should not do: 'there should be no disturbance at the level of language, no challenge to our [adults'] own sexuality, no threat to our status as critics, and no question of our relation to the child' (20). While she accepts the demands are 'impossible' for an individual child, she claims they persist in the aspirations of those who mediate between children's fiction and child readers, holding at bay complex questions about sexuality, origin, and meaning.

Children's literature and the aesthetic of transformation

> The impressions of childhood are those that last longest and cut deepest.
>
> Virginia Woolf in *The Common Reader*, quoted in Greenway, 2005: xv.

Where Jacqueline Rose sees children's literature as largely regressive, arrested, and antipathetic to literary modernism, Juliet Dusinberre argues that children's literature plays a seminal role in bringing about cultural change, including preparing the way for modernism. Indeed, she credits a single children's book – *Alice in Wonderland* – with ushering in the modernist movement in all its forms. According to Dusinberre, for the generation to which her central subject, Virginia Woolf, belonged:

> ... cultural change was both reflected and pioneered in the books which children read. Radical experiments in the arts in the early modern period began in the books which Lewis Carroll and his successors wrote for children.
>
> (5)

There is, she argues, a 'symbiotic relationship between children's books and adult writing' (xv), or to put it another way, the books read in childhood lay the foundations of a writer's literary aesthetic; they provide the models, the anti-models, and the springboards for subsequent generations. This is not always conscious, but it is undeniable that the stories we encounter as children perpetually 'inhabit the landscape of childhood, what Bachelard calls "the oneiric house of memory" or the realm of dreams and imagination' (Natov, 2003: 6). Like childhood itself, these stories do not disappear, but continue to unfold and inform how we interpret the world. In the case of writers and other creative artists, they provide the kind of fund of remembered images that Dusinberre says Carroll's books provided for Woolf's generation. In this way they become seedbeds of creativity.

Dusinberre attributes the importance of the Alices and the children's books they inspired to the way they challenged authority, released subversive energies, refused to condescend and preach to readers, and, particularly for modernists, foregrounded issues to do with language as the medium of meaning.

> The question of mastery over language, structure, vision, morals, characters and readers was to become the central concern, not only of children's authors, but of many adult writers – Virginia Woolf, Henry James, Joyce – in the shift of consciousness at the turn of the twentieth century. ...
>
> 1987: xvii

This is a far cry from Rose's account of the direct nature of language in children's literature.

As its title suggests, *Alice to the Lighthouse* is primarily concerned with the relationship between Carroll's Alice books and Woolf's writing, but in passing, Dusinberre points to other key children's texts and writers that demonstrably contributed to the rise of literary modernism and the modernist consciousness. Her list includes the influence of Frances Hodgson Burnett on D.H. Lawrence; *The Rose and the Ring* and *Black Beauty* on Roger Fry, and the Alices, *Treasure Island* and *Huckleberry Finn* on just about all the best-known modernists. The extent to which writers are aware of their debt to children's literature is in itself an interesting area of study (I should say that I distinguish between books written for an audience of children and books that are read in childhood as this makes it possible to focus on the creative space specifically represented by children's literature and arising from the constraints associated with its audience at any given moment). A small amount of work has already been done on the relationship between writers and their childhood reading, beginning with Humphrey Carpenter's (1989) entertaining analysis of the role Beatrix Potter played in shaping the modern literary sensibility. Carpenter traces a line from Potter through W.H. Auden, George Orwell, and Evelyn Waugh to Blake Morrison, who uses two characters from Potter's *The Tale of Tommy Tiptoes* in a 1987 sonnet:

> They are holed up in some bar among the dives
> Of Deptford, deep in their cups, and a packet
> Of cashew nuts, like Chippy Hackee and cute
> Little Tommy Tiptoes hiding from their wives.

Carpenter notes particularly the debt to Potter acknowledged by Graham Greene:

> Of course there was Beatrix Potter. 1 have never lost my admiration for her books and 1 have often reread her, so that 1 am not surprised when 1 find in one of my own stories, 'Under the Garden', a pale echo of Tom Kitten being trounced up [*sic*] by the rats behind the skirting-board and the sinister Anna Maria covering him with dough, and in *Brighton Rock* the dishonest lawyer ... hungrily echoes Miss Potter's dialogue as he watches the secretaries go by carrying their little typewriters.
>
> From *A Sort of Life* in Carpenter, 1989: 272

Greene was convinced that childhood reading (referring both to children's writers such as Potter and books read in childhood) is profoundly influential. His autobiography, *A Sort of Life* (1971), sums up his belief that creative writers are for ever in thrall to the visions and perceptions of childhood and adolescence: 'The influence of early books is profound. So much of the future lies on the shelves: early reading has more influence on conduct than any religious teaching' (in Sinyard, 2003: 23). Greene's essay The Lost Childhood' (1951) also explores this idea, concluding,

> Perhaps it is only in childhood that books have any deep influence on our lives. In later years we admire, we are entertained, we may modify some views we already hold, but we are more likely to find in books merely a confirmation of what is in our minds already ... But in childhood all books are books of divination, telling us about the future, and like the fortune-teller who sees a long journey in the cards or death by water *they influence the future*.
>
> Sinyard: 31; my emphasis

Betty Greenway's edited collection of essays, *Twice-Told Tales: The Influence of Childhood Reading on Writers for Adults* (2005) similarly maintains that 'artists are made by the books they read as children' (xxiv). Greenway emphasises that it is not just the words in the books that shape future writers but books as objects, and the range of sensory and emotional responses evoked through their pictures, words, sounds, and even the weight, feel, and smell of their pages. Not every text necessarily has a physical form, and influences from oral sources can be as powerful and enduring as those from printed texts. For Sylvia Plath, the rhythms, images, and sometimes earthy language of nursery rhymes helped her articulate deeply ambivalent feelings about family relations, childhood, and the literary tradition (Castle, 2005: 114). In the case of Salman Rushdie, it was the 1939 MGM film adaptation of L. Frank Baum's *The Wonderful Wizard of Oz* (1900) that provided a seminal experience. That childhood narratives are experienced in various forms and media is assumed in the approach to and selection of children's 'literature' in the following pages, though the handheld book is given primacy.

Probably the most sustained and probing exploration of the uses and enduring impressions made by children's literature on an individual writer is Francis Spufford's *The Child that Books Built* (2002), an autobiographical account of himself as a young reader. As Spufford explains, he undertook the project because he recognised that in many ways he had read himself into the kind of adult and writer that he is:

> the words we take into ourselves help to shape us. They help form the questions we think are worth asking; they shift around the boundaries of the sayable inside us, and the related borders of what's acceptable; their potent images ... dart new bridges into being between our conscious and unconscious minds, between what we know we know and the knowledge we cannot examine by thinking. They build and stretch and build again the chambers of our imagination.

21–2

While the detail in Spufford's reflections on himself as a consumer of fiction suggest that at some level he always understood himself in relation to what he was reading, the author Eva Figes did not realise that the fairy tales she encountered as a child were at work, shaping her thinking and behaviour, until she began to read them to her first grandchild. In *Tales of Innocence and Experience* (2003), she writes about how she gradually became aware that reconnecting with stories remembered – and misremembered – she had heard and read when young, was releasing and giving expression to lost, repressed or unacknowledged childhood experiences. In her case, sharing fairy tales with her granddaughter allowed her to realise that she had unconsciously used the tales to understand the experience of fleeing from Nazi Germany and resettling in an alien world. That insight has made it possible for her to write about both the events and the way the tales continue to shape them for her.

All the examples provided so far focus on the role played by children's literature on the formation of adult writers rather than why writing for children appeals to writers. In an essay on Kipling's late short story, 'Fairy-Kist' (1928), Judith Plotz sets a series of interesting ideas in motion, ideas which support the notion that children's literature both directly influences the way its readers who become writers write, and represents a valuable cultural space for writers. (Inevitably this influence is recognised long after the first reading; it is never possible to recover initial responses to works read in childhood, though many writers testify to strong memories of being powerfully affected by what they recall as first encounters with particular books, comics and stories in periodicals.) In what at first appears to be a corrective to Dusinberre's claims for children's literature, Plotz carefully establishes that, publicly at least, the main figures in literary modernism dismissed children's literature, just as they did writing by women (Greenway, 2005: 183; see also Hughes in Hunt, 1990). She concludes that by the turn of the nineteenth century, male modernists had begun variously to 'appropriate, fear, obscure and diminish' children's literature as part of a lesser, female tradition that serves 'larger male cultural needs' (183).

Dusinberre is not interested in the therapeutic value of children's literature, but she does point to the way writing for children releases visionary potential during periods of upheaval and uncertainty: 'in times of great change', she says, 'some of the most radical ideas about what the future ought to be like will be located in the books which are written for the new generation' (1987: 34). This ability to envisage and engage young readers with possibilities for new worlds and new world orders strikes me as central to the transformative power of children's literature, both socially and aesthetically. The stories we give children are blueprints for living in culture as it exists, but they are also where *alternative* ways of living arc often piloted in recognition of the fact that children will not just inherit the future, but need to participate in shaping it.

New visions may operate primarily at the levels of plot and content, but they may also inspire stylistic innovation, new narrative forms, and fresh explorations of the book as medium, resulting in intellectual platforms from which to build new thinking. Such platforms are necessary but rare. In the absence of new ways of thinking or creative alternatives to the way society works, writing for children may take up a diagnostic position, identifying problems as a first step towards formulating solutions. For instance, in the United Kingdom and the United States, the Thatcher–Reagan era coincided with (or provoked?) a wave of political dystopias and concerns about the environment, globalisation, and the ethics of some scientific/technological developments, a wave which has been gathering force as the extent of the problems becomes more apparent. Whether intellectual, social or creative in their focus, as Graham Greene recognised, children's books have the potential to influence the future.

The uses of children's literature

Alice to the Lighthouse is specifically concerned with the radicalism associated with modernism, but Dusinberre's thesis can be applied more generally. This is not a question of tracing influences, entertaining as that can be, but of refuting Rose's claim that children's literature is becalmed as an art form, and demonstrating that many textual experiments are given their first expression in writing for children. Children's literature, then, is both a breeding ground and an incubator for innovation. There are certainly many very ordinary children's books – at least as many as there are banal books for adults – but there are also aspects about writing for children that result in a kind of wild zone where new ways of thinking are explored, given shape, and so made part of the intellectual and aesthetic currency of that generation of child readers.

Dusinberre's Introduction complains that children's literature has not been treated seriously – that the critical establishment perceives it as 'belonging to a separate sub-culture which has never been allowed a place in the discussion of high culture' (1987: xvii). As I see it, however, this lack of visibility contributes significantly to the freedoms available to those who create children's literature – there is a clear distinction between the amount of regulation and scrutiny applied to narrative forms such as television, films, comics, magazines, and computer games, and that given to children's literature. *Learning from the Left* (2006), Julia Mickenberg's fascinating study of the role played by children's literature in the United States in disseminating and preserving left-wing thinking during the rigours of the McCarthy era and the Cold War, celebrates the fact that commercial children's literature (as distinct from textbooks) flies under the cultural radar and so is able to cross any number of official and unofficial boundaries. Precisely because children's books, then as now, were generally assumed to be good for children, she explains, they 'escaped the stigma attached to commercial culture and often maintained an aura of purity that could ward off would-be censors' (14). Although Mickenberg traces an enduring leftist legacy in American children's publishing – which largely holds for Britain too as the two publishing industries are closely allied – the cultural and aesthetic wild zone at the centre of children's literature is a space for dissenters of all kinds.

Mickenberg's research provides evidence to support Dusinberre's claims that at times of cultural change, children's literature becomes a place of visionary thinking and, Mickenberg would add, political engagement. For instance, she gives examples of books written during the depression 'designed not simply to enlighten children and set their spirits free, but to radicalize them' (50), while the increasing prosperity and industrialization of the post-war period inspired children's books that stressed the power of the imagination and creative thinking as an antidote to creeping mechanisation in most areas of work (40). In the same way, the Cold War years 'when the child became a focal point for national anxiety: anxiety about violence, social control, changing social norms, and "alien" – both extranational and extraterrestrial – influences' (132) stimulated children's book makers to create books that looked outside isolationist paranoia and featured narratives about social justice, freedom of thought and how technology could be used to solve the problems of the past. In other words, children's books encouraged young readers to think optimistically about the future and the pioneering roles they could play in improving society for all.

Avoiding the cultural spotlight is one reason why writers may find themselves drawn to write for children; especially if, consciously or not, they are exploring ideas that they feel may not sit comfortably within the literary establishment or other cultural institutions. There is a kind of liberation in writing for children that stems in part from what Philip Pullman calls their lack of sophistication (though it might be more accurate to relate this to their lack of experience of life and texts). This may be because writers assume children will be less judgemental than adults (and know that their views are unlikely to carry much critical weight). Even when writers consciously adhere to the various unwritten rules about what kind of material is suitable for children, there is abundant textual evidence suggesting that addressing a child audience removes some of the censors and filters that come into play when writing for adults. There are, for instance, many studies that identify Victorian and Edwardian children's fantasies and adventure stories as vehicles for a range of desires or unorthodox ideas that did not find expression so readily in adult fiction (see Brooks, 1969; Carpenter, 1985; Kincaid, 1992; Reynolds, 2000; Rose, 1984).

Another appeal of children's literature for writers and illustrators comes from the oneiric dimension of childhood; the logic of dreams, fantasy, play, and the imaginary, all associated with the young, is seen to be more permeable and plastic than the rationality assigned to adulthood. This plasticity is reflected in children's literature's lack of generic rigidity; it not only tolerates but embraces generic mutation, and also takes in and nourishes kinds of literature that have temporarily fallen from favour in writing for adults, creative activities considered in more detail below.

For me, a crucial part of the explanation for why children's literature is so good at stimulating and nurturing innovation is that many children's texts operate two semiotic systems simultaneously: the visual and the textual, and the entire domain is bound up in interactions between formats and media that are beginning to change the nature and delivery of narrative fiction. The word-image dynamic is particularly adept at giving expression to meanings and concepts that reside at the edges of language – things for which the vocabulary and grammar that regulate verbal communication may currently be inadequate. Those texts that combine visual and textual elements have been especially successful and active in preparing the way for new concepts to be called into language and introducing complex ideas to a juvenile readership.

The way children's literature and associated narrative playthings such as toy theatres and, more recently, book-related merchandise including multimedia products, lay down the foundations of aesthetic taste was well understood by the late-Victorians, as can be seen in the following quote from a review in the 12 December 1865 number of *The Bookseller*.

> There is no department of book-manufacture that requires more skill and conscientious art combined with good taste, than that of children's books; as a general rule, this has been overlooked; it is thought that any rubbish will do for a child. Cruel mistake! Were it possible, only the beautiful, the pure, and the good should be presented to the sensitive eye and ear of childhood.
>
> Masaki, 2006: 10

I am less concerned than Dusinberre about the way children's literature tends to be excluded from the high table of culture, not least because at least in Britain the situation has changed noticeably in recent years. For instance, since 2004 the National Theatre has staged works by Philip Pullman,

Jamila Gavin, and Michael Morpurgo, reviews of children's books are frequently placed alongside those for adults in the broadsheet newspapers, and individual writers, notably Philip Pullman and Michael Morpurgo, regularly contribute to news and cultural affairs programmes. The creation of the Children's Laureate, who is mandated to speak on behalf of the children's book world, has added to the enhanced status and visibility of children's literature in British culture. Despite these improvements, cultural contributions made by children's literature continue to be largely invisible. One of the least recognised areas of creative enrichment and transformation takes place around the way children's literature both incubates genres that have ceased to be used in adult fiction and participates in generic innovation. In this way it functions both as restorative – receiving and returning in rejuvenated form genres originally associated with adult fiction – and as a wellspring from which adult writers can draw.

In and out of the nursery

This movement of genres between writing for children and adults is noted by Jacqueline Rose, who sees children's literature as being charged with the care of certain older forms of literary texts such as myths and legends as a means of preserving and eventually restoring values perceived as being 'on the point of collapse' in contemporary culture (1984: 44). In *Retelling Stories* (1998), John Stephens and Robyn McCallum draw attention to the way that the stories cultures choose to preserve and repeat serve a purpose. They disseminate values, pass on traditions, prop up what Stephens and McCallum call the Western metaethic, with its adherence to qualities such as loyalty, honour, courage, humility, duty, and responsibility. These are all characteristics shared by the majority of early heroes whose stories continue to be handed down from generation to generation; they are also attributes that make for good and governable subjects and citizens, which explains why so many retellings are directed at juvenile audiences.

Although traditional forms may be saved from extinction by being retold to the young, as Rose sees it, consignment to the nursery is ultimately damaging because in the process, the genres are infantilised and impoverished (50). She has a point. Largely to meet the needs of educationalists, many retellings of such cultural staples as myths, legends, and the plays of Shakespeare have been so vigorously adapted for children, so sanitised, flattened out, and restricted in their choice of vocabulary, that they have indeed lost their vigour and purpose. But the problem lies in the nature of the retelling; it is not a direct consequence of such materials being classified as 'children's literature'. Not only can the adjustment to a juvenile audience – which may involve no change to the text but, for instance, the inclusion of illustrations – result in high-quality and largely faithful retellings for new generations of readers such as those by Roger Lancelyn Green, Rosemary Sutcliff, Kevin Crossley-Holland, and Geraldine McCaughrean, but it can also lead to highly original new works that pay subtle homage to established genres and texts. For instance, a range of classic children's texts celebrates Arcadian pastoral literature, among them Kenneth Grahame's *The Wind in the Willows* and A.A. Milne's Pooh books (see Carpenter, 1985). Both books may express a regressive desire to retreat from the demands associated with mature masculinity, but both equally offer original and enduring literary experiences. More recently, writers such as Allan Ahlberg, Christopher Bing, Anthony Browne, Kevin Crossley-Holland, Neil Caiman, Jon Scieszka, and Diana Wynne Jones have produced outstanding fictions that are deeply indebted to traditional sources.

The intertextual richness of children's literature is part of the process by which children are inducted into culture. In the same way, there is a clear logic in giving genres that have fallen from favour in adult fiction space in the 'nursery' of children's literature. A nursery is both a place for the young and a place of development; far from necessarily languishing and becoming aesthetically inert when directed at a juvenile audience in the way Rose suggests, such genres are often refreshed and developed for use in new ways. It is also important to remember that children of nursery age are in the process of learning the primary narratives of culture as well as the more fugitive tales that will become part of the shared stock of cultural references for their particular generation. (Though the preponderance of the latter now come from television, film, and other media – just as for recent generations they were generated by radio and comics – many will still have their origins in books, not least because for Western children, education is an almost universal experience and learning to read print remains central to the curriculum.)

There is a certain affinity between acquiring traditional literacy skills and learning the tales that have helped pass on cultural knowledge for centuries, since such tales also contain basic information about genres, narrative conventions, and the styles associated with different kinds of narratives. Just as we never leave childhood behind, so the narratives ingested in childhood endure and shape adult thinking and behaviour at many levels. This has been discussed above with reference to writers, but it is true more generally as well; Mickenberg, for instance, sees a connection between the student-led radicalism of 1960s America and the children's literature of the 1950s, which actively urged the young to change the world (2006: 26).

Children's literature is not just capable of preserving and rejuvenating outdated or exhausted genres; it also contributes to the creation of new genres and kinds of writing, though to date this has gone unacknowledged because, as Dusinberre notes, there is a widespread assumption that children's literature is a second order of creativity that lags behind and imitates what happens in adult fiction. Until something is identified and named by the cultural establishment, which deals almost exclusively in art directed at mature audiences, it is culturally invisible. Magic(al) realism is a case in point and one that demonstrates well children's literature's role in aesthetic and social innovation and transformation as well as the tendency of children's literature towards generic hybridity.

That children's literature should have given rise to this curious literary hybrid is not surprising; the affinities between the two can quickly be established. At a primary level, magic(al) realism, with its emphasis on transformation, corresponds closely to the conditions of childhood and adolescence, which are intrinsically about change, metamorphosis, and growth of body and mind. Magic(al) realism's requirement that readers accept the improbable – even what is held to be impossible – also minors the constant mental adjustments the young make as they undergo new experiences and encounter new ideas.

References

Brooks, Peter. 'Towards Supreme Fictions' in Peter Brooks (ed.) *Yale French Studies: The Child's Part*. 1969, pp. 5–14.

Burman, Erica. 'The Pedagogics of Post-Modernity: The Address to the Child as Political Subject and Object' in Karín Lesnik-Oberstein (ed.) *Children in Culture: Approaches to Childhood*. Basingstoke: Macmillan, 1998, pp. 55–88.

Carpenter, Humphrey. *Secret Gardens: A Study of the Golden Age of Children's Literature*. London: George Allen and Unwin, 1985.

———. 'Excessively Impertinent Bunnies: The Subversive Element in Beatrix Potter' in Gillian Avery and Julia Briggs (eds) *Children and Their Books: A Celebration of the Life and Work of Iona and Peter Opie*. Oxford: Clarendon Press, 1989.

Castle, Luanne. 'Higgledy Piggledy, Gobbledygoo: The Rotted Residue of Nursery Rhyme in Sylvia Plath's Poetry' in Betty Greenway (ed.) *Twice-Told Tales: The Influence of Childhood Reading on Writers for Adults*. London and New York: Routledge, 2005, pp. 109–24.

Chesterton, G.K. *Autobiography*. London: Arrow Books, 1959.

Dusinberre, Juliet. *Alice to the Lighthouse: Children's Books and Radical Experiments in Art*. Basingstoke: Macmillan, 1987.

Figes, Eva. *Tales of Innocence and Experience: An Exploration*. London: Bloomsbury, 2003.

Greenway, Betty (ed.) *Twice-Told Tales: The Influence of Childhood Reading on Writers for Adults*. London and New York: Routledge, 2005.

Higonnet, Anne. *Pictures of Innocence: The History and Crisis of ideal Childhood*. London: Thames and Hudson, 1998.

Hunt, Peter. (ed.) *Children's Literature: The Development of Criticism*. London: Routledge, 1990.

———. *Criticism, Theory and Children's Literature*. Oxford: Basil Blackwell, 1991.

Kincaid, James R. *Child-Loving: The Erotic Child and Victorian Culture*. London: Routledge, 1992.

Lesnik-Oberstein, Karin. 'Childhood and Textuality: Culture, History, Literature' in *Children's Literature: Criticism and the Fictional Child*. Oxford: Clarendon Press, 1994.

Masaki, Tomoko. *A History of Victorian Popular Picture Books: The Aesthetic, Creative, and Technological Aspects of the Toy Book through the Publications of the Firm of Routledge 1852–1893*. Tokyo Kazamashobo, 2006.

McCallum, Robyn. *Ideologies of Identity in Adolescent Fiction: The Dialogic Construction of Subjectivity*. New York and London: Garland, 1999.

Mickenberg, Julia L. *Learning from the Left: Children's Literature, the Cold War, and Radical Politics in the United States*. New York: Oxford University Press, 2006.

Natov, Roni. *The Poetics of Childhood*. London and New York: Routledge, 2003.

O'Malley, Andrew. *The Making of the Modern Child: Children's Literature and Childhood in the Late Eighteenth Century*. New York and London: Routledge, 2003.

Paul, Lissa. 'Sex and the Children's Book' in *The Lion and the Unicorn*, vol. 29, no. 2, April 2005, pp. 222–35.

Reynolds, Kimberley. 'Fatal Fantasies: The Death of Children in Victorian and Edwardian Fantasy Writing' in Gillian Avery and Kimberley Reynolds (eds) *Representations of Childhood Death*. Basingstoke: Macrnillan, 2000.

———. *Children's Literature in the 1890s and the 1990s*. Plymouth: Northcote House, in association with the British Council, 1994.

Rose, Jacqueline. *The Case of Peter Pan, or, The Impossibility of Children's Fiction*. Basingstoke and London: Macmillan, 1984.

Rudd, David. 'Children's Literature and the Return to Rose' on *Working Papers on the Web* (www.shu.ac.uk/wpw/). Sheffield Hallam University: Autumn, 2006.

———. 'Theories and Theorising: The Condition of Possibility of Children's Literature' in Peter Hunt (ed.) *International Companion Encyclopedia of Children's Literature*, 2nd edition, vol. 1, London: Routledge, 2004, 29–43.

Sinyard, Neil. *Graham Greene: A Literary Life*. Basingstoke: Palgrave, 2003.

Spufford, Francis, *The Child that Books Built*. London: Faber and Faber, 2002.

Stephens, John and Robyn McCallum. *Retelling Stories, Framing Culture: Traditional Stories and Metanarratives in Children's Literature*. London and New York: Garland, 1998.

Tucker, Nicholas. *Suitable for Children? Controversies in Children's Literature*. Berkeley and Los Angeles: University of California Press, 1976.

Zipes, Jack. *Fairy Tales and the Art of Subversion: The Classical Genre for Children and the Process of Civilization*. New York: Routledge, 1991 (first published in 1983).

2
Publishing, Prizes and Popularity

Introduction
Janet Maybin

As Matthew Grenby pointed out in Part 1, children's literature became established as a distinct branch of print culture in Britain in the mid-eighteenth century. Following this, children's books began to be stocked in libraries and also became available for purchase from specialist shops. By the mid-nineteenth century, children's literature had diversified across a wide range of markets and genres. The essays in this section examine social practices connected with the consumption and valuing of this burgeoning body of literature, ranging from Victorian explorations of young people's reading preferences and controversies over the moral tendency of 'penny dreadfuls' to the twentieth and twenty-first centuries and the popular phenomenon of Enid Blyton, changing publishing practices, and the business of awarding literary prizes.

Children's literature has traditionally been subject to a range of different kinds of evaluation, especially from the perspectives of educational and literary criteria. The criteria used for evaluation within practices connected to these domains are linked to different ideas about the nature and purposes of children's literature and to particular conceptions of childhood. Those who want to promote the aesthetic and literary value of children's literature often place importance on the formal quality of the writing, applying criteria similar to those used for assessing literary writing for adults. From this perspective, children are expected to learn to appreciate adult literary aesthetics through the apprenticeship offered by reading good-quality children's literature. However, children's books may also be judged primarily according to their perceived pedagogic value, which means that they will be valued for the insights they provide about 'real life', or for their promotion of particular moral positions. In contrast to these didactic purposes, which are often allied to a view of childhood as a training ground for adulthood, a model of childhood as a time for freedom and play produces the valuing of literature which offers children a rich imaginative world, and perhaps an escape from harsh reality. This tension between valuing instruction and valuing delight is cross-cut by values connected with the social and cultural dimensions of particular historical contexts (for instance, the privileging of certain class values, the promotion of particular forms of family life and gender roles, the construction of specific national identities).

The essays

The section starts with providing a historical insight into the kinds of literature (books, poetry, magazines) which appealed to young people at the end of the nineteenth century. What children actually read in the nineteenth century depended on a range of factors, including their family circumstances and wealth, their access to education and the kinds of books believed by adults to be appropriate for them. It is difficult to gather information, other than from anecdotal evidence, about the children's own role in choosing their reading matter. However, Edward Salmon's essay provides a rare snapshot of young people's views and preferences, discussing the results of a remarkable survey carried out in 1884, which collected responses about favourite authors and reading matter from approximately two thousand 11–19-year-old school students. Salmon is especially interested in comparing and contrasting the choices reported by boys and girls. As he points out, although the young people's responses have to be interpreted with some caution, they reveal a wide range of reading practices and some surprising findings in the case of the girls who refused to be restricted to the less prestigious books designated for their gender. (It is interesting to compare Salmon's data with the results of more recent surveys: see Further Reading).

The data discussed by Salmon came from young people who were probably relatively socially privileged, since they were still in school at a time when compulsory education for children finished at the age of 10. In the next essay, Joseph Bristow focuses on a different social sector of the British population and identifies a significant source of popular reading during the Victorian period which wasn't mentioned by the respondents in Salmon's study: the cheap sensationalist booklets known as 'penny dreadfuls'. Featuring stories about murderers, vampires and highwaymen, these circulated widely among the lower classes. Bristow argues that penny dreadfuls were the first kind of true mass reading. When this readership shifted to become largely juvenile, he suggests, middle-class anxieties about the effects of the penny dreadfuls on working-class boys led to the wholesale borrowing and repackaging of their violent content in the form of stories of manly valour and patriotism featured in more respectable boys' books and magazines, where heroes fought and killed in the service of the British Empire. In Bristow's thesis, this respectably violent reading matter, endorsed by educationalists, was intended to wean working-class youth away from the seditious dreadfuls and to facilitate the more general recruitment of boys, via the colonial adventure story, into a distinctly imperial version of masculinity.

While Bristow is most interested in inscribing literacy practices and gender within a postcolonial analysis of the boys' adventure story, he discusses both literary and educational notions of quality in relation to controversies over the penny dreadfuls. He also describes the bleeding between popular and respectable genres which suggests that quality and non-quality literature are not watertight categories, and that their designation as such may be politically or ideologically motivated. In the next essay, questions about quality are central to Nicholas Tucker's discussion of the trends in British children's books and reading during the twentieth century, which he traces in relation to sociopolitical change and growing competition from other media. Like Bristow, Tucker uses adult-like literary criteria as one reference point for evaluating children's books, criticising those produced between the wars as undemanding, backward-looking, riddled with archaic, chauvinist class values and largely uninteresting to adults. He places a high value on realism and so praises post-1960s children's literature which he sees as depicting the diverse lives of ordinary children and constructing a realistically complex moral world. Tucker's preferences here suggest the prioritisation of an educational aim, in his assumption that literature should reflect real life and teach children about how the world really is. His strong emphasis on realist literature is striking: there is no discussion of the famous fantasy fiction which was published by British authors such as C.S. Lewis and Alan Garner in the 1950s–1970s.

In the same way as the judgements of critics are underpinned by particular assumptions about the nature and purpose of children's literature, the awarding of literary prizes to particular kinds of books, as Kenneth Kidd points out, reveals the cultural values underpinning judges' choices. Taking the most famous American children's book prize, the Newbery Medal (inaugurated in 1922), as a case study, Kidd charts how early meritocratic expectations about excellence gave way, under the influence of progressive social movements in the 1960s and 1970s, to more pluralist notions of literary value, although African-American children's literature continued to be marginalised. He points out that the Newbery has typically been adjudicated by librarians, mainly middle-class white women, who lobbied schools to encourage children's supplementary reading and worked closely with teachers. Thus Kidd suggested that the Newbery became an 'educo middlebrow' project, troubled by the contradictions implicit in identifying distinction within a liberal ethos of democratisation. He suggests that there is an equation between education, women and middlebrow, in contrast to the dominance of male critics and authors in the adult literature prize committees. While Kidd argues that the Newbery and other prizes have played a significant role in establishing hierarchies of value in the field of US children's books, it is also worth noting that lists of past prize-winners include titles which are now largely forgotten, although this does not necessarily affect his argument about the changing regimes of value.

Prizes signify a book's prestige in the eyes of the critics, but they are not necessarily an indication of its appeal to children (although in recognition of this a number of prizes now include children in the judging process). Alongside respected works of literature, popular children's reading matter has always existed, whether in the form of chapbooks, penny dreadfuls, comics and magazines or best-selling children's fiction. It is interesting to note that a popular work or form immediately becomes suspect in the eyes of critics and educationalists for whom popularity signifies a lack of intellectual depth or the absence of improving challenge. In the next essay, David Rudd engages with notions of value in relation to the twentieth-century queen of children's popular fiction, Enid Blyton. Blyton, often cited as the epitome of 'non-quality' children's writing and a negative reference point against which other authors can be more favourably judged, is still the best-selling children's author of all time. Defending her against regular accusations of limited vocabulary, flat characterisation and formulaic plots, Rudd claims that Blyton's skilful use of structure and techniques to produce immediacy and presence make her a master story-teller, who should be judged in terms of a popular oral-narrative tradition, rather than within the narrow strictures of a writerly set of literary criteria. She creates, he argues, a fantasy space similar to that of an orally inflected fairy tale.

In contrast to discussions about the literary or educational value of children's books, soaring sales at the turn of the century and rapidly changing marketing and promotion practices have foregrounded the commercial potential of children's literature. In the final essay included in this section, Claire Squires discusses recent developments in British children's book publishing, highlighting the increasing competition and the market-focused commodification of children's literature. Against the criticism that quickly produced and derivative publishing is now valued above literary quality, she argues that children's books and authors are receiving recognition as never before and suggests, somewhat provocatively, that current publishing practices may be more in touch with the twenty-first-century child, as well as more in line with other media and leisure industries. This, Squires suggests, could be regarded as a healthy state of affairs, counteracting the misplaced nostalgia for the earlier Golden Ages of children's literature which has often characterised publishers' lists in the past.

Further reading

Barker, K. 1998. 'Prize-fighting', in Kimberley Reynolds and Nicholas Tucker (eds) *Children's Book Publishing in Britain Since 1945*. Aldershot, Scolar Press.

Dickinson, P. 1970. 'A Defence of Rubbish', *Children's Literature in Education*, 3: 7–10.

Hade, D. 2001. 'Curious George Gets Branded: Reading as Consuming', *Theory into Practice*, 40 (3): 158–65.

Hall, C. and Coles, M. 1999. *Children's Reading Choices*. London, Routledge & Kegan Paul.

National Centre for Research in Children's Literature, 2007. *Young People's Reading in 2005: The Second Study of Young People's Reading Habits*. London, University of Roehampton.

Reynolds, K. 1998. 'Publishing Practices and the Practicalities of Publishing', in Kimberley Reynolds and Nicholas Tucker (eds) *Children's Book Publishing in Britain Since 1945*. Aldershot, Scolar Press.

Whitehead, F., Capey, A.C., Maddren, W. and Wellings, A. 1977. *Children and Their Books*. London, Macmillan Education.

Boys' and Girls' Reading, 1884
Edward Salmon

Of the many anxieties which every Christmas brings to the parental mind, none is greater than that involved in the answer to the question, What shall the children read? Sons and daughters equally have grown to look upon the gift of a book as an indispensable accessory to their holiday. Paterfamilias would have little peace were the gaily-covered volume not forthcoming as regularly as the turkey, the plum-pudding, the crackers, and other Yuletide delights. To conscientious parents the choice of a work suitable to the young mind may pardonably present many difficulties. What are the books and periodicals issued for the special edification of their children? and what is the influence which these works are calculated to exercise? Such are the problems which have to be faced, and the parent who faces them courageously and solves them satisfactorily discharges an onerous duty in a manner to be commended.

In the circumstances, therefore, it is not surprising that slowly but surely two questions are beginning to occupy a place in the literary discussions of

Originally published as 'Chapter I. Introduction. I. What Boys read II. What Girls read', in E. Salmon, *Juvenile Literature As It Is* (London, Henry J. Drane, 1888), pp. 11–31.

the day. First, What do children read? second, What is written for them? Little seems to he known by the general public on either point. Everyone can tell you what he or she read in early youth; but beyond this personal experience acquired in the course of a few years' reading by way of amusement, no reliable data exist as to the work of individual writers for the young, or the precise nature of the books read by the rising generation.

To answer both questions is important. What children read I am able, through the kindness of Mr Charles Welsh, to show in a way as nearly conclusive as it possibly can be; with what is written for them, I have been at considerable pains to make myself acquainted.

Four years ago, Mr Welsh, who has been long and actively engaged in the preparation and production of books for the young, took up the inquiry into the extent and character of children's reading in an earnest and practical spirit, and stress of engagements alone prevented him from working out the results of his inquiries. He despatched to numerous schools for boys and girls a circular containing several questions such as 'What is your favourite book, and why do you like it best?' 'Who is your favourite author?' and 'Who is your favourite writer of fiction?' 'Which of his books do you like best?' 'What other writers of fiction do you like?' 'Which is your favourite magazine, and why do you prefer it?' 'What others, if any, do you read?' 'What histories have you read?' 'What biographies?' 'What travels?' 'What other books?' 'What pieces of poetry do you like best?'

The interest taken in these questions by boys and girls, as well as by masters and mistresses, is proved by the ready replies given on the one hand, and the assistance rendered in securing them on the other. In all, some two thousand answers were received, and a curious jumble of ignorance and intelligence, application and laziness, they present. These I have analyzed, and the analysis will serve fitly as a basis for much that I shall have to say. The indication which they afford to the literary likes and dislikes of our boys and girls may not be in every case reliable; but the consensus of feeling, gathered as it is from widely differing sources, is sufficiently consistent to be of immense value.

I. What boys read

First, let us take the replies of the boys, whose ages, like those of the girls, range from eleven to nineteen. Their positions in life are those equally of all scholars, from the ordinary Board schoolboy to the young collegian. Tabulating together the answer to the two questions, 'Who is your favourite author?' and 'Who is your favourite writer of fiction?' the distinction between these two being somewhat subtle, we arrive at the following list of the favourite authors among seven hundred and ninety boys: –

C. Dickens,	223	C. Lever,	11
W.H.G. Kingston,	179	Thackeray,	10
Sir W. Scott,	128	Lord Tennyson,	10
Jules Verne,	114	H.C. Adams,	10
Captain Marryat,	102	C. Reade,	9
R.M. Ballantyne,	67	Miss Braddon,	9
H. Ainsworth,	61	George Eliot,	9
Shakespeare,	44	Rev. J.G. Wood,	8
Mayne Reid,	33	Cowper,	8
Lord Lytton,	32	Whyte Melville,	7
C. Kingsley,	28	Wilkie Collins,	6
Defoe,	24	Hans Andersen,	6
J. Grant,	12	Longfellow,	6
Fenimore Cooper,	12	A.R. Phillips,	5
Macaulay,	11		

Among the many names which fail to secure many votes are: – Byron, 4; Bunyan, 4; Carlyle, 3; Mark Twain, 3; Dumas, 3; Archdeacon Farrar, 3; Aimard, 3; A.R. Hope, 2; Dr G. Stables, 2; whilst Mr Henty, Mr Hughes, Erckmann-Chatrian, and Mr Ruskin, figure in a group whose constituents are accorded one each.

The books mentioned as favourites are: –

Robinson Crusoe,	43	Around the World in	
Swiss Family Robinson,	24	Eighty Days,	7
Pickwick Papers,	22	Midshipman Easy,	7
Ivanhoe,	20	David Copperfield,	7
Boys' Own Annual,	17	Every Boy's Annual,	6
The Bible,	15	Ernie Elton,	6
Tom Brown's Schooldays,	15	Peter Trawl,	6
Valentine Vox,	13	Scalp Hunters,	6
Vice Versâ,	12	Nicholas Nickleby,	6
St Winifred's,	11	Eric,	6
Arabian Nights,	10	Uncle Tom's Cabin,	5
Westward Ho!	9	Peter Simple,	5
Oliver Twist,	9	Twenty Thousand Leagues	
The Three Midshipmen,	8	under the Sea,	5
Charles O'Malley,	7	Masterman Ready,	5

The papers and magazines read by these young gentlemen find favour in the following degrees: –

The Boys' Own Paper,	404	The Daily Telegraph,	8
Tit Bits,	27	The Morning Post,	8
The Standard,	20	Little Folks,	7
The Union Jack,	16	The Boys of England,	6
The Boys' World,	16	Harper's Magazine,	5
Punch,	14	The Graphic,	5
The Field,	13	Cassell's Family Magazine,	5
Young England,	11	Chatterbox,	5
Rare Bits,	11	Youth,	5
Chambers' Journal,	10	Boys' Comic Journal,	5
Young Folks,	10	The Sunday at Home,	4
The Times,	8	The Daily News,	4

The Century secures 3; *The Globe*, 3; *Longman's Magazine*, 3; *The Nineteenth Century*, 2; *The Spectator*, 2; *Every Boy's Magazine*, 2; and *St Nicholas*, 2.

Pieces of poetry liked best graduate thus: –

Lady of the Lake,	99	The Revenge,	15
Marmion,	65	Casabianca,	14
Horatius,	60	Childe Harold,	12
Gray's Elegy,	55	The Fireman's Wedding,	12
The Charge of the Light Brigade,	45	L'Allegro,	11
The Battle of Bannock-burn,	38	The Eve of Waterloo,	11
Lay of the Last Minstrel,	37	Mary, Queen of Scots,	10
My Mother's Picture,	33	The Deserted Village,	10
John Gilpin,	31	The Inchcape Rock,	9
Paradise Lost,	27	The Merchant of Venice,	8
The Burial of Sir John Moore,	24	The Battle of Blenheim,	8
The Spanish Armada,	23	William Tell,	8
The Ancient Mariner,	21	Macbeth,	7
The Battle of Flodden,	20	St Crispian's,	6
Evangeline,	19	Hiawatha,	5
Macaulay's Lays,	16	The Ingoldsby Legends,	5
The Village Blacksmith,	15	The Curfew Bell,	5

In the department of Biography and Travel, boys have read chiefly such lives as those of Stephenson, Wellington, Nelson, and Cook, and delight in the stirring records of Livingstone, Stanley, Columbus, and other well-known explorers. In the department of history, some mention Macaulay's History, some Hume's, Smith's, or McCarthy's, but in the majority of cases they are content with the simple statement that they have read English history, supplemented, perhaps, by a history of some other country or countries, ancient or modern.

It is interesting to turn from a bare record of what these young gentlemen have read to some of their reasons for liking 'best' one book or magazine. These are generally summed up in the words, 'because it is interesting,' or 'because it is full of adventures:' in other, words, because it is what it is. Thus, one young gentleman responds that he prefers 'Robinson Crusoe' because it tells you about a man on a desert island; another 'Vice Versâ' or 'Valentine Vox,' because it is 'funny and makes you laugh;' another likes poetry, 'because it comes in rhyme.' Several prefer certain books which they can read more than once without being wearied. The Bible, when it is declared a favourite, is accepted as such because, to put into a phrase the varying responses of the lads, it is the book of truth and comfort, and 'any one of its sentences contains more than any sentence in any other book.' *The Boy's Own Paper* is liked best because it has 'no slang,' and no 'sensational tales,' and indulges, as one young gentleman, more graphically than elegantly, puts it, in 'no blood and thunder.' The majority of its readers give as their reason for liking it, its admirable combination of instruction and amusement. More than one answer concerning particular books goes to prove that boys place immense faith in what they read. Two lads, both aged thirteen, in different schools, accept as their favourite book 'The Swiss Family Robinson.' One writes that he likes it best because 'it informs you what to do when shipwrecked;' the other 'because it shows you how to get on when shipwrecked, and have no civilized people to help you.' A lad of sixteen likes 'Old St Paul's,' 'because when you sit down to a book of this sort you ought to get thoroughly worked up by it,' as he doubtless was. Another of the same age likes 'The Cloven Foot,' 'because it is exciting, and has a murder.' 'Daniel Deronda' finds favour with a third lad of sixteen, of a more critical and humane temperament, 'because of the plot, the vigour of the characters, and the close attention paid to human nature.' Master Hopeful, aged fifteen last birthday, writes with conviction: 'I never yet came across a magazine worth reading except *Hunt's Universal Yachting Magazine*.' Of newspapers two emphatic opinions are expressed by lads of sixteen. One has a preference for the *Standard*, 'because in it they write everything short and true;' the other, in close agreement, on one point, with the journalistic verdicts of Mr Gladstone, the late Mr Hayward, and the *Pall Mall Gazette*, declares, 'I like *The Morning Post* because its opinions are genuinely Conservative. Should prefer the *Times* if it did not shift.'

Had these questions been submitted to boys four years later, that is, today, there are two names that would assuredly have found some mention – Mr Robert Louis Stevenson and Mr H. Rider Haggard. Both gentlemen have now secured a place in the hearts of English lads. I will therefore conclude this glance at what boys read with some remarks from the pen of a lad of fifteen, who writes to me under date November 1886. He says: 'I have read Charles Dickens' "Nicholas Nickleby," and like it very much; but I do not care about "The Pickwick Papers" and others of Dickens' works, because they are too jocular. I prefer a book of the more "serious" type, such as "Peter Biddulph," by W.H.G. Kingston. I have now taken in two volumes of *The Boys' Own Paper*, because of the adventurous stories that appear in it, and intend to take in a third. I have read in them "School and the World," by Paul Blake, and "Reginald Cruden," by Talbot Baines Reed, but although they are very interesting, giving instances of school and business life, I would again much rather read such stories as "Kormak the Viking; or the Shield-Borne Boy," by Professor Hodgetts, and "Roger Kyffin's Ward," by W.H.G. Kingston, for the reason already given. I hail the monthly numbers of it with pleasure, knowing that, as well as simply reading, I shall also be instructed. I esteem *The Boys' Own Paper* very greatly. I prefer it to *Young Folks' Paper*, for one reason, that the illustrations are better; but, of course, opinions differ. Then, again, it is printed on better paper; that is, if you keep *Young Folks' Paper* in your pocket for a week (not having had the chance of reading it in less time) it wears out, whereas *The Boys' Own Paper* does not. The latter likewise is more comfortably carried in the pocket, it not being such a large book. Although Mr Louis Stevenson's "Kidnapped" in *Young Folks' Paper* was very highly praised, for myself, "Treasure Island" was the more attractive. Just finished also in this latter magazine is "Iron Trials," by G. Manville Fenn, which is very interesting, but to me seems written in a careless fashion. "The Adventures of a Three Guinea Watch" is also a book illustrative of school-boy life, and of how boys may be led into scrapes, if not upon their guard, by bad companions. As it is a "personal" narrative, the watch telling its own story, it makes it very interesting. "Self Help," by Dr Smiles, is likewise instructive – it showing how ragged boys have risen to be members of Parliament. One passage that particularly struck me contains the words, "An idle brain is the devil's workshop," and it has taken such a hold of me that I have, since I first saw it, tried to keep a busy brain.'

II. What girls read

The replies from girls number a few more than a thousand. A perusal of the statistics which are the result will prove generally more surprising, and on

that account more instructive, than in the case of the boys. The favourite
authors are: –

Charles Dickens,	355	Miss Braddon,	13
Sir Walter Scott,	248	Harrison Ainsworth,	13
C. Kingsley,	103	Miss Worboise,	12
C.M. Yonge,	100	Bunyan,	11
Shakespeare,	75	Mrs H.B. Stowe,	11
Mrs Henry Wood,	58	Lord Tennyson,	10
E. Wetherell,	56	Miss Montgomery,	9
George Eliot,	50	R.D. Blackmore,	9
Lord Lytton,	46	Miss Havergal,	9
Andersen,	33	W. Black,	8
Longfellow,	32	Defoe,	8
A.L.O.E.,	32	Mark Twain,	8
Hesba Stretton,	27	C. Brontë,	8
Canon Farrar,	27	F. Smedley,	7
Grace Aguilar,	23	Carlyle,	7
Jules Verne,	22	John Ruskin,	7
Grimm,	20	Miss Edgeworth,	6
Thackeray,	20	R.M. Ballantyne,	6
Mrs Walton,	20	Lewis Carroll,	5
W.H.G. Kingston,	19	Mrs Gaskell,	5
Whyte Melville,	18	Mrs Hemans,	5
Mrs Craik,	15	Mrs E. Marshall,	5
Macaulay,	15	Captain Marryat,	5
Miss Alcott,	14	F. Anstey,	5

Books in the greatest favour are voted as follows: –

Westward Ho!	34	Kenilworth,	12
The Wide, Wide World,	29	The Pickwick Papers,	11
The Bible,	27	Little Meg's Children,	10
A Peep Behind the Scenes,	27	Good Wives,	9
John Halifax, Gentleman,	25	Christie's Old Organ,	8
David Copperfield,	22	Queechy,	8
Little Women,	21	Scottish Chiefs,	8
Ivanhoe,	18	The Channings,	8
The Days of Bruce,	16	Uncle Tom's Cabin,	8
The Daisy Chain,	13	Lorna Doone,	8
The Heir of Redcliffe,	12	Eric,	8

St Winifreds,	8	The Heroes,		6
Hereward the Wake,	8	Two Years Ago,		5
Pilgrim's Progress,	8	Little Dot,		5
The Mill on the Floss,	7	Melbourne House,		5
The Lamplighter,	7	Home Influence,		5
The Swiss Family Robinson,	6	The Newcomes,		5
John Inglesant,	6	Hypatia,		5
Last Days of Pompeii,	6	East Lynne,		5
Last of the Barons,	6			

Among those books which secure four votes are: 'Vanity Fair,' 'The Talisman,' 'The Dove in the Eagle's Nest,' 'The Arabian Nights,' 'The Old Curiosity Shop,' 'The Prince of the House of David,' and 'Tales from Shakespeare.' 'Robinson Crusoe' is only liked best by two, and 'Alice in Wonderland' by one. In reply to the question as to favourite magazines or papers, the young ladies bestow the badge of merit in the following manner: –

The Girls' Own Paper,	315	Good Words,	15
The Boys' Own Paper,	88	Harper's Magazine,	15
Little Folks,	71	The Temple Bar,	12
Cassell's Family Magazine,	35	The Chatterbox,	12
Quiver,	29	Aunt Judy,	11
Punch,	24	The Child's Companion,	10
Monthly Packet,	22	St Nicholas,	9
The Child's Own Magazine,	19	The Graphic,	8
Scribner and The Century*	18	Every Girl's Magazine,	8
Sunday,	18	The Argosy,	8
Chambers's Journal,	17	The Magazine of Art,	7
Sunshine,	17	The Prize,	7
The Children's Friend,	17	The Leisure Hour,	7
Sunday at Home,	17	The Cornhill,	5

Of the magazines which score less than five, *Longman's* and *The Union Jack* secure four each; the *Nineteenth Century*, *Little Wide Awake*, *Our Darlings*, and *Macmillan's Magazine*, three. Girls, according to this list, do not affect newspapers much, and society papers not at all.

---

*These two names are used indifferently to distinguish the magazine, the original *Scribner's* a year or two ago having become *The Century*.

The various pieces of poetry mentioned as liked best are the following: –

Evangeline,	186	My Mother's Picture,	32
The Lady of The Lake,	185	Ancient Mariner,	32
Marmion,	89	In Memoriam,	30
The May Queen,	80	Horatius,	30
The Lay of the Last Minstrel,	75	Spanish Armada,	30
Mary, Queen of Scots,	59	Deserted Village,	27
Hiawatha,	59	Burial of Sir John Moore,	25
Idylls of the King,	54	Wreck of the Hesperus,	25
Enoch Arden,	51	Merchant of Venice,	24
Paradise Lost,	51	Excelsior,	24
Lays of Ancient Rome,	48	Battle of Troy,	24
Psalm of Life,	41	Casabianca,	22
Gray's Elegy,	37	Courtship of Miles Standish,	20
The Princess,	34		
The Charge of the Light Brigade,	33		

Among those pieces which are voted less than twenty are: – 'Village Blacksmith,' 16; 'Song of a Shirt,' 14; 'The Tales of a Roadside Inn,' 14; 'Golden Legend,' 14; 'John Gilpin,' 14; 'Lord of the Isles,' 13; 'Childe Harold,' 12; 'Ingoldsby Legends,' 11; 'Maud,' 11; 'The Cry of the Children,' 10; 'Dream of Eugene Aram,' 10; 'The Revenge,' 9; 'L'Allegro,' 8; 'The Raven,' 5; 'Fairy Queen,' 4

Shakespeare's poetry, as a whole, secures eighteen votes; Longfellow's, fifteen; Scott's, eight; Tennyson's, eight; Mrs Hemans', seven; Cowper's, four; Wordsworth's, three; Hood's, two; Byron's, two.

In response to the questions, What biographies have you read? only very familiar names – Shakespeare, Raleigh, Johnson, Isaac Walton, Pusey – are mentioned; and in the case of books of travel, 'A Voyage in the Sunbeam,' has been read by nearly every other young lady appealed to. The frequent mention of Lady Brassey's work is, in fact, one of the most remarkable features of the replies.

The majority of the reasons given by the girls as to why they prefer a particular book, are very simple. One likes 'Ernie Elton' because the hero is so mischievous; another likes 'Little Women' because there are more than one in the family; another of fifteen likes 'Westward Ho!' 'because the navy is my favourite profession.' 'The Heir of Redclyffe' is a favourite with one young lady of sixteen, because she has read it through so many times and never gets tired of it. 'It always seems new and interesting.' 'The First

Violin' is 'natural, homely, and touching.' 'The King's Namesake' is admired because of the character of Charles I. Of 'David Copperfield' a young lady of fifteen writes, 'he is one of my favourites. I like it because the characters are true to life. They are human beings; not romantic creations of the author's imagination. The story itself is interesting, and simply and graphically told.' 'Vanity Fair' appeals to a young lady of eighteen, because 'it is a book written with a definite purpose, and reveals hollowness of life in a certain class at that time. Author is plain spoken; very sarcastic.' Pronouncing Charles Kingsley to be her favourite author, the same young lady says of 'Westward Ho!': 'It abounds in truly *noble* characters, men who are marked by their loyalty and love for the English Church. My favourites are Amyas and Frank Leigh.' 'My favourite book,' declares a young lady of sixteen, 'is "The Scottish Chiefs" by Jane Porter. I like it best because it gives you such a good idea of what used to go on in the days of such heroes as Wallace and Bruce, and because it is so graphic a description, that you can imagine the scenes to yourself as you read.' The following comment on 'John Inglesant' from a pen of seventeen is interesting. 'It shows that men were the same in every age. I like analysis of character, and Inglesant's is so well analyzed. Also, I like the charity with which all sects of religion are dealt with, and I like the splendid descriptions of churches and music. I like the mystical religion in it too.'

If we glance now at the voting as a whole, we shall see that it affords ground for general satisfaction. Boys and girls equally have proved that they recognise and appreciate the best in literature, whether or not they always read it. Who could wish hoys to adopt as their favourite authors, better men than Dickens, Kingston, Scott? as their favourite books, better works than 'Robinson Crusoe' or 'Ivanhoe'? as their favourite magazine, a better than *The Boys' Own Paper*? as favourite pieces of poetry, better than 'The Lady of the Lake,' or 'Marmion,' or 'Horatius'? With the girls, the choice is equally gratifying – Dickens as a favourite author, 'Westward Ho!' as a favourite book, *The Girls' Own Paper* as a favourite magazine, and 'Evangeline' as favourite poetry, leave little to be desired in a general way. One striking fact in connection with the replies of the girls is that already noted, viz., the almost complete absence of reference to society papers or papers chiefly gossipy in character. Only one declared in favour of *The Queen* as a favourite paper. *Truth* and *The World* are hardly mentioned. Two prefer, above other papers, *The Family Herald*. Even, therefore, though we assume that the voting is not in all particulars quite sincere, there is at least the satisfaction of knowing that girls recognise the propriety of accepting, as entitled to the first place, only books and periodicals of an irreproachable kind.

Not the least suggestive item in the result of the voting on the part of girls is the popularity of *The Boys' Own Paper* and several purely boys' books. The explanation of this, as will be shown, is that they can get in boys' books what they seldom get in their own – a stirring plot and lively movement. Probably, if we were to take the country through, we should find that nearly as many girls as boys have read 'Robinson Crusoe,' 'Tom Brown's Schooldays,' and other long-lived 'boys' stories.' Nor is this liking for heroes rather than heroines to be deprecated. It ought to impart vigour and breadth to a girl's nature, and to give sisters a sympathetic knowledge of the scenes wherein their brothers live and work.

The general feeling of English girls is, I fancy, fairly accurately expressed in the following notes sent me by a young lady, who says: 'Charlotte Yonge's stories are pretty, and if they were not quite so goody-goody, would be very nice stories of home and everyday life. Anne Beale is still more goody-goody in her style. I think if the "Wide, Wide World" and "Queechy" had been English stories, they would not have gained a quarter of the popularity they have – the American writing is so much more life-like than the English. American stories for girls are always more true to nature than English stories. A great many girls never read so-called "girls' books" at all; they prefer those presumably written for boys. Girls as a rule don't care for Sunday-school twaddle; they like a good stirring story, with a plot and some incident and adventures – not a collection of texts and sermons and hymns strung together, with a little "Child's Guide to Knowledge" sort of conversation. This is also, I am sure, why girls read so many novels of the commoner type – they have, as a rule, nothing else in any way interesting. People try to make boys' books as exciting and amusing as possible, while we girls, who are much quicker and more imaginative, are very often supposed to read milk-and-watery sorts of stories that we could generally write better ourselves. Among some good authors of books which girls read, are Jessie Fothergill's "The First Violin" and Mrs Gaskell's "Wives and Daughters," &c. Being an omnivorous reader myself, I am not perhaps a very good judge of what girls generally like to read, but America holds the palm, I think, in its school-girl literature and children's books. When I was younger I always preferred Jules Verne and Ballantyne and "Little Women" and "Good Wives" to any other books, except those of Charles Lever.'

To those who have any idea at all of 'girls' literature,' the foregoing lists suggest some curious reflections. Hardly one of the recognised writers for girls is in high favour; and without attributing any want of frankness to the young ladies who have voted so emphatically for Dickens and Scott, the question may fairly be asked, do their replies really represent what girls like best in literature? Three things, at least, I should say, contributed to make

them vote as they have done. In the first place, doubtless they considered
it proper to vote for such names as Scott and Dickens, although, perhaps,
they had not read two of the works of either; in the second, Dickens' or
Scott's works are probably in the school or home library, and hence easily
get-at-able; in the third, personal inquiries induce me to believe that young
ladies do not take particular notice of authors' names, and such household
words as Scott and Dickens would occur to their minds more readily than
the patronymics of the authors who devote their energies solely to writing
for girls. Miss Sewell, for instance, is not mentioned as a favourite once;
neither is Miss Maggie Symington. Miss Sarah Doudney is mentioned only
four times, Mrs Ewing only once, and Marian Farningham once. To imagine that Carlyle is more popular with girls than any one of these is absurd.
In reply to the question, 'What other books have you read?' many books
published for girls are enumerated, and, with every respect for the judgement
of the young ladies appealed to, I venture to think that their voting has been
hardly as uncoloured by circumstances, doubtless more or less accidental, as
that of the boys.

At the same time, unless these lists are to be entirely discredited, they must
open the eyes of parents to the real needs of our girls. Mr Welsh is doubtless
correct when be surmises that much of the popularity, from the publishers'
point of view, of books for girls, is due to the fact that they are bought by
parents and friends for the purpose of presentation. If girls were to select their
own books, in other words, they would make a choice very different from
that which their elders make for them. Allowing, therefore, that the table now
given at all represents the degrees of regard in which the various authors are
held by girls, it should induce those who aspire to write especially for girls to
think twice before giving to the world another story on the usual lines.

Empire Boys
Joseph Bristow

The penny dreadful

The origins of the penny dreadfuls – increasingly referred to by that name
in the 1860s – lay in the gothic novel. The tales of Sweeney Todd and Varney
the Vampire count among the celebrated examples of melodramatic stories

---

Extracted from 'Reading for the Empire', in J. Bristow, *Empire Boys: Adventures in a Man's
World* (London: HarperCollins, 1991), pp. 4–52.

constructed in a simple narrative style where the emphasis is more on incident than character.[1] Bizarre and fantastic events prevailed in these eight-
page publications, usually made attractive by a sensational engraving on the
cover. Some of these stories sold not by the thousand but the million. They
were the first kind of truly mass reading. By 1870 their market had largely
shifted to a 'juvenile' readership (as it was by then named), and the majority of self-defined cultured people was . . . appalled by the content of these
works. The well-educated middle classes were aghast at the unforeseen consequences of teaching working people how to read.

As early as 1858, Margaret Oliphant, a conservative novelist and regular
contributor to *Blackwood's*, decried the failure of charitable organizations
(such as the Societies for the Diffusion of Knowledge) whose Penny Magazines and Cyclopaedias packed with 'useful' information were not favoured
by the mass reading public. Instead, as Oliphant said, the working classes
preferred to consume despicably low-grade fiction, and their interest in
cheaply produced sensational tales where the 'characters may be the merest
puppets of invention; the springs of the machinery may betray themselves
at every movement; the language may be absurd, the invention miserable'
was sustained by the seemingly simple pleasures of 'narrative'. Oliphant
accounted for this fascination for technically unaccomplished but none
the less stimulating narratives in a revealing analogy: 'What does a child
care for the probabilities of fiction, for the wit of dialogue, or the grace of
style? It is likely they bore him, detaining him as they do from the current
of events'.[2] The middle-class child and the literate adult worker supposedly
shared much in common. Both had to be trained to read literature of a more
improving kind. An article such as Oliphant's (one of many on this topic)
discloses how the increasing emphasis on culture at this time rested upon
a much older and well-established idea of moral sustenance promoted by
evangelical groups, Sunday schools, and religious publishing houses.

By the 1880s, middle-class denunciations of the penny dreadfuls grew
increasingly infuriated. B.G. Johns provided a typical summary of this type
of popular fiction in the 1887 volume of the *Edinburgh Review*. Throughout his discussion of 'The Literature of the Streets', Johns made it clear that
the penny dreadfuls exploit that all too conspicuous lack of restraint that
fundamentally violates culture. According to him, the working classes were
presumably as wild, sick, and populous as the 'trash' they read. Sewers of
this so-called filth overflowed the streets of Britain's cities, and swarms of
poor people were everywhere consuming this dangerous stuff:

[T]he fountain head of the poisonous stream is in great towns and cities,
especially in London itself; and it is with that we now have to deal. Here the

readers are to be numbered by hundreds of thousands, and the supply exceeds the wildest demand. There is now before us such a veritable mountain of pernicious trash, mostly in paper covers, and all 'Price One Penny': so-called novelettes, tales, stories of adventure, mystery and crime; pictures of school life hideously unlike reality; exploits of robbers, cut-throats, prostitutes, and rogues, that, but for its actual presence, it would seem incredible. To expect our readers to wade through such a nauseous mass would be useless, even if the task were possible. All that can be done is to select from the whole heap a few specimens. Widely and carefully chosen, that may serve as types of the mental diet now provided for millions of poor children, who buy and devour it with intense relish. It matters little where we begin, so we take the first –

'*Joanna Polenipper, Female horse-stealer, Footpad, Smuggler, Prison-Beater and Murderer*', a complete romance in eight quarto pages, four chapters of small print, as a sample of the entire series. For, in point of general style, colour, incident, and character of the *dramatis personae*, all these volumes of trash are as like each other as peas in a single pod. Every sentence fairly bristles with adjectives of tremendous and fiery strength; the characters are of but two kinds, whether angels or demons in mortal guise; fools or sharpers; rogues or the victims on whom they prey. Every page is crammed with incidents of the most astounding kind, which succeed each other as swiftly as the scenes in a transpontine drama. Bombastic rant, high-flown rhodomontade, and the flattest fustian from the lips of all speakers alike; and 'Joanna' is no exception to the rule.[3]

The penny dreadfuls may have excited their readers but the very thought of them being read by the unruly multitude set Johns's prose into an equally violent motion. Since there are many instances of sensational narratives going as far back as the medieval period, it is worth inquiring exactly what it was that Johns objected to. Bad style, cheap format, excesses of expression, implausible plotting – these were the points that violated Johns's and his contemporaries' cultured sensibilities. Yet in his account of these pitched battles between heroes and villains, their unlikely adventures and wickedly perpetrated crimes, Johns was disgusted not only at the thought of the working classes degrading themselves but also – and this is the point – of the degradation of reading itself. In their overwhelming numbers, working people were obviously not reading what was thought best for them by the cultured few. And it was the working classes' consent to consume such 'trash' that threw Johns into such a quandary. Their reading was uncontrollable, in terms of both its extravagant sales figures and overworked plots.

Such 'literature of the streets' was clearly at a far remove from the fairy stories and other acceptable narratives Johns had so highly praised in an earlier article published in 1867, where he claimed: 'Fiction seldom paints life as it truly is, though the stream of life is so chequered that no incident can be devised which has not some counterpart in reality. And yet fiction ought to be, and is, in some sense a picture of life; and so far has the power, and ought, to teach true things'.[4] Johns upheld Mrs Barbauld's moral tales (popular evangelical stories from earlier in the century), as ideal reading matter.

In *A Plea for the Revival of Reading*, published in 1906, the well-known journalist, W.T. Stead, invited comments from his readers on good and bad reading for children. His central chapter – on 'A Lads' and Lasses' Library' – focused on the debate about the dreadfuls. Stead claimed that 'the verdict is that boys take penny dreadfuls as children take measles, and they usually recover'. Quoting one of his correspondents, he says:

> In the penny 'blood' a boy gets his money's worth, and that is what he wants. This type of literature is much abused; it is not nearly so harmful as the ordinary newspaper. All the boys I ever knew to read 'dreadfuls' have, after a spell, turned their thoughts to higher forms of literature. You cannot climb the ladder without commencing at the bottom, and the bottom rung must not be despised because of its position.[5]

Stead's aim was to get children consuming as many stories and poems as possible. It does not, for the moment, really matter what they read, as long as they are reading. And the reading that children enjoy is largely made up of adventure fiction. One woman reader told Stead: 'I didn't want a good book for girls, I wanted to read the books my daddy read.' Thereafter, reading deemed unsuitable for children, and particularly unsuitable for girls, would find its way, in modified form, into school reading schemes.

Surveying the changing markets for juvenile fiction, Dunae writes that the texts 'one generation of critics had denounced as "blood and thunder" came, in a slightly altered form, to be regarded by the next generation as wholesome and patriotic.'[7] The school system, therefore, would gradually take some control over the consumption of fiction by legitimating a range of classic tales of adventure – such as Stevenson's *Treasure Island* (1883) and *Kingsley's Westward Ho!* (1855) – not dissimilar in theme from those to be found on sale as penny publications. For the purpose of study, these books were often abridged and adapted to present what was considered to be a suitable ordering of language. Unnecessary literary idioms were edited from the originals to make them into suitable elementary school readers. Rose has analysed the Report of the 1910 Board of Education, pointing out how it moves in opposed directions where literature for distinct groups of younger and older students is concerned.[8] In the earlier age range (up to fourteen years), the use of 'natural' language – applicable to concrete experience – was favoured in the development of reading skills. Such a policy governed the education of most working-class pupils. The

Report states that older, secondary pupils (twelve to sixteen years) are to be offered a distinctly literary approach to language where, implicitly, ideals of Arnoldian culture stand paramount. Students with the middle-class advantage of staying on at school until sixteen had the opportunity to improve their style and to appreciate felicitous phrasing (contact with Chaucer, Shakespeare and Milton was possible). By 1910, then, the only introduction to high culture a working-class child might receive would have been in the form of an instructive adaptation: a good read with practical applications, something, surely, remote, from the world of sweetness and light. A child's (not to be confused with childish) language would be offered to this kind of pupil. It was a utilitarian language stripped of any affectation. Simple and innocent, it rendered classic narratives accessible in terms of literacy.

By contrast, most penny dreadfuls were aimed at a working-class readership to provide access to a specific type of literary writing – at a great distance from concrete experience, and, paradoxically, with plenty of aspirations to high culture. To their infuriated critics, these publications debased literary models by making fiction repetitious in style and predictable in plot. In his contribution to the debate on the detrimental effects of popular fiction, Francis Hitchman complained:

> 'Turnpike Dick' is described as the true history of all the celebrated highwaymen, and who appears to be a hash-up of the moral and improving biography of Dick Turpin and his 'gallant companions'. The hero is always in company with a magnificent horse; is always armed with sword and pistols, and always sumptuously dressed; he has a 'rich, mellow voice', in spite of his 'nocturnal rambles' and frequently repeated 'draughts of brandy'; he is of matchless physical strength, and is naturally beloved by the most adorable of women; and he beguiles his leisure with wine and song amidst a select crew of 'Knights of the road', whom he treats in a 'haughty yet affable manner'. The moon is always 'shining merrily' on his gallant exploits, and fortune is ever on the side of the handsome hero, and as constantly unfavourable to the stupid, cowardly, and ill-looking constables and their assistants.[9]

For all his irritation with these penny publications, Hitchman none the less discloses their enduring popularity with the working classes. Narratives of this type fulfil specific expectations – in terms of length (standard format of eight pages); idiom (emphatic use of adjectives and adverbs); and characterization (making heroes out of criminals). Each aspect shows no respect for the refinements of literariness. The text is practically worthless (it costs only one penny); it tries in no respect to be original (authorship is unimportant); and it has no moral sense (it flouts the law). But Turnpike

Dick, who outwits the police, carouses with his mates, pulls the women, and thereby plays the role of a notorious Jack-the-Lad, is a complete master of his environment (see Plate 2). All these points are represented in language that is easy to understand. Yet the language used to describe Dick's exploits is far from natural, concrete, or literal. The text deploys an antiquated register – glimpsed in that telling reference to the 'Knights of the road' – that is appropriate to an old-fashioned kind of romance.

Educating British boys

Given the extension of the franchise in 1867 and the marked rise in the working-class population, the boy was now identified as a political danger to the nation. He had to be trained not only to read the right things, to turn his mind away from the debasing effects of penny fiction, but he had also to meet the demands of becoming a responsible citizen. Imperialism made the boy into an aggrandized subject – British born and bred – with the future of the world lying upon his shoulders. But the country of his birth was not in itself the guarantee of his ability to participate in ruling a globe with ever-increasing amounts of red on it. It was, time and again, his class affiliation that threatened his imperial superiority:

> These are the future electors who will exercise so much influence on the world's destiny. The constituents of an imperial race, they ought to be educated with a view to the power they will wield. Every Englishman ought to know something about the dependencies of England, as one of the heirs of such a splendid inheritance; he should understand English interests, something about her commerce, her competitors, the productions and trade of other lands. He ought to know his country's historical as well as her geographical position. He cannot, with safety to the empire, be allowed to be so ignorant as to be unfit for his political trust, like loose ballast in a vessel, liable, in any agitation that may arise, to roll from side to side and so to destroy national stability.[10]

In order to discover more about his national rather than class, origins, two areas of knowledge in particular had to be bequeathed to him – history and geography. From the late 1870s onwards, as Tory designs on the world influenced educational policy, geography earned an increasingly important place among the upper grades of schools. It took until 1900, as Pamela Horn notes, for history – and history of a politically motivated kind – to become a subject to be studied 'as a rule' in elementary education. Before that time, state schooling was preoccupied with teaching basic skills, the 3Rs, and curriculum planning had been largely left in the hands of pragmatic liberals. Horn quotes from a document produced by the Board of Education in 1905 which gives clear reasons for teaching these disciplines:

> from . . . geography lessons the scholars know that Great Britain is only one country among many others. It is, therefore, important that from the history lessons they should learn something of their nationality which distinguishes them from the people of other countries. They cannot understand this . . . unless they are taught how the British nation grew up, and how the mother country in her turn has founded daughter countries beyond the seas.[11]

By the end of the century, then, tenets of imperialism were shaping the ideological dimensions of subjects studied in school. Yet these new rulings on the teaching of history and geography were not imposed by fiat on the world that schoolchildren were learning to appreciate. Instead they reinforced already established imperialist assumptions that had for many years acted as the main precepts guiding the production of adventure fiction for children. Jacqueline Rose has traced the continuity between overtly didactic children's books, such as Thomas Day's *Sandford and Merton* (1783–89), and the realistic narratives of boys' adventure stories (by Captain Marryat, W.H.G. Kingston, and R.M. Ballantyne) which 'are the inheritors of a fully colonialist concept of development, and a highly specific and limited conception of the child.'[12] Gradually, the imperialist knowledge supplied in school lessons would converge with the world-view laid out in what became a canon of children's literature reaching back into the colonial past of the mid-eighteenth century. This trend would be set by Jarrold's *Empire Readers*, published in the 1880s, and adopted by the London School Board. Slightly earlier, between 1865 and 1875 Cassell published adaptations of classics in words of more than one syllable. These were highly popular readers, and included a retelling of Day's eighteenth-century colonial narrative.[13]

Schooling was supposed to be a model of efficiency. It left very little room for creative development (except in the playground). In the 1870s, reading for pleasure, therefore, took place in leisure time rather than at school. Fictional narratives that absorbed the adventurous militarism of this new and rising imperial ideology now had a prime opportunity to enter into that comparatively unrestricted world: a world that belonged to the individual boy and not the school he went to. But these adventures would not be excluded from the school curriculum for long. Towards the end of the Victorian period, the type of adventures absorbed outside school would be modified and so make their way into the classroom. If the Schoolboy was also a Scout, he would, in Edwardian Britain, find most of his time, both in and out of school, taken up with the ideals of empire.

The restricted concern with literacy in schools had other, far-reaching effects on attitudes to literature. At roughly the same time, educators perceiving themselves as Arnold's heirs were attempting to secure the serious study of literary writing in all areas of education, and, as Reports of the Board of Education bear witness, this initiative played a key role in establishing concepts of Englishness vital to imperialism. Newbolt was Rudyard Kipling's and W.E. Henley's most notable descendant as poet of empire. His poem, 'Vitai Lampada' (1908) contains the famous chant, 'Play up! play up! and play the game!'. Similarly, 'Clifton Chapel' upholds the idea that boys hailing from the public schools embody a superior race.[14] That poetry should be used as a vehicle for patriotism was never very far from the minds of key literary educators. It would appear that between 1870 and 1900 narratives celebrating empire and techniques in teaching reading and writing gradually converged, although this is not to suggest that schoolchildren were by the turn of the century only interested in stories adapted to imperialist ends. The point is, both inside and outside the classroom, there was more and more emphasis on heroic adventure, and this involved a number of shifts in attitude towards juvenile publishing and curriculum design.

As Britain expressed its needs for stronger bodies and healthier minds among its working-class male population, two related models of educational knowledge came into the world of boyhood, and both of these, at their inception, were defined against what was seen as the mindless inculcation of facts preoccupying elementary education. One was the practical survivalist education of Scouting and the military structure of youth organizations such as the Boys' Brigade which would provide skills not present in the school curriculum. The other was embodied in the adventure story which would take the boy into areas of history and geography that placed him at the top of the racial ladder and at the helm of all the world.

Boys' magazines

After 1866 the market for boys' penny fiction was driven in two directions, dividing roughly across working-class and middle-class lines. With the astonishing increase in juvenile periodicals, particularly in the late 1860s and 1870s, a split in the readership appeared. Working-class boys were tempted by *The Bad Boy's Paper*, set up in 1875 by Charles Fox, one of the penny dreadful magnates. It was a short-lived enterprise. More extreme was the celebrated *Wild Boys of London*, suppressed by the police in the 1890s. Brett's lower middle-class *Boys of England* lasted longer, running until 1899. It was followed by numerous rival publications under the control of the Emmett brothers. George Emmett's *Young Englishman's*

Journal (1869) was matched by Brett's *Young Men of Great Britain* (1868). Both publishers put out a host of other magazines with almost identical titles. Many of them were lucrative. *Boys of England* had a circulation of no less than 250,000 in the 1870s. Recognizing the huge success of boys' papers in a juvenile market in which it had a diminishing share, the Religious Tract Society (RTS) reconsidered how it might take hold of the minds of young men by using a similar format that was altogether higher in quality. In 1866 the Rev. J. Erskine Charles had attempted to improve boys' reading with *Chatterbox*. His journal, however, seems to have found favour only in middle-class homes. It ran for only two years. Over a decade later, *Boy's Own Paper* (B.O.P.) successfully brought together different classes of reader under the influence of a unifying ideology: imperialism.

Boy's Own Paper ran from 1879 to 1967. Until the First World War its contents and layout hardly varied from one week to another. Its sister paper *Girl's Own Paper* (G.O.P.) was set up in 1880. Although both were remarkably successful, *G.O.P.* reached a wider audience in terms of class and occupation (young single and married women). Exact records of sales and circulation figures are not available. However, Jack Cox, the historian of *B.O.P.*, reckons 250,000 to be a fair estimate of the number of young readers.[15] Kirsten Drotner notes how juvenile weeklies benefited from technological advances in Linotype printing developed in the 1880s, and adds: 'the general expansion in retail trades created a national network of local tobacconists, sweetstalls, and cornershops to which adolescents swarmed on their way from school or work to get the Wednesday or Saturday weeklies'.[16] Competitively priced at one penny, *B.O.P.* appeared in a sixteen-page octavo format. Every year readers could purchase coloured binders for a substantial volume running to 800 pages. In 1914 the paper changed to a monthly publication. Two years later the price rose sharply to one shilling. In style the journal most closely resembled the *Boy's Own Magazine*, published by Samuel O. Beeton from 1856 to 1874. *B.O.P.* aimed to address Beeton's readership along with young men whose families read the popular RTS weeklies, such as *The Leisure Hour* (1852–94), which managed to combine 'instruction and recreation' on the Sabbath in the lower middle-class Victorian home. What is more, these journals redefined earnest Sunday reading as a form of leisure.

From the late 1860s the RTS had voiced the need for an appropriate journal to counter what was perceived as the criminal influence of the penny dreadfuls. At the annual general meeting of the Society in 1878, serious discussions took place to establish a good boys' weekly. The Society's Annual

No. 1.—Vol. I.   SATURDAY, JANUARY 18, 1879.   Price One Penny.
[ALL RIGHTS RESERVED.

MY FIRST FOOTBALL MATCH.

BY AN OLD BOY.

IT was a proud moment in my existence when Wright, captain of our football club, came up to me in school one Friday and said, "Adams, your name is down to play in the match against Craven to-morrow."

I could have knighted him on the spot. To be one of the picked "fifteen," whose glory it was to fight the battles of their school in the Great Close, had been the leading ambition of my life—I suppose I ought to be ashamed to confess it—ever since, as a little chap of ten, I entered Parkhurst six years ago. Not a winter Saturday but had seen me either looking on at some big match, or oftener still scrimmaging about with a score or so of other juniors in a scratch game. But for a long time, do what I would, I always

seemed as far as ever from the coveted goal, and was half despairing of ever rising to win my "first fifteen cap." Lately, however, I had noticed Wright and a few others of our best players more than once lounging about in the Little Close where we juniors used to play, evidently taking observations with an eye to business. Under the awful gaze of these heroes, need I say I exerted myself as I had never done before? What cared I for hacks or bruises, so only that I could distinguish myself in their eyes? And never was music sweeter

"Down!"

Figure 7   Front page of the first issue of *The Boy's Own Paper*, No. 1, Vol. 1, 18 January 1879.

Report of 1879 revealed the tension the Committee felt existed between boys' reading and religious instruction. Cox cites the following passage:

> Juvenile crime was being largely stimulated by the pernicious literature circulated among our lads. Judges, magistrates, schoolmasters, prison chaplains, and others were deploring the existence of the evil and calling loudly for a remedy, but none seemed to be forthcoming. The Committee, fully admitting the terrible necessity of a publication which might to some extent supplant those of a mischievous tendency, yet hesitated upon the task. To have made it obtrusively or largely religious in its teaching would have been to defeat the object in view. Yet it did not seem to come within the scope of the Society's operations if this were the case. It was therefore hoped that some private publisher would undertake the task of producing a paper that should be sound and healthy in tone, and which the boys would buy and read. But no one would incur the risk of pecuniary loss which such a publication seemed to threaten . . . It was thus forced upon the Committee to attempt an enterprise from which the others shrank.[17]

How, then, would the RTS, one of the country's most respected religious bodies, guarantee its investment against the vagaries of a market of which it had little knowledge? They appointed George Hutchinson, who came to them with twelve years' experience of editing *Night and Day*, a magazine for Dr Barnardo's boys. Yet he found it hard to persuade the Committee that the proposed *B.O.P.* would be appropriate to the work of the RTS. His pilot issue was not acceptable to the Society's governing board. Hutchinson was obliged by them to find a formula which, as Cox says, would be 'a compromise between the kind of paper boys would read, and buy; the kind of paper parents and teachers would approve; and the kind of paper the Society, as responsible Christian publishers, wanted to reproduce.[18]

When it went out on sale, *B.O.P.* gave pride of place to fiction – more than half of its contents, in fact. It usually ran three serials concurrently. Up to thirty instalments of 2,000–3,000 words took turns to feature on the front page. The opening paragraphs were laid out next to a large illustration detailing the high points from that week's thrilling episode. Inside, printed text dominated, although high quality engravings were sometimes given a full-page spread. Visual materials were scattered here and there. Yet they were supplementary to the three-ruled columns of adventure, short essays, and correspondence. *B.O.P.* was clearly not to be looked at; it demanded to be read. It carried some advertisements, notably for books in the *B.O.P.* library. Occasional and rather lavish fold-out colour plates were issued to be bound into the page opposite specific articles on general knowledge. Poems, songs (including the scores), a regular brainteaser on chess, and shorter pieces on field sports stood alongside essays providing all sorts of information about hobbies, the military, and 'strange but true' stories. Competitions, ranging from music to carving, were set each week, and subsequent winners were duly listed. A short column entitled 'Doings for the Month' provided useful tips on a variety of topics. Caring for animals was frequently one of them. These materials were understandably geared towards young men. But it is striking how exclusively male the contents are. Women rarely appear in *B.O.P.*. (There was, however, a proportion of women authors. The paper advertised for such things as perambulators, so it seems that mothers were expected to cast an approving eye on its pages.) If the stories and features are not concerned with boys and men, they depict a 'Jungle Book' of predatory creatures – foxes, bears, tigers – along with domestic cats and dogs. These beasts were, then, both fierce and friendly, exciting and sentimental at once, in a domain based on emotional extremes of protecting and fighting.

Here nothing presents itself as overtly political. No news is in evidence. Most of the paper, however, is devoted to information directly connected with the world (the expanding empire). But this is a world defined according to a highly selective version of history and geography. Ancient culture and far-off places are particular sources of interest. Remote in time and place, they (rather than present-day events) are shaped by the contemporary imperial context. Such a world appropriately excited but did not threaten the boy. And this is simply because this world was bounded by his leisure: hobbies, adventures, sports and games. In fact, *B.O.P.* had no explicit ties with time spent at either school or work. (The public-school story, which ran in practically every issue, may seem aberrant here. Yet adventure rather than education is the focus of the schoolboy narrative.) Instead, the paper brings together selected aspects of imperialist ideology – aggressive, competitive, and yet gentlemanly behaviour – to make the most of the boy's free time. This is not to say that the paper is jingoistic. Rather, it appears respectably patriotic. Yet its patriotism celebrates not just the empire but also the boy himself. One of its many rollicking songs, 'Boys of England', makes this point in its title. Singing the praises of his country, the boy was idealizing a quality he himself enshrined. Empire and boyhood, then, were mutually supportive. Everywhere the nation's young hero encountered texts and illustrations that made him the subject of his reading. Here the boy was both the reader and the focus of what he read.

B.O.P. was the first journal, and the most enduring of its kind, to be welcomed by the critics of penny fiction. Yet, as E.S. Turner writes, it 'may not have been strictly blood-and-thunder, but it was a long way from milk-and-water.'[19] Arnoldian ideals of culture had certainly not found their way to the nation's increasing numbers of young men. Instead, imperialism took on all the attributes of moral and educational improvement. Those virtues so highly praised in culture – sweetness and light – were overshadowed by a more literary middle-class version of those violent narratives that made their bad-mannered working-class readers objects of ridicule, fear, and contempt. The migration of cultural values was, in effect, moving in two directions, up and down. Up towards a more respectable ideology of securing the empire, and down towards a more popular kind of narrative celebrated by the reading of the masses. (This vertical model, of aspiration and degradation, is a persistently Victorian one.) In the context of late Victorian popular boys' reading – whether in Brett's *Boys of England* or the RTS's *B.O.P.* – the rarefied atmosphere of culture no doubt seemed irrelevant to a world governed by adventure, survivalism, and, as the end of the century approached, war.

Notes

1. Extracts from Thomas Peckett Prest, 'Sweeney Todd' (1846) and James Malcolm Rymer, 'Varney the Vampire' (1840s) can be found in Peter Haining, (ed.), *The Penny Dreadful: Or, Strange, Horrid and Sensational Tales!* (London; Gollancz, 1975), pp. 95–133.
2. Margaret Oliphant, 'The Byways of Literature: Reading for the Million', *Blackwood's Edinburgh Magazine*, 84 (1858), p. 205.
3. B.G. Johns, 'The Literature of the Streets', *Edinburgh Review*, 165 (1887), pp. 42–3.
4. B.G. Johns, 'Books of Fiction for Children', *Quarterly Review*, 122 (1867), pp. 60, 80–1.
5. W.T. Stead, *A Plea for the Revival of Reading* (London: Stead's Publishing House, 1906), pp. 75–6.
6. Ibid., p. 73.
7. Dunae, 'Penny Dreadfuls: Late Nineteenth-Century Boys' Literature and Crime', *Victorian Studies*, 22 (1979), p. 150.
8. Jacqueline Rose, *The Case of Peter Pan or The Impossibility of Children's Fiction* (London: Macmillan, 1984), pp. 119–25.
9. Francis Hitchman, 'Penny Fiction', *Quarterly Review*, 171 (1890), p. 153.
10. David Vincent, *Literacy and Popular Culture: England 1750–1914* (Cambridge: Cambridge University Press, 1989), p. 133.
11. *Suggestions for the Consideration of Teachers and Others Concerned in the Work of Public Elementary Schools* (London: HMSO, 1905) cited in Pamela Horn, 'English Elementary Education and the Growth of the Imperial Ideal: 1880–1914' in J.A. Mangan, (ed.), *Benefits Bestowed? Education and British Imperialism* (Manchester: Manchester University Press, 1988), p. 42.
12. Rose, *The Case of Peter Pan*, p. 57.
13. A brief overview of elementary school readers can be found in Alec Ellis, *Books in Victorian Elementary Schools*, Library Association Pamphlet, no. 34 (London: The Library Association, 1971); see, in particular, pp. 21–36.
14. Henry Newbolt, *Poems: New and Old* (London: John Murray, 1912), pp. 76–9.
15. Jack Cox *Take a Cold Tub, Sir! The Story of the Boy's Own Paper* (Guildford, Surrey: Luttermorth Press, 1982), p. 18.

16. Kirsten Drotner, *English Children and their Magazines 1751–1945* (New Haven, Conn.: Yale University Press, 1988), p. 124.

17. Cited in Cox, *Take a Cold Tub, Sir!* p. 18.

18. Ibid., p. 20.

19. E.S. Turner, *Boys Will Be Boys; The Story of Sweeney Todd, Deadwood Dick, Sexton Blake, Dick Barton, et al.* (London: Michael Joseph, 1948), p. 94.

Twentieth-Century British Publishing
Nicholas Tucker

The year 1945 was a crucial one in British history. The six-year war that came to an end saw many social and political changes, with more still to come. But while radical legislation helped transform social policy, cultural life and the values that informed it often went on very much as before. There were a number of reasons for such enduring conservatism. A war in which many civilians suffered badly was not seen by any branch of opinion as a good time for rocking the political boat at home, socially or otherwise. Much of British war-time propaganda, therefore, had concentrated on celebrating shared values dating from the past rather than looking to the future. In this world of universal food and energy shortages, travel restrictions and common danger, it was natural to look backwards for contrasting and consoling images of a time before total warfare.

This was particularly true of the small world of children's literature. Comics and a few novels did take up immediate war themes, just as they had done during the First World War, but accompanying contemporary social issues were portrayed at a very over-simplified, nationalist level. More subtle political analysis of happenings both at home and abroad simply did not happen in children's literature. Nor were many criticisms of Britain heard in terms of its still existing class barriers and the economic inequality that accompanied them. Pre-war silence about such topics in the world of children's books and general popular entertainment continued largely as before.

Voices from abroad, in terms of American or Commonwealth children's writers, were not a significant factor at this early stage. An initially debt-ridden post-war Britain had enough trouble financing its own children's literature, let alone buying in material or translations from abroad. The American influence upon British publishing was in time to become an important one. But in 1945 British children's literature and publishing remained strongly parochial.

Extracted from 'Setting the Scene', in K. Reynolds and N. Tucker, *Children's Book Publishing in Britain Since 1945* (Aldershot: Scolar Press, 1998), pp. 1–19.

With little modern British children's fiction published as possible competition, it was not surprising that sales of A.A. Milne's children's stories – already very popular – greatly increased during the war. Modern best-sellers that also looked to the past, like Richmal Crompton's William books, with their full complements of cooks, gardeners and maids, were as sought after as ever. Immensely popular writers like Enid Blyton and W.E. Johns (see Plates 6 and 8) continued to write stories reflecting a world of middle-class prejudice against selected foreigners, half-castes and gypsies. Home-grown villains as often a not continued to be portrayed as surly working-class characters, generally with designs on other people's property. This was how children's books had always been, and there was as yet little pressure for change.

Damage caused in bombing raids to publishers' stocks and printing plates also meant that up to twenty million children's books suddenly disappeared altogether, often with no hope of republication. This led to shortages of well-known nineteenth-century titles such as Charles Kingsley's *The Water-Babies* and Louisa M. Alcott's *Little Women*. At the same time, paper rationing during the war and for some time afterwards was strictly enforced. In these circumstances, it made commercial sense to allocate what resources there were to those authors who had always sold best. This meant that tried and tested conservative writers such as Crompton, Blyton and Johns took up a disproportionate percentage of children's book sales up to and after 1945. In Blyton's case, some of fifty-three different publishers with whom she had dealings made over the bulk of their paper quotas to her books.[1]

Keen child readers who could not get hold of these best-sellers were often forced back to long-past children's literature wherever they could find it. My older brother and I, aged six and four when the war started, made constant use in the next six years of our grandfather's ancient bound copies of the *Boy's Own Paper*. One of my friends was reading Walter Scott's *Ivanhoe* in 1945. Like child readers in previous centuries when more appropriate contemporary literature was also scarce, one soon learned to track down what little there was by way of child-centred entertainment and then make the best of it.

Children's comics continued to thrive, but again in a non-innovatory manner. Weekly comic-strips in Britain regularly featured up to 20 per cent of recycled material; hardly strong encouragement for any radical new approaches. The popular *Dandy* and *Beano* comics (see Plate 7), produced by the publishing firm D.C. Thomson in Dundee, had always been somewhat backward-looking, featuring teachers wearing gowns and mortarboards who handed out daily canings or the dunce's cap long after such practices were beginning to diminish or disappear from British schools. Such anachronisms were part of the traditional knock-about humour so popular in these comics. But they also symbolised a general unwillingness to portray the modern world.

Disagreeable contemporary happenings like the war itself could hardly be ignored altogether in children's literature, although the popular Rupert Bear comic strip in the *Daily Express* did its best here, hardly ever referring to wartime conditions between 1939 and 1945. There were comic-strips elsewhere featuring Nazi characters forever getting the worst of the situation, such as *Addie and Hermy, the Nasty Nazis*, appearing in the *Dandy*, and *Musso the Wop – He's a Big-a-da Flop*!, coming out in the *Beano*. But these strips both closed by 1942. After that, comic Nazis tended to make more fleeting appearances in other regular comic-strips often still happy to feature pre-war characters living in an unchanging world. In the *Beano's* strip *Lord Snooty and his pals*, originating in 1938 and running for years afterwards until comparatively recently, characters still wore Eton collars and were surrounded by traditional British comic-strip icons like irascible old colonels with gouty feet.

Children's literature [was] also in a generally quiescent state so far as political issues were concerned. George Orwell argued before the war for a socialist children's literature possibly backed up by the Trade Union Council, but this was little more than an after-thought and never got anywhere.[2] The pre-war Left Book Club published only one collection of stories aimed at children. As a young man Geoffrey Trease wrote a pair of Marxist adventure stories: *Bows Against the Barons* and *Comrades for the Charter*, both published by Martin Lawrence in 1934. These never proved hugely successful, and after the war Trease reissued his earlier adventure stories stripped of Marxist ideology in tune with his own later renunciation of communism.

This lack of political engagement was nothing new in children's literature. But the type and extent of worldly innocence it represented made it increasingly difficult for adults to find anything they occasionally wanted to read in children's literature. This was a reversal of the situation found at the turn of the century, when Robert Louis Stevenson, Frances Hodgson Burnett, Kenneth Grahame and many other children's writers had once been read and appreciated by all ages. But reading habits had begun to change after the First World War. Adult readers began to lose the habit of enjoying books written around a formula that children also liked.

A few books continued to span the child–adult divide. Richmal Crompton's William stories appeared in adult magazines before publication in book form, and some popular adult writers still appealed to older children, too. W.E. Johns' undemanding, juvenile Biggles stories, starring a heroic British aviator, also commanded some adult readers, including young airmen who fought in the Battle of Britain. But, increasingly, adult and child readers

Figure 8   Frontispiece, Richmal Crompton, *William the Conqueror*, illus. 'Thomas Henry' (Thomas Henry Fisher) (1926), London: George Newnes Ltd, 1931. By kind permission of Macmillan Children's Books.

were occupying different camps. While many adult novels were reaching out towards new sophistication, sometimes eschewing the happy endings and moral tidiness common in former times, twentieth-century children's books in their turn tended to become more exclusively child-centred.

Enid Blyton's huge success from the 1930s onwards was perhaps the final factor in turning the children's adventure story firmly away from any remaining adult interest. Her use of a repetitive formula whereby child characters regularly won all before them in an evidently unreal universe had little to offer mature readers. But most children adored these stories at the time and many still do today. Yet Enid Blyton was rarely an author that children took with them into late adolescence and adulthood in the way that sometimes used to happen with writers such as Robert Louis Stevenson and Louisa M. Alcott. Just as Blyton was often the most-loved of all children's authors, so was she often mocked by the very same readers once they felt they had truly left their childhood behind them.

Popular fantasy and comedy writing for children were hardly any more demanding in the immediate post-war period. Amiable, comically muddled adult characters like Hugh Lofting's Doctor Dolittle or Norman Hunter's Professor Branestawm continued to offer charming, uncomplicated entertainment but only to the very young. Fairy story collections were also by now increasingly infantilised, dropping the sophisticated art-work and more complex texts of some Victorian editions in favour of child-centred simplicity throughout. The enduring success of Disney's film version of *Snow White* was another factor in the general reorientation of fairy tales towards the overall sentimentality now thought to reflect the needs and understanding of the young.

The provision of fiction in lessons and school libraries was hardly any more exciting. While comics with their classless readership would routinely be condemned or even confiscated by irate parents or teachers, classics from the past, almost invariably written from a decidedly establishment point of view, continued to be thought most suitable. These were the books, according to Geoffrey Trease,[3] which continually took the side of the cavaliers against the roundheads, or which pictured the French Revolution chiefly in terms of the number of aristocrats guillotined on the scaffold. But since it was largely middle-class parents who bought books at the time, it was hardly surprising that such books tended to take a less than revolutionary line when it came to dealing with social issues either past or present.

It followed, therefore, that the stories set in modern times available to school libraries in 1945 were still largely of the type that rarely got far away from the imaginary lives and activities of comfortably off young people having fun on their holidays. As was also the case with novels written for adults around this time, few children's stories existed devoted entirely to descriptions of working-class life. One such was Eve Garnett's *The Family from One End Street*, published in 1937 and appearing in Puffin Books in 1941. The picture it conveyed, however affectionate, was always one of amiable caricature, with the Ruggles family fundamentally content in their lowly position in life if only there were a little more ready money to purchase new shoes.

This dearth of fiction featuring ordinary children with ordinary emotions eventually produced a reaction from authors themselves, sometimes prompted by the reading needs of their own children. Nina Bawden writes in her autobiography about being

> depressed by the books my sons were reading which seemed dull to me, chiefly because the characters were wooden, and uninvolved in any kind of reality I

recognised. I think I wanted to give my children something that would encourage them to feel they could make a difference to what happened in the world, show them fictional children who were people like themselves, bright and gutsy and determined, able to think, to reason, to hold a moral view.[4]

Her first children's book, *The Secret Passage*, appeared in 1963 after innumerable rejections from other publishers. After that,

I might not have written a second novel for children, if children had not sent me the kind of letters that surprised and delighted me. What had interested them in my story was what I had hoped would interest them. Not the plot, although they seemed to find it exciting enough, but the emotions, the feelings, of the characters. 'I didn't know', they wrote, 'that other people felt like that.'[5]

Until writers like Bawden had started writing, even if state school libraries had wanted to stock books describing the everyday lives of ordinary children in a way that avoided both cliché or caricature, they would not have known where to look. While no children's authors went out of their way to be systematically anti working-class, in many of their books this class simply did not exist outside minor supporting roles such as servants, helpful artisans or occasionally uncouth villains. He who pays the publisher calls the stories, and it is hardly surprising that middle-class book purchasers wanted stories reflecting their mode of life or that of those wealthier than themselves. In this way, it was hoped their children could be provided with suitable social aspirations while also enjoying a good story.

Demand for a wider range of books might have been expected from the Public Library system. But this too was both permanently strapped for cash while also firmly cast in the direction of self-improvement, often preferring classics of the past to children's best-sellers of the present. Although membership had long been free, this was a right much less taken up by potential readers from the manual working class, sometimes for obvious reasons. The children's writer Robert Leeson, describing his life in the 1930s, remembers how 'My mother got a ticket for the library in the next town – there wasn't a library in our own place – and because she was a council tenant she had to get somebody to vouch for us to get a library ticket.'[6]

Children from a working-class background who did use libraries would therefore be a minority in their own community where reading for pleasure was not usually seen as a particularly valued skill in either sex. As Leeson recalls, 'To most of the people on our estate, I should think reading, except the occasional comic, was an alien exercise. It wasn't for us.'[7] Boys who read a lot might even be seen as effeminate; girls who did the same could be suspected of not fully pulling their weight in the domestic chores seen as their lot in life.

The British working class after the war was roughly double the size of the middle class. Working-class child readers, although proportionately fewer, still numbered about the same as middle-class child readers. But they were seldom made to feel at home in a library system stocked with books reflecting a largely middle-class social background. Nor was the reading environment noticeably inviting. Eileen Colwell, who established a pioneering children's library in Hendon between the wars, remembered 'no good libraries at any time during my childhood and youth, least of all at school. It was possible theoretically to provide separate children's rooms ... but few followed this example for reasons of expense and through pure indifference to the needs of children.'[8]

It was some time after 1945 that this dismal picture started to show any real improvement. The placid world of post-war publishing for children chose to spend its energies arguing over different issues, such as the amount and supposed poor quality of Enid Blyton's writing and its alleged bad effects on young readers. The gravest charge here was her limited vocabulary: a serious crime in the eyes of parents who wanted their children to gain practical advantage in the English language while also enjoying themselves with a book. But this concern apart, middle-class parents still generally liked seeing their children reading, albeit respectable books, and so building up and perfecting the literacy skills necessary for them in their educational and social advancement. Library visiting was therefore generally encouraged, sometimes as part of a family event. Only the occasional bookworms, thought to read too much, were seen as something of a problem, although comics or other 'low' literature bought direct by young readers were sometimes accused of exerting a bad influence.

As for children themselves, with almost no competition from television at the time, many of them turned to fiction for their main imaginative entertainment. For really keen readers, it was not so much a question of finding a particularly suitable book – any story that was not too boring would do in order to provide the cherished temporary escape from reality. Middle-class children found themselves better catered for here in terms of a sense of shared identity with the stories they were reading. Working-class children in search of good reading might take longer to realise that, however much they loved their favourite books, they still came to them more as outsiders.

This point is made by Robert Leeson about his own childhood reading: 'Fantasy stories were distinctly class-oriented, and the working-class child had to indulge in two flights of fantasy ... one to get into the characters, and the second to get into the adventure. That seemed to me to be a big effort and a colossal waste of time.'[9]

Voices were raised during the post-war period questioning the power of radio to divert children from suitable hobbies such as reading. But like many other fits of moral panic about the malign influence of various media on the young, this fear was very exaggerated. Radio was indeed popular, but again particularly with middle-class audiences. In times of peace Radio Luxembourg's commercial station constantly attracted more listeners, many from the British working class. By contrast, BBC programmes aimed specifically at children were usually middle-class in tone, with presenters who either came directly from private school teaching or who sounded as if they had. BBC's famous *Children's Hour* also reflected the conservative reading tastes of the time in its radio adaptations. Stories chosen included classics written by Kenneth Grahame, A.A. Milne, John Masefield and E. Nesbit. Modern fare was well represented too, with some plays written for radio later appearing in book form. But these again tended to be safe choices, such as Anthony Buckeridge's popular Jennings stories, set in a boarding preparatory school in the countryside.

This conservative cultural background that generally informed children's book publishing continued to operate for some years to come. Those who worked for publishers tended to share the values common at the time while often having a particular enthusiasm for reading for its own sake. Providing children with attractive books which also reflected a positive, optimistic view of childhood was seen as particularly important. For some editors this represented a chance to offer children the type of book not available when they were young. Such books had above all to be well written, breaking away from the clichés and mechanical plots formerly so often found in hurriedly produced books and comics for the young. After that, the 'good' book had to satisfy the editor on more amorphous grounds of taste and general suitability. For Eleanor Graham, first editor of the enormously influential Puffin Story Book series, defining such books had proved a persistent problem during her years as a children's bookseller in London. 'Mothers, aunts, and the rest came in with only the haziest ideas of what to choose – but it had always to be a "*good*" book. I got so tired of that word.'[10]

Graham wrote in a previous article that she was 'frequently urged to get some Blyton on our list, but I never did. It was not intended for that kind of public.'[11] In similar vein, Barbara Ker Wilson coming to Bodley Head in 1956 as a young editor of children's books, was 'dismayed to discover five early Blyton titles on the list, and set about selling them off to William Collins's Glasgow publishing offices, where they were received with delight. (In a similar move, OUP had sold off W.E. Johns's Biggies titles to Hodder & Stoughton.)'[12] While the intention of both publishers was to uphold literary standards, the effect was also to limit the appeal of their books to a more educated audience. Middle-class children also often enjoyed Blyton and Biggles books, but their parents and teachers required that more demanding fare was also always available for them, either as suitable birthday or Christmas presents or else as approved choices from the public library system. This was not just in order to fulfil ideas of self-improvement; it was also using the choice of a certain type of literature and the language, values and modes of address principally associated with it as one way of defining membership of a particular social class.

As for children different from the norm, such as the disabled or the generally dispossessed, these were largely invisible in children's fiction. It was still commonly thought that one important if unstated aim of children's fiction was to set appropriate role models for young readers. Books dwelling on less fortunate children or very different child characters would therefore have been seen as pointless, unable to suggest any suitable examples for emulation. Describing society's outcasts in fiction, however well done, was also too reminiscent for some of the Victorian type of moralising in fiction from which parents and teachers were now keen to move.

Setting good examples to children had always been seen as the responsibility of everyone closely involved with the young, including those writing children's books. Failure to do this was thought highly undesirable, leading to the possibility of direct imitation of inappropriate behaviour by inexperienced young readers. This particular view of child psychology is a long-standing one, still heard today in arguments about the supposedly noxious effects of violent films and videos on the young. Anecdotes about such ill-advised imitation of art into life have always been around. In performances of J.M. Barrie's *Peter Pan*, mention is made of Peter having to apply special fairy dust to the Darling children before they could attempt to fly like him. Without this piece of stage-craft, it was feared that some children in the audience might go home and try flying from an open window for themselves. This was not an entirely idle anxiety; Barrie was asked by the London Ambulance Service to add this line, 'so many children having gone home and tried it from their beds and needing surgical attention'.[13]

It was easier to blame some books, comics or films for influencing the mass of children in a particular way, rather than to look at other more pervasive social or individual factors in children's lives that might also help explain their attitudes and behaviour. When the relationship between child and culture is seen in these simple terms, undesirable films or reading matter would naturally be considered as a bad influence on a young audience: a point made in the parliamentary debates about banning Horror Comics in 1955. In such a climate, it was understandable that books, radio, films and comics aimed at children at the time all tended to play reasonably safe most of the time.

Changes 1960 onwards

One particularly important agent for the immense changes in children's literature that eventually started to occur in the 1960s was the growth of children's libraries. As early as 1945 new regulations required the establishment of libraries in schools. Such changes were slow to come, but gathered pace over the years. By 1964 there was a 30 per cent increase in overall expenditure on public libraries, with children's needs often foremost in mind.[14] With their enlarged budgets and improved facilities, children's librarians became an important force for publishers to bear in mind. Many of the best-equipped children's libraries were in inner-city areas, reflecting the controlling local Labour Party's traditional commitment to higher spending in education.

The librarians concerned could not help but notice that the huge majority of books in stock still reflected broadly middle-class backgrounds. While this would once have been seen as part of the natural order of things, some librarians in the 1960s began to question this picture. In a less class-conscious and prejudiced cultural climate, celebrating working-class lifestyles for their own sakes soon came to seem a legitimate aim for children's literature. Publishers and writers duly followed suit, with school stories in particular changing from favourite boarding-school settings to the state, day schools of most of today's children's fiction.

Inner-city librarians and teachers also became conscious that young readers from the new ethnic minorities also had little to read reflecting their own experiences. After trying her hand at selling children's books in an East London Saturday street market, Elaine Moss concluded in 1974 that 'the desperate need for picture books with black or Asian children in them is evident every minute of the day. Britain has been very slow off the mark in this respect.'[15] Those black characters that did appear in children's fiction were often patronizing stereotypes left over from former colonial attitudes. Once again publishers responded with new books reflecting new attitudes. Pioneering movements like Anne Woods' *Federation of Children's Book Groups* encouraged book purchasing across all social classes, with some success. School bookshops helped distribute these books to a wider audience than before.

Another important influence for change was the new insistence on the changing role of girls and women in fiction as in life. Previous attitudes in picture books often meant that boys were shown taking most of the action while girls tended to be relegated to supporting domestic roles. In reading primers like the *Janet and John* series, produced by the London firm of James Nisbet from 1949 onwards and by 1968 estimated to be in use in over 80 per cent of British primary schools, fathers always seemed to take the active role while mothers busied themselves domestically either washing up, cooking or ironing in the background. The new women of the 1970s wanted something better than this, and gradually, often against considerable opposition, began to get some of their way. The 1980s also saw new demands for widening children's literature's catchment area even further, for example by including more disabled characters in stories. The battle to make children's books more truly representative of all the nation's children still goes on.

Consciousness of a widening children's market made up of individuals coming from very different backgrounds finally destroyed the former, unitary image of the child reader as essentially white, middle-class and privately educated. The influential Plowden Report into Primary Education in 1967 was scathing about existing reading primers. It considered 'their middle-class world represented by the text and illustrations often alien to children'.[16] At the same time, competition among children's publishers became fiercer once it was realised that children's books could also be money-spinners at a time when profit margins elsewhere were sometimes becoming severely squeezed.

But the books they then came to publish faced new, important rivals for children's attention from other sources. Widespread television viewing by children in the 1960s and beyond was the most important challenge confronting children's publishers at the time and increasingly so as more electronic equipment continued to come on the market. Faced by this opposition, quality publishers' allegiance to the 'good' book became rather more tenuous.

As finances became squeezed and the demand for accessible literature for a wider social group of children grew, the whole concept of what a 'good' book for children consisted of began to change. Literature as a source of desirable role-models conveyed through characters always talking to each other in standard English began to give way to fiction containing characters who were more earthy and often less idealised than before. Controversies about the desirability of best-sellers like Blyton and Dahl, who did not always appear to set high literary or moral standards in their books, became less important at a time when there seemed a real question whether some television-obsessed children would ever willingly pick up a book written for them at all.

Another important factor in this new atmosphere was the dramatic growth of paperback editions for children. For years Puffin Books had been the market leaders in this area of publishing, successfully battling it out against other publishers, unwilling to sub-lease their best titles, and against librarians, who disliked the less durable paperback for both practical and aesthetic reasons. But, with more spending money around in the 1960s, paperback purchases grew quickly, with more publishers eager to get in on the act. The self-improving tone of so many Puffin Books, typified by revivals of titles like Mrs Molesworth's *The Cuckoo Clock* (1977) gave way to fiction that was more lively and contemporary. This was important, since children's books could not afford to look unduly staid compared with their new media rivals. In particular, children had now begun to view a good deal of adult material on television, leading to a gradual but inevitable erosion of what was once considered suitable material for the young.

In response, children's books also began to take on once-controversial themes unknown to previous generations of readers. Many of the social problems formerly unspoken about in front of children started appearing in the works of some children's authors. Homosexuality, child abuse, incest, rape, drug-taking, alcoholism: it was all there in the older ranges of children's literature during and after the 1970s. The language of children's books also began to change. Swear-words and rude jokes as well as slang and what was once seen as slipshod, ungrammatical speech could now sometimes be found in print, however upsetting to those parents who still looked to literature to set higher standards for their children. But the 'Piss off!' so objected to by some parent-purchasers in Richard Adams' epic *Watership Down*, first published in 1972 and later appearing as a Puffin book, did nothing to hinder its vast sales. Roald Dahl, meanwhile, became a millionaire by providing books which, among other things, contained moments of scatological humour irresistible to children.

Parents were not always happy with this new literary frankness, although toleration of the same type of thing on television or film was usually much greater. Children's books for most adults still broadly stood for something different and better than ordinary reality – a reversion to the older norms by which stories were once expected to set high standards for children by chiefly concerning themselves with idealised child characters. Yet, given that literacy skills remained as important as ever for academic success, the parents of the 1960s mainly had to accept the new types of book their children were reading, even though they may not always have approved of everything within them.

In tune with cultural changes, children's books became more concerned with themes of individual fulfilment, with less emphasis given to the importance of community-based values such as duty, loyalty and always doing the right thing by others. The self-improving children's book of old, with its painstaking attention to accuracy in matters of educational detail, became less valued for its own sake. The historical novel for children also began to lose popularity, with young readers generally preferring stories set in the present or, in the case of science fiction, well into the future.

The decline of deference and the growth of satire in British culture also helped erode the establishment values once generally reflected by traditional casts of characters in children's fiction. Adults, previously respected as part of the social status quo, now as often as not found themselves on the wrong side of juvenile ridicule. Parents and teachers, once the butt of humour only in comic-strips and a few novels, frequently saw themselves sent up or at least generally criticised in all types of children's literature. Respect for elders now had to be well and truly earned in children's books; the total parent-worship found in nineteenth-century novels like *Little Women* or *The Swiss Family Robinson* was over. Nor did other traditional values always do well in this new, more critically-minded mood. Environmental concerns and a general fear of warfare once nuclear weapons came on the scene gradually turned children's literature away from its former celebration of fighting in favour of more pacific attitudes. Widely accepted principles, such as always telling the truth, remaining honest, and showing kindness and respect to the old, were now challenged by numbers of new writers keen to point out that defining moral behaviour could sometimes be a far more complex business than the mere following of absolute rules.

Notes

1. Sheila Ray (1982), *The Blyton Phenomenon: The Controversy Surrounding the World's Most Successful Children's Writer* (London: André Deutsch), p. 26.
2. Geoffrey Trease (1974), *Laughter at the Door: A Continued Autobiography* (London: Macmillan), p. 26.
3. Geoffrey Trease (1964), *Tales Out of School: A Survey of Children's Fiction* (London: Heinemann), p. 104.
4. Nina Bawden (1994), *In My Own Time: Almost an Autobiography* (London: Virago), p. 154.
5. Ibid., p. 156.
6. Interview with Robert Leeson, 12 July 1995.
7. Ibid.
8. Eileen Colwell (1974), 'At the beginning', *Signal* no. 13, p. 30.
9. Interview with Robert Leeson.
10. Eleanor Graham (1972), 'The Bumpus years', *Signal* no. 9, p. 98.
11. Eleanor Graham (1973), 'The Puffin years', *Signal* no. 12, p. 122.
12. Barbara Ker Wilson (1995), 'Grace abounding', *Signal* no. 78, p. 78.
13. Andrew Birkin (1979), *J.M. Barrie and the Lost Boys* (London: Constable), p. 162.

14. Alec Ellis (1971), *Library Services for Young People in England and Wales 1830–1970* (London: Pergamon), p. 102.

15. Elaine Moss (1974), 'A mirror in the market place', *Signal* no. 15, p. 113.

16. *Children and their Primary Schools: A Report of the Central Advisory Council for Education*, vol. 1, 1967, p. 213.

Prizes! Prizes! Newbery Gold
Kenneth Kidd

Despite repeated criticisms of their efficacy – they 'have a predictability for literature on about the level of crystal gazing or astrology,' complains Fred B. Millett in 1935 – literary prizes have mushroomed since the establishment of the Nobel Prizes in 1901 and especially since the 1960s. Literary prizing has been a remarkably effective mechanism for publicity, sales, and scandal, if not always for the production of Literature. Prizing, moreover, has middlebrow as well as highbrow features and effects; it encourages both the making and unmaking of canons, underwrites but also undercuts faith in popularity. So ubiquitous is cultural prizing more broadly that James English, in his recent study *The Economy of Prestige*, argues that the prize

> *is* cultural practice in its quintessential contemporary form. The primary function it can be seen to serve – that of facilitating cultural 'market transactions,' enabling the various individual and institutional agents of culture, with their different assets and interests and dispositions, to engage one another in a collective project of value production – is the project of cultural practice as such. (2005: 26)

To prize children's literature presumably means to assert its value beyond the merely or crudely utilitarian. Among the questions we might ask: What are the mechanisms of distinction in and around children's literature, how successful are they, and how do we in turn assess (perhaps prize) them? Given that children's literature is not generally held in high regard, does prizing boost its status or contribute to its devaluation? Do prizes ensure or threaten its literariness? What 'cultural market transactions' are achieved by or through or against children's book awards? Who are those 'individual and institutional agents,' and how do they operate? How does the prizing of children's literature compare to and intersect with the prizing of so-called adult literature?

Extracted from K. Kidd, 'Prizing Children's Literature: The Case of Newbery Gold', in *Children's Literature*, 35 (2007), pp. 166–90.

Rather than examining children's literature prizing at large, I offer here a provisional case study of the Newbery Medal, first examining how the Medal established a beachhead in the economy of prestige, and then addressing the culture of critique and proliferation characteristic of the more contemporary American children's book award scene. Founded in 1921 by the American Library Association (ALA) and named after the eighteenth-century publisher and bookseller, John Newbery, the Medal has been awarded annually to 'the most distinguished contribution to American literature for children published in the United States during the preceding year.' To date, there are eighty-five Medal winners and several hundred Honor Books or runners-up. Honor Books are not mandated but are usually selected by the Newbery Medal Committee, largely made up of librarians specializing in children's materials. The Medal scheme proved so successful that in 1938, a second award was created for excellence in picture book art, named for the English illustrator Randolph Caldecott. Children's literary prizing is now nearly as varied as its adult counterpart, but the ALA, now some 60,000 members strong, is the largest and most influential evaluating body, administering twenty book and media awards and reviewing most, if not all, of the roughly five thousand children's and young adult titles published each year in the United States.[1] The Medal remains the most prestigious of the ALA awards, and has come to signify the broader culture of children's literary prizing as well as a critique of such.

Although the Medal carries no cash prize, it can more than double the sales of a book, as well as increase sales of the author's other books. More important, the Medal keeps titles and authors in circulation for decades. Whereas the average shelf life of a children's book today is roughly eighteen months, many Newbery titles are still in print, and most can be found in public and school libraries. People with only basic familiarity with children's literature often recognize Medal titles, if not also their authors. Walk into any large bookstore and you'll likely see a section or shelf of Newbery titles, their covers graced with the trademark gold seal.

On the one hand, the Medal is the oldest and arguably the most influential such award, and deserves focused analysis; on the other, it is not necessarily representative of American children's book awards (any more than Newbery titles are representative of American children's literature). For better and for worse, however, the Medal represents both a tradition of merit and a growing dissatisfaction with such. There's a tradition of professional commentary on the Medal that can be brought into dialogue with more recent theorizations of cultural capital and literary value. The Medal merits more than a footnote in the history of prizing, and this essay takes the Medal as its principal subject, in an attempt to discover what might be learned about the prizing of American children's literature more generally.

If, as English asserts, the Nobel Prize has served as a baseline for the modern prize, inspiring envy and imitation, the Newbery Medal arguably has had a similar role in the children's literature scene and its own particular 'logic of proliferation.' 'Each prize that achieves a premier position in a particular field,' he notes, 'and that becomes, however contestably, the "Nobel" of that field, produces a host of imitators with various legitimating claims of similitude and difference' (2005: 65). Giving coherence to a specialized market, the Newbery Medal helped establish the modern awards system for children's literature, in the process ensuring that ALA librarians would continue to serve as tastemakers. With adult literary prizing, by contrast, critics and authors are usually the credentialed authorities.

Medal books are instant classics, the selection process an ostensible simulation of the test of time. They are 'minor' classics in at least two senses of the phrase: classics for kids, and respectable if not remarkable achievements in their own right. If not exactly a canon, the Medal is part of the canonical architecture of children's literature. At the same time, the Medal stands for a good education, for what we might call 'edubrow' culture – the middlebrow culture of public schools and libraries.

That said, the Medal's pre-eminence within the field of American children's literature has been challenged on the grounds that it doesn't, in fact, sufficiently promote the common good, or that its ideology of distinction is incompatible with a democratic program of literary citizenship. It's clear that the Medal has long been a selective, even separatist affair. We can see in the history of the Medal a representative shift from meritocratic, formalist expectations about excellence to a more pluralistic understanding of literary and cultural merit. The Medal, in fact, has come to embody our ambivalence about distinction in the wake of progressive social movements, canon reform, and widespread faith that literature, especially that for children, should be an equal opportunity employer.

Browbeating the medal: the Newbery economy of prestige

In her important study *Kiddie Lit: The Cultural Construction of Children's Literature in America*, Beverly Lyon Clark reminds us that nineteenth-century American authors often wrote for children and adults alike, contributing to *Youth's Companion, St. Nicholas*, and other children's periodicals – so much so, in fact, that the contents list for such read like a *Who's Who* of American letters. Children's books were reviewed regularly in *The Nation, Harper's, Scribner's, Lippincott's, The Dial, The Critic, North American Review,* and *Catholic World.* All three editors of the *Atlantic Monthly* on the job between 1871 and 1898 – William Dean Howells, Thomas Bailey Aldrich, and Horace E. Scudder – published children's books without jeopardizing their reputation as men of letters (Clark, 2003: 55). Soon after, however, luminaries such as Henry James and Bliss Perry claimed irreconcilable differences between children's literature and literature for adults, such that the former 'generally disappeared from the purview of the cultural elite' (181). Clark blames not merely cultural elitism, but also anxiety about American immaturity:

> Not for nothing was a 1915 manifesto of early-twentieth-century criticism by Van Wyck Brooks – a book whose memorable contribution was the coining of *highbrow* and *lowbrow*, thereby providing terms for discussing and indeed fostering such separations as that between children's and adults' literature – titled *America's Coming of Age.*
>
> 58

Advocates for children's literature responded to this devaluation by insisting upon levels of distinction, in effect creating a middlebrow tradition of children's literature, and perhaps positioning 'children's literature' as a middlebrow formulation more generally. Even as space for adult literature was being carved out, anxiety about ostensibly lowbrow forms such as the dime novel and the series book led to arguments for more respectable or legitimate writing for children. Better books were sorely needed, it was thought, along with better venues for their display and distribution. To this end, more and more people – most of them middle-class women – got involved in the children's book scene. In 1917, Macmillan created the first children's book department within a major publishing house, with others soon following. Just the year before, Bertha Mahony had opened in Boston the first children's bookshop, described by Alice Jordan as 'a center for those who choose to take children's books seriously as a branch of literature' (qtd. in Viguers, 1953: 429–30). Mahony and partner Elinor Whitney distributed book lists, which evolved into *The Horn Book Magazine*, still thriving today, as well as into library science and education textbooks. The Medal and subsequent ALA prizes also have partial origin in those lists.

Librarians, of course, were the mainstay of the Medal. Mostly white women of genteel or middle-class backgrounds, they saw library work as a form of public service as much as a modern profession. By 1900 they already were focused on the reading lives of children; as Dee Garrison reports, the first publication of the ALA was Caroline Hewins's book list *Books for the Young* (1882), and the first specialized area within librarianship was children's services. In 1918, Anne Carroll Moore of the New York Public Library began reviewing children's books in *The Bookman*. She insisted upon the importance of the children's reading room, and of professional commentary on children's literature. By the 1920s, librarians were working closely with the book industry to set standards for production and reception. Whereas earlier librarians pushed for mere acceptance of children's books, Moore and her cohort stressed their aesthetic value, linking that value to the public good. 'Despite their perceived passivity,' notes Anne Lundin, 'librarians can be defined as canon makers who reproduce social hierarchy in a systematic act of tradition bearing' (2004: 30).

At the same time, ALA leaders insisted on certain standards in shaping their public. While originally the selection process involved the larger membership of children's librarians, since 1928 that process has been a committee affair, due to practical concerns as well as anxiety about the process of selection. Writing in 1922, Clara Hunt insists that the judges be 'people of high standards and experience,' for '[i]f a majority vote of all so-called children's librarians determines the award, it is entirely possible for a mediocre book to get the Medal' (qtd. in Smith, 1957: 40). Thus the formation of a special committee, the structure of which remains principally unchanged. Of the fifteen librarians who serve each year, seven are elected by the general membership, as is the Chair, who appoints the other seven.

The first Newbery Medal winner was Hendrik van Loon's *The Story of Mankind* (1921), a Eurocentric history of the world approaching five hundred pages. Rubin cites van Loon's book as an example of the middlebrow 'outline' genre devised by Will Durant and H.G. Wells (1992: 216–19). Although Rubin doesn't mention the Medal, and dates the term 'middlebrow' to 1933 (xii), the appeal of van Loon's tome to adult as well as child readers is telling. H.L. Mencken called it 'stupendous'; Carl Van Doren described it as 'the chief historical primer of the age.' Anne Carroll Moore predicted it would be 'the most influential children's book for many years to come' (qtd. in van Loon, 1972: 128). Although subsequent Newbery titles weren't as widely lauded – van Loon was already something of a celebrity, and outlines were all the rage – the Medal books from the 1920s were generally admired by the literati. At first, then, Newbery literature seemed destined for literary or proto-highbrow status. As the decades wore on, however, and as the Medal succeeded as a middlebrow project beyond the specificity of its titles, the Newbery books were understood primarily as minor classics rather than as classics that children might read. Thanks largely to its association with the ostensibly feminine professions of librarianship and teaching, the Medal became less a public affair and more a professional domain. Furthermore, writing for children was and remains a highly gendered enterprise; most of the Newbery titles were written by women. In the end, Anne Carroll Moore was right; van Loon's history became 'the most influential children's book' rather than a work of Literature.

The attempt to legitimize children's literature through the Medal contributed to the ongoing separation of children's and 'serious'/adult literature. There were other factors at play here – among them, the turn toward realism in adult writing – but as Anne Scott MacLeod notes, the professionalization of children's literature by the ALA effectively removed children's literature from broader public ownership, despite (or rather through) those claims about fashioning a public. As a result, writes MacLeod,

> children's literature became an enclave. All the creative activity, all the knowledgeable producing and reviewing and purveying of children's books, took place a little apart from the larger world of literature. By about 1920, children's literature was a garden, lovingly tended by those who cared about it but isolated as well as protected by the cultural walls that surrounded it.
>
> 1994: 125[2]

The sphere of children's literature launched in the 1920s wasn't just middlebrow, but also edubrow. Beginning in the late nineteenth century, librarians successfully lobbied public schools to introduce supplemental reading into their programs, and to furnish school libraries much in the manner of public libraries. As a result, teachers as well as librarians became invested in the Medal. Contemporaneous schemes such as Scherman's Book-of-the-Month Club, notes Radway, capitalized on the desire for educational goods in the wake of the expansion of the educational apparatus but also helped shore up that apparatus, with its systems of evaluation and accreditation. 'Indeed,' she writes, 'these enterprises played an important role in defining the parameters of an extracurricular public space where school-derived knowledge might be further exercised' (1997: 162). So, too, with prize-winning children's literature, claimed as a curriculum of enrichment. Generally speaking, teachers and librarians have seen themselves as partners in edubrow culture. Granted, there have been some struggles for authority staged around the Medal. As Christine Jenkins reports, in the late 1930s some cantankerous male teachers, editors, and authors challenged the jurisdiction of women librarians over the Medal, accusing them of bias against boys and boy books. While the gender politics of this turf-war are significant, the turf itself is what I want to emphasize: by the 1930s, the Medal had come to be as closely associated with the educational mission as with library work.

As I've noted, the early Newbery books were strongly invested in history, geography, and comparative cultural study, which resonated with John

Dewey's praise of geography and history as 'the information studies *par excellence* of the schools' (1966: 210) and his linking of these subjects with the cultivation of aesthetic 'appreciation . . . an enlarged, an *intensified* prizing, not merely a prizing' (237). While they are sometimes incorporated into curricula, often in geographical/historical or social studies units, and in 'gifted and talented' classes, Medal books are not usually primary teaching texts. Instead, they form a kind of secondary or supplemental curriculum, part of that 'extracurricular public space.' The existence of Newbery-themed pedagogical materials affirms such and also tacitly acknowledges doubts about the appropriateness of Newbery titles for elementary students especially. The Medal is thus an edubrow project with literary tendencies or aspirations.

In passing, I note that the early twentieth-century scene of children's literature has interesting resemblances to the character-building movement and may be a reinvention or extension of it. It's no coincidence that the Chief Librarian of the Boy Scouts (a man) was involved in Children's Book Week. Librarians presided over reading and reading rooms in much the same way that Scoutmasters and other boy workers supervised more outward-bound pursuits. Children's literature might be understood as a less masculinist and more literary venture in character building as well as an edubrow formation.

Medal privilege and American subjects

Newbery excellence is defined loosely, with interpretations of the terms, definitions, and criteria as set forth in 1921 largely left up to the annual Committee.[3] While 'there are no limitations as to the character of the book, except that it must be original work' ('Terms and Criteria'), the award is restricted to citizens or residents of the United States, and books originally published elsewhere are ineligible. Authors had to be certifiably American, and their work had to make 'original' contributions to American literature.

At the same time, most of the Newbery Medal titles in the first two decades of the award were set in other countries and/or indigenous North American cultures. Historical fiction, folklore, and comparative cultural fiction dominated the early Newbery scene.

For all their worldliness, the early Medal books had little in common with either progressive education or with the progressive children's books of the day. Even so, the trend was so obvious that Sophie Goldsmith, in a 1931 essay for *The Bookman* assessing the first decade of the Medal books, irritably calls for authors to turn homeward and to 'interpret some phase of the last ten years, or even the last twenty or thirty' (314). Goldsmith didn't see that the early titles affirm WASP American society precisely by depicting other cultures as exotic, primitive, and 'historical,' subject to the inexorable processes of modernization. Janice M. Alberghene puts it more generously when she notes that the 1930s winners were about the frontier and/or about folk cultures – either way, they functioned to clarify 'that which is American – even when the books are ostensibly about other cultures' (1981: 10). In any case, had Goldsmith surveyed the scene again in the 1940s, she likely would have been pleased. Whereas some earlier winning authors had been born abroad, all ten in the 1940s were born in the States, and only one spent any significant time abroad. More to the point, six of those authors wrote about non-indigenous American life, and declared more explicitly their patriotism, as in *Daniel Boone* (1939) and *Johnny Tremain* (1943). Since the 1940s, books set outside the contemporary United States have appeared with some regularity, but no longer dominate the scene. Books with decidedly American settings and themes have since been a staple. While historical fiction remains a preferred genre, the Newbery books are now more varied than they once were with respect to subject, setting, and even style.

For the first several decades, then, Medal committees and thus the larger credentialing body of the ALA gave priority to American work, defined not by setting but by authorship, theme, and values. What was American was established through and against contact with the cultural other, usually safely removed across time and/or space. If we include the Honor Books in our analysis, our picture of the Medal shifts somewhat, as the Honor Books are often more progressively engaged with the vexing theme of Americanness. Doris Gates's *Blue Willow* (1940), for example, narrates the trials and triumphs of an itinerant worker's family in California, and Florence Crannell Means's *The Moved-Outers* (1945) was the first children's book to focus on the internment of Japanese Americans during WWII. Arna Bontemps's *The Story of the Negro* (1948), the first title by an African American to garner Newbery laurels, was an Honor rather than a Medal Book. Moreover, while the Medal heavily favors the genre of historical fiction, the Honor Books are more diverse with respect to genre. To some extent, then, the Honor Books offset the relative conservatism of the Medal books, forming a shadow-canon of sorts that's safely contained. Very few Honor Books are as widely known as the Medal winners.

Whether asserted through portraits of exotic folk cultures or through the later domestic/patriotic turn, Medal faith in literary American talent was not extended to African-American authors or their works. Whereas immigrant subjects were granted Newbery citizenship, African-American subjects were excluded from the scene, in keeping with social practices of segregation. The institutional racism of the ALA can be traced both within the Newbery tradition and within ALA prize culture at large. What makes this resistance particularly disturbing is the contemporaneous existence not only of African-American children's literature, but also of African-American literary prizing, which, like ALA prizing, was linked firmly to ideals of education and uplift.

The Newbery Medal was founded in 1921, one year after the NAACP, under the guidance of W.E.B. Du Bois, launched *The Brownies' Book* magazine. Although it folded a year later, the magazine achieved a monthly circulation of around five thousand subscribers. *The Brownies' Book*, moreover, is only the best-known example of an expansive children's literature of the Harlem Renaissance, as Katharine Capshaw Smith demonstrates in her engaging study of that material (2004). By her account, the black child became the 'race leader' (xix) and an icon 'of emerging cultural nationalism' (xxiii), and children's literature was central to the movement. Du Bois and others 'prized' children and their material, if not through children's book awards.

All along, however, many prominent figures had their doubts about prizing, including Du Bois. Langston Hughes and Zora Neale Hurston, themselves prize winners, came to see prizes as part of an infantilizing white patronage system. Jessie Redmon Fauset, editor of *The Brownies' Book*, voiced similar concerns, and Claude McKay, in a letter to Arthur Schomburg (1925), even called the prestigious NAACP Spingarn Medal (established in 1915) 'an insult to the intelligence of the American negro – like a tick attached to a thoroughbred horse.' African-American authors took issue with the ethos of competitive individualism that made difficult a sense of community.

The dominant Newbery genre has long been historical fiction, and as Dianne Johnson emphasizes, historical fiction was likewise a dominant genre of African-American children's literature from the 1940s forward. That's partly why Bontemps's *The Story of the Negro*, in part a corrective to *The Story of Mankind*, was the first title by an African American to garner 'near miss' laurels. Separate and unequal traditions of children's literature long prevailed. Not until mid-century did a title about African Americans actually win the Medal, and that title was a historical novel of assimilation written by a middle-class white woman, Elizabeth Yates. Yates was one among a handful of white authors in the 1950s writing about slavery and its ills.

Difference is tolerated until it threatens native soil; then it must be contained. Hence the comparativist ethos of the early Newbery books yields by the 1950s to a more anxious insistence on the universality of human experience, as racial otherness at home became harder to handle. Nearly twenty years passed before the Medal went to another book about African-American life, also written by a white author: William H. Armstrong's *Sounder* (1970), a melancholic novel about father–son separation and the compensatory power of letters. Finally, in 1974, the Medal went to an African-American writer, Virginia Hamilton, for *M.C. Higgins, the Great* (1974). In fits and starts, the ALA began to respect and honor African-American literature. A common assumption is that the Medal is now more often awarded to books that grapple directly with social issues. But even now, most of the Medal books that address racism, for instance, are historical novels that give priority to the folk/vernacular and are set no later than the Depression.

All that glitters

The Medal is no longer the only game in town; several hundred prizes are now awarded to children's titles in English alone. The proliferation of prizes has in turn given rise to an apparatus of bibliographic summary, pedagogical application, and collection management. This expansion is hardly incidental to shifts in literary content and context; it embodies and accompanies new contingencies of value.

To be sure, civil rights and other progressive social movements have helped diversify prizing, through the creation of new awards and through critique of the Medal. Debate about the Medal's value has been heated of late. In her 1998 essay 'What Color is Gold?' for example, Bonnie J.F. Miller deems the Medal a racist institution, taking issue not with the basic concept of the award (or of awards more generally) but rather with the selection process, and arguing that children's literature should be more representative of diversity. 'When ... a body of literature with the power of Newbery gold lacks even one text by a minority writer or about a minority lead,' writes Miller, 'the message sent to children is that the 'most distinguished' protagonists and authors are white' (1998: 34). Others defend the Medal's aims and ends. From the other end of the prizing wars, in an essay entitled 'Slippery Slopes and Proliferating Prizes,' Marc Aronson deplores the expansion of prizing and chalks it up to the success rather than (as for Miller) the failure of identity politics. Citing the Coretta Scott King (CSK) Awards and the Pura Belpré Medal, founded in 1969 and 1996 for distinction in African-American and Latino/a children's writing, respectively, Aronson (2001) holds that children's literature has yielded to special interests. Aronson urges judges to 'honor content alone, not identity. Use the very best judges and set the very highest standards' (278). Otherwise, he implies, to quote the Dodo in *Alice in Wonderland*, '*everyone* has won, and *all* must have prizes.' 'Who will bet,' asks Aronson, 'how soon mixed-race authors, *those* with disabilities, Muslims (and thus Jews, which, of course, then means Christians), will demand awards of their own? How can ALA say no to any of them?' (277).

Miller is right: the Newbery Medal has slowly and inadequately adapted to social change. Aronson is right, too: new prizes have shifted or at least pluralized the terms of distinction. The CSK Awards, for example, go to titles that help young readers 'comprehend their personal duty and responsibility as citizens in a pluralistic society.'[4] What Aronson and other defenders of the Medal fail to see is that the identitarian critique may be the logical outcome of the Medal's edubrow mission. Still unclear is the impact of progressive prizes on the institution of the Medal as well as the field more broadly. On the one hand, after the critique of Miller and others we've seen some improvement in the Medal's identity politics. Replacing yesteryear's explorations of world culture are more self-consciously pluralistic titles like Linda Sue Park's *A Single Shard* (2002 Medal) and Cynthia Kadohata's *Kira-Kira* (2005 Medal). On the other hand, the Newbery's contemporary track record isn't that impressive overall, and newer awards have done more to alter the scene of prizing. Progressive prizes may have forced greater consideration of social identity within the Newbery evaluation process without necessarily improving its representational politics. The CSK Awards have gained influence even as few books by and/or about African Americans have since won the Newbery. After the 1977 selection of *Roll of Thunder, Hear My Cry*, the Medal did not go to another African American – authored book until 2001. Some observers have declared the 1980s and 1990s a golden age of African American children's literature, while others disagree, pointing to the white sheen of the Medal and to the low numbers of books published annually by and/or about African Americans. And never has a book with lesbian/gay/bisexual content received Newbery recognition (not even Honor status), in spite of or perhaps thanks to the ALA's creation of the Stonewall Book Awards in 1971.

The Medal remains the ALA's pre-eminent award, at once continuing its mission of certifying achievement while also serving as a touchstone for debate about the politics of representation. If the Medal has no intrinsic merit, it attempts to generate merit, thereby establishing children's literature not only as a form of legitimate culture but also as a vital component of public life. Progressive prizes are likewise understood as useful tools for publicity and public making; prizes get the word out. Such is the paradox that prizing represents, at once the stuff of distinction and democratization.

Notes

1. As with adult awards, emphasis sometimes goes to general excellence, sometimes to achievement within a certain genre, as with the Edgar Allan Poe Prize for juvenile mystery. In addition to the ALA prizes, U.S. awards are sponsored by individual states, among them the Colorado Children's Book Awards, the Georgia Children's Book Award, the Nene Award (Hawaii), the Mark Twain Award (Missouri), and the Dorothy Canfield Fisher Award (Vermont). Not surprisingly, children's book awards now tend toward the multicultural and the pedagogical, as with the Carter G. Woodson Book Award, sponsored by the National Council for Social Studies and designed to promote social science books that 'treat topics

related to ethnic minorities and race relations sensitively and accurately.' For an overview of children's book awards, see *Children's Books Awards & Prizes*. The Children's Book Council, the publisher of this guide, also hosts a subscription database called Awards and Prizes Online: <http://awardsandprizes.cbcbooks.org/>. Another online resource is the Book Award Annals Web site: <http://book.awardannals.com/home/>.

2. Anne Lundin takes the garden metaphor further, arguing that the librarians and their collaborators were heirs to Romantic ideals about childhood, nature, and the imagination; the centerpiece of their vision was the children's reading room, that Edenic space or secret garden wherein children could experience the natural joys of literature.

3. In identifying distinguished writing in a book for children, Medal Committee members must consider the following criteria:

   - interpretation of theme or concept.
   - presentation of information, including accuracy, clarity, and organization.
   - development of plot.
   - delineation of characters.
   - delineation of setting.
   - appropriateness of style.

   Works under consideration need not show excellence in all of these areas, but a book should be distinguished in all of the elements pertinent to it. Also, the committee members must consider excellence in presentation for a child audience, even though the book need not be written exclusively for children. They are to focus on a book's literary and social value, and ignore aspects such as illustration and design unless they distract from the actual narrative. Reprints and compilations are ineligible. For more information, see <http://www.ala.org/ala/alsc/awardsscholarships/literaryawds/newberymedal/newberyterms/newberyterms.htm>.

4. This is criterion 'g'; see <http://www.ala.org/ala/emiert/corettascottkingbookawards/corettascott.htm>.

References

Alberghene, Janice M. 'From Frontier to Foreign Shores: Seeing Ourselves in the Thirties.' Peterson and Solt, 10–12.

Aronson, Marc. 'Slippery Slopes and Proliferating Prizes.' *The Horn Book Magazine* (May/June 2001): 271–78.

Clark, Beverly Lyon. *Kiddie Lit: The Cultural Construction of Children's Literature in America.* Baltimore: Johns Hopkins UP, 2003.

Dewey, John. *Democracy and Education.* New York: Free P, 1966.

English, James F. *The Economy of Prestige: Prizes, Awards, and the Circulation of Cultural Value.* Cambridge: Harvard UP, 2005.

Garrison, Dee. *Apostles of Culture: The Public Librarian and American Society, 1876–1920.* New York: Free P, 1979.

Goldsmith, Sophie L. 'Ten Years of the Newbery Medal.' *The Bookman* (Nov. 1931): 308–16.

Jenkins, Christine A. 'Women of ALA Youth Services and Professional Jurisdiction: Of Nightingales, Newberies, Realism, and the Right Books, 1937–1945.' *Literary Trends* 44.4 (Spring 1996): 813–39.

Lundin, Anne. *Constructing the Canon of Children's Literature: Beyond Library Walls and Ivory Towers.* New York: Routledge, 2004.

MacLeod, Anne Scott. *American Childhood: Essays on Children's Literature of the Nineteenth and Twentieth Centuries.* Athens: U of Georgia P, 1994.

McKay, Claude. 'To Arthur Schomburg,' 17 July 1925. Claude McKay Correspondence. Special Collections, the Schomburg Center for Research in Black Culture, New York City.

Miller, Bonnie J.F. 'What Color is Gold? Twenty-One Years of Same-Race Authors and Protagonists in the Newbery Medal,' *Joys* (Fall 1998): 34–39.

Millett, Fred B. 'Literary Prize Winners.' *The English Journal* 24.4 (April 1935): 269–82.

Moore, Anne Carroll. 'The Reviewing of Children's Books.' 1926. *My Roads to Childhood: Views and Reviews of Children's Books.* Boston: The Horn Book, Inc. 1961. 221–29.

Peterson, Linda Kauffman, and Marilyn Leathers Solt. Introduction. Ed. Linda Kauffman Peterson and Marilyn Leathers Solt. Spec. section, 'Newbery and Caldecott Medal and Honor Books,' of *Children's Literature Association Quarterly* 6.3 (Fall 1981): 7.

Radway, Janice. *A Feeling for Books: The Book-of-the-Month Club, Literary Taste, and Middle-Class Desire.* Chapel Hill: U of North Carolina P, 1997.

Rubin, Joan Shelley. *The Making of Middlebrow Culture.* Chapel Hill: U of North Carolina Press, 1992.

Smith, Irene. *A History of the Newbery and Caldecott Medals.* New York: Viking P, 1957.

Smith, Katharine Capshaw, *Children's Literature of the Harlem Renaissance.* Bloomington: Indiana UP, 2004.

van Loon, Gerard Willem. *The Story of Hendrik Willem van Loon.* Philadelphia: J.B. Lippincott, 1972.

Viguers, Ruth Hill. 'Childhood's Golden Era: An Introductory Survey.' *A Critical History of Children's Literature.* Ed. Cornelia Meigs, Anne Thaxter Eaton, Elizabeth Nesbitt, and Ruth Hill Viguers. New York: Macmillan, 1953. 427–47.

In Defence of the Indefensible? Some Grounds for Enid Blyton's Appeal
David Rudd

While no one would dispute that Enid Blyton is a cultural icon, a phenomenon, there is much dispute about why this should be the case, with many people still preferring to sweep her out of sight, as someone who compromises the academically respectable study of children's literature. But Blyton is hard to steer around, to change metaphors, given the huge shadow she casts across the terrain, topping polls amongst readers since the 1950s right through to the millennium, and her work continues to be hugely popular, despite the fact that she died in 1968. She consistently sells some 11 million copies of books a year and currently seems to be the only children's author to have outsold J.K. Rowling.[1]

The word 'phenomenon' is itself usefully vague, connoting something 'noteworthy' but also, simultaneously, something 'not worthy': something not really deserving any more time and analysis than merely to be noted. However, Blyton is such an influential figure (on Rowling no less than others) that children's literature criticism has to make some sense of her. Over the years this criticism has generally been negative, seeking to belittle her achievement, seeing her as a mere writing machine, a hack, or worse: simply as 'slow poison' (Fisher, 1983: 4120), leading readers to a life of *Reveille* and strip cartoons (Woods, 1955). With the advent of social criticism, it was not just her literary qualities that were suspect; she was also seen as being racist, sexist or simply 'classist', reflecting the values of jaded little Englanders. Regardless of this, Blyton's books persisted in popularity (and in fact often became more popular), such that critics had to take her work more seriously and look for the positive qualities that might be engaging readers, especially as her original readership had not only matured but, contrary to some critics' expectations, turned into successful adults. Indeed, a number were to take English literature further, as writers or critics, and were intrigued at the attraction that Blyton once held for them (Fraser, 1992). I deliberately use the past tense here, for Blyton does seem to be one of the few children's writers whom adults do not read from choice (unlike, say, Ransome, Sutcliffe, Wynne Jones or Pullman). Not only that, she's also a writer whom many former fans find, as adults, unreadable, perplexed at their former fascination. In this chapter I intend to try and make some sense of this: to find, in short, the secret mechanism that unlocks the mystery, the seeming contradiction, of Blyton's popularity.

In order to do this, the ground first needs clearing by revisiting various alternative conceptions of Blyton. As a number of critics have pointed out, until the 1950s Blyton was generally rated positively as a writer. In the 1920s, when her writing career began, her work appeared alongside many celebrated writers of the day (e.g. de la Mare, Kipling, and Masefield (Stoney, 1974: 49)). Also a respected educationalist, Blyton edited and wrote a number of influential volumes (e.g. a three-volume *The Teacher's Treasury* (1926b) and six-volume *Modern Teaching* (1928), aside from many class readers and lesson ideas (e.g. story openings that children had to complete themselves (Blyton 1926a)). But what comes across most strongly is Blyton's tendency to narrativise her material. Blyton's weekly column, 'From my Window', which ran in *Teachers World* from 1923 to 1927 (and then, perhaps significantly, was consigned to the 'Junior' section and retitled 'Letter to Children'), is notable in this, with its heavily personified and romantically tinged descriptions of nature: flowers that 'smiled at the sun', 'peeping blossoms', and spots where she half expects a 'tired elf or weary gnome' to appear (Blyton, 2003a: 17; 2003b: 18).

It is not surprising, then, that she might have felt restricted by more traditional, educational work, much of which must have come her way thanks to her then husband, Hugh Pollock, an editor at George Newnes, her main publisher. As Blyton herself was later to admit, writing non-fiction was a slow and laborious process: 'I find it more difficult to write this short article, than to write a 40,000-word book for children!' (Blyton, 1959a). She had to 'think hard – deliberate – write a sentence or two – erase one – rewrite – think again, and so on' (McKellar, 1957: 138), whereas fiction came to her 'like cotton from a reel' (from Blyton's letter to Peter McKellar, quoted in Stoney, 1974: 135). She often describes it using similes of a screen on which she would watch events unfold then type them up, later to read them through as though for the first time. It was not fanciful, then, when she claimed to be a 'storyteller' rather than a writer.

One can certainly witness a shift from writer to storyteller in Blyton's writing as she takes increasing control of the process. The obscure publishers Birn Brothers are particularly interesting in this regard, with previously unknown Blyton works of theirs continuing to reappear. They were a cheap, ephemeral press (hence their scarcity, slipping through bibliographical nets), but the respected Blyton clearly enjoyed writing for them because they allowed her to experiment, in the process producing work that would result in her more famous series.

So, although initially seen as an educationalist, there is a sense that Blyton's real passion lay in storytelling and, specifically, in the fairy-tale format which, as Jack Zipes (1997: 3) defines it, 'emanated from an oral tradition in which small groups of people interacted with a storyteller, generally a member of the group, who responded to their needs and demands'. Blyton's community was children, and she was happiest addressing them directly, as she had been doing most overtly in her fortnightly *Sunny Stories for Little Folks* (1926–37). Initially consisting of traditional tales retold by Blyton, in 1937 it changed its title to *Enid Blyton's Sunny Stories*, and she began to publish longer, serialised tales as well. Admittedly very episodic at the outset, they show her consolidating her earlier work with Birn and elsewhere, making the child figure increasingly central. In her stories for the younger ages, these children tend to consort with imaginary figures based on folk and fairy tale; for the older years, the children inhabit more realistic though still glamorous environments, such as the circus or seaside. *Adventures of the Wishing Chair* (1937) was one of the first of these serials to be published in book form, with the even more successful 'Magic Faraway Tree' series soon following (Blyton, 1939; 1943).[2] These more fantasy-based stories can be contrasted with a relatively realistic trend established in *The Secret Island* (1938b).

The ideas in these, and the distinctive way in which she wrote them, will be returned to. But first let me continue to outline her writing life. The period I have now reached, the late 1930s and the 1940s, was to be her golden age, a time when her personal life also underwent upheaval: she raised two daughters, divorced her first husband and married a second and, at the end of the 1940s, created her most popular and infamous character, Noddy – the last, really well-known figure with which she would be associated. But it is also at this time that some negative criticisms of her work started to appear, which would grow throughout the 1950s. Blyton's production rate was certainly climbing: in the early 1950s she was averaging over 50 new titles a year, with a record 70 in 1955 (approximately one every five days). For a literary writer, such an output would be extraordinary, but it is less so for someone who saw herself spinning everyday yarns, rather than fashioning an haute couture ball-gown.

As Sheila Ray (1982) has pointed out, after the Second World War children's literature was becoming more respected. Bespoke posts were available for trained children's librarians, some of them subsequently moving into publishing, head-hunted to run the equally new children's book divisions of presses. In building up their stable of writers, Blyton was their nemesis: the antithesis of the literary writers who were then being fêted and to whom the equally new literary prizes were being awarded (indeed, some publishers deliberately divested themselves of Blyton titles, as did Barbara Ker Wilson (1995: 162) with Bodley Head). In many ways, then, one can see a replay of the battle that had been waged by Henry James and others for the 'literary' adult novel in the late nineteenth century. Children's writers like E.B. White were being lauded as part of some 'great tradition', while Blyton and others were equally castigated. The large Schools Council survey of children's reading consolidated this, categorising authors as either 'quality' or 'non-quality' (Whitehead et al., 1977).

But if literary critics dominated the critical landscape in the post-war period, the 1960s initiated a change with the rise of social criticism, challenging the former for their middle-class elitism, their norm of whiteness and denigration of all things foreign, and, most prominently, their marginalisation of females in favour of the male. However, such criticism would not help Blyton who, if anything, was seen as equally an offender in these terms. Whatever the criteria, then, Blyton was damned: she was the scapegoat. And yet, despite socially concerned adults seeking to remove Blyton from their children's bedrooms, schoolrooms, and libraries, her works continued to be immensely popular.

We arrive, then, at the key question: what is the basis of her success? Adults seldom return to her work and enjoy it as they do, say, *Winnie-the-Pooh*, *Alice's Adventures in Wonderland* or *Tom's Midnight Garden*. This is where earlier attempts to evaluate Blyton seem to founder, though, in trying to measure the quality of her work on some literary yardstick.

Let me now look at these criticisms in more detail, before suggesting that a default literary or educational approach to her books has pre-empted others.

Roy Nash (1964) sums this up in an amusing article where Big-Ears declares: 'We're redundant in Toyland ... Children want literature now. Literature with a capital L.' This said, it was not children so much as gate-keeping adults who wanted 'Literature' (e.g. Holbrook, 1961). We thus find Blyton set up like an Aunt Sally against a variety of writers before being ritually trounced: Leon Garfield (Fisher, 1986), Beatrix Potter (Fisher, 1964), Alan Garner (Coupland, 1982), William Golding (Hildick, 1970), Robert Louis Stevenson and Leila Berg (Dixon, 1974), A.A. Milne (Welch, 1958), William Mayne (Hollindale, 1974), E. Nesbit ('simply about 1700 times more intelligent', Sullivan, 1982), Jean Webster and L.M. Montgomery (Lehnert, 1992), amongst others.

Without doubt, Blyton is different. For a start, her language is not figuratively rich. Margery Fisher (1986: 386–87) laments Blyton describing some rocks as 'a curious red colour' without this having further import. In Blyton's defence, the colouration is central to the plot ('And now I know why it's red. It's coloured by the copper deposits' (Blyton, 1944c: 126)),[3] and red does customarily connote danger, but there is certainly no special metaphorical association. Blyton's writing has also been accused of being cliché-ridden – seventy-five per cent so, according to Peter Hunt's analysis of one passage (1978: 144). However, Barbara Wall's (1991: 190) description of Blyton's prose as 'direct and practical' seems more apposite, in that she uses the oral strengths of cliché, colloquialism and collocation which usually become debased only after repeated written usage. Blyton certainly avoids any words likely to detract from her story (precisely because of their possible, figurative associations), but her vocabulary is not limited. Ironically, it is in revised editions that popular notions of the Blytonesque have been consolidated, such that Noddy is no longer 'becalmed', he simply 'isn't moving' (Blyton, 1959b: 44); likewise, a number of her typographical and grammatical idiosyncrasies have been amended (see below).

Moving on to a second area, Blyton's characters have also been criticised for being flat and 'unmemorable' (Cadogan and Craig, 1976: 338); as Bob Dixon (1974: 52–53) puts it, their 'literary destiny is, clearly, to figure in the stories of *Woman's Own*'. They may not be psychologically rounded, but this does not make them unmemorable, any more than Brer Rabbit or Red Riding Hood are; indeed, many are fondly remembered by readers: the Saucepan Man, Mr Pink-Whistle, Moonface, Noddy, Big-Ears, Mr Plod, Amelia Jane, Darrell, George, Fatty, and so on.[4] It is precisely their dependability that appeals, just like the figures of the old Greek romances where, as Bakhtin (1981: 110) notes, 'there is no potential for evolution, for growth, for change ... What we get is a mere affirmation of the identity between what had been at the beginning and what is at the end.' Thus, in the Famous Five, Anne is notorious for being the '[p]roper little housewife' (Blyton, 1949b: 28), Julian for being bossy, Dick for greediness and George for stubborn independence. Fred Inglis (1981: 65) is quite candid about this: 'Partly I read them for the untaxing safety of their stereotypes ... I was hardly troubled by the notion of "character" at all.'

Her figures readily fit the types that Vladimir Propp (1968) delineated in his *Morphology of the Folktale* (e.g. heroes, villains, victims, helpers, and so on). So whether a helper is a boy, a girl or a dog is irrelevant, as long as this person moves the plot on; likewise the villains can be anything from Nazis (Blyton, 1941) to a local postman (Blyton, 1961). Roland Barthes's ([1970] 1974) discussion of narrative codes is also helpful here, with his more neutral description of character in terms of 'semic' elements (e.g. tall, dark, mean, and so on), which we will decode according to cultural disposition – although we are equally likely to be deceived in this, as we shall see.

I want to query just one other area where Blyton has been read inappropriately, for she has also been criticised for her formulaic plots, even of having but one plot: 'Enid Blyton demonstrated that children are so hungry for *stories* that they will read the same story over and over, slightly disguised', as Elaine Moss claims (1977: 336). Others just see her plotting as full of 'flaws' (Dixon, 1974: 54), by which they seem to mean contrivances, citing exactly the sort of devices that we find in such canonical writers as Dickens or Hardy – both also notable for having been influenced by popular culture, and for experiencing audience reaction through serial publication.

For each of these aspects, then – language, character and plot – I am suggesting that Blyton is seen as inadequate only if she is judged according to the fairly narrow (and recent) strictures of literary criticism. I have also indicated that, outside this, her work sits far more appositely within a different tradition: one more associated with an oral, popular culture. Here storytelling – that is, the story itself and how it is related (or plotted) – is paramount, with setting and character taking second place, making her tales easily transportable across cultures and classes, each providing their local colouring. To examine this in more detail, then, the story must come first.

Moss's suggestion that Blyton knew but one plot could not be more wrong. There are varying typologies, but if we take Christopher Booker's *The Seven Basic Plots* (2005), Blyton covers all but one. She has 'rags to riches' stories (e.g. Fenella, an orphan in *Mr Galliano's Circus*, is even called 'Cinderella' (Blyton, 1938a)). She also wrote 'quest' narratives, as in her series about Barney, a circus performer looking for his father (Blyton, 1949d). Booker's third plot type, 'voyage and return', features most obviously in the 'Magic Faraway Tree' series; his fourth, 'over-coming the monster', is also there, though less frequent (in *The Adventurous Four* (Blyton, 1941) the children help in defeating a German enemy base). In contrast, 'rebirth', where a Scrooge-like character is redeemed, is particularly popular, perhaps especially in the school stories (in 'Malory Towers' (see Plate 8). with the brash American, Zerelda Brass, the self-centred Amanda and the boasting Jo), as is his sixth category, 'comedy'. It is only the last, 'tragedy', that proved unacceptable to Blyton. As she once said, 'No murders. No ghosts. No horror. No blood' (Blyton, n.d.).

Of course, plot types being so few, the skill lies in their deployment. Blyton showed herself adept not only at helping readers become attentive to how plots function, but also at manipulating their conventions. Thus Timmy the dog is established as being particularly sensitive to a character's qualities (wagging his tail or growling accordingly), but, like any good storyteller, Blyton then has him growl at a Mrs Janes, who is old, toothless and looks exactly like a witch (Blyton, 1957: 56). Of course, she then turns out to be completely innocent. As Charles Sarland (1983: 170) puts it, Blyton skilfully teaches readers 'the basic 'grammar' of narrative stance and narrative function'.

I used the word 'plot' above, but the present participle, 'plotting', is in many ways preferable, as it conveys another facet of the storyteller's art: the idea that the tale is related 'on the hoof'. There might be a general sense of where the story is going but beyond this lies improvisation. Thus, in *Noddy Goes to Sea*, the Captain tells Noddy that they will 'land on an island somewhere' (Blyton, 1959b: 30), but does not name it till later – clearly, at the point at which a name was needed. Whereas many writers would go back and amend the earlier text, with Blyton it remains intact. This notion of 'making it up as you go along' certainly helps give a sense of immediacy to her tales. And, as noted earlier, she herself always maintained that she watched her own stories unfold, coming back to them later as though for the first time. This lack of careful revision, of course, accounts for her ability to write so much, whereas a more literary writer, seeking the *mot juste*, must revise endlessly.

It also follows that stories plotted 'on the hoof' are going to be looser in their construction. To use terms from linguistics, they are more likely to be 'paratactic' than 'hypotactic'; that is, to be episodic, joining elements with coordinating conjunctions ('and', 'also'). In hypotaxis, elements are causally linked (whether psychologically or materially). Paratactic construction is plainly seen in folk and fairy tale, where events move from one thing to another (as they do in other children's works that have an oral, dreamlike original, such as *Alice's Adventures in Wonderland*). Blyton's early full-length books have this loose structure too. Over time her plots did become tighter, but paratactic elements remain, even at the level of individual sentences: 'How lovely to wake in a strange place at the beginning of a holiday – to think of bathing and biking and picnicking and eating and drinking – forgetting all about exams and rules and punishments!' (Blyton, 1953: 37), rejoices the narrator or, perhaps, one of the characters (see 'free indirect discourse' below). The 'ands' are particularly effective in this sentence, showing how all is levelled out, the hierarchical nature of school having been removed.

From making the plot central, other points follow, with versions varying according to the current preoccupations of the teller, not to mention the nature of the audience. The whole notion of there being an original, sacrosanct text is thereby undermined: there will be different tellings only – just as the plot of *Noddy Goes to Toyland* (1949c) has an earlier outing in *Tales of Toyland* (1944b). Plagiarism is not an issue for oral tellers: all draw from a common stock of character types and plots. And the tale can be tailored for an audience likewise: for older children, the characters will also be older and will use a wider vocabulary, and the story will be longer. Likewise, when Blyton wrote for a religious press, such as Lutterworth, she would give the story a Christian flavour, and so on. Blyton was a master of adaptation, and could even tailor stories according to the time available (e.g. *Five Minute Tales* (1933) and *Ten Minute Tales* (1934)).

Following from this, two further points of contrast with the literary tradition need making. First, the notion of a discrete art object, or verbal icon, in which each part contributes to a coherent whole, is less applicable, for characters, scenes and plotlines can readily be swapped around. There is seldom any polishing of an earlier story; instead, a new one is fashioned. The Saucepan Man, a popular figure from the 'Magic Faraway Tree' series, for instance, can easily be reintroduced in 'Noddy'. In this manner, oral tales have more in common with soap opera: they are open-ended, ongoing, open to revisions of the narrative's history, and even to changes in a character's appearance (just as another actor takes over a particular role). As a result, narrative closure does not bear the ideological freight that it does in canonical texts. Secondly, just as the text itself becomes less significant (in its precise wording, its delineation of character), so the reader becomes more so (as with individual audience members at a performance). So readers can internalise their own versions of Blyton's stories and characters, just as fairy-tale readers have been found to appropriate and personalise works (e.g. Bernheimer, 2002; Westland, 1993). Moreover, not only is the reader empowered, but the reading occasion itself becomes significant (it, too, is a performance). Thus a great many readers, even if hazy on plot, could distinctly remember where and when they read Blyton (the particular venue itself often being important, whether in a cupboard, behind a chair, up a tree, or, most commonly, under the bedclothes).

In stressing the importance of reader and reading occasion, then, the text becomes more of a personalised production, or daydream, with events unfolding in the 'here and now' – a quality that Blyton captures in a variety of ways. One of these is her tendency to be repetitive, which gives the oral teller valuable thinking time to consider what happens next. Bob Dixon (1974: 55) complains about this, at how the sea, which 'shone as blue as cornflowers' in one book, continues to do so 'thirteen years and twelve books ... later'. But stock, or formulaic, phrases are a staple of oral narrative, and equally prevalent in Homer, for whom the sea was forever 'wine dark'.

Deixis is another feature more explicit in oral storytelling. Deictics are words that indicate particular spatial and temporal relations, as the phrase 'here and now' itself demonstrates. Once again, they create a sense of events unfolding before the listener's or reader's eyes. Pronouns function in this way, being dependent on who or what is being referred to; for example, the phrase 'he said' depends on who, precisely, 'he' is. Blyton's work is sometimes quite complex in this regard, with constructions like, 'We'll take him with us and say we'll set him on to them if they don't clear out' (Blyton, 1944a: 130). However, for a reader picturing the scene (or, indeed, for the writer), ambiguity is less likely. There are parallels here, both with what Vygotsky (1962: 139) calls 'inner speech', itself often being 'disconnected and incomplete' to an outsider, although quite clear to the initiated and with what Basil Bernstein (1971) terms 'restricted speech', characteristic of more close-knit groups (Blyton, interestingly, was accused of writing in just this 'restricted' manner – Dyer, 1969: 16).

I am not suggesting that Blyton used these techniques deliberately; rather, she was simply conveying to the reader what she herself saw unfolding, being of the opinion that readers would see it too. She is thus a very sensory-oriented writer, always preferring the concrete to the abstract – as the oral tradition generally does (Ong, 1982). Furthermore, Paul Bourdieu (1984) has shown that popular culture is generally more 'hands on', in contrast to the distantiation of the highbrow. The ability to evoke things visually has generally been frowned upon by critics from Plato onwards, a more detached, transformative re-creation being preferred. However, Ellen Esrock (1994: 131), reviewing the whole area, quotes research showing that visual imagery is 'an important contributor to reading pleasure', encouraging reader involvement.

Just look at him! There he stands,
With his nasty hair and hands.
See! his nails are never cut;
They are grim'd as black as soot;
And the sloven, I declare,
Never once has comb'd his hair;
Any thing to me is sweeter
Than to see Shock-headed Peter.

Plate 1 'Shock-headed Peter', from Heinrich Hoffmann, *The English Struwwelpeter* (1845), Limpsfield: Dragon's World Ltd, 1996. By kind permission of Pavilion Children's Books, Anova Books Ltd. © Pavilion's Children's Books 1996. One of the first books to use the method of cheap colour-printing called chromolithography. Invented in Germany, it was this process which first made it possible to mass-produce cheap coloured books for children. Such books were usually printed in garish and crudely mixed colours, and their standard of production contrasts strongly with the expense and expertise lavished on, for example, *Alice's Adventures in Wonderland*.

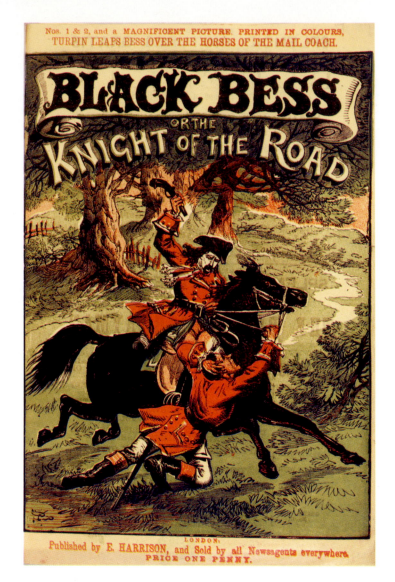

Plate 2   Edward Viles, 'Black Bess, or 'The Knight of the Road', cover of a 'penny dread-ful' magazine (1866). By kind permission of the British Library. © British Library Board. All Rights Reserved, shelfmark C.140.a.15, cover. Chromolithograph. Penny dreadfuls were mass-produced cheap sensational series fiction, priced at a penny, which accounts for the crudity of the lithographic illustration. Usually by multiple anonymous authors and illustrators, they were originally aimed at a mass readership of adults and children, as this cover's choice of subject would suggest. This Dick Turpin saga ran to 254 weekly parts, and was published in its entirety in 1868. Middle-class anxiety over boys' consumption of this material resulted in the provision of 'healthier' reading for them in the shape of high-minded boys' magazines.

Plate 3 'Alice and the Duchess', from Lewis Carroll, *Alice's Adventures in Wonderland*, illus. John Tenniel (1865), London: Macmillan & Co. Ltd, 1962. By kind permission of Macmillan Children's Books. Tenniel's elaborate colour illustrations were what made *Alice* a luxury product. They were reproduced through the use of as many as thirty separately coloured engraved woodblocks per page.

Plate 4 'The Queen of Hearts', from the series *R.D. Caldecott's Collection of Pictures and Songs*, London: Routledge, 1881. By kind permission of Cotsen Children's Library, Princeton University Library, Department of Rare Books and Special Collections. Call number Eng 19 13172. Like Tenniel's, Randolph Caldecott's illustrations to nursery rhymes and eighteenth-century light verse were reproduced through wood-block engraving, in this case by Edmund Evans, and represent a pinnacle of achievement in this type of colour-printing.

Ladies in act to smile, and pages in attendance wait;
The horses slept within their stalls, the dogs about the gate.
The King's son presses on, into an inner chamber fair,
And sees, laid on a silken bed, a lovely lady there;
So sweet a face, so fair—was never beauty such as this;
He stands—he stoops to gaze—he kneels—he wakes her with a kiss.

Plate 5 'Sleeping Beauty', from *The Sleeping Beauty Picture Book*, illus. Walter Crane, London: Routledge and New York: Dodd Mead & Co., 1911. By kind permission of the Children's Center, The New York Public Library, Astor, Lenox and Tilden Foundations. One of the most popular and important English illustrators of the late nineteenth century, Crane produced an extremely successful series of illustrated traditional and fairy-tale texts in association with the wood-block engraver Edmund Evans and Routledge from 1865 onwards. This example shows his characteristic filling of the whole frame, clear line, strong use of black, and care for detail of decoration, dress and furniture, all of which made his illustrations one of the high-water marks of late nineteenth-century children's illustration.

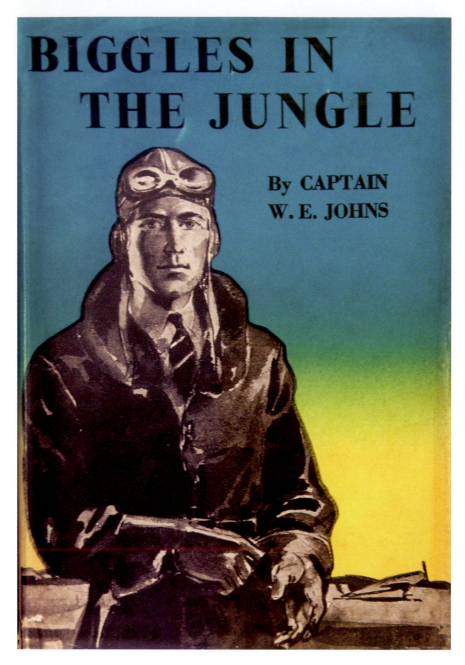

Plate 6 'Biggles' from Captain W.E. Johns, *Biggles in the Jungle*, London: Oxford University Press and Geoffrey Cumberlege, 1949. By kind permission of Alamy Ltd. © Antiques & Collectables/Alamy. Johns's hero first appeared in a magazine of the early 1930s, and the series began to be published soon after.

Plate 7 Front cover, *Beano* magazine (no. 367, 30 July 1949), illus. Dudley D. Watkins, Dundee: D.C. Thomson. By kind permission of D.C. Thomson & Co. Ltd. The cartoon-style illustrations of this magazine launched for boys in 1938 strongly contrast with earlier and contemporary publications aimed at boys, which are markedly realist and heroic in pictorial mode, from the 'penny dreadful' to *The Boy's Own Paper*, through to the Biggles books.

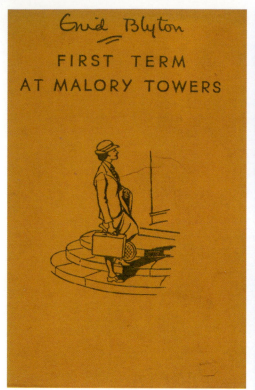
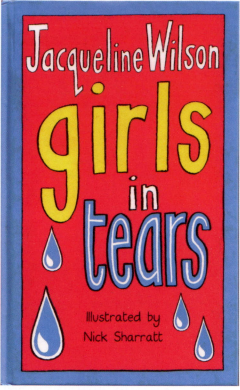

Plate 8   Front cover, Enid Blyton, *First Term at Malory Towers*, first edition, illus. Stanley Lloyd, London: Methuen & Co. Ltd, 1946. By kind permission of Tony Summerfield, The Enid Blyton Society. A famous and prolific illustrator in the first half of the twentieth century, Stanley Lloyd illustrated all the first editions of the Malory Towers series (1946–51), Blyton's belated but successful excursus into the genre of the girls' school story. Lloyd's illustration for the hardcover of the first book depicts the anticipation of the new girl, on the brink of discovering the joys of active, youthful female friendship.

Plate 9   Front cover, Jacqueline Wilson, *Girls in Tears*, London: Doubleday, 2002. By kind permission of The Random House Group Ltd. This cover to one of Wilson's very successful series for girls illustrates the way that realist fiction around the turn of the twenty-first century was conspicuously marketed by gender; books for girls were typically pink, and often embossed and shiny in imitation of the sex-and-shopping airport novels of the 1990s, while books for boys, by contrast, tended to imitate airport action-thrillers.

Plate 10   Front cover, Bertha Upton, *The Adventures of Two Dutch Dolls*, illus. Florence K. Upton, London & New York: Longmans Green & Co., 1895. By kind permission of V&A Images, Victoria and Albert Museum. Image no. 2006AN2215. Displaying unusual boldness and clarity of colour for the time, this was the book that sparked a craze for golliwogs.

Plate 11   From Julius Lester, *Sam and the Tigers*, illus. Jerry Pinkney. Illustration copyright © 1996 by Jerry Pinkney. First published in the United States by Dial Books for Young Readers. All rights reserved. By kind permission of www.penguin.com and Sheldon Fogelman Agency, Inc. Lester and Pinkney re-version Helen Bannerman's original *Little Black Sambo*. In an effort to retain the appeal of the original story while sidestepping its racist representation of the child and his family, Lester reconceives Bannerman's vague setting (an amalgamation of Africa and India) as a vague historicism, equipping Sam with period clothing.

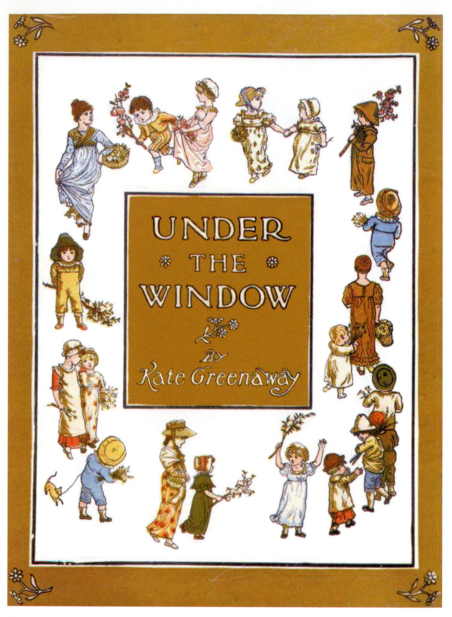

Plate 12 Front cover, Kate Greenaway, *Under the Window*, London: G. Routledge & Sons, 1879. Project Gutenberg Greenaway's characteristic vision of sunlit children clothed in imaginary eighteenth-century costume, which inspired countless imitations and a persistent fashion in children's dress, is well represented here in the cover to her first book of drawings and verses. Edmund Evans engraved four or five colour blocks plus the outline per page, a costly procedure which meant the book was priced at 6 shillings (compare the sixpenny and shilling toy books then dominating the market), but the first edition nevertheless sold out almost immediately, launching Greenaway on a long and successful career.

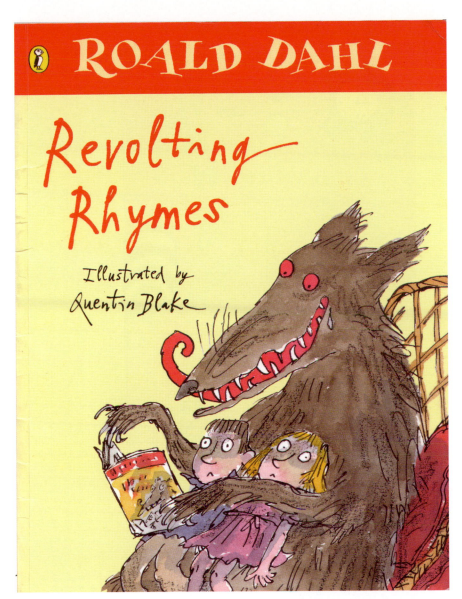

Plate 13   Front cover, Roald Dahl, *Revolting Rhymes*, illus. Quentin Blake, London: Puffin Books, [1984] 2001. Text copyright © Roald Dahl Nominee Ltd, 1982. Illustrations copyright © Quentin Blake, 1982, 1984, 2001. By kind permission of Penguin Books Ltd. Quentin Blake's cover expresses the anarchic spirit of Dahl's rewrites of fairy tales with a characteristic inversion of normality; in place of the maternal Nurse Lovechild featured in the frontispiece to *Tommy Thumb's Songbook*, we have a wolf reading to two frankly terrified children perched uncomfortably on his lap.

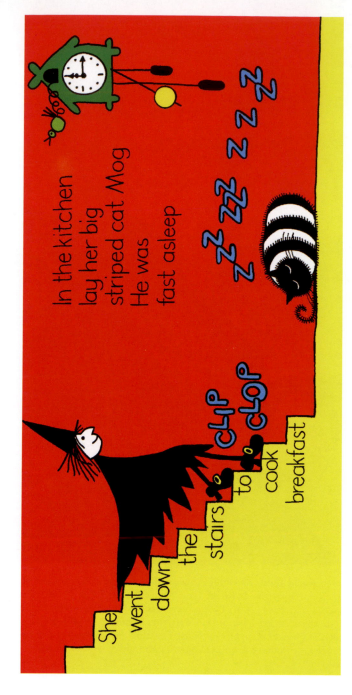

Plate 14 From Jan Pieńkowski and Helen Nicoll, *Meg and Mog*, London: Puffin Books, 1972. This is the first of 16 Meg and Mog books collaboratively produced by Jan Pieńkowski and Helen Nicoll. Pieńkowski's vivid, exuberant colours and simple bold images, imaginatively combined with Nicoll's text, brought the well-meaning, inept witch and her cat to life for numerous young children and early readers.

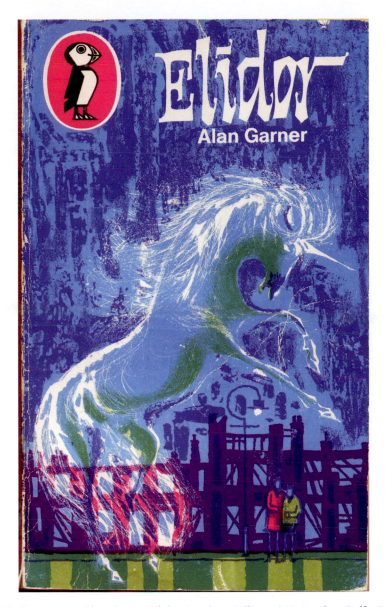

Plate 15 Front cover, Alan Garner, *Elidor*, London: Collins, 1965; London: Puffin Books, 1967. Copyright Alan Garner, 1965. By kind permission of Penguin Books Ltd. Cover illustrated by Charles Keeping. The intrusion of myth into the modern world is dramatised by the white figure of the unicorn set against the energetically realist portrayal of decaying urban Manchester, and evokes the mix of fantasy and gritty topicality that characterised much fiction of the Second Golden Age. Paperbacks such as this published for children by Puffin (launched in 1941) fuelled this new Golden Age; not only were the books cheap, but Puffin's novel ambition was to publish 'the best of the *new* classics of the new generation'.

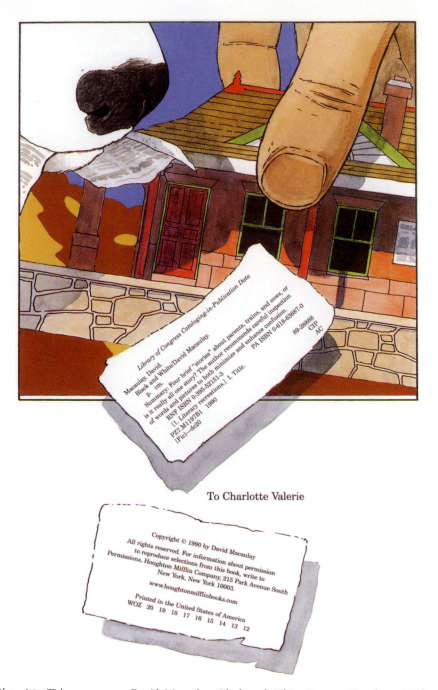

Library of Congress Cataloging-in-Publication Data

Macaulay, David.
Black and White/David Macaulay.
p. cm.
Summary: Four brief "stories" about parents, trains, and cows, or
is it really all one story? The author recommends careful inspection
of words and pictures to both minimize and enhance confusion.
RNF ISBN 0-395-52151-3   PA ISBN 0-618-63687-0
[1. Literary recreations.] I. Title.
PZ7.M1197B1 1990   89-28888
[Fic]—dc20   CIP
                                                          AC

To Charlotte Valerie

Plate 16   Title-page verso, David Macaulay, *Black and White*, Boston: Houghton Mifflin, 1990. Copyright © 1990 by David Macaulay. By kind permission of Houghton Mifflin Harcourt Publishing Company. A picture book demanding much work from young and older readers alike, *Black and White* is not so much a story, as four stories which may, or may not, be connected.

Plate 17 'I think ... someone's out there' from David Wiesner, *The Three Pigs*, New York: Clarion Books, 2001. Copyright © 2001 by David Wiesner. By kind permission of Clarion Books, an imprint of Houghton Mifflin Harcourt Publishing Company. All rights reserved. A contemporary American picture book often cited as a prime example of postmodern visual storytelling, *The Three Pigs* won the Caldecott Medal in 2002.

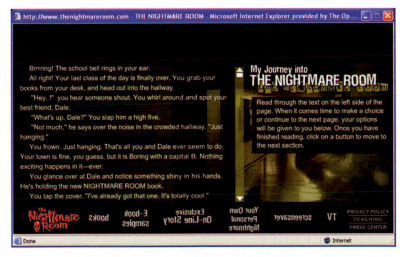

Plate 18 'The Nightmare Room', http://www.thenightmareroom.com, by R.L. Stine. Accessed 2001–2. Used by permission of HarperCollins Publishers. This screenshot illustrates hyper-media at the beginning of the twenty-first century. The multimodal affordances of words, music, images and sound are used to enhance a horror story. The technology allows the reader to select whether to read the story, link to a game, or download a screensaver. There are also links to educational material which allows the site to be used for teaching purposes.

Plate 19 From Robert Sabuda, *Alice's Adventures in Wonderland*, a pop-up adaptation of Lewis Carroll's original tale, New York: Little Simon, 2003. Copyright © 2003 Robert Sabuda. By kind permission of Little Simon, an imprint of Simon & Schuster Children's Publishing Division. This pop-up book is a modern instance of the permeability between toy and book that dates back to the eighteenth century, as well as an example of one of the ways in which children's classics are particularly prone to adaptation.

Plate 20 From *His Dark Materials*, adapted in two parts from Philip Pullman's trilogy of the same name by Nicholas Wright, directed by Nicholas Hytner, National Theatre, 2003–5 seasons. The revival of 2005. By kind permission of photographer Catherine Ashmore. Lyra Belacqua and the polar bears, realised through bunraku puppetry.

Blyton is certainly adept at this; as an 8-year-old boy in my own research put it, 'when you're reading them, you feel like you're in the picture'. She not only conjures up scenes that are easy to visualise, but also often explicitly instructs readers to attend to them. This was particularly common in the original 'Noddy' series, where there is explicit pictorial support: 'Have a look at it' (Blyton, 1954a: 28), she states, or 'Here it is' (Blyton, 1956: 33). But Blyton is equally likely to hail the reader through other senses. Of a song being sung she says, 'I'll pop my head in at the window and hear it for you. Listen!' (Blyton, 1954b: 60). Visual and aural senses are easiest to evoke, but she seeks to induce taste, too, regularly tantalising readers with lavish descriptions of food and feasting.

Blyton also uses other techniques to suggest immediacy and presence. Thus she tries to emulate the exact sound of things. In 'Malory Towers', for instance, we find phonetic spelling ('Wunnerful!', from Zerelda (Blyton 1948: 9); ('g-g-g-gone to be m-m-m-mended' from the nervous Mary-Lou (1946b: 134)). We also have such typographical conventions as capitalising and italicising words, for both volume and emphasis ('How *dare* ...? And HOW DARE ...', Blyton 1946b: 137), often picking out single syllables for emphasis ('so ex*a*sperating', Blyton 1951: 60; 'EVERYbody', Blyton, 1954a: 31). She seems to rejoice in onomatopoeia, too (e.g. 'EEEE-ee-OOOOO-oo-EEEEEEEEAH-OOO!', Blyton, 1962: 140), and sometimes collapses words altogether to convey haste (as in the breathless 'couldyoulookafter-theponyhereforme?' (Blyton, [1954] 1968: 94)). Of course, we should not forget the countless exclamation marks, used even in chapter titles ('Well done, Mary-Lou!' (Blyton 1946b: 133)).

All the above help give the reader a sense of being there, of having an exact report of events. But Blyton also achieves this effect grammatically. Occasionally she uses a shift of tense from past to present, particularly evident in 'Noddy' again. For instance, when he encounters a crab, we are told to 'Look at it, holding on with its claws' (Blyton, 1953b: 42). Likewise, at the end of this book, Blyton brings everyone together in the continuous present: 'So now they are having a perfectly wonderful tea-party' (58). We are invited, or sometimes even directed, to *picture* the scene. In these instances the Blyton persona can itself be heard to speak, while at other times we quietly slip into the consciousness of a character, in what is known as 'free indirect discourse'. However, there are degrees of this device, and Blyton likes to blur the divide. For instance, in the final 'Malory Towers' book, the narrator informs us that 'Darrell looked at Gwen's silly, weak face ... Nobody ... could make any impression on Gwen!' (Blyton, 1951: 41). Clearly this is not an objective account. Presumably it is Darrell's view we are experiencing, and the exclamation mark at the end also suggests a more subjective consciousness – or would do, were such exclamations not so prolific in Blyton.

However, although she is without doubt an intrusive storyteller, this is not the whole story, for Blyton herself often seems to lack complete control – something that we might link to her compositional methods (watching her own story unfold) – hence the consequent ambiguity at times. Thus if Blyton intrudes, then so too do her characters, with spoken and inner discourse often merging, for example:

> 'I wish I was like George,' [Anne] thought. 'She wouldn't really mind that toad. I'm silly. I ought to try and like all creatures. Oh my goodness, look at that enormous spider in the corner of the sink! It's sitting there, looking at me out of its eight eyes! Wilfrid, Wilfrid – PLEASE come and get this spider out of the sink for me!'
>
> Blyton, 1962: 49

Readers, I suspect, won't have problems comprehending this, or even notice the shift from inner to outer speech, but it makes Dorrit Cohn's (1978) term for free indirect discourse, 'narrative monologue', seem especially apt. For this is closer to what an oral teller does: not just relating a story but also performing it, imitating voices and sounds, giving us characters' thoughts and commenting on their actions as well as adding her (or their) asides. Here I am thinking of what is known as apostrophising, a standard device in Homer – as it is in much classical drama. This is one example from the 'Famous Five':

> If danger was about, [Julian] could deal with it better than George could. After all, she was only a girl!
>
> Yes, Julian, she is – but, as you've often said, she's just as brave as a boy. Don't be too sure about tonight!
>
> Blyton, 1963: 129

This narrator is blatantly in the 'telling' not the 'showing' mould. Yet, once again, such metafictional comments also seem to originate from the characters themselves. *In the Fifth at Malory Towers* has an example where one teacher comments on another's untidy desk: 'You'll probably find the Speeches made at the Opening of the First Term at Malory Towers if you look a little further into your desk' (Blyton, 1950: 126). *First Term at Malory Towers* is, of course, the opening book of the series. We seem to have an in-joke here, to be shared by audience and storyteller alike, but also one that draws attention to the fact that Blyton seems to occupy both roles.

While I don't think that Blyton was aware of her technique at this level, she certainly utilised many of the elements traditionally associated with tellers of folk and fairy tales. Indeed, simply being a female writer was conducive: the

'Mother Goose' figure, seated with her distaff as she spun yarns both meta-phorical and literal, closely associated with hearth and home. Blyton conjures up this image in a number of titles, like *Chimney Corner Stories* (Blyton, 1946a) and *Fireside Tales* (Blyton, 1966), besides more generally celebrating her home, Green Hedges, as in, most famously, *A Story Party at Green Hedges* (1949a). The first page of this book even has an invitation for readers to complete, in order that they too might attend; guests are then told stories tailored to each of them. But the whole atmosphere of an oral story session, of sitting round a hearth, feasting while tales are told, is thereby evoked. Moreover, if Green Hedges is metonymic of its author, Blyton managed to incorporate her own, iconic name in the title of more than a hundred of her books (again foregrounding the teller). A final point about storytellers, though, is that they tell the tales of their community, which, for Blyton, as I said earlier, comprised children almost exclusively. She certainly emphasised the importance of listening to children's own tales, encouraging their feedback through her weekly and fortnightly magazines. Whether or not she actually made use of their ideas is irrelevant; what is important is the fact that she cultivated such a persona.

Conclusion

In the above I have taken issue with a number of Blyton's earlier critics for misconstruing her work. Seen in the tradition of oral storytelling, as part of popular culture, many of what appear to be her weaknesses can more fruitfully be viewed as strengths, helping to explain her particular appeal. From this perspective, children are not mindlessly imbibing what Fisher termed Blyton's 'slow poison'. Why would they? Given that most of her readers are not middle-class, white, English, home-counties or male – and neither are they seeking literary or educational improvement – then their pleasure in her texts clearly lies elsewhere. I have suggested that it lies precisely in the fantasy space that her stories evoke, one that is similar to that of the orally inflected fairy tale. It is a space where to take part is to take 'time out' from reality, from educational and other concerns, and to savour, alongside their mythical childhood heroes, the present-centred pleasures of the text, and, moreover, to emulate their adventurers by reading in secretive locations armed with personal feasts, in a space that is, at least symbolically, removed from the adult world.

The 'Famous Five' series, Blyton's most successful, is perhaps so because it perfectly captures this: being on holiday not just literally but psychologically, too, escaping from school and parental influence in the company of one's celebrated peers. And, for all their adventures, this usually involved setting up an alternative home or family unit, where the Famous Five could enjoy each other's friendship, feasting and, to adapt a Blyton title, having plenty of extra-mural fun. As Zipes (1997: 4) puts it, 'to read a fairy tale is to follow the narrative path to happiness' and, with Blyton's perennially 'Sunny Stories', this is certainly the case.

References

AFP 2008. 'JK Rowling Wins Privacy Ruling over Photo of Son', 7 May, www.afp.google.com/article/ALeqM5jgv8ALgPziQENLv7J68K8Xf_KJeA>, accessed 19 June 2008.

Bakhtin, M.M. 1981. *The Dialogic Imagination: Four Essays*, trans. Michael Holquist and Gary Emerson. Austin, University of Texas Press.

Barthes, R. [1970] 1974. *S/Z*, trans. Richard Miller. New York, Hill & Wang. [orig. Paris, 1970].

Bernheimer, K. (ed.) 2002. *Mirror, Mirror on the Wall: Women Writers Explore their Favorite Fairy Tales*, 2nd edn. New York, Random House.

Bernstein, B. 1971. *Class, Codes and Control, Vol. 1*. London, Routledge & Kegan Paul.

Blyton, E. (ed.) 1926a. *Tales Half Told*. London, Nelson.

Blyton, E. (ed.) 1926b. *The Teacher's Treasury*. London, Newnes.

Blyton, E. (ed.) 1928. *Modern Teaching*. London, Newnes.

Blyton, E. 1933. *Five Minute Tales: Sixty Short Stories for Children*. London, Methuen.

Blyton, E. 1934. *Ten Minute Tales*. London, Methuen.

Blyton, E. 1937. *Adventures of the Wishing Chair*. London, Newnes.

Blyton, E. 1938a. *Mr. Galliano's Circus*. London, Newnes.

Blyton, E. 1938b. *The Secret Island*. Oxford, Blackwell.

Blyton, E. 1939. *The Enchanted Wood*. London, Newnes.

Blyton, E. 1941. *The Adventurous Four*. London, Newnes.

Blyton, E. 1943. *The Magic Faraway Tree*. London, Newnes.

Blyton, E. 1944a. *Five Run Away Together*. London, Hodder & Stoughton.

Blyton, E. 1944b. *Tales of Toyland*. London, Newnes.

Blyton, E. 1944c. *The Island of Adventure*. London, Macmillan.

Blyton, E. 1946a. *Chimney Corner Stories*. London, National Magazine.

Blyton, E. 1946b. *First Term at Malory Towers*, illus. by Stanley Lloyd. London, Methuen.

Blyton, E. 1948. *Third Year at Malory Towers*, illus. by Stanley Lloyd. London, Methuen.

Blyton, E. 1949a. *A Story Party at Green Hedges*. London, Hodder & Stoughton.

Blyton, E. 1949b. *Five Get Into Trouble*. London, Hodder & Stoughton.

Blyton, E. 1949c. *Noddy Goes to Toyland*. London, Samson Low.

Blyton, E. 1949d. *The Rockingdown Mystery*. London, Collins.

Blyton, E. 1950. *In the Fifth at Malory Towers*, illus. by Stanley Lloyd. London, Methuen.

Blyton, E. 1951. *Last Term at Malory Towers*, illus. by Stanley Lloyd. London, Methuen.

Blyton, E. 1953a. *Five Go Down to the Sea*. London, Hodder & Stoughton.

Blyton, E. 1953b. *Noddy at the Seaside*. London, Samson Low.

Blyton, E. 1954a. *Noddy and the Magic Rubber*. London, Samson Low.

Blyton, E. 1954b. *Noddy Gets into Trouble*. London, Samson Low.

Blyton, E. 1956. *Be Brave, Little Noddy!* London, Samson Low.

Blyton, E. 1957. *Five Go to Billycock Hill*. London, Hodder & Stoughton.

Blyton, E. 1959a. 'Writing for Children', *New Statesman*, 9 May: 649.

Blyton, E. 1959b. *Noddy Goes to Sea*. London, Samson Low.

Blyton, E. 1961. *Shock for the Secret Seven.* Leicester, Brockhampton Press.

Blyton, E. 1962. *Five Have a Mystery to Solve.* London, Hodder & Stoughton.

Blyton, E. 1963. *Five are Together Again.* London, Hodder & Stoughton.

Blyton, E. 1966. *Fireside Tales.* London, Collins.

Blyton, E. [1954] 1968. *The Children at Green Meadows.* London, Collins.

Blyton, E. 2003a. 'From My Window: Enid Blyton's Weekly Talk, No. 1: Cherry-Tree Farm', *Teachers World*, 27 April 1925, reproduced in *The Enid Blyton Society Journal*, 20: 17–19.

Blyton, E. 2003b. 'From My Window: Enid Blyton's Weekly Talk, No. 2: Hideaway Corner', *Teachers World*, 17 June 1925, reproduced in *The Enid Blyton Society Journal*, 21: 18–19.

Blyton, E. (n.d.) 'How I Regard Writing for Children', Enid Blyton Society Archive.

Booker, C. 2005. *The Seven Basic Plots: Why We Tell Stories.* London, Continuum.

Bourdieu, P. 1984. *Distinction: A Social Critique of the Judgement of Taste*, trans. R. Nice. London, Routledge.

Cadogan, M. and Craig, P. 1976. *You're a Brick, Angela! The Girls' Story, 1839–1985.* London, Gollancz.

Cohn, D. 1978. *Transparent Minds: Narrative Modes for Presenting Consciousness in Fiction.* Princeton, NJ, Princeton University Press.

Coupland, J. 1982. 'What's in a Story: Narrative Structure and Realisation in Children's Fiction', in Peter Hunt (ed.) *Further Approaches to Research in Children's Literature: Proceedings of the Second British Research Seminar in Children's Literature, Cardiff, September 1981.* Cardiff. Dept of English, UWIST: 85–93.

Dixon, R. 1974. 'The Nice, the Naughty and the Nasty: The Tiny World of Enid Blyton', *Children's Literature in Education*, 15: 43–61.

Druce, R. 1992. *This Day Our Daily Fictions: An Enquiry into the Multi-Million Bestseller Status of Enid Blyton and Ian Fleming.* Amsterdam-Atlanta, Rodopi BV.

Dyer, C. 1969. 'Anatomy of a Blyton', *Lines*, 2, 7: 16–18.

Esrock, E.J. 1994. *The Reader's Eye: Visual Imaging as Reader Response.* Baltimore, MD and London, Johns Hopkins University Press.

Fisher, M. 1964. *Intent Upon Reading: A Critical Appraisal of Modern Fiction for Children*, 2nd edn. Leicester, Brockhampton Press.

Fisher, M. 1983. 'A Reputation Considered', *Growing Point*, July: 4119–20.

Fisher, M. 1986. *The Bright Face of Danger.* London, Hodder & Stoughton.

Fraser, A. (ed.) 1992. *The Pleasures of Reading.* London, Bloomsbury.

Hildick, W. 1970. *Children and Fiction: A Critical Study in Depth of the Artistic and Psychological Factors Involved in Writing Fiction for and about Children.* London, Evans Bros.

Holbrook, D. 1961. *English for Maturity.* Cambridge, Cambridge University Press.

Hollindale, P. 1974. *Choosing Books for Children.* London, Paul Elek.

Hunt, P. 1978. 'The Cliché Count: A Practical Aid for the Selection of Books for Children', *Children's Literature in Education*, 9, 3: 143–50.

Hunt, P. 1994. *An Introduction to Children's Literature.* Oxford, Oxford University Press.

Inglis, F. 1981. *The Promise of Happiness.* Cambridge, Cambridge University Press.

Jones, N. 2007. 'Why Blyton Was Another Breed', *Sunday Telegraph*, 30 June, www.telegraph.co.uk/arts/main.jhtml?xml=/arts/2007/06/30/nosplit/boblyton130.xml>, accessed 19 June 2008.

Lehnert, G. 1992. 'The Training of the Shrew: Socialization and Education of Young Women in Children's Literature', *Poetics Today*, 13 (1) 1992: 109–22.

McKellar, P. 1957. *Imagination and Thinking: A Psychological Analysis*. London, Cohen & West.

Moss, E. [1974] 1977. 'The Adult-eration of Children's Books', in Margaret Meek, Aidan Warlow and Griselda Barton (eds) *The Cool Web: The Pattern of Children's Reading*. London, Bodley Head: 333–37.

Nash, R. 1964. 'As Big Ears Said to Noddy Yesterday', *Daily Mail*, 7 February.

Ong, W. 1982. *Orality and Literacy: The Technologizing of the Word*. London, Methuen.

Propp, V. 1968. *Morphology of the Folktale*, 2nd edn, trans. Laurence Scott. Austin, University of Texas Press [orig. Russia, 1928].

Ray, S.G. 1982. *The Blyton Phenomenon: The Controversy Surrounding the World's Most Successful Children's Author*. London, André Deutsch.

Rudd, D. 2000. *Enid Blyton and the Mystery of Children's Literature*. London, Palgrave Macmillan.

Sarland, C. 1983. 'The Secret Seven vs The Twits: Cultural Clash or Cosy Combination?', *Signal*, 42, Sept.: 155–71.

Stoney, B. 1974. *Enid Blyton: A Biography*. London, Hodder & Stoughton.

Sullivan, M. 1982. 'Land of Noddy', *Sunday Telegraph*, 25 July.

Vygotsky, L.S. 1962. *Thought and Language*. Cambridge, MA, MIT Press.

Wall, B. 1991. *The Narrator's Voice: The Dilemma of Children's Fiction*. London, Macmillan.

Welch, C. 1958. 'Dear Little Noddy: A Parent's Lament', *Encounter*, 10, 1: 18–23.

Westland, E. 1993. 'Cinderella in the Classroom: Children's Responses to Gender Roles in Fairy Tales', *Gender and Education*, 5, 3: 237–49.

Whitehead, F., Capey, A.C., Maddren, W. and Wellings, A. 1977. *Children and their Books: Schools Council Research Project into Children's Reading Habits, 10–15*. Basingstoke, Macmillan Education.

Wilson, B.K. 1995. 'Grace Abounding', *Signal*, 26: 151–65.

Woods, F. 1955. [Letter] *Journal of Education*, 87: 404.

Zipes, J. 1997. *Happily Ever After: Fairy Tales, Children, and the Culture Industry*. London, Routledge.

Notes

1. This is based on estimates that Rowling has currently sold some 350 million copies (AFP, 2008), whereas Blyton is reckoned to have shifted around 410 million (Jones, 2007).

2. Peter Hunt found amongst his literature undergraduates that *The Magic Faraway Tree* 'was by far the best-remembered book of their childhoods' (Hunt, 1994, p.116).

3. Unfortunately both Blyton and Fisher failed to notice that copper-veined rocks should rightfully be green, as they are in more recent editions.

4. This, and other findings, draws on my research, conducted in the early 1990s, which attracted responses from both contemporary and past readers of Blyton: some 500 children, and 400 adults from different social classes, countries and ethnic backgrounds (Rudd, 2000).

Marketing at the Millennium
Claire Squires

Introduction: market contexts

For British children's books and the industry that produced them, the turn of the twentieth and twenty-first centuries was a period of transition and high visibility. In marked contrast, during the preceding decades, as Kimberley Reynolds argues in 'Publishing Practices and the Practicalities of Publishing' (1998), the children's sector was underprivileged and undervalued, occupying a marginal position within the larger publishing industry. As late as 1999, in a short contribution on children's fiction for *The Writer's Handbook*, the author Philip Pullman complained about the paucity of review space, the lack of marketing spend on children's books, and the less lucrative prize purses of children's literary awards. Put simply, children's literature was taken less 'seriously' than books written for adults (Pullman, 1999: 217).

All this would soon change. Between 1997 and 2007, the seven volumes of J.K. Rowling's Harry Potter series appeared, with each volume generating more excitement, greater promotional activity and stratospheric sales. This most spectacular literary and publishing phenomenon brought close attention to the market sector. By 2002, the US trade journal *Publishers Weekly* (*PW*) was claiming the period was 'A Golden Time for Children's Books' (Eccleshare, 2002), and many other commentators on the contemporary publishing scene would echo the sentiment that children's books had entered a new Golden Age, of which Rowling's boy wizard was only one indicator. Julia Eccleshare, the author of the *Publishers Weekly* report (and the children's books editor for the *Guardian* newspaper) further chronicled the shift which brought children's books from the margins to the centre of the publishing industry in 2004: 'The received wisdom about children's books is being challenged. Their hallmark was once a long life in the slow lane. Not so any more. Children's books are now up front big sellers and the barriers to their success are tumbling down' (2004: 16). Eccleshare's report cited eight authors in the UK children's market selling at adult levels, including home-grown talents Rowling, Pullman and Jacqueline Wilson, and US imports Meg Cabot and Lemony Snicket. Sales were led by the Harry Potter series, but others contributed strongly to the commercial success. Jacqueline Wilson conducted marathon book-signing events, including one session lasting over eight hours, in which she signed books for approximately three thousand fans (Meek 2004). The 2004 Public Lending Right figures revealed that Wilson had overtaken the saga writer Catherine Cookson as the most borrowed author from libraries. By 2006, loans of her books totalled over two million (Public Lending Right, 2004, 2006). The 'crossover' phenomenon, which saw authors including Rowling, Pullman and Mark Haddon reaching an adult as well as a children's readership, excited much commentary in the media, and energised publishers' efforts to target a dual audience.

Following the success of these leading writers, there has been a substantial level of attention focused on the British children's book world, and a consequent heightened level of hype surrounding its marketing. Many children's authors now have literary agents, an unusual arrangement at the beginning of the 1990s. Some children's authors receive large advances for the rights to publish their properties. The Bologna Book Fair, which concentrates on books for children and young adults, is a focal point for rights trading and international publication deals, and also, more recently, for film scouts to prospect for the hottest children's books to turn into television and films. Children's book characters are developed as merchandised properties, with associated toys, games and stationery. Several celebrities (often with the aid of a ghostwriter) have begun writing books for children, including the models Katie Price and Sophie Dahl and the pop stars Madonna and Geri Halliwell. Since 2004 a *Children's Writers' and Artists' Yearbook* has been published annually, offering tailored advice for aspiring authors and illustrators.

By 2007, UK customer purchases of children's books amounted to £545 million, representing nearly 16 per cent of overall publishers' sales in the domestic market. The volume of children's books sold represents a greater market share: in 2007, 25 per cent of total copies sold in the market were children's books (the disparity between these two figures is explained by the average lower selling price of children's books). The children's market sector has been characterised by strong growth, well ahead of adult trade books (books intended for a general readership and sold through bookshops) with an 18 per cent growth in volume and 29 per cent growth in value in the four-year period from 2004 to 2007. This pattern of growth is perceptible even if J.K. Rowling's sales figures are excluded (11 per cent growth in volume and 14 per cent by value in the same period) (Richardson and Taylor, 2008: 11, 29, 31).

Such figures demonstrate that children's publishing is a serious economic force at the turn of the twentieth and twenty-first centuries, 'despite competition from other media', as the Publishers Association reports (Richardson and Taylor, 2008: 31). The publishers contributing to this success replicate the pattern of publishing companies throughout the UK publishing sector. The sector is dominated by a small number of very large conglomerates: HarperCollins (part of the News Corporation media group), Hodder Headline and Orion

(Hachette), Puffin (Penguin/Pearson), and Random House (Bertelsmann). However, the children's publishing market is also populated by a number of independent and small-to-medium-sized publishing companies whose output successfully challenges the stranglehold of the conglomerates. Such companies include Bloomsbury (Rowling's publisher), Usborne, and Walker Books. Oxford University Press also continues its tradition of children's publishing.

Yet, for all the positive economic indicators, the global success of UK children's writers, and the dawn of another perceived Golden Age, there are more negative narratives which demonstrate anxiety around children's books and children's reading patterns. In contradiction to the positive message conveyed by the Publishers Association, the proliferation of other media competing for children's leisure time – television, film, DVDs, computer games and the internet – presents a genuine threat to the more traditional activity of reading (Horn, 2008). With such a plethora of competing activities it is evident that publishers have to think creatively about how to make their products relevant to twenty-first-century children. In this respect, the potential for multimedia synergies and merchandising – with literary characters and storylines being repurposed for a variety of different media – show that books can also contribute to and benefit from these competitors. Picture-book characters such as Lucy Cousins's Maisy and Lauren Child's Charlie and Lola, and storybook characters including Jacqueline Wilson's Tracy Beaker, demonstrate where books have been extremely successful progenitors of newer media including TV programmes, videos and interactive websites.

Further concerns over the competence and extent of children's reading remain, though, with frequent complaints in the media and from politicians about declining standards in literacy and reading (Garner, 2002; Clark, 2007). A range of literacy and literary development campaigns such as Bookstart, Booktime and Booked Up (which give free books to babies, children and teenagers respectively), the annual World Book Day, the National Years of Reading (in 1998 and 2008), and organisations such as Booktrust, The Reading Agency, and the National Literacy Trust have been developed in response to these trends, and to help counteract them. The National Literacy Strategy, implemented by the UK Government in 1998 (and incorporated into the Primary National Strategy in 2003), was indicative of the national mood in its concerns about children's reading patterns. Boys' disinclination to read caused particular concern, prompting gender-specific campaigns promoted by sports stars to get boys (and their dads) into reading.

Negative attitudes around children's reading have affected the opinions of children themselves, as a survey into young people's self-perceptions as readers by the National Literacy Trust in 2008 revealed (Clark et al., 2008). Perhaps unsurprisingly, when asked to imagine someone who reads, 58 per cent of the sample thought of someone who was 'clever' and 'intelligent', but a large minority (just over a third of the sample) envisaged someone who was 'geeky' or 'a nerd'. In response to being asked how reading made them feel, a third also stated that reading 'bored' them. The study found that many young people – even those who did read – did not designate themselves as readers. Being a 'reader' was closely linked to reading fiction or poetry (the reading thought to be encouraged in schools), but not with magazines or websites. It is possible that by overvaluing certain types of reading and books, adults may be persuading children to internalise literary hierarchies, and so to fail to see themselves as readers at all.

Another concern sometimes expressed by commentators on children's publishing relates to the perceived quality of the (undeniably commercially successful) children's publishing industry in the 1990s and 2000s – and to a sense of literary hierarchy. This commercial success has derived from a mass-market approach, in which, some might say, quickly produced and derivative publishing is valued above literary quality (Reynolds, 1998). While the 1990s and 2000s have undoubtedly been an age of commerciality and market excitement in children's publishing, it is also possible to argue that there has been an emphasis on content and quality of writing for children, and recognition of the strength of children's books both within and beyond their primary audience. The range of children's books available in the early twenty-first century is explored in the next section.

Genre

Diversity is a key aspect of the children's publishing market sector. It produces everything from baby and bath books that have to be rigorously tested to conform to safety standards for children's toys, to storybook series heavily branded with pink and glittering covers, to manga versions of Shakespeare and to hard-hitting fictional accounts of drugs, death and teen sex. A visit to the children's section of a bookshop sustains this impression, divided as they often are into bays for different age groups, for picture books, for educational books, and into sections akin to toy shops, with a variety of novelty titles and tie-in merchandise. Teen titles are usually given shelving within the children's department of general bookshops, although occasionally bookshops distance teen titles from the rest of the children's books. This is done for divergent reasons: first, perhaps, to distance the more controversial titles produced for teenagers from younger children; secondly, to give teenagers an area in which to browse for books which is more attractively 'adult' to them than one populated by soft toys and younger siblings.

At the youngest end of the market, which overlaps the early years toy market, are board and bath books. These may employ images without text, but their structure replicates the codex – the traditional book format that existed before the development of the printing press, and has survived through its 500-year history – thus preparing the child for a lifelong reading habit. Books are carefully produced to standards which make them able to withstand the physical wear and tear of life in baby and toddler hands – and mouths! Early books include Usborne's *That's Not My ...* (tractor, penguin, robot, etc.) series, which incorporates simple, repetitious text with images and materials (such as corrugated card and mirrored paper) designed to stimulate a number of the senses.

Picture books – the next section of the market in age terms – display a level of complexity which grows alongside children's psychological development and understanding of narrative (both visual and textual). They also frequently speak to a double audience, keeping the adult reader entertained alongside the child. Established writer/illustrators such as Janet and Allan Ahlberg, Helen Oxenbury and Mick Inkpen co-exist with newer talents including Julia Donaldson and Axel Scheffler (*The Gruffalo*), Lauren Child, and Oliver Jeffers. Picture books were thought to have suffered from a lack of attention at the end of the twentieth century, being in the shadow of writers such as Rowling, Pullman and Wilson. Trade reports detail a 'challenging' market in the 2000s, with declining picture-book sales and some retailers reducing their range of titles stocked (Horn, 2006). For publishers their high production costs compare unfavourably with storybooks, and the media excitement directed at writers for older children rather neglect the crucial importance of books for the very young. Moreover, the popularity of television tie-in books (for example, books based on the character Bob the Builder) threaten to crowd out the market for originally produced picture books. In one attempt to counteract this, The Big Picture campaign was announced in 2008, with the aim of promoting and enhancing picture books and the art of illustration.

As children's literacy and facility with textual narrative develops, the books produced for them also become more sophisticated. Slightly older children (*c.*5–8 years) are catered for with simple storybooks, often featuring black and white illustrations. These books are frequently published in series, which encourage return sales through brand identity and collectability. Daisy Meadows's spectacularly successful 'Rainbow Magic' series falls into this category, as do Francesca Simon's tales of Horrid Henry. The quantity of output required by some of these series is provided by 'fiction factories' rather than by individual authors. Lucy Daniels, for example, is an invented author of the 'Animal Ark' books (who handily sits next to the ever-popular Roald Dahl on the bookshop shelf) with titles under her name commissioned from a number of jobbing writers. Other series demonstrate a clear gender segmentation. The sparkly, pretty 'Rainbow Magic' books are obviously targeted at girls, and such series reinforce gender stereotypes in their content and marketing. Publishers know they have a much readier young female market, but could be criticised for feeding a vicious circle in which boys are put off reading by the overwhelming pinkness of the book-shop shelves.

It is perhaps no surprise that in terms of quality of output, the market for storybooks for 5–8 year olds attracts less praise than books for both younger and older audiences. The appearance of various celebrities as writ-ers for younger readers, including glamour model Katie Price and former Spice Girl Geri Halliwell, did nothing to dispel an anxiety that children's books were becoming increasingly commodified (Hoyle, 2008). Jacqueline Wilson's books for this age group are a very notable exception – although still published with collectability in mind, with strongly branded covers and internal illustrations from Nick Sharratt.

Older fiction (*c.*9–12 and teens) is also published in series, though argu-ably less formulaically than books for the younger age group. These series also frequently follow (and often play with) the genre demarcations of books for the adult market: Darren Shan, horror; Louise Rennison and Meg Cabot, chick and tween lit; Anthony Horowitz, Charlie Higson and Robert Muchamore, spy novels and thrillers; and Julia Golding, historical adven-ture. Science fiction and fantasy in particular has figured large in the wake of Harry Potter and Pullman's *His Dark Materials*, with authors in this field including Eoin Colfer, Garth Nix and Jenny Nimmo.

The teen market varies widely: from the mass-market 'Gossip Girls' series to more literary and sometimes stand-alone titles (e.g. Malorie Blackman's 'Noughts and Crosses' series and books by Jenny Downham and Siobhan Dowd) and hard-hitting social realist teen books. The ever controversial Melvin Burgess falls into the latter category – his *Doing It* (2003) occa-sioned heated debate on its publication. Its frank and explicit depictions of teen sex proved provocative to many readers, including the author Anne Fine who made an unprecedented attack on it in the *Guardian*, calling it a 'grubby book' containing 'vile, disgusting musings'. She concluded that 'all of the publishers who have touched this novel should be deeply ashamed of themselves' (Fine, 2003). Other critics took the opposite line, and Burgess continues as an acclaimed, prize-winning writer of the genre (Sexton, 2003; Spring, 2003). The debate around this particular book – and around his other works, including *Junk* (1996) and *My Life as a Bitch* (2001) – foreground how altering conceptions of the 'child' (or the teenager in this case) can cause both controversy and anxiety among consumers and reviewers and within the children's publishing industry.

The backlist (previously published, in-print titles) and classic children's authors still play an important role in the sector. Nostalgia for their own childhood reading undoubtedly plays a greater role in purchasing decisions by parents, carers and other adults than in any other market sector. Long-lived classics include picture books such as Eric Carle's *The Very Hungry Caterpillar* and Judith Kerr's *The Tiger Who Came to Tea* and the work of Enid Blyton, Roald Dahl and C.S. Lewis. Publishers attempt to keep the classics alive through a number of strategies, including the refreshing of covers and tie-in editions to film or television adaptations. Oxford University Press and Great Ormond Street Hospital commissioned Geraldine McCaughrean to write a sequel to J.M. Barrie's *Peter Pan and Wendy*, published as *Peter Pan in Scarlet* (2006), spurring sales of Barrie's original, particular when rejacketed in a similar design to the newer book. Similarly, Lauren Child's illustrated version of *Pippi Longstocking* introduced Astrid Lindgren's heroine to a new generation of children more familiar with Charlie, Lola and Clarice Bean.

The turn of the century also witnessed a renewed interest in comic books and graphic novels, and an explosion of manga (Japanese and Japanese-style comic books) in the UK, with imported Japanese titles joining UK-commissioned work. There are manga versions of classic stories, and graphic novel adaptations of current favourites such as the adaptation by Donkin (2007) of *Artemis Fowl* (Colfer, 2001). Other contemporary trends include tie-in and merchandised publishing (including books and annuals relating to film and television series such as *Doctor Who*), activity, colouring and sticker books, and popular non-fiction series such as the *Horrible Histories* and *Horrible Science*.

While British children's books have proved a national and global success story, and the industry that produces them is the envy of other countries, there are international trends that have yet to catch on in the UK. The British market may have taken manga to its heart, but another, more recent Japanese publishing phenomenon should give the children's publishing sector in Britain much food for thought. In 2007, the Japanese bestseller list was dominated by books that started life as 'mobile phone novels' – literary content specifically written for digital delivery. That Japanese teenagers are both producers and heavy consumers of these novels puts paid to the idea that new technologies will necessarily kill off reading (Parry, 2007).

The diverse products of the children's publishing industry overviewed make a variety of different appeals to multiple audiences, using – as the next section on marketing and promotion explores – a range of different marketing strategies.

Marketing and promotion

Increasingly, the marketing of children's books at the turn of the century has followed the sales promotional path of the adult trade book market. Authors are introduced with large-scale promotional campaigns, targeting the mass market through consumer advertising, sales promotions (three-for-the-price-of-two offers), and digital marketing activities. The marketing of books occurs through a series of intermediaries, both from within the supply chain (e.g. publishers, wholesalers and distributors, retailers) and outside it (e.g. the media, librarians) (see Figure 9).

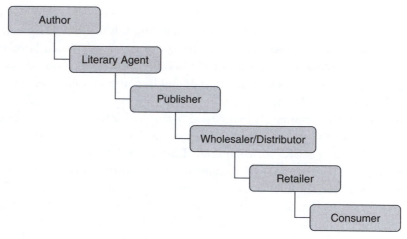

Figure 9   The book supply chain (adults').

Marketing strategies for books divide into 'push' and 'pull' activities. Push marketing is directed at the intermediaries (particularly retailers and the media), with the assumption that the intermediaries will push the communication along the supply chain, eventually arriving at the consumer. Pull marketing is focused at the consumer, through direct marketing (e.g. advertising campaigns and websites) which encourages consumers to go to retailers to make their purchases. An example which clarifies the difference between these two strategies is in the marketing of Meg Cabot. When her publisher Macmillan sent out publicity packs for *The Princess Diaries* containing miniature branded champagne bottles, they were clearly targeting booksellers and the media rather than the teen reader. But in their search for a cover girl for Cabot's new series 'Allie Finkle's Rules for Girls' through *Go Girl* magazine, the tween audience was directly addressed. Marketing campaigns for any trade book (children's or adults') will typically include a mix of push and pull marketing, with a range of activities targeted at intermediaries and consumers, communicating information about new products and converting interest into purchase.

By comparison, the passage of children's books from publisher to consumer, as Figure 10 shows, is further complicated by a series of key intermediaries or gatekeepers, through whom marketing messages pass and by whom purchasing decisions are made, principally parents, teachers and librarians. Although purchase on behalf of others is an important element of the adult book market (the Christmas gift market is crucial to the industry's annual viability), it is self-evident that in the children's book market – particularly but not exclusively at the younger end – adults are key purchasers. More than half (53 per cent) of the market for children's books is gift purchases by adults, with many more titles (44 per cent) being purchased by adults but not explicitly viewed as gifts (the *Books and the Consumer* figures survey only those aged 12+, so miss pocket-money purchases from the under-12s) (Book Marketing Limited, 2008).

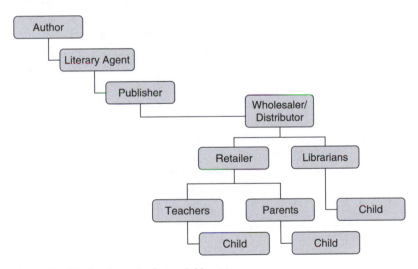

Figure 10   The book supply chain (children's).

The child is therefore only one of a number of individuals and agencies towards whom marketing is directed and, depending on the age of the child or teenager, there is an array of gatekeepers in the marketing communications for children's books. The websites of children's publishers demonstrate this: companies such as Random House (www.randomhouse.co.uk/childrens/home.htm) and Scholastic (www.scholastic.co.uk) have dedicated website sections specifically for teachers, parents and families, providing book-related activities and reading and literacy advice, in addition to book and author recommendations and promotion from their own lists.

The marketing departments of children's publishing companies have therefore created multifaceted marketing strategies, appealing to the book trade, a number of different gatekeepers, and children themselves. Authors are heavily involved with the promotion of their own books, participating in readings and book-related events in schools, libraries and bookshops and at literary festivals. The success Jacqueline Wilson has had in terms of sales and library borrowing figures is not solely the result of the appeal of her writing to its audience, but also of her concerted efforts over several years to *create* that audience via readings, public appearances and, eventually, the prolonged signing sessions for her fans mentioned earlier.

The digital age has presented opportunities for innovation in marketing and promotion. For marketers of children's books, the internet allows both publishers and authors to interact directly with their intended audience, in a medium that is familiar and attractive to their youthful audience. Publishers and authors have built promotional websites, which have developed from simple informational pages to a complex mix of free downloads, embedded video and podcasts, quizzes, messageboards and the chance to communicate directly with the author. Authors including Eoin Colfer (www.eoincolfer.com) and Robert Muchamore (www.cherubcampus.com) have websites which add value to their print products, attract attention to those products, encourage sales, and work towards creating communities of readers – and purchasers. Publishers and authors are also harnessing the power of online social networking, via sites such as Bebo, Facebook and MySpace. In 2007, Penguin created Spinebreakers (www.spinebreakers.co.uk), an online books-based teen community with teen editors – an idea developed from the earlier, independent reviews website Cool Reads (www.cool-reads.co.uk). The site is stuffed with downloads, competitions, and 'webisodes' – short, filmed extracts of new books, including Melvin Burgess's *Sara's Face*. Penguin has shown a perceptiveness about teen tastes and reading habits: the company branding (which is heavily marketed in other sectors) is toned down and has none of the cuteness of Puffin (their children's list), and promotes books both from its teen list but also from grown-up Penguins. For example, Spinebreakers features both Charlie Higson's *Young Bond* series and the rejacketed *Casino Royale* (riding on the interest of the film remake), alongside non-fiction including Eric Schlosser's *Fast Food Nation*.

The challenge in making such digital marketing efforts effective is to provide content that is genuinely interactive and that attracts its audience without making an offputting hard sell. Moreover, it is labour-intensive as content needs to be very regularly updated, and the channels of communication kept open. A Bebo page that has not been updated for several months is unlikely to hold the attention of a group of young people used to instant connectivity. For the moment, Penguin's Spinebreakers is full of good ideas – and intentions – but seems experimental. The extent to which it will push sales and develop reading habits is debatable. If more high-street retailers took the approach to the teenage section of their bookshops that Penguin is taking online, however, by including both teen and adults books, and siting this area away from the younger children's section, a more conducive bookshop environment for teenagers might well result.

In the rush to connect with children and young adults online, some publishers may have given less priority to marketing towards schools and libraries, through the provision, for example, of attractive marketing materials for classrooms and children's sections. Although surveys such as that of the National Literacy Trust (Clark et al., 2008) infer that there is a distinction made by children between types of reading for education and leisure, in school and out of school, schools in particular remain central to children's reading habits via their curricula, exam syllabuses and free reading. Reports on school set texts by the Qualifications and Curriculum Authority (QCA) in 2005, however, indicated some level of anxiety about the use of books in schools. Concerns and trends included children being set the same book across several years (examples include the classic *The Diary of Anne Frank* and Charles Dickens's *A Christmas Carol*), teachers often concentrating on perennial favourites (such as Philippa Pearce's *Tom's Midnight Garden* and Robert Westall's *The Machine Gunners*) rather than venturing towards newer books, and that an 'orthodoxy' was developing around newer books, with 'a relatively limited range of fiction' read in class (National Literacy Trust, n.d.). The politicisation of reading and books is inevitable in such debate, as the Government and its political opposition take positions on education and literacy. What is clear from the perspective of children's publisher's marketing departments is that they have to work hard to get their books read in schools, but that the dividends from such activity are potentially great.

In 2008, the UK Publishers Association (PA) introduced a scheme to classify books according to age. The aim behind the plans was to market books more effectively by providing a clear indication of the approximate age that any given book would appeal to in order to make purchasing decisions simpler, as with the DVD, film and computer games markets. After conducting market research, the PA decided to go ahead with plans to 'age-band' books with an indicated 'age plus' range located on the bar code on the back of both new and backlist books. The plans proved very controversial, and leading children's writers, including Philip Pullman, Anne Fine and J.K. Rowling, established an online petition (www.notoagebanding.org), which, by the planned implementation time, had amassed over four thousand signatories. Their principal objection was that age-range limitations on books would put off as many children as it would attract. A smaller, but vocal, constituency of authors (including Philip Reeve and Meg Rosoff) declared themselves in favour of the scheme. At the time of writing this chapter, it was unclear whether the PA's plans would be derailed by the authors' intervention. The authors' concerns were legitimate, but the argument for providing clearer guidance for less confident buyers, and for bringing books into line with other child-oriented products, link directly to industry and broader concerns to expand the book-buying market and to sustain and raise levels of reading.

One of the principal arguments put forward by the authors was the potential for books to be read by those whose age is both lower and higher than its core market and designated age range. The success in recent years of 'crossover' books would seem to support this argument. Pullman's own 'His Dark Materials' trilogy has been read by children, teenagers and adults, and Mark Haddon's *The Curious Incident of the Dog in the Night-Time* (2003) was successfully published in simultaneous children's and adults' editions from imprints of the same company (David Fickling Books and Jonathan Cape). The enormous fan base of Rowling's Harry Potter series consists of adults as well as children. David Fickling (who is also Pullman's editor) has stated that crossover is nothing more than an act of 'professional categorisation' or, in other words, a description of how books are sold and where they are shelved in bookshops and libraries. Crossover is, to Fickling, 'purely commercial and practical', as sales and marketing teams attempt to maximise exposure for titles by getting them displayed in as many locations as possible (Squires, 2006). Haddon stated that it was only with hindsight that this strategy was deemed successful, as 'the same book is reviewed in different places, advertised in different places and, most importantly, placed on two different shelves, and often in two different rooms, in the same bookshop' (www.commonwealthwriters.com/worldreaders/haddon.html). Fickling's and Haddon's comments might seem dismissive of the marketing efforts that have paid them such rewards, but nonetheless they give a clear indication of how marketing and sales strategies can radically influence the ways in which books are consumed and read, and by which children, teenagers, and adults come to books.

Literary awards

Another way in which children and teenagers may find their way to books is via literary prizes and book awards. These perform two key functions in the children's sector: rewarding achievement and promoting particular authors and genres. The former function casts prize judges as literary gatekeepers, while the latter allies prizes closely to the marketing and promotional activities of publishers and to the sales strategies of retail outlets. Prizes have been important in establishing and maintaining the careers of writers: J.K. Rowling was recognised early in her career by the award of the Smarties Prize to *Harry Potter and the Philosopher's Stone* (1997), and the Carnegie Medal was awarded to Philip Pullman for the first instalment of 'His Dark Materials'. The award of the Whitbread Book of the Year Award to Pullman for *The Amber Spyglass* (2000) denoted a changing environment in which children's books could be valued alongside those for adults – and occasionally be judged more successful.

There are a number of long-established British literary awards for children's books, notably the Carnegie and Greenaway Medals (established 1936 and 1955, respectively), followed by the *Guardian* Children's Fiction Award (1967), the Children's Whitbread (latterly Costa) Book Award (established 1972) and the Red House Children's Book Award (1980) (Allen 2005). By the 1990s and 2000s, the children's literary award scene was in a state of flux, both with the introduction of several new prizes, controversy over others (notably the Nestlé/ Smarties Children's Book Prize, which was withdrawn in 2008 after several years of bad press surrounding its sponsor) and new methods of judging. Traditionally, prize judges have been drawn from the gatekeeping community: Carnegie, for example, is judged by children's librarians; judges on other prize panels frequently include children's literary critics from newspapers, children's literature journals and universities. In more recent years, innovations have been introduced, as children have begun to play a role in the judging process, often by reading a shortlist selected by adult judges. Prizes such as the Smarties, Red House and Blue Peter Book awards are decided by a combination of young judges and popular vote, and although Carnegie retains its librarian judges, it has a very widespread shadowing scheme run via schools. This turn away from traditional gatekeepers can be interpreted in a number of different ways: as indicative of a more market-focused approach to prizes; as an attempt to engage children directly in literary prizes rather than via a series of intermediaries; as a belief that children may value different books from traditional gatekeepers; as a loss of faith in traditional gatekeeping and literary valuation systems; or as a desire to be seen as relevant in a changing world, in which cultural decisions are frequently turned over to popular vote.

Some prizes have rather different purposes. The Marsh Award for Children's Literature in Translation, for example, aims to highlight and encourage the production of books from non-English-language-speaking countries in UK translated editions. (The UK has, in comparison to other EU countries, a notoriously low rate of imported, translated books.) The Big Picture campaign's Best New Illustrators list, alongside its programme of events and exhibitions, similarly aims to promote a particular set of books within the larger sector. Prizes typically award particular types of books, or books with a particular target age group, with categories varying from award to award. The Blue Peter's categories of The Book I Couldn't Put Down, The Best Book to Read Aloud and The Best Book with Facts set up categories which differ from the standard criteria of literary 'quality', echoing some of the wider current debates about value versus readability, and culture versus commerce, in the children's book market.

Conclusion: the commodification of children's books

The publishing industry that has produced children's books at the turn of the century has retained its differences from the adult trade book sector, and yet it has also experienced a time of change. Much more emphasis is placed on generating income from the frontlist (titles in a company's current publishing programme), whereas the traditional economic model of children's books was based on the slower development of the backlist, and on books and authors with a lengthy shelf life. Commodification of children's books has thus followed the pattern of book publishing in the adult trade sector: heavily marketed, highly competitive and very market-focused. This change in the market – perceived (and mourned) by the children's editors and authors quoted in Kimberley Reynolds' 1998 article on the children's book market – has intensified considerably in more recent years.

Yet it would be wrong to tell only a negative story of the children's book market in the 1990s and 2000s. Children's authors in this period have received recognition – and sales – as never before. Children's books may be commodified, but it is also possible to argue that the market-focused approach of many children's publishers shows them to be in touch with the twenty-first-century child, who may harbour little nostalgia for earlier Golden Ages of children's books. Some of the current activities of children's publishers bring them and their products more in line with other media and leisure industries. But, in an environment in which books must struggle to retain their relevancy and appeal alongside newer technologies and competing leisure interests, this may be no bad thing.

References

Some of the material contained in this chapter previously appeared in different forms in Claire Squires's *Marketing Literature: The Making of Contemporary Writing in Britain*, 2006 (Basingstoke: Palgrave Macmillan) and in 'Living Happily Ever After?', *Publishing News London Book Fair Daily*, 15 April 2008.

Books and articles

Allen, R. 2005. *Winning Books*. Lichfield, Pied Piper Publishing.

Book Marketing Limited. 2008. *Books and the Consumer Summary Report*. London, BML/TNS.

Children's Writers' and Artists' Yearbook 2005. 2004. London, A&C Black.

Clark, C., Osborne, S. and Akerman, R. 2008. *Young People's Self-Perceptions as Readers: An Investigation Including Family, Peer and School Influences*. National Literacy Trust.

Clark, L. 2007. 'English Children's Literacy Levels "Among the Worst in the Developed World" ', *Daily Mail*, 28 November.

Colfer, E. 2001. *Artemis Fowl*. London, Viking.

Donkin, A. 2007. *Artemis Fowl*. (Graphic novel adapted from the original by Eoin Colfer.) London, Puffin.

Eccleshare, J. 2002. 'A Golden Time for Children's Books', *Publishers Weekly*, 18 February: 20–24.

Eccleshare, J. 2004. 'A Fast Track for Children's Books', *Publishers Weekly Special Report: British Publishing 2004*. 8 March: 16–18.

Fine, A. 2003. 'Filth, Whichever Way You Look at It', *Guardian*, 30 March.

Garner, R. 2002. 'School Literacy Hour Fails to Halt Decline in Reading Skills', *Independent*, 27 November.

Horn, C. 2006. 'Picture Books Fight Back', *The Bookseller*, 26 May.

Horn, C. 2008. 'Are the Kids All Right?', *The Bookseller*, 16 October.

Hoyle, B. 2008. 'Katie Price Causes Storm in a Literary D-Cup', *The Times*, 22 March.

Meek, J. 2004. 'To 3,000 Little Fans, with Love', *Guardian*, 11 March.

Parry, R.L. 2007. 'It ws bst f tms, it ws wrst f tms: Japan's Mobile Phone Literature', *The Times*, 6 December.

Pullman, P. 1999. 'Writing Children's Fiction: or You Cannot Be Serious', in Barry Turner (ed.) *The Writer's Handbook 2000*. London, Macmillan: 216-218.

Reynolds, K. 1998. 'Publishing Practices and the Practicalities of Publishing', in Kimberley Reynolds and Nicholas Tuckers (eds), *Children's Book Publishing in Britain Since 1945*. Aldershot, Scolar Press.

Richardson, P. and Taylor, G. 2008. *A Guide to The UK Publishing Industry*. London, Publishers Association.

Sexton, D. 2003. 'Boys' Own Stories', *Evening Standard*, 14 April.

Spring, K. 2003. 'Beastly Boys', *Observer*, 13 April.

Squires, C. 2006. Personal communication with David Fickling, 25 January.

Websites

Colfer, E. www.eoincolfer.com

Cool Reads. www.cool-reads.co.uk

Haddon, M. www.commonwealthwriters.com/worldreaders/haddon.html, accessed 22 May 2006.

Muchamore, R. www.cherubcampus.com

National Literacy Trust. n.d. www.literacytrust.org.uk/Database/natcur.html, accessed 1 September 2008.

www.notoagebanding.org

Public Lending Right. 2004. 'Wilson Topples Cookson', www.plr.uk.com/trends/pressrelease/feb2004.htm, accessed 22 May 2006.

Public Lending Right. 2006. 'Jacqueline Wilson: UK's Most Borrowed Author for Third Year Running', www.plr.uk.com/trends/pressrelease/feb2006(1).htm, accessed 22 May 2006.

Random House. www.randomhouse.co.uk/childrens/home.htm

Scholastic. www.scholastic.co.uk

Spinebreakers. spinebreakers.co.uk

3
Poetry

Introduction
Nicola J. Watson

The essays in this section are groundbreaking in their focus, because it has only been relatively recently that specialists in children's literature have turned their attention squarely to examining the phenomenon of poetry for children.

This new interest in poetry has perhaps derived from a revival of the saleability of poetry written specifically for children, in the shape of single-author collections such as Michael Rosen's *Mind Your Own Business* (1974), Roald Dahl's *Revolting Rhymes* (1982) or Grace Nichols's *Come into My Tropical Garden* (1988). Such has been the increase in the visibility of poetry for children that poets who have hitherto written solely for an adult audience – such as Carol Ann Duffy – have been publishing work for children inspired by their own experiences of parenting. These relatively recent collections can trace their lineage back to a handful of landmark collections of poetry for children from the First Golden Age, such as the English translation of *Struwwelpeter* (1848), Christina Rossetti's *Goblin Market* (1862), R.L. Stevenson's *A Child's Garden of Verses* (1885) and A.A. Milne's *When We Were Very Young* (1924) and *Now We Are Six* (1926).

But arguably the history of poetry for children is not satisfactorily encompassed in the history of such collections. Nor is it adequate to concentrate on the works of individual poets whose verse (often included within prose texts) has proved a firm favourite with a century or more of children: Lewis Carroll, Edward Lear, Hilaire Belloc and Rudyard Kipling amongst them. It may be, instead, that the history of poetry for children should be conceived so as to include or even privilege the history of the anthology. This is because the body of rhyme, verse and narrative poetry available to children, originally orally transmitted, has been made available to the literate and well-heeled child since the mid-nineteenth century largely in the form of the anthology pioneered in 1862 by Coventry Patmore's *Children's Garland* (1862) and the American poet John Greenleaf Whittier's *Child Life* (1871).

It is perhaps the hybrid and miscellaneous nature of the category of poetry for children, showcased in the form of the anthology, which has proved the real barrier to thinking about such poetry in generic terms, and it may be worth pausing here on this point. Pick up any children's poetry anthology, obscure or celebrated, and the difficulties and ambiguities inherent in endeavouring to discuss at any level of generalisation the nature of 'poetry for children' become plain. This is not merely because the category of children is impossibly inclusive, ranging from toddler to teens, or even because children as readers have been imagined quite differently at different historical periods. It is because such an anthology will be compounded of pieces deriving from peculiarly miscellaneous sources. There will be material that was originally oral and never had 'literary' pretensions, such as nursery rhymes (which, as the Opies showed, are often decayed political jingles, mutilated broadsheet ballads or songs from stage productions as well as lullabies and counting rhymes). There will be much other material originally designed for an adult audience in mind, and often excerpted from much longer works so as to represent illustrious, canonical authors, such as Shakespeare, an exercise which tends to change meanings (the witches' chant from *Macbeth*, often anthologised, becomes in the context of children's poetry both a surreal meditation on cooking with mother in the kitchen and an attractive exercise in imagining gross things to eat). On the other hand there will be some material specifically written for and addressed to children, which will often consciously mimic older oral forms such as lullabies and ballads. There will be generic variation – lyric, and narrative; there will be tonal variation – morality facing down anarchic nonsense; there will be stylistic variation, if only because the material will have been drawn from across historical periods.

Faced with this disparity of material, anthologists have typically displayed a need to make sense of it. They may foreground their selection criteria; there may be an effort to select verse felt to appeal across an age range. The books will be designed implicitly or explicitly with a notion of how they are to be used: to be read aloud from, to be read from together by adult and child, as a gift or a school prize for solitary reading by a bookish child with the not-so-hidden agenda of educating their taste towards poetry for adults. They may be designed to appeal to the eye, with extensive illustration, or principally to the ear, the extreme modern instance of this being the audiobook. In this sense anthologies successively describe the ways in which childhood and its relation to literature have been constructed and have changed over time, and this is because poetry for children is produced or designated by adults for an imaginary child, whether that is a childhood self remembered, a real child or an envisaged and implied child audience.

The essays

The first essay included here, Morag Styles's ' "From the Garden to the Street": A History of Poetry for Children', offers a history of verse written specifically for children condensed from her pioneering book-length survey. It describes the dual origins of such verse in Puritan efforts to teach religious, spiritual and moral lessons to the very young, and in eighteenth-century mothers' efforts to educate and entertain their children in the nursery. Styles argues that this verse then developed a Romantic view of childhood located in an idealised Arcadian or magic space in the early nineteenth century, a sensibility which remained dominant until the 1970s when it gave way to a relocation of poetry for children to urban spaces, whether street or school playground. She also outlines the parallel career of comic verse for children, which may also plausibly trace its origins back to the nursery rhyme. Styles's account offers a starting-point for those wishing to map individual poems in relation to generic traditions, or to think about single-author collections of poems as revisions of those traditions.

Styles's focus upon the relation of poetic form to changing notions of childhood provides a macro-narrative of poetry; by contrast, Lesley Jeffries concentrates upon the internal, stylistic evidence of the poetic text, endeavouring to identify stylistic commonalities within a modern anthology containing a wide range of poetry, some of which has been written expressly for children and some of which has been assigned to them. Her broad conclusion is that such poetry tends to be strongly invested in the aural, rather than in the visual. She notes, for example, a prevalence of strong, formal sound-patterning, whether rhythm, rhyme in its many forms or other forms of repetition and parallelism, and a tendency towards a strong sense of spoken language in the dramatic depiction of voice whether in monologue or dialogue.

Finally, 'From the Best Poets? Anthologies for Children,' also by Morag Styles, compares the practices of anthologising poetry originally designed for adults and poetry originally written expressly for children and comes to the polemical conclusion that 'poets writing for children are half as likely to be included in anthologies as those writing for adults', particularly if they are women, because 'poetry for children' has conventionally endeavoured to act as a stepping-stone to the national canon. Styles makes a powerful argument for revaluing the poets and poetry that specifically appeal to children, *because* of their appeal to children.

Further reading

Rosen, M. 2009. 'The Contexts of *A Child's Garden of Verses*', in H.K. Montgomery and N.J. Watson (eds) *Children's Literature: Classic Texts and Contemporary Trends*. Basingstoke, Palgrave.

Styles, M. 1998. *From the Garden to the Street: An Introduction to 300 Years of Poetry for Children*. London, Cassell.

Wullschläger, J. 2009. 'A.A. Milne: *When We Were Very Young*', in H.K. Montgomery and N.J. Watson (eds) *Children's Literature: Classic Texts and Contemporary Trends*. Basingstoke, Palgrave.

'From the Garden to the Street': The History of Poetry for Children
Morag Styles

Openings

In 1744 two significant books for children appeared. *A Little Pretty Pocket Book* and *Tommy Thumb's Song Book* came onto the market through the good offices of publisher John Newbery and bookseller Mary Cooper, respectively. These tiny books, both of which contained verse and were decorated with simple woodcuts, have been widely regarded as the first genuine children's literature (Darton, 1982: 1). In constructing this historical account of the development of children's poetry, however, I will first be going back in time to the precursors of these two little books, considering both the oral tradition on which *Tommy Thumb* was based and the literary tradition out of which it emerged. I will then turn to exploring how 'children's poetry', as represented in any number of 'classic' anthologies, evolved between the middle of the eighteenth century and the middle of the twentieth century from a mixture of oral and literary traditions: a cocktail of nursery rhymes, religious verse, romantic lyrics, nonsense and cautionary tales. I will be taking account of the changing sociocultural contexts in which poetry for children appeared, reflecting on the different ways in which childhood has been constructed within verse. I shall be considering in particular the importance of poets who specialised in writing for children, especially those who were most successful at writing in the voice of a child, even though their work has typically been marginalised by many anthologists and critical commentators over the years (see Styles, 1990, 1996, 1998). I will also be discussing the ways in which the field of children's poetry has always drawn from the adult canon. I will conclude with an exploration of how poets in late twentieth- and early twenty-first-century Britain writing for children have sought to revise and rethink the legacy of children's poetry.

My general argument is that, apart from comic verse which has had an important life and history of its own, most verse for a young audience has until very recently located itself in a rural setting, or a magic space, a metaphorical garden often associated with an Arcadian innocence connected to childhood. Kenneth Grahame revealingly described his role as editor in his preface to the *Cambridge Book of Poetry for Children* (1916) in just such terms:

> His task is to set up a wicket-gate giving admission to that wide domain, with its woodland glades, its pasture and arable, its walled and scented gardens here and there, and so on to its sunlit, and sometimes misty, mountain-tops [...] Always he must be proclaiming that there is joy, light and fresh air in that delectable country.
>
> Grahame, 1916: v

This idealised and highly Romantic view of poetry for the young dominated from the early nineteenth century until about 1970 when a post-Romantic verse (sometimes called 'urchin verse') came to prominence. Since then, poetry has moved to urban locations and developed a streetwise informality and a tendency to playfulness, breaking rules, flouting conventions, and changing the expected order of things.

The Puritan tradition

Before the growing impact of the thought of Locke and Rousseau in the latter half of the eighteenth century, and the influence of Romanticism which followed hard upon it, most children's literature was highly didactic. Poetry was no exception: the chief aim of its proponents was to teach children how to be dutiful, obedient, hard-working and God-fearing, in accordance with the Puritan religious project which dominated seventeenth-century England. As one historian of childhood notes, 'sustained interest in children in England began with the Puritans who were the first to puzzle over their nature and their place in society ... [and] to write books exclusively for children' (Somerville, 1992: 23).

One great Puritan writer turned his hand to poetry for children as well as fiction. John Bunyan's variously titled *Divine Emblems* (also called *A Book for Boys and Girls* and which became *Country Rhimes for Children*, 1686), is the earliest collection of verse for the young which is worth serious examination. It is also an excellent example of what Heather Glen has described as the 'ambivalence of intention' of some key Puritan writers, displaying a 'conflict between the desire to appeal to the child's sensibility' and the desire to serve a larger didactic purpose. She notes that 'there is a vivid colloquial life about much of the poetry – an imaginative effort to enter the child's way of seeing the world – which must have been very attractive to young readers' (Glen, 1983: 10–12). In his preface, Bunyan acknowledges to the adult reader that in order to save the souls of his young audience, he must play with them, and make them forget that there is a serious adult addressing them:

> Wherefore good reader, that I save them may,
> I now with them, the very Dottrill play.
> And since at Gravity they make a Tush
> My very Beard I cast behind the Bush.
> And like a Fool stand fing'ring of their Toys,
> And all to show them they are Girls and Boys.

Poetically, there is something to applaud in *Country Rhimes:* the butterfly whose 'all her all is lighter than a feather'; the snail who 'tho' she doth but very softly go,/ However, 'tis not fast, nor slow, but sure'; the frog who is by nature 'both damp and cold/ Her mouth is large, her belly much will hold'; the hen who 'About the yard she cackling now doth go,/ To tell what t'was she on her nest did do'. Darton praises the 'touches of homeliness' and 'queer gentleness' (Darton, 1982: 64–65) that Bunyan's verse here displays, while Christopher Hill talks of his depiction of 'familiar natural objects' as 'invariably far livelier and in better verse than the moral drawn' (Hill, 1989: 270).

Other religious poets with an interest in a young audience included Isaac Watts, who wrote *Divine Songs Attempted in Easy Language for the Use of Children* some twenty years later in 1715. It was a best-seller for a century after its publication. Lewis Carroll's parody of Watts's typically industrious busy bee ('How doth the little busy Bee/Improve each shining Hour,/And gather honey all the day/From every opening Flower!' (Watts, 1971: 238)) with his ironical crocodile ('How doth the little crocodile/Improve his shining tail') in *Alice's Adventures in Wonderland* (Carroll, 1973: 37) is a tribute to the continuing popularity of his verse in Victorian culture. Darton comments on the subtle changes in the way children were perceived by the early eighteenth century which are suggested by Watts's verses: 'They must ever be a landmark, early but clear, in the intimate family history of the English child, who was at last beginning to be seen to be a little adventurous pilgrim worth watching with love and care' (Darton, 1982: 110–11). Despite a fair amount of moralising, Watts had a lyric gift and a kinder tone than Bunyan: 'Hush! my dear, lie still and slumber, / Holy angels guard thy bed!' (Watts, 1971: 267).

Religious poetry in the early eighteenth century would largely have been experienced by most children in the form of the hymns they sang at church on Sunday. Some of them had fine lyrics by poets such as Charles Wesley, Christopher Smart and Anna Barbauld. Later in the nineteenth century, the Taylor sisters wrote hymns which are largely forgotten, but several by Cecil Frances Alexander are still popular today, such as 'Once in Royal David's City' and 'All Things Bright and Beautiful'. The prolific Eleanor Farjeon wrote poetry and hymns for children during the first half of the twentieth century. 'Morning Has Broken' is a good example of her light touch and shows how religious verse modified over the centuries to become much more tender and child-centred.

Out of the nursery

If the eighteenth century saw the evolution of religious verse for children, it also saw the entry of the oral tradition of verse into the realm of print culture. An important dimension of poetry is its aural quality and its invocation of the spoken voice, so we must not overlook that body of verse which flows from mother to child and from child to child over generations – a key part of the oral tradition in all its variety, some of it very ancient indeed in origin. This body of verse encompasses many genres, ranging from lullabies and nursery rhymes (sometimes called Mother Goose rhymes) to nonsense and playground rhymes. John Goldthwaite emphasises the range of reference of these 'random snatches of silliness' which begin with 'lullabies for the newborn' and end 'in the town churchyard'. Goldthwaite also comments on their universality and longevity and on the consequent difficulty of pinning down the origins, geographical or historical, of nursery rhymes ('New songs are piping into existence in odd corners of the planet every day') and he notes their foundational cultural importance: 'This is the only book in the world that everyone in the world, literate and illiterate alike, knows some of by heart' (Goldthwaite, 1996: 14).

In *The Oxford Dictionary of Nursery Rhymes*, Iona and Peter Opie, the best-known collectors of this fine tradition, remind us that most of these rhymes were not 'composed' for children at all, suggesting that they are, rather, fragments of ballads, folk songs, street cries, proverbs, stage productions, rude jokes, counting rhymes, lullabies, old customs and much more besides. The most robust nursery verse is decidedly oral in origin and transmission, handed

down by word of mouth and is created or re-created by the young themselves –
playground rhymes that may accompany skipping or ball games or are chanted
and sung for the sheer fun of it – the ruder the better!

> Donkey walks on four legs
>   And I walk on two;
> The last one I saw
>   Was very like you.

Opie, 1992: 33

Tommy Thumb's Song Book (Cooper, 1744) was the first attempt to put
nursery rhymes from the oral tradition into print. Some of the ruder ones,
no doubt, delighted the young of their time, just as similar rhymes do today:
'Piss a bed/Piss a bed/Barley butt/Your bum is so heavy/You can't get up'.
(see Figure 11). Contemporary books of nursery rhymes still tend to include

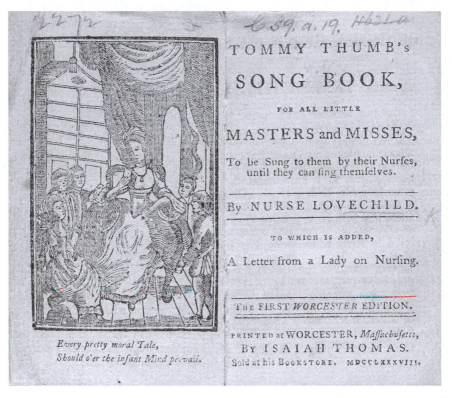

Figure 11 Frontispiece, 'Nurse Lovechild', *Tommy Thumb's Song Book* (1788), London:
Mary Cooper, 1788, copperplates. By permission of the British Library. © British Library Board.
All Rights Reserved. Shelfmark: C.59.a.19.

some that were in *Tommy Thumb's Song Book*; 'Tommy Tucker', 'Baa Baa Black Sheep', 'Mistress Mary', 'Ride a Cock Horse' and many others were first printed in this collection. Modern literary rhymes are often parodies of these originals. For example, the ending of 'Monday's Child' that I learned as a child – 'The child that's born on the Sabbath day/Is bonny and blithe and good and gay' was rewritten by Colin McNaughton in 1987 as:

> And the child that's born on the seventh day
> Is a pain in the neck like the rest, OK!

At the same time, playground rhymes continue to develop. Because they are essentially oral, changes over time are less documented, but I am aware of several rhymes which I learned in north-east Scotland as a child still being chanted and sung in southern English playgrounds, but in updated form.

From the beginning of the nineteenth century, women had much to do with the literary development of the nursery rhyme as they wrote little ditties to please young children. For example, Sarah Martin published 'Old Mother Hubbard' in 1805 and the super-talented dog and her owner have delighted children ever since. Here's a verse:

> She went to the hosier's
> To buy him some hose;
> But when she came back
> He was dressed in her clothes.

Mary Howitt composed 'The Spider and the Fly' in 1834, a Mrs Pearson is thought to have written 'Dame Wiggins of Lee' in 1823, and it was certainly Sarah Hale who wrote 'Mary Had a Little Lamb' in about 1830. But although these rhymes are still known today, and although scholarship has unearthed their authorship, the women who composed them are rarely credited in collections old and new.[1]

One of the most famous and well-loved of these women-authored nursery rhymes must be 'Twinkle, Twinkle, Little Star' written by Jane Taylor in 1806, cited as 'anonymous' in several anthologies between the nineteenth century and the present day. 'The Star', to give it its proper title, is a flawless piece of nursery verse, so light it rings like a bell. The glory of the night sky is conveyed in simple language, using clear but striking imagery, giving her young audience more space in which to 'wonder' than any other poem that went before. It is accessible, child-centred, domestic, asking questions instead of telling the child what to think, leaving room for young readers to imagine the starlight 'peeping' through their bedroom curtains and to conjure up their own 'travellers in the dark'. This apparently modest little rhyme is a landmark in children's poetry because it is one of the first non-didactic poems ever composed for the young. Two years before, Jane had co-authored *Original Poems for Infant Minds* (1804) with her sister Ann and other contributors, a collection which made quite an impression on middle-class nurseries. It was quickly followed by *Rhymes for the Nursery* (1806). Both volumes sold in large numbers and others were quick to take up this new, more child-centred style of poetry. Charles and Mary Lamb published *Poetry for Children* in the same mode in 1809, though their poems were less accomplished and appealing to children than those of the Taylor sisters. Individual poems from the two collections became so well known that they were repeatedly parodied, most notably again by Lewis Carroll:

> Twinkle twinkle little bat,
> How I wonder what you're at.
> Up above the world so high
> Like a tea-tray in the sky!

Carroll, 1865

One reason why the Taylors were so popular was the way they explored and vocalised the bond between mothers and babies:

> Come, dear, and sit upon my knee,
> And give me kisses, one, two, three,
> And tell me whether you love me,
> My baby.

'The Kind Mamma', Taylor, 1806

A direct line can be drawn from the Taylor sisters to the Victorian poet Christina Rossetti, who produced her only volume of poetry for children, *Sing-Song: A Nursery Rhyme Book*, in 1872, a volume which is also notable for its celebration of the mother–baby relationship:

> Love me, – I love you,
>   Love me, my baby;
> Sing it high, sing it low,
>   Sing it as it may be.
> Mother's arms under you,
>
> Her eyes above you
>   Sing it high, sing it low,
> Love me, – I love you.

While the Taylors' verse should be recognised and cherished for its newly tender nature, *Sing-Song* is of a different order, with a quality of prosody and range of tone more musical and assured. It includes a sensuous expression of love between the mother and the child in many poems, as well as nonsense, nature poems, songs, riddles, kind lessons in verse, finger rhymes and lullabies. It is a model of how playful nursery verse can sing both high and low. Rossetti's poems are deceptively simple and unobtrusive, yet subtle. *Sing-Song* is hard to get hold of these days, though a few individual poems from it are still regularly anthologised, such as this powerful riddle:

> What are heavy? sea-sand and sorrow:
> What are brief? today and tomorrow:
> What are frail? spring blossoms and youth:
> What are deep? the ocean and truth.

Romantic visions

The most long-lasting collection of poetry for children in the eighteenth century and beyond has proved to be William Blake's *Songs of Innocence* (1789), reissued with *Songs of Experience* in 1794 as a pair 'shewing the two contrary states of the human heart'. While some scholars do not regard Blake as in any sense a children's writer, others challenge that view (Glen, 1983; Leader, 1981; Watson, 2001). Indeed, it is difficult to argue that a collection of poetry which contains the following lines in the opening poem does not include children in its address: 'Piper, sit thee down and write/ In a book that *all* may read ... /And I wrote my happy songs /*Every child* may joy to hear' (my italics). As Darton put it, with these two volumes 'a great imaginative writer had ... broken into the narrow library that others were toiling so laboriously to fill for children' (Darton, 1982: 179). As I've already remarked, children's poetry in Blake's time tended to be severe and authoritarian and to offer little light relief. There were certain exceptions; cheap chapbooks, hawked by peddlers the length and breadth of the country and performed within communities by those who could read, contained the popular literature of the day – exciting tales, including songs and rhymes. There were also the companions and descendants of *Tommy Thumb* being published and sold by Newbery and other enterprising publisher/booksellers from the middle of the eighteenth century, but these books would have been beyond the pocket of any but middle- and upper-class children, as, indeed, would have been the case with Blake's *Songs*. The importance of *Songs of Innocence* for scholars of children's literature lies primarily in the way that it is felt to have challenged the prevailing didactic tone of writing for children at the end of the eighteenth century. Victor Watson argues that 'Blake was addressing children in ways which were radically new, challenging parents' assumptions about instructional verse.' He notes their new range – 'some are expressions of a young child's developing sense of goodness; some are poems for bedtime; one is a nonsense poem; in others, children take on the language of adults to address creatures smaller than themselves' – and their dramatisation of the new domestic tenderness being more generally celebrated at the time: 'He was the first great poet to draw on the oral traditions of the eighteenth-century nursery, capturing the gentle rhetoric of mothers singing and talking with their children' (Watson, 2001: 662).

Songs of Innocence opens with a laughing child demanding that the author/piper 'pipe that song again'. It challenges the prevailing common sense that adults know best and this theme is echoed in poem after poem. In 'Nurse's Song', for example, although she tells her charges to 'come home, my children, the sun is gone down, / And the dews of night arise', it is the children, not the nurse, who really decide when it's time to go to bed ('Well, well, go and play till the light fades away, / And then go home to bed'). Watson notes that this is counterpointed by 'hints of a darker reality' perceptible primarily to the adult reader: 'Blake was the first writer to employ a kind of irony unique to children's literature.' 'The Chimney Sweeper', superficially like other children's verse typical of the time, while offering a simple reassuring message to a very young child, simultaneously challenges the adult with a set of questions about the exploitation of children (Watson, 2001: 662).

Blake's work did not reach a wide readership in his own time, partly because it was too original to be valued by most contemporaries, partly because of Blake's eccentric reputation and partly because the books themselves were so expensive, as Blake printed, bound and hand-coloured each elaborately illustrated copy himself. (With hindsight, these books were pioneering examples of picture-book poetry, achieving, in place of the more common and often rather crude woodcuts in black and white, a symbiotic union between word and image in an imaginary pastoral setting.) However, anthologies of poetry for children since the 1830s (when the first affordable publication of *Songs of Innocence* appeared in print) have regularly included Blake's poetry. It is hard now to imagine a 'classic' collection of poetry for children without a Blake poem at its heart because of the power of his poetry still to move and inspire both old and young readers more than two hundred years after it was first written.

Blake's successors – Coleridge, Wordsworth, Clare, Byron, Shelley – did not write with children in mind, except for Keats who occasionally composed poems for his little sister, Fanny, including the delightful 'Meg Merrilies' which showcases Keats' lyric gift and narrative flair. It is, however, worth drawing attention to poems by the Romantics, as they have become a mainstay of children's classic anthologies since the first half of the nineteenth century. Their shorter and simpler poems have often been regarded as especially suitable for children because they make links between childhood and the natural world. In this way, some adult poems become part of the canon of children's poetry; Wordsworth's 'Daffodils', for example, is so well known through having been anthologised for the young as to have become almost a cliché. Coleridge's long narrative poem in ballad form, 'The Rime of the Ancient Mariner', was certainly not originally intended for children, but the poem, which frequently appears whole or in excerpts in various anthologies for children, has been proven to hold a young audience with its combination of spell-binding imagery, powerful storytelling and memorable (and memorisable) lines, such as 'Water, water, everywhere / And all the boards did shrink. / Water, water everywhere, / Nor any drop to drink'.

Nonsense

So far, I have been dealing mainly with a tradition of moral verse, whether overtly didactic or not, but running alongside it (and often making sardonic comments upon it, as in the case of Lewis Carroll) is a tradition of nonsense verse. If Romantic poetry can be traced back to Puritan poetry, nonsense can be traced back to the wildness of the nursery rhyme. Humour is an important strand in children's poetry – it always has been and probably always will be. Kornei Chukovsky notes children's delight in puns and riddles as 'not just turning word meanings upside-down, but playing with the effects of two meanings considered simultaneously, or [transforming] parts of words for new effects'. He also stresses the universality of nonsense, identifying 'the inexhaustible need of every healthy child of every era and of every nation to introduce nonsense into his [sic] small but orderly world'. He accounts for the appeal of nonsense by suggesting that it actually strengthens the child's sense of reality. 'Why is it', he asks, 'that so many typical children's rhymes, approved by millions of youngsters in the course of many centuries, cultivate with such persistence the obvious violation of reality? ... [T]o be able to respond to these playful rhymes the child must have a knowledge of the real order of things' (Chukovsky, 1976: 601–6). Anthony Burgess described the British nonsense tradition in a similar vein as 'only a bizarre way of making sense ... it is a *playful*, pragmatic way of interpreting the universe' (Burgess, quoted in Tigges, 1987: 18–21). Edward Strachey defined nonsense as bringing 'forward the incongruities of all things within us and without us ... through its contradictions' (Strachey, 1994: 7–8). For whatever reason, children the world over seem to find it hilarious to turn the 'real order of things' upside down.

The typical yoking of nonsense content with strong verse form, however, balances such disorder against rigid order. Elizabeth Sewell points to the dialogic character of nonsense verse which 'consists in the mind's employing its tendency towards order to engage its contrary tendency towards disorder, keeping the latter perpetually in play and so in check' (Sewell, 1952: 48). The famous children's illustrator Quentin Blake similarly comments:

> There is one respect in which nonsense poetry isn't the least bit crazy: it is the way the poems are made. The rhymes, the metre, the verse-forms are just as regular as, and in many cases identical with, those of more serious poems. Indeed, it's the fact that nonsense poems preserve this decorum that makes them so effective.
>
> Blake, 1994: 5

Two great nonsense poets, Edward Lear and Lewis Carroll, dominated the Victorian period, and their poems have stood the test of time since, even though the latter only wrote a handful of nonsense poems embedded within his fiction plus 'The Hunting of the Snark' which has never been a childhood favourite. 'Jabberwocky', with its brilliantly inventive language and mock-heroic style, was probably the pinnacle of that anarchic imagination realised in verse. Lear's talent first saw the light of day in *A Book of Nonsense* (1846) which featured limericks accompanied by his own exuberant drawings. 'The Owl and the Pussycat' (from *Nonsense Songs and Stories*, 1872) was voted the Nation's Favourite Children's Poem in Britain a few years ago. Artist, musician, writer, Lear offered readers the delights of his lavish imagination in drawings as well as through limericks, songs and stories, creating a cornucopia of extravagant characters and settings in writing that is very close to music.

A popular comic form related to the irreverence of nonsense which developed during the nineteenth century was cautionary verse. This featured 'over-the-top', tongue-in-cheek tales of warning, usually directed at naughty children – Hilaire Belloc's Matilda, for example, 'told lies and was burned to death'. The extremity of the punishment is not meant to be taken seriously, though the form did evolve from moral tales in verse which *were* intended as stern lessons for the young. Heinrich Hoffmann's *Struwwelpeter* (1845) was written to amuse his son, but if 'The Story of Little Suck-a-Thumb' and its accompanying illustrations is anything to go by, it would have terrified the child half to death! Belloc's *The Bad Child's Book of Beasts* (1896) and subsequent collections sold in huge numbers. Marriott Edgar gave the form a Yorkshire spin in the endearing 'The Lion and Albert' and the twentieth-century American humorists Shel Silverstein and Ogden Nash were also partial to the cautionary; in Silverstein's case, the zany, surreal drawings which accompanied his verse added strongly to its appeal. More recently, Roald Dahl reworked the tradition with his updated versifications of fairy tales in *Dirty Beasts* and *Revolting Rhymes*; his 'Red Riding Hood' serves as a cautionary tale not to girls, but to wolves (see Plate 13). Wendy Cope has also favoured this form on occasion and her poem 'Kenneth' is a good example of her dry wit.

The best of plays

The nineteenth century also saw the publication of what many regard as the most significant collection for children of all time. Robert Louis Stevenson's *A Child's Garden of Verses* (1885) has never been out of print. Its significance for the history of children's poetry is that this was the first time a major poet had written for children in the first person, as if in the voice of a child. It was also ground-breaking in being an extensive evocation and celebration of children's play. In analysing why these poems have continued to resonate for so many children and adults half a dozen generations after they were written, Darton argues for the authenticity of the depiction of child experience: 'there are few thoughts in that little 1885 volume ... that children have not felt' and 'even though the grown-up can be detected using his literary art to express them ... the substance is the fabric of a child's mind' (Darton, 1982: 314).[2] An example of this is 'Shadow March'. Stevenson suffered night terrors as a child, partly as a result of chronic illness which induced high temperatures and sleeplessness and partly because his devoted and adored nurse filled the invalid's head up with her hellfire-and-damnation Calvinist beliefs. In this stanza from 'Shadow March' some of the anxieties of childhood seep into the child's voice:

> The shadow of the balusters, the shadow of the lamp,
> The shadow of the child that goes to bed –
> All the wicked shadows coming tramp, tramp, tramp,
> With the black night overhead.

The collection's long-standing success may also be attributed to its ability to appeal to both child and adult audiences. The juxtaposition of make-believe and reality may be the prerogative of childhood but it also has particular attraction for adults, something Stevenson exploited brilliantly in his poetry. 'From a Railway Carriage' has always been one of the most popular poems with older readers with its hallucinatory evocation of the landscape 'whistling by'. The key to the whole collection is the final poem. Addressed 'To Any Reader', it meditates upon the position of the adult reader, facing up to the fact that childhood cannot last forever (the child 'has grown up and gone away') and that adults will always view childhood with regret and nostalgia, and through the imagination:

> And it is but a child of air
> That lingers in the garden there.

But perhaps one of the overwhelming reasons for the collection's success is that Stevenson sought to celebrate the pleasures and playfulness of childhood, mostly editing out the miseries which most of us experience as well.

Story and song

I have already touched on Victorian narrative poetry in the form of the non-sense verse of Lear and Carroll, but there are many other famous instances. Browning's inventive verse melodrama, 'The Pied Piper of Hamelin', Longfellow's appealing and much-parodied 'Song of Hiawatha' and Tennyson's heroic Arthurian tale, 'The Lady of Shalott' are all still favourites in classic anthologies for children. They appeal to children because their language is accessible, they have strong story-lines, and they are written in memorable verse with a strong metre. Narrative verse continued to be popular as a mode in the first half of the twentieth century. I might cite here Alfred Noyes's dramatic 'The Highwayman'. This continuing vitality of narrative verse was counterbalanced in the first half of the twentieth century by gentle, lyrical, song-like verse largely in the romantic tradition, and here Walter de la Mare is the key figure in children's poetry. *Peacock Pie* (1913) established his name and he went on to write many more collections of poetry and stories. De la Mare was famous for a 'mysterious otherworldliness' (Alton, quoted in Watson, 2001:201), exemplified by the opening of 'Silver':

> Slowly, silently, now the moon
> Walks the night in her silver shoon;
> This way, and that, she peers, and sees
> Silver fruit upon silver trees ...

But the lyrical could coexist with narrative; de la Mare could also tell a story in verse. 'The Listeners' is one of his most famous poems and its whispering mystery still beguiles young readers. He also merits mention as an anthologist who mixed both modes: his outstanding anthology, *Come Hither* (1923), dedicated to 'the young of all ages', is even today regarded as a model of its kind.

In most respects the poetry of the second half of the twentieth century would move decisively away from this romantic lyric tradition, and this can be seen by looking briefly at the output of two of the most important poets writing for children at the time, Charles Causley and Ted Hughes. Causley is famous as a balladeer, writing for children and adults alike, making no great distinction between them as audiences. Although Causley's verse can be tender and lyrical, his other modes include protest ('Timothy Winters', 'The Jolly Hunter', 'My Mother Saw a Dancing Bear', 'On St Catherine's Day'), the autobiographical ('Tavistock Goose Fair' is a powerful but understated memory of his father before he died in the First World War), magic and mystery in poems like 'Tell Me Sarah Jane', and humour, creating memorable comic characters in collection after collection, including Colonel Fazackerley in *Figgie Hobbin* (1970). He was also a gifted, meticulous anthologist and his *Puffin Book of Magic Verse* and *Puffin Book of Salt-Sea Verse* are classics of their kind, as is *The Sun, Dancing*, a book of Christian verse with plenty to offer non-religious readers. He was teamed with some outstanding illustrators, including Gerald Rose, Charles Keeping, Michael Foreman and John Lawrence. Like Causley, the sometime poet laureate Ted Hughes wrote for both children and adults. Hughes is about as far away from the Romantic tradition, and especially from the Romantic treatment of childhood, as you can get. Indeed, he doesn't write about children in his poetry, although he was committed to writing for them. His muscular nature poetry makes few allowances for young readers because Hughes believed that children 'will accept plastic toys, if that's all they're given, but their true driving passion is to get possession of the codes of adult reality – of the real world' (Hughes quoted by Pirrie, 2001: 351). His first poetry book for children was *Meet My Folks* (1961), but most critics agree that *What is the Truth?* (1984) is Hughes' greatest work for children – a farmyard fable where God comes down to earth to speak the 'truth' about human beings as well as animals. Hughes's poetry falls into two categories which frequently overlap: starkly realistic descriptions of the animal world with occasional reference to human beings' relationships with them, and the evocation of a numinous, mythic, mystical world in collections such as *Moon-Whales* (1991) and *The Mermaid's Purse* (1999). Hughes' powerful poetry was illustrated by some exceptional artists, including Leonard Baskin and R.J. Lloyd, noted for their power rather than for lyricism.

Streetwise poetry

From the vantage-point of the early twenty-first century, what has changed most dramatically over the last two and a half centuries is that which is considered suitable to amuse a young audience. The best recent poetry is no longer just written for children or about children, but aspires to be in the playground *with* children. Today, there are no poets writing for children who are not playful at least some of the time and who do not conspicuously value playfulness. Other great departures from the past include the setting of poetry in urban rather than rural environments, the favouring of gritty realism, and a marked willingness to explore difficult and provocative subjects. John Rowe Townsend coined the term 'urchin verse' to describe this new wave of poetry which was ushered in with Michael Rosen's *Mind Your Own Business* in 1974. This verse looked like scraps and jottings. The poems came without titles, contained little punctuation, few rhymes or regular metre, and frequently took the form of incomplete conversations between a child and adult, making the reader work to understand who was saying what. This informality of language and form deliberately broke with the past by adopting in this way the voice of a child, and the subject of the poetry is an interrogation of authority and hierarchy within the family and beyond from a child perspective. Rosen does this again and again in poems such as 'Rodge Said' (from *You Tell Me*, 1979), where the protagonist complains that 'Teachers ... want it all ways.' The child's voice continues, 'You're jumping up and down on a chair / or something' when the teachers 'grab hold of you', saying, 'Would you do that in your own home?' If you answer 'No', the poem explains, they say, 'Well don't do it here then.' If the answer is 'Yes', the reply is 'Well, we don't want this kind of thing / going on here / thank you very much.' Thus, according to Rodge, 'they get you all ways.'

Rosen's debut was quickly followed by collections by Roger McGough, Kit Wright, Gareth Owen, Adrian Mitchell, Allan Ahlberg, Brian Patten, Adrian Henri, Jackie Kay and others. In the same period, talented Caribbean/British poets began to experiment with a colloquial mixture of Creole and standard English in children's poetry – James Berry, John Agard, Valerie Bloom, Grace Nichols and Benjamin Zephaniah are some of the best known of these writers. Celebrating the vitality and orality of dialect poetry on the page and in live performance, these poets opened up issues of race and identity in a playful and ironic way, revising inherited representations of childhood and children's voice to include the everyday experience of black children in Britain.

Urchin verse is various in form. Some writers are steeped in the literary traditions of English poetry, while others experiment with the oral, embodying vernacular voices in free verse. But what is common to urchin verse is the celebrating and seeking to be inclusive of previously excluded groups and promoting the value of each child's individual experience. It focuses on personal experience within real-life settings, favours the weak and relatively powerless over the powerful and authoritarian, and makes emotional relationships a central part of its subject matter, detailing the joy, pain and comedy of changing family and peer-group experience. Urchin verse (good and bad) aims deliberately to foreground a new conception of childhood for the twenty-first century, in touch with the way many children live now.

Notes

1. For more information about the women from the past whose poetry for children deserves to be better known, see Styles, 1990: 177–205 and the essay elsewhere in this section reprinted from Styles, 1998.
2. For further information on critics' views of Stevenson's poetry, see Styles, 1999.

References

I have, in some instances, drawn in small ways on commentary on poets and poems from Styles 1998 and 2006.

Blake, Q. 1994. *The Puffin Book of Nonsense Verse*. London, Penguin.

Carroll, L. [1865] 1973. *Alice's Adventures in Wonderland*. London. Puffin.

Chukovsky, K. 1976. 'The Sense of Nonsense Verse', in J. Bruner et al. (eds) *Play: Its Role in Development and Evolution*. Harmondsworth, Penguin.

Cooper, M. 1744. *Tommy Thumb's Song Book*. London.

Darton, F.J. Harvey. 1982. *Children's Books in England*, 3rd edn, revised by B. Alderson. Cambridge, Cambridge University Press.

de la Mare, W. 1944. *Collected Rhymes and Verse*. London, Faber.

Glen, H. 1983. *Vision and Disenchantment: Blake's Songs and Wordsworth's Lyrical Ballads*. Cambridge, Cambridge University Press.

Goldthwaite, J. 1996. *The Natural History of Make-Believe*. Oxford, Oxford University Press.

Grahame, K. (ed.) 1916. *The Cambridge Book of Poetry for Children*. Cambridge, Cambridge University Press.

Hill, C. 1989. *A Turbulent, Seditious and Factitious People: John Bunyan and His Church 1628–1688*. Oxford, Oxford University Press.

Leader, Z. 1981. *Reading Blake's Songs*. London, Routledge & Kegan Paul.

McGough, R. and Rosen, M. 1979. *You Tell Me*. London, Penguin.

Opie, I. and P. 1992. *I Saw Esau: The Schoolchild's Pocket Book*. London, Walker.

Pirrie, J. 2001. 'A Measure of Grace: The Teacher's Story', in N. Ganmage (ed.) *The Epic Poise: A Celebration of Ted Hughes*. London, Faber & Faber.

Rosen, M. 1974. *Mind Your Own Business*. London, André Deutsch.

Sewell, E. 1952. *The Field of Nonsense*. London, Chatto & Windus.

Somerville, C.J. 1992. *The Discovery of Childhood in Puritan England*. London, University of Georgia Press.

Stevenson, R.L. 1885. *A Child's Garden of Verses*. London, Longmans & Green.

Strachey, E. 1994. Introduction to *Complete Nonsense of Edward Lear*. Ware, Wordsworth.

Styles, M. 1990. 'Lost from the Nursery: Women Writing Poetry for Children 1800–1850', *Signal*, 63: 177–205.

Styles, M. 1997. '"Of the Spontaneous Kind": Women Writing Poetry for Children from Vane Johnson to Christina Rossetti', in M. Hilton, M. Styles and V. Watson (eds) *Opening the Nursery Door: Reading, Writing and Childhood 1600–1900*. London, Routledge.

Styles, M. 1998. *'From the Garden to the Street': 300 Years of Poetry for Children*. London, Cassell.

Styles, M. 1999. 'The Best of Plays', in E. Bearne and V. Watson (eds) *Where Texts and Children Meet*. London, Routledge.

Styles, M. 2000. '"Play-business": Issues Raised by R.L. Stevenson's Classic Collection, *A Child's Garden of Verses*', in E. Bearne and V. Watson (eds) *Where Texts and Children Meet*. London, Routledge.

Styles, M. 2006. 'Poetry', in P. Hunt (ed.) *International Companion for Children's Literature*. London, Routledge.

Tigges, W. 1987. *Explorations in the Field of Nonsense*. Amsterdam, Rodopi.

Watson, V. 2001. *The Cambridge Guide to Children's Books*. Cambridge, Cambridge University Press.

Watts, I. 1971. *Divine Songs*. Intro. J.H.P. Pafford. Oxford, Oxford University Press.

Woollcott, A. (ed.) 1989. *The Complete Works of Lewis Carroll*. London, Nonesuch.

The Language of Poems for Children:
A Stylistic Case Study
Lesley Jeffries

What is the language of poems for children? Is it significantly different from
the poetic style that is used in poems for adults? These questions, of course,
assume that there *is* such a thing as literary or poetic language, which is
controversial (Leech, 2008: 56). However, to the extent that poetic language
has been described at all, we can make some comparisons (Leech, 1969;
Jeffries, 1993). To make the task manageable, I focus on a recent collection
edited by Roger McGough, *100 Best Poems for Children* (2002). A first
glance at this anthology confirms further difficulties in proposing the category of 'poems for children', since this volume, like many others intended
for children, includes a number of poems which were written for adults,
and are read by adults, including Matthew Arnold's 'Dover Beach', William
Blake's 'The Tiger' and Alfred, Lord Tennyson's 'The Lady of Shalott'. However, I am going to make the assumption that the inclusion of these poems
in an anthology for children reflects a sense of their relative appropriateness
and accessibility for younger readers, and so I will not exclude any of the
poems on the grounds that they are *not* poems for children.

A second glance makes clear that this, like other anthologies for children,
contains a large variety of poems from different eras, with different subject matter and probably accessible to different ages. The reader interested
in linguistic style will note a number of stylistic features common to the
majority of these poems. These stylistic features are linked to the question
of the *function* of poetry in children's lives. Though, for the adult, poetry
reading tends to be a solitary activity, for children it is more often an experience shared with carers, teachers and peers. The result is that, whether
the poems are actually read aloud or silently, most of them foreground the
music of the language to a marked degree. Although the anthology contains
a small number of poems in free verse (unrhymed, no regular rhythm), the
overwhelming majority of them have some kind of regular poetic form,
whether that is a regular or patterned metre, or rhyme scheme, or both. We
may surmise that this is because children appreciate above all the musicality
of formal poetry, knowing that they love to make up nonsense songs and
rhymes for themselves and that they seem to take a delight in the sounds
for their own sake. Indeed, this morning, I was listening to a pair of small
children at the local gym, and they were chanting something like 'the keys
are in the kitchen, yum, yum, yum' over and over again, though there was
no situational link to kitchens and the content of the chant was therefore

secondary to the sound. My approach, therefore, has been to make stylistic notes on each poem in the collection and to draw up a cumulative picture of the range of linguistic/stylistic features that were present, and their relative (though not quantified) frequency in the collection.

A preliminary note on foregrounding

During its early development in the mid-to-late twentieth century, stylistics as a discipline developed from linguistics and literary criticism and depended on the conviction that 'language is not simply a "medium" for 'content', but a significant part of the whole experience we call literature' (Wales, 1993: 89). Early stylistics developed a particular application of the Russian formalist view that the distinctive feature of literary (as opposed to non-literary) texts was the presence of expressions that made the everyday and familiar seem strange and new. By using the more precise descriptions that linguistics had made possible, stylistics pointed out exactly how this 'making strange' was carried out in textual form. This resulted in the theory of 'foregrounding', and though this is no longer considered unique to literary texts, the notion that one of the features of a text may be foregrounding has become the bedrock of stylistic research. Short describes 'foregrounded features' as 'the parts of the text which the author, consciously or unconsciously, is signalling as crucial to our understanding of what he has written' (Short, 1996: 36).

Much of what follows will draw on the notion that features worth discussing are those that stand out in some way from their surroundings and/or from the language in general. However, there will also be some discussion of the more 'backgrounded' features which form the basis of any text. Such features (foregrounded or backgrounded) may be at any level of language – from phonetics to text structure. There are at least two different ways in which a feature can be foregrounded, and though these are not always clearly distinct, the extreme versions are useful reference points. Thus, features may seem to 'break the rules' of the language as a whole, and go against all experience that the reader has of 'normal' texts. This is known as 'external deviation'. Leech describes it as follows:

> Just as the eye picks out the figure as the important and meaningful element in its field of vision, so the reader of poetry picks out the linguistic deviation in such a phrase as 'a grief ago' as the most arresting and significant part of the message, and interprets it by measuring it against the background of the expected pattern.
>
> Leech, 1969: 57

Also common in poetry is 'internal deviation', whereby a norm for that text is established and the foregrounded features are those which deviate from this norm. Short explains:

> Internal deviation is deviation against a norm set up by the text itself. Suppose that a poem is written in rhyming couplets, but then the fifth couplet does not rhyme. The rhyme is a pattern of parallelism at the phonetic level, which is then broken at stanza five.
>
> Short 1996:59

Of course, these distinctions between internal and external deviation are sometimes challenged by 'real' examples, but they may serve us as reference points. Parallelism, mentioned above by Short, is another common type of foregrounding, which is not deviant in the expected way, because it doesn't obviously confound any expectations. Commentators on stylistics nevertheless see parallelism as a kind of foregrounding, as here in 'Wha Me Mudder Do' (McGough 78) by Grace Nichols:

> Mek me tell you wha me mudder do
> wha me mudder do
> wha me mudder do

The musical structure of poems for children

I noted earlier that the sounds of poems are very important to children. It is noticeable, for example, that there is only one poem in this anthology which uses layout as a structuring device (Jo Shapcott's 'Penguin Complaints' (100)) whereas 82 out of 100 use some kind of musical structuring, whether metrical, rhyming or both. The sounds of poetic text can have *purely* musical effects, but in adult poetry, at least from the twentieth century onwards, there is an increasing tendency to use sound effects for *meaningful* as well as musical reasons (see Jeffries, 1993: 39–56). This growth in symbolic use of sound probably coincided with the relaxation of the requirement of strict form in poetry. As the convention of using strict metre and rhyme weakened, the choice to use particular sound effects in poems became meaningful. In fact, the poet's use of metre and rhyme *at all* begins to have a meaningful, symbolic effect (see Jeffries, 1993: 42). Ho wever, in children's poetry the musical use of sound is perhaps still dominant, unlike in adult poetry. The almost universal use of metre and rhyme for children's poems, then, implies that these features of the language of the poems are *not* foregrounded as meaningful except where they take an unusual form or deviate *within* the form in some way. They remain, therefore, one of the backgrounded features of this subgenre. Below I discuss examples of both foregrounded and back-grounded metre, as well as deviation within metrical patterning.

The regularity of metre in children's poems at first sight may seem to be a background feature of the genre, and one that has little impact on the meaning or the literary effect, beyond perhaps marking a text out as being poetic. However, this is far from true, since particular metrical patterns can be indicative of a particular type of poem, and the choice to vary the metre or choose no metre at all is also significant.

What we might call the 'basic metre' in all English verse is the iambic foot (dee-dum). This is the combination of unstressed (ˇ) and stressed (ʹ) syllables which is often combined in four feet in children's poetry. See, for example, the many 'cautionary tales' of both Victorian and more recent provenance. Here are the opening lines (respectively) of Hilaire Belloc's 'Matilda' (15) and Wendy Cope's 'Kenneth' (25):

> Mǎtílda tóld sǔch Dréadfǔl Líes,
>
> Ǐt máde ǒne Gásp ǎnd Strétch ǒne's Éyes:
>
> The chíef deféct ǒf Kénněth Plúmb
>
> Wǎs chéwǐng tóo mǔch búbblě-gúm.

These poems also use the most basic rhyme scheme, the rhyming couplet, where each pair of consecutive lines has a matching final rhyme. Once established, there is little, except the occasional metrical variation, to disturb the story, though the disciplinary nature of the metre can also cause the reader to change the 'normal' stresses in a word to fit the pattern, usually to comical effect. This happens to the word 'defect' in 'Kenneth', where the normal stress (in British English at least) would fall on the first syllable, but here the metre encourages us to change it to the second.

Though many commentators suggest that iambic feet are natural to the speaking rhythms of English and are more common as a result, there is also quite a lot of trochaic metre in this collection. The trochee is the reverse of the iambic foot, and has a stressed syllable followed by an unstressed syllable (dum-dee). This may result in an other-worldly feel about the poems in which this metre dominates, such as Henry Wadsworth Longfellow's 'Hiawatha' (62) or Richard Edward's 'The Word Party' (36):

> Lóvǐng wórds clútch crímsǒn rósěs,

Rúde wŏrds snĭff ănd pĭck thĕir nŏses,

Slў wŏrds cŏme drĕssed ŭp ăs fŏxes,

Shŏrt wŏrds stănd ŏn cărdbŏard bŏxes

Notice how the word 'words' occurs in a stressed position in the first line, when it is first introduced, but as it becomes secondary to the description ('rude', 'sly', 'short') in the following lines is downgraded to the unstressed position. Here is a short extract from 'Hiawatha' for comparison:

Ănd thĕ smŏke rŏse slŏwly, slŏwly,

Thrŏugh thĕ trănquĭl ăir ŏf mŏrning,

Fĭrst ă sĭnglĕ lĭne ŏf dărkness,

Thĕn ă dĕnsĕr, blŭer văpŏur

Though we may see children as appreciative of simple rhyme schemes, children of course come in different ages and a good anthology will prepare them for the delights of both unrhymed and unmetrical poetry and also for poems with more complex rhythms and rhyme schemes. A common pattern is the abcb type of rhyme scheme, whereby each four-line stanza (though not all are actually divided in this way) rhymes the second and last line. Waltes de la Mare's 'The Listeners' (29) takes this pattern:

And a bird flew up out of the turret,	(a)
Above the Traveller's head:	(b)
And he smote upon the door a second time;	(c)
'Is there anybody there?' he said.	(b)

This pattern with the 6 rhymes (head/said) gives enough structure for musicality, while allowing for some freedom of sounds in the intervening lines (turret/time). Some poems, such as Thomas Hardy's 'Paying Calls' (43) have abab schemes, in which the first and third lines also rhyme. This poem in particular is notable for its apparent lightness of theme, echoed in the regular rhyme scheme. When it turns out that the calls are being paid to friends who are now dead ('But they spoke not to me'), the clash between the levity of form and the solemnity of theme is all the more effective.

A more sophisticated version of a four-line rhyme-scheme is evident in 'Stopping by Woods on a Snowy Evening' (42) by Robert Frost. Though not written as a children's poem, it has a long history of being included in school anthologies (and used for speaking competitions!). The rhyme scheme is combined with a judicious mixture of run-on lines and end-stopping, making it very satisfying musically. The rhyme scheme uses an aaba pattern which is repeated in each verse by picking up the minor rhyme (b) as the main rhyme in the second verse and likewise picking up the minor rhyme (c) in the third verse (so, bbcb, ccdc), with the final verse bringing the sleepiness of the narrator to our attention by using the same d rhyme throughout. Here is the third verse:

> He gives his harness bells a shake
> To ask if there is some mistake.
> The only other sound's the sweep
> Of easy wind and downy flake.

Note the c rhymes ('shake'/'mistake'/'flake') which continue from the previous verse ('lake') and the d rhyme ('sweep') which is repeated at the ends of all the lines in the final verse ('deep'/'keep'/'sleep'). The first and third lines also have the effect of pushing forward the grammatical sense, because they do not finish a clause. The third and fourth lines, in particular, break up a noun phrase ('the sweep of easy wind and downy flake') and it therefore challenges a reader to balance the demands of the rhythm with maintaining the ongoing sense and grammatical structure.

Other sound effects in poems for children

So far we have been considering the foundational patterns of stresses and rhymes as background over which all other stylistic effects are laid. More foregrounded, because rarer in anthologies for children, are poems written without specific metre or rhyme. These would include a poem such as Seamus Heaney's 'Mid-Term Break' (45) which has no rhyme-scheme or clear metrical pattern, though it has mostly ten syllables a line, which prevents it from being entirely formless. Examples of others lacking both metre and rhyme are Liz Lochhead's 'Poem for My Sister' (61) and James Reeves's 'The Sea' (92) which, without metrical pattern and only a sporadic pattern of end-rhymes (abbccdddcceffghhhccc), gives a sense of order breaking out into chaos. This is the only clear case where *the rhyme-scheme itself* may be taken to represent in some way the meaning of the poem. The choice of end rhyme (rather than no rhyme) but in an ever-changing – if not quite random – pattern is what causes this meaning potential to arise because it is a foregrounded decision.

Beyond metre and rhyme, there are many other possible patterns of sound in poetry, in particular, alliteration and assonance. Available effects vary more than these terms conventionally indicate since they have traditionally been used only to refer to sequences of *words beginning with the same sound* (or often the same letter), whereas many poetic effects may result from a preponderance of similar sounds rather than identical ones (e.g. a lot of plosive phonemes such as t, d, k, b, d, g or long vowels like 'ee' and 'oo') and in a range of positions in word and syllable. Such concentrations of sound *may* be simply one of the enriching patterns of music that are overlaid onto the metre and end rhyme, but they may also be meaningful in a range of ways.

The most obvious way in which sounds can be meaningful is when they reflect the referent directly and are therefore onomatopoeic. These words are often thought of as attractive to children, probably because they seem to contradict the general rule that words have a purely arbitrary relationship with their referents. However, the poems here provide remarkably few examples of conventionally onomatopoeic words (like 'miaow' for a cat's cry) though Roger McGough's 'The Sound Collector' (69), predictably perhaps, uses a wide range of such words:

> The *hissing* of the frying-pan
> The *ticking* of the grill
> The *bubbling* of the bathtub
> As it starts to fill

Though conventional lexical onomatopoeia is associated with children's language, there is a less blatant type of reflection of sounds possible in poetry which usually occurs across a longer stretch of text and may result from a concentration of similar or identical sounds, as here in Walter de la Mare's 'The Listeners' (29):

> 'Is there anybody there?' said the Traveller,
>   Knocking on the moonlit door;
> And *his horse* in the *silence ch*amped *the* grasses
>   *Of the* forest's *ferny floor* ...

Here, the most significant onomatopoeic effect is found in the alliterative use of the fricative sound /f/ in the *forest's ferny floor*. The fricative sound is one where the air leaving the lungs is channelled through a very small opening between two parts of the mouth, and this leads to a 'whistling' or 'breathy' sound. The effect of the horse's chewing sound in amplifying the silence around it is also anticipated by a concentration of other fricatives (/h/, /s/, /ð/ and /z/ and /tʃ/) in the lead-up to this phrase, as we can see if we highlight the fricative sounds: 'and *his horse* in *the* silence *ch*amped *the* grasses *of the* forest's *ferny floor*'. The breathy quality of the fricative consonants thus effectively summons up the stillness within the house by comparison with the relative noisiness of the horse eating, oblivious to the uncanny silence.

Though direct reflection of sound is one of the generic features of poetry, and found relatively often in children's poems, another type of sound-symbolism which features a great deal in adult poetry may also be relevant here. Short describes an expanded 'sound-symbolism' as consisting in 'similar relations between the sounds of words and other aspects of the things which the word refers to, like size or brightness' (Short, 1996: 115). Alastair Reid's 'A Spell for Sleeping' (93) displays some sound-symbolism. It is a mesmeric lullaby with little clear narrative, though small sections of the poem seem to describe different scenes of gathering dusk. Though it can be a risk to read too much into phonemic patterns, many of those in this poem do seem to enhance the meaning rather than being simply harmonic:

> Curtains are clouding the casement windows.
> A moon-glade smurrs the lake with light.
> Doves cover the tower with quiet.

The first noticeable sound pattern is the alliteration of /k/ sounds in the first line, where the velar plosive sound requires a complete closure of the vocal tract at the soft palate. This physical closure, which is the defining feature of the rather sharp kind of plosive consonant represented by /k/ here, may be taken to emulate the closing of curtains one after another at different windows. The sound patterning in the rest of the stanza is more vowel-based, with the high concentration of long vowels and diphthongs in the middle line seeming to symbolise the visual effect of the moon on the lake, in particular the /ɜ/ of 'smurrs' where the smudgy reflection, elongated by the ripples on the water, is reflected by the length of the vowel sounds. This sound-symbolism turns aural again in the final line when the cooing of the doves is evoked by the two short vowels in *doves cover*, whether that is two /ʌ/ sounds (for Southern British English accents) or two ʊ sounds, (for Northern British and many American accents of English). These shorter sounds are foregrounded in the context of so many long vowels, and this foregrounding is retrospectively reinforced by the two triphthongs in the final lexical words of the stanza, *tower* ʊ and *quiet* /ɪ/ which begin to turn the whole world of the poem into a blurry blanket of vowels, with relatively few of the distinctive landmarks of the consonants to give them shape.

Word-play in poems for children

Perhaps the most 'expected' feature of poems for children, after musicality, is concentrated 'word-play'. A poem for children will either be playful with the rules of word construction and combination or it will not, and where it is playful, it tends to be humorous. The creation of new words is one of the joys of learning your first language when you are growing up. This form of word-play may be reflected back to the child-reader by poems. There are at least two ways that words can be 'constructed' and these reflect the phonological (sounds), graphological (written spellings) and morphological (word-structure) levels of language.

Laura E. Richards's 'Eletelephony' (94) describes the efforts of an elephant to use a telephone. The fun in the poem comes from the playful way in which the words 'elephant' and 'telephone' are first of all made more similar ('elephant'/'telephant' and 'telephone'/'elephone') and then are varied further to match the rhyme-scheme ('trunk'/'telephunk', 'free', 'telephee' and 'song'/'telephong'). Note that the graphological/phonological similarity of the words (mainly the 'ph' representing the sound of /f/) is one of the drivers of the game that the poem is playing, and the physical resemblance of the trunk of an elephant with the curled wires of a landline telephone is also implied by this muddling up of the words (and the accompanying illustration with the wire round the elephant's trunk). Spike Milligan's 'On the Ning Nang Nong' (71) is perhaps an even more extreme version of the purely phonological playfulness that can be found in children's poems. Spike Milligan seems to have captured the very kind of made-up words that children themselves tend to invent by changing just one of the sounds in a nonsense word a few times to produce a chain of musically similar words (e.g. *Ning Nang Nong; Jibber Jabber Joo*).

On a morphological level of inventiveness, there are occasional derivations whereby a word has its word class changed, for example from noun to verb, as in the word 'dustbinized' from Pam Ayres's 'The Dolly on the Dustcart' (13). This word displays internal deviation because the rest of the poem is written in a fairly strong regional dialect but does not contain invented words apart from this one. The word is separated out from the rest of its line: 'No longer prized ... dustbinized!' This describes the throwing away of the dolly who has been on the dustcart for so long that she becomes damaged and out of date and is eventually thrown away. The poet chooses to make a clear foregrounding of this word, as its position and the exclamation mark show. These foregrounding devices, as well as the internal rhyme of 'prized' with 'dustbinized' help to demonstrate a reflective awareness by the narrator (the doll herself) that she is making a word up and there is a sense of triumph at her cleverness in the foregrounding by all these means.

What Short (1996: 45) would call 'lexical deviation' is demonstrated by those poems that invent rather more than the occasional word. The most famous, and perhaps most satisfying, of these is Lewis Carroll's 'Jabberwocky'

(20), where normal English derivational processes are used to create apparently 'real' words on the basis of non-existent and yet strangely familiar base forms. Thus, the suffix –y, which is normally added to nouns to make adjectives (e.g. greasy, bony, etc.) is added in this case to a non-existent base, 'slithe', creating the adjective 'slithy' as a result. The fact that we know the word class of these neologisms means that the reader can at least make out the grammatical relationships between them, and thus knows for certain that it is the 'toves' which are 'slithy', even while not knowing exactly what toves are, or what the characteristic of being 'slithy' entails. Notice, however, that Carroll makes use of the patterns of sound-symbolism in English to help us a little further with decoding his work. Thus, the initial 'sl' of 'slithy' is recognisably a member of the group of sl-words in English which have a smooth or slippery aspect to their meaning: slippery, slimy, slur, etc. This gives the reader a clue; being 'slithy' is an unpleasant and smooth quality.

Another kind of word-play is when words are used alongside other words with which they would not normally occur. Margaret Atwood's 'Song of the Worms' (12) is a poem about the rising up of worms, literally and metaphorically. It suggests that worms 'come out into the open air at /night only to love/ which disgusts the soles of boots'. Here, we have an unusual combination with the verb 'disgust', which normally requires a human object (e.g. the 'smell disgusted him') but here has the 'soles of boots' instead. The result is that the reader will either personify the soles of the boots as having the capacity to be disgusted, or perhaps more likely reads it as a metonymic reference to the owner of the boots, and the way in which human beings recoil when they find they have stepped on entangled worms.

Craig Raine's 'A Martian Sends a Postcard Home' (90) is one of the adult poems included for their presumed accessibility to children or for their potential to appeal to the child's appetite for the musical or for the strange. The topic of the poem (an alien's view of human life on Earth) is presented through a classic example of 'making strange'. The Martian's best guesses as to what the human beings are up to and what their objects are used for makes for some amusing results, many of which are achieved through the use of unusual combinations of words. Thus the night is described as 'when all the colours die', though the verb 'die' normally requires an animate subject; books are described as 'mechanical birds' though the adjective 'mechanical' normally describes a machine or other piece of technology rather than a bird; and books are said to 'cause the eyes to melt' (cry), though the verb 'melt' normally requires a frozen subject. Each of these images is achieved through the juxtaposition of words which do not normally co-occur.

Voice

Poets of the twentieth century have typically been interested in experimenting with the vernacular in poetic contexts, and poets writing for children are
no exception. A number of these poems use dialect forms, either throughout
the poem as in the Caribbean dialect poem 'Wha Me Mudder Do' (78) or in
the occasional lexical item, as in the use of the Scottish word for hopscotch –
'peever' – in 'Poem for My Sister' (61). 'The Dolly on the Dustcart' (13) and
Marriott Edgar's 'The Lion and Albert' (33) adopt a slightly stereotyped
version of their respective regional dialects. This extract from 'The Dolly on
the Dustcart' features the irregular possessive pronoun 'me' (instead of 'my')
the non-standard negative of 'haven't ('ain't') and the double negative combining 'ain't' with 'no' rather than 'any'. Note that a consistent representation of the quasi-Cockney accent suggested here would have also dropped
the 'h' from 'had', but that this writer has chosen to represent only the lexical and grammatical features of the dialect, rather than the accent:

> There's dirt all round me face,
> And all across me rosy cheeks,
> Well, I've had me head thrown back,
> But we ain't had no rain for weeks.

In 'The Lion and Albert', which was written to be performed, and is
perhaps therefore more concerned with phonology, the poet shows the
dropped aitches of the working-class Lancashire accent he is trying to represent, in particular where it would have most comic impact by its repetition. In the following stanza, for example, he doesn't drop the aitch in
'his' in line two, but manages to drop *four* of them in the following line,
making it surprisingly hard to articulate, and thus sounding like a rather
deliberate pronunciation as opposed to the lazy carelessness of the common stereotype:

> A grand little lad was their Albert
> All dressed in his best; quite a swell
> 'E'd a stick with an 'orse's 'ead 'andle
> The finest that Woolworth's could sell.

The effort required to pronounce the third line of this stanza with features
of a stigmatised lower-class accent symbolises the efforts at self-improvement of Albert's family represented by 'in his best, quite a swell' and 'the
finest that Woolworth's could sell'. Contemporary audiences for Stanley
Holloway's famous renditions of these monologues would accordingly have
been made acutely aware of the aspirations of Albert's family – and their
dismal failure – to seem richer and more cultured than they were.

The form and structures of Edgar's northern dialect are exemplified in a number of places elsewhere in the poem. He describes the waves, for example, as 'fiddlin'' representing Northern phonology by eliding the 'g' to indicate an alveolar nasal sound, rather than the more standard velar one. The most noticeable features of non-standard dialect in the poem are the non-standard forms of the verb, 'to be', whereby the plural of the past tense is identical to the singular 'they was' and the hypercorrect double past tense of the verb 'drown', whereby the standard, but irregular, form, 'drowned', is the core of the item, but another past tense morpheme (ed) is added for good measure, resulting in the phrase 'nobody drownded'. This double past tense gives a sense of the family's own voice, and shows them to be attempting to sound educated by using the 'correct' form, when of course they fail miserably. The final line in the same stanza has a structure with part missing, 'Fact', which hints again at the voice of the family, being a contraction of the phrase 'in fact' which would be used in conversation amongst them as they discuss their day so far. This extract also demonstrates the use of 'free direct style' whereby the voice of the protagonists is used within the narration.

These dialect poems are less common than poems that use general features of spoken interaction such as the kind of language used between children and schoolteachers (Joyce Armor's 'Excuses Excuses' (83); Peter Dixon's 'Please Sir' (31)), exemplified most effectively by Alan Ahlberg's 'Please Mrs Butler' (6), which combines the sing-song rhythm of three stresses per line and an abab rhyme scheme in four-line stanzas to mimic the chant of children 'telling' on their classmates. In addition to mimicry, the poem also uses structures familiar in British classrooms whereby each new complaint is prefaced by a 'politeness' marker, 'Please', and followed by the double-noun phrases known as appositional phrases containing both a description and the name of the accused: 'This boy Derek Drew'. In other circumstances we might expect an indefinite article (a boy) rather than a demonstrative adjective (**this** boy), and in some ways the appositional phrase is redundant. But in the classroom context, the repeated referent 'this boy' and 'Derek Drew' is often used for emphasis, and it certainly sounds like part of the normal register of the schoolroom. The repeated nature of these lines is also part of the foregrounding of the poem, where the parallelism of the structure is both regular and also reminiscent of a repeated (empty) conversation between chronic complainer and harassed teacher.

Another poem that evokes a particular type (register) of language is Brian Patten's 'The Race to Get to Sleep' (85). This depicts an adult using the register of the racing commentator to encourage children into their pyjamas and into bed:

> She's got one sock off! Now the other's off!
> But Matthew's still winning! No, he's not!
> It's Penny! Penny's in the lead!

The features of commentating which Patten uses here include the repetition of names, the exclamatory structures ('It's Penny!') and the use of the present (and present continuous) tense to describe a scene as it unfolds. The present tense is not often used in this rather literal way.

Although it is not a universal feature, evoking spoken language appears to be an important stylistic feature of poetry for children.

Structures in poems for children

Stylistic approaches to poetry typically focus more on linguistic choices made *within* the constraints of a chosen poetic form than on the form itself. There are, nevertheless, some comments worth making from a stylistics angle about the boundary between song and poem, which is more blurred in children's poems than in the adult genre. Those poems that appeal to children often show a similarity to song form, often featuring refrains and parallelism.

Roger McGough's 'The Sound Collector' (69), William Blake's 'The Tiger' (17) and William Allingham's 'The Fairies' (7), for example, each feature a first stanza repeated with minor changes as the last stanza. These repeated stanzas take the reader back to the beginning again, though there is often a subtle difference in the repetition which shows that we are not back to exactly the same spot, as we can see by comparing the first and last stanzas of 'The Tiger':

> Tiger! Tiger! burning bright
> In the forests of the night,
> What immortal hand or eye
> Could frame thy fearful symmetry?

> Tiger! Tiger! burning bright
> In the forests of the night,
> What immortal hand or eye
> Dare frame thy fearful symmetry?

This minimal change of the modal verb (from 'could' to 'dare') demonstrates the power of a single word, as Blake moves from considering the nature of creation in the first stanza to marvelling at the stupendous and fearful daring of a possible creator. This poem, like one or two others in the collection, is based firmly on the interrogative structure, which works against the closure suggested by repetition.

One of the structuring devices that seems to take the place of formal metrical structure in some recent poems is the conversation. Harold Munro's

'Overheard on a Salt Marsh' (74), Colin McNaughton's 'Sometimes I think you don't listen to a word I say!' (70) and Trevor Hardy's 'The Painting Lesson' (44), for example, are typical of this form, which begins with a question and may supply a punch-line ending. In 'The Painting Lesson' for instance, the teacher tells the child that s/he should paint a realistic picture of mummy, rather than the green and orange splodges that are appearing. The denouement of the poem demonstrates that the child was obediently following instructions after all. The child's voice records with glee that the teacher

> ...turned white
> At ten to three
> When an orange-green blob
> Collected me.
> 'Hi, Mum!'

The foregrounding in such poems is the unexpected response and it is just one of the ways in which the transgressive nature of poetic 'worlds' can appeal to the imagination of the child.

Other structuring devices, usually aimed at younger children and possibly having a pedagogic function in addition to their poetic function, are those structured around numbers. John Agard's 'What Turkey Doing?' (5) and Moira Andrews's 'November Night Countdown' (9) are two such poems, the latter using a countdown from ten to one, and featuring a great deal of onomatopoeia reflecting the sounds of fireworks:

> Eight jumping jacks
>   leaping on the ground.
> Seven silver sparklers
>   whirling round and round.

Note that this poem, like many of those structured around lists or numbers, uses minor sentences, with no main verb throughout. In this case, the clauses all use the present continuous form (e.g. 'sizzling', 'reaching', 'leaping'), ungoverned by an auxiliary verb. The result is that there is a timelessness about the poem, which describes a 5 November which lasts indefinitely.

A similar effect is achieved by different means in Ted Hughes's 'Amulet' (51) in which the minor sentences are characterised by the lack of any verb at all. Each line in this poem is structured on a prepositional phrase beginning with 'Inside' and a following noun phrase, after a comma, namely 'Inside the X, the Y'. The comma represents the verb 'to be', but its omission leaves the poem unanchored in time as no tense is supplied. Rather than saying 'Inside the wolf's fang **is** the mountain of heather' or 'Inside the wolf's fang **was** the mountain of heather', then, we are left with the timeless:

> Inside the wolf's fang, the mountain of heather.
> Inside the mountain of heather, the wolf's fur.
> Inside the wolf's fur, the ragged forest.

The parallelism of the line-structure is supplemented by the movement of each noun phrase to the prepositional phrase of the next line. The poem ends, as another circular poem, with the initial noun phrase of the first line:

> Inside the North star, the wolf's fang.

While there is no indication within the vocabulary of the poem that there is much more to it than a kind of listing of the features of a bleak northern landscape, there is some potential for interpretation of the structure itself as symbolising a stable and complete, if unforgiving, world of nature.

Positioning the child-reader

Though not all descriptive poems use minor sentences, a relatively large number of poems for children display present-tense description as their main stylistic characteristic. These include Matthew Arnold's 'Dover Beach' (10) Robert Frost's 'Stopping by Woods' (42) Kenneth Grahame's 'Ducks' Ditty' (43) Edward Thomas's 'October' (116) and James Reeves's 'The Sea' (92), amongst others. These poems have the very strong effect of taking the reader into the focal 'centre' of the text. The present tense, first-person narrative and a strong sense of place create a focal point from where the scene being described is 'viewed' and this becomes the reader's viewpoint. Extracts from 'Dover Beach' and 'October' all demonstrate how viewpoint is produced:

> The sea is calm to-night...
> The tide is full, the moon lies fair
> Upon the straits...   (10)

> and now I might
> As happy be as earth is beautiful,
> Were I some other or with earth could turn
> In alternation of violet and rose.   (116)

In these instances the present tense seems to refer to the 'present' of the narrator, and so readers are invited to imagine themselves into the moment of composition. This effect is enhanced in the opening of 'October' (116) by time adverbs, such as 'to-night' and 'now'. The place in which the narration is happening is also evoked by deictic words and structures (something is 'deictic' when it directly points to something, here, the specifics of place). In some cases this is the definite article (**the** sea, **the** tide, **the** moon) which presupposes the existence of these things, and thus evokes a scene in which they are necessarily present. The use of the first-person pronoun is more complicated, but always evokes a deictic centre (the viewpoint of the 'I' character) and depending on whether there is also a second-person addressee ('you'), the reader may adopt the first- or second-person position in the narrative.

In the case of 'October' there is no direct addressee, and the reader is thus invited to take up the viewpoint of the narrator himself/herself. 'Dover Beach', on the other hand, has a number of references to another person, at first in the imperative forms ('Come to the window' and 'Listen!') and later in direct address ('Ah, love, let us be true/To one another!'). This is the only first-person love poem in the collection, and as such represents one of the stepping stones for children from 'their' poetry which is musically regular and often light-hearted towards the subjects of adult poetry, love, religion and politics. The poem's positioning of the reader inside this heavily emotional situation is one of the reasons for its power. Poems participate in the discourse levels envisaged by Short amongst others, whereby literary works have both internal addresser and addressees, and external addresser (the poet) and addressees (the readers). The scope for merging of these identities is very broad and any focal centre is likely to be strongly suggestive of the imaginative position that a reader should take up.

Another, larger, group of children's poems are straightforwardly narrative in content, reflecting this in using a past tense and third-person narrative. These include Neil Adam's 'The Hero of the Match' (2), Hilaire Belloc's 'Matilda' (15), Robert Browning's 'The Pied Piper of Hamelin' (18), Samuel Taylor Coleridge's 'The Rime of the Ancient Mariner' (24), Thomas Hardy's 'Paying Calls' (43), Seamus Heaney's 'Mid-Term Break' (45) and, one of the most famous, Alfred Noyes's 'The Highwayman' (79):

> The wind was a torrent of darkness among the gusty trees,
> The moon was a ghostly galleon tossed upon cloudy seas,
> The road was a ribbon of moonlight over the purple moor,
> And the highwayman came riding –
> > Riding – riding –
> The highwayman came riding, up to the old inn-door.

This opening stanza describes the landscape over which the highwayman comes, which narrows as he arrives at the inn: 'Over the cobbles he clattered and clashed in the dark inn-yard.' Between these descriptive elements, the action progresses ('He whistled a tune to the window'). The reader is taken by the omniscient narrator from one part of the scene to another, privileged in knowing all, and suffering to the full the dramatic irony of the knowledge of Bess's impending sacrifice as the unsuspecting highwayman approaches on his horse and the soldiers crouch in ambush:

> *Tlot-tlot, tlot-tlot!* Had they heard it? The horse-hoofs ringing clear –
> *Tlot-tlot, tlot-tlot*, in the distance? Were they deaf that they did not hear?

The most recent developments in stylistics have included cognitive approaches to the experience of readers as they read texts and we have already touched on one of these – the notion that the features of a text may create a kind of imaginative 'centre' which the reader is most likely to adopt as her/his viewpoint (see Gavins and Steen, 2003). In a roving third-person narration like that of 'The Highwayman', the centre shifts regularly and readers are invited to change their viewpoint accordingly.

Another cognitive theory which has been used to date mainly to describe the effects of prose narration is text world theory. This defines the ways in which texts create and 'furnish' a text world which may differ from the actual world of the reader, and which the reader is invited to recreate mentally as s/he reads. This theory depends upon detailed description of language choices to determine how the picture of the text world is built up in the reader's mind. Many of the examples of foregrounding above play a part in creating such a text world. Another textual practice seems particularly prevalent in creating the worlds of children's poetry – the use of 'negation'. 'The Listeners' (29), for example, is a poem which appeals to children through its spooky atmosphere. The title of the poem hints at the presence of people (or ghosts?). The first stanzas evoke the feelings of the traveller knocking on the door and getting no answer:

> But no one descended to the Traveller;
>> No head from the leaf-fringed sill
> Leaned over and looked into his grey eyes,
>> Where he stood perplexed and still.

The description of what does *not* happen is as vivid and detailed as what does happen, and this creates an interesting text world for the reader who can imagine both the scene as described (with no answer to the knock) and also the one that could have happened, but doesn't. This coupled with the evocation of a 'host of phantom listeners', who do not behave in the normal fashion by opening the door, lends an eerie quality to the scene. This conjuring up of scenes by negation is a very common, but underrecognised, phenomenon which adds texture to a scene by commenting not only on what is, but on what might be, or might have been. Another poem in this collection, Gerald Bullett's 'November Evening' (19), describes winter darkness in the countryside by such negation:

No moon or stars, no glimmer
    Of lamp, nor means to tell
Hedge from house or haystack
    But by feel and smell

Conclusion

It is probably true to say that there *is* a stylistic tendency in children's poems towards the formal, rhythmical, rhyming and humorous poem. However, since there is no clear boundary between children's poetry and adult poetry, this can only be a tendency, since the best practice in creating general anthologies for children (as opposed, say, to those for very young readers) must construct a bridge between those poems which appeal most to the sense of musicality and fun that children have and the place of poetry in the adult world, which is, by and large, about intensity of meaning produced through the subtle inventiveness of multiple linguistic processes. The anthology studied here, like many others, brings children into their own world of poems to share with carers, teachers and other children. At the same time, they are also led toward the more subtle uses of language that they will find in adult poetry books.

References

Gavins, J. and Steen, G. 2003. *Cognitive Poetics in Practice*. London, Routledge.
Jeffries, L. 1993. *The Language of Twentieth Century Poetry*. Basingstoke, Palgrave Macmillan.
Leech, G. 1969. *A Linguistic Guide to English Poetry*. London, Longman.
Leech, G. 2008. *Language in Literature: Style and Foregrounding*. London, Longman.
McGough, R. (ed.) 2002. *100 Best Poems for Children*. London, Penguin.
Short, M. 1996. *Exploring the Language of Poems, Plays and Prose*. London, Longman.
Wales, K. 1993. 'Teach Yourself "Rhetoric": An Analysis of Philip Larkin's "Church Going"',
    in P. Verdonk (ed.) *Twentieth-Century Poetry: From Text to Context*. London, Routledge.

'From the Best Poets'? Anthologies for Children
Morag Styles

'From the best poets' is the sub-title to Coventry Patmore's highly regarded anthology of poetry, *The Children's Garland*, which was published in 1862. Patmore, like many anthologists of the past and present, was a poet himself

Extracted from 'From the Best Poets? How the Canon of Poetry for Children is Constructed', in M. Styles, *From the Garden to the Street* (London: Continuum, 1998), pp. 186–96.

and he explains the reasons for his selection of poetry in his preface – something many anthologists feel the need to do. He writes:

> I have excluded nearly all verse written expressly for children and most of the poetry written about children for grown people ... this volume will, I hope, be found to contain nearly all the genuine poetry in our language fitted to please children.[1]

Thus Patmore introduces several of the ideas I want to deal with here: the extraordinary exclusion from anthologies of nearly all *verse written expressly for children*; the notion of 'genuine' poetry which ought to be included in a good anthology; the concern to 'please children'.

Now pleasing children is a difficult idea to grapple with, when the notion of children or 'childhood' has been constructed in many different ways and is constantly evolving. Untangling what might be meant by 'pleasing' one young person, let alone children in their infinite variety, is also tricky. Sales figures and regularity of new editions are helpful indicators, but we must not forget that it is adults, by and large, who buy children's poetry – and write, sell, publish and teach it. And adults are often dismissive of children's taste. More importantly, there is Patmore's extraordinary determination to avoid poetry written specifically for children. This exclusion is even more perplexing when one learns that it was commonplace: Patmore, as we shall see, was by no means alone in taking such a stance.

To help us grapple with this issue, it might be instructive to ask some questions. What did Patmore actually select for children? What did he mean by 'genuine' poetry? What did he think would please children? Why was he so firm about excluding poetry written with children in mind?

E.V. Lucas (1868–1938) was another distinguished anthologist with a wide knowledge of and interest in children's poetry. In one of the earliest essays dealing seriously with poetry for children (1896), he takes Patmore's *The Children's Garland* to task:

> As a collection of poems about childhood each in its own way is delightful, although even then not satisfactory. It is as vehicles for the entertainment of young readers that they are so sadly to seek ...[2]

Lucas's view of childhood was as a time of 'fun and irresponsibility' where literature 'should amuse and delight from first page to last'. Do we seem to have a champion for children's poets? Not quite; in the Introduction to Lucas's own anthology, *A Book of Verses for Children*, he writes:

> When you feel ... that these pages no longer satisfy, then you must turn to the better thing. You must understand that there is a kind of poetry that is finer than anything here, poetry to which this book is only a stepping stone.[3]

My argument is that Patmore and Lucas, despite their disagreements, held views about poetry and children in common which also had currency with most anthologists of influence who preceded them and with many who have succeeded them. They believe in a canon of great or 'genuine' poetry which children must read, sooner or later. They believe that what is written with children in mind is inferior to what is written by 'great' poets for adults. They want to please young readers, but that does not necessitate being interested in what they actually choose to read. Despite the protestations of many anthologists that they are guided by their own personal preferences, clear patterns and continuities of editing poetry for children have developed over time. The established canon of poetry for children which has emerged over time marginalizes the very poetry actually written for young readers. The main reason for this has been the role played by editors of anthologies for children, many of whom, while believing they were making unique and fresh collections, have actually been strongly influenced by a tradition of anthologizing from the so-called 'best poets'.

Early anthologizing

One of the earliest, if not the first, poetry anthology for children, is *Mother Goose's Melody*, 1760,[4] a delightful chapbook compilation of nursery rhymes, plus a selection of Shakespeare's songs. The contemporary reader immediately recognizes at least two familiar features of the poetry anthology – nursery rhymes and poems by Shakespeare. It does not seem surprising that as soon as anthologies started to be published for children, nursery rhymes were considered suitable material with their lively rhymes, humour, melody, enjoyable repetitions and simple forms, though they were not widely considered respectable until the middle of the nineteenth century. However, the successful children's publishers of the eighteenth century believed that giving pleasure to children in their reading (as well as instruction) was desirable and commercially advantageous. So a trend began in the mid-eighteenth century for attractive compilations of nursery rhymes which is still in evidence as Mother Goose collections are a mainstay of children's bookshops today. As for Shakespeare 'that sweet songster', the same extracts were chosen in *Mother Goose's Melody* that anthologists have drawn on ever since: 'Where the bee sucks', 'When icicles hang by the wall', 'Under the greenwood tree', 'Ye spotted snakes' ... .[5] Lucy Aikin did not select any nursery rhymes in *Poetry For Children*, 1801, but she did include two Shakespeare poems. Since then Shakespeare has had a consistent place in anthologies for children. As I write, a new, handsomely illustrated book of Shakespeare's poetry, *Something Rich and Strange*,[6] is doing good trade in the shops.

That set me wondering about other poets writing for adults. Who get anthologized for the young, and why? Which poets pass that test of time? In order to make the investigation manageable, I decided to concentrate on a handful of poets who fulfilled the criteria described in the list below.

1. They were included in the Opies' *Oxford Book Of Children's Verse* (1973)[7] because it was a historical landmark of poetry for children, and/or Lucy Aiken's *Poetry for Children*, 1801,[8] because it was one of the earliest selections for children and because she included a wide cross-section of the poets of her time.
2. They were widely anthologized for children for some time after their deaths.
3. They were considered by many to be fine poets, either in their day or by posterity.
4. Their main poetic output was for adults rather than children.

In my choice of poets I tried to span the most popular genres and to be representative of the overall output of published poetry. I also tried to select equal numbers of men and women, but there were not enough published women poets to fulfil my stated criteria. In the end I chose Robert Burns, John Clare, William Cowper, Oliver Goldsmith, Felicia Hemans, Thomas Hood, Alexander Pope, Alfred Tennyson and William Wordsworth who straddle between them the eighteenth and nineteenth centuries.

I then set about choosing some key anthologies, from the nineteenth century to the present day, in order to trace the representation of my chosen poets. I added a number of large, mainstream anthologies of poetry for children by well-qualified editors published more recently. My rough rule of thumb has been (a) poetry for children aged roughly between 6 and 12 and (b) one or two anthologies per decade. My sample contains most of what would be widely regarded as the influential anthologies of my chosen period. I included poetry books intended for school use and those for sale to the general reader, though the latter predominate.

What can we make of the pattern that emerges? The most obvious point is that poets who write for adults are very popular in anthologies for the young. Some poets quickly get incorporated into the children's canon and maintain their popularity right up to the present day: Wordsworth, Tennyson and Burns share that distinction. Some poets are popular for a while, then disappear from view. Whereas Cowper has fallen out of favour since the 1960s, Goldsmith and Pope seem to go in and out of fashion, But in my final anthology representative of 1995, all but two of the poets (Clare and

Table 1   Anthologies for children from 1801 to 1995

Title	Editor
Poetry For Children, 1801	Lucy Aikin
First Book Of Poetry, 1820	W.F. Mylius
Poetry For Children, 1825	Lucy Aikin
The Children's Harp, 1850	unknown
The Golden Treasury of Songs and Lyrics, 1861	Francis T. Palgrave
The Children's Garland, 1862	Coventry Patmore
Easy Rhymes And Simple Poems, 1864	unknown
Child Life, 1874	John Greenleaf Whittier
Poetry For The Young, 1883	unknown
Blue Poetry Book, 1892	Andrew Lang
A Book of Verses for Children, 1897	Edward Lucas
Poems Every Child should Know, 1904	Mary Burt
Another Book of Verses for Children, 1907	E.V. Lucas
The Golden Staircase, 1910	Louey Chisholm
Come Hither, 1923	Walter de la Mare
Tom Tiddler's Ground, 1931	Walter de la Mare
A Poetry Book for Boys And Girls, 1933	Guy Pocock
A Puffin Book of Verse, 1953	Eleanor Graham
The Faber Book of Children's Verse, 1953	Janet Adam Smith
This Way Delight, 1957	Herbert Read
The Cherry Tree, 1959	Geoffrey Grigson
The Dragon Book of Verse, 1977	Harrison & Stuart-Clark
A New Treasury of Poetry, 1990	Neil Philip
Classic Poems to Read Aloud, 1995	James Berry

Hood) are included; and they feature in Philip's *New Treasury* of 1990. One might wonder if Pope's poetry would seem dated for the young, yet he is included in nine out of 24 anthologies.

Lucy Aikin drew extensively on Cowper, Shakespeare and Pope in the first edition of *Poetry For Children*, but in the 1825 edition she cut down on Pope and brought in Wordsworth. She did *not* choose to include popular children's poets like Ann and Jane Taylor, William Roscoe or Elizabeth Turner and she drops Isaac Watts after the first edition. She does not offer any clues as to the reasoning behind the selection in her Introduction, which is liberal and enlightened about both children and poetry. Whatever her reasons, Lucy Aikin preferred to draw from what she presumably considered to be the best poetry of her day that was accessible to children. *And that is what anthologists have done ever since.*

How then do the poets fare who *are* well known for writing for children in the same anthologies? Was I right in believing that this poetry was under-represented? This time I chose children's poets who were popular in their day and who fulfilled the criteria outlined above: Mary Howitt, Edward Lear, A.A. Milne, William Roscoe, R.L. Stevenson, Jane Taylor and Isaac Watts. I added four more poets whose work was or is equally well known for children and adults – Anna Barbauld, Charlotte Smith, Christina Rossetti and William Blake.

What conclusions can we draw? Poets writing for children are half as likely to be included in anthologies as those writing for adults. The poor representation of some poets is remarkable. Milne remains popular in early-years classrooms today, yet only one out of ten possible editors chose to include him. Although Lear and Stevenson are well represented, Lear is ignored in 14 out of 21 and Stevenson in four out of 15 poetry books. Compare that with the representation of Wordsworth or Tennyson in Table 2. Of course, many will argue that Wordsworth and Tennyson are anthologized for children simply because they wrote some of the best poetry ever written. Best poetry *for whom*?

None of our children's poets was included in Andrew Lang's influential *Blue Poetry Book.*[9] Sixteen editors chose to include only two or fewer of our representative children's poets in their anthologies, Women poets writing, for children do better in this table than the last. Mary Howitt and Jane Taylor fare pretty well until this century; William Roscoe hardly survives his lifetime, though Isaac Watts lasted right up to 1953 and is still occasionally anthologized today.

Once Blake's poetry was well known and widely circulated, he solidly maintained his place in children's anthologies. Not so Rossetti, who is excluded (10 omissions) more often than she is included (she is selected in eight texts). There is neither rhyme nor reason for this neglect and it certainly cannot be justified on any grounds to do with the quality of the poetry. Barbauld and Smith are even more poorly represented. As relatively few women were able to get published at all, it would appear that because of the marginalized status of poetry written for children, they suffer a double disadvantage. The neglect of women poets from anthologies is a sad part of this tale.

This evidence seems to confirm my suspicions that children's poets are less likely to gain a place in anthologies for the young than poets writing for

Table 2   British poets writing for adults represented in key anthologies for young readers from 1801–1995 (Note: The date given below each poet's name is the date of first publication of a book of poetry likely to be used by anthologists for children. The dates in the left-hand column represent the poetry anthologies)

	Burns 1780	Clare 1820	Cowper 1782	Golds 1760	Hemans 1834	Hood 1825	Pope 1730	Tennyson 1842	W'worth 1798
Aikin 1801		x	*	*	x	x	*	x	
Aikin 1825			*	*	x	x	*	x	
Mylius 1820	*	x	*	*	x	x	*	x	
Harp 1850	*		*		*				*
Palgrave 1861	*	*	*	*		*	*	*	*
Patmore 1862			*	*	*			*	*
Easy 1864					*	*		*	*
Whittier 1874			*		*	*		*	*
Young 1883	*		*		*	*			*
Lang 1892	*		*	*		*			*
Lucas 1897	*		*	*		*			
Lucas 1907						*		*	*
Burt 1904	*				*	*		*	*
de la Mare 1923	*	*	*	*	*	*	*	*	*
de la Mare 1931	*		*			*		*	*
Pocock 1933		*							*
Graham 1953		*	*						*
Smith 1953	*	*	*	*				*	*
Read 1957		*						*	*
Grigson 1959	*	*	*			*			*
Dragon 1977	*	*		*			*	*	*
Philip 1990	*	*		*		*			*
Berry 1995	*		*	*	*		*	*	*

* = at least one poem included in anthology
x = couldn't be included in anthology because writing at a later date.

Table 3   British poets writing for children represented in key anthologies for young readers from 1801 to 1995. (Note: The date given below each poet's name is the date of first publication of a book of poetry likely to be used by anthologists for children)

	Howitt 1834	Lear 1846	Milne 1923	Roscoe 1809	Stevenson 1885	Taylor 1804	Watts 1715
Aikin 1801	x	x	x	x	x	x	x
Aikin 1825	x	x	x		x		x
Mylius 1820	x	x	x		x		
Harp 1850	*		x		x		
Palgrave 1861			x		x		
Patmore 1862			x		x		
Easy 1864			x		x	*	*
Whittier 1874	*	*	x			*	
Young 1883	*		x		x	*	*
Lang 1892							
Lucas 1897	*	*	x	*	*	*	
Lucas 1907			x		*	*	
Burt 1904	*		x		*	*	*
de la Mare 1923	*		x		*		*
de la Mare 1931	*				*	*	
Pocock 1933					*		
Graham 1953		*			*	*	*
Smith 1953		*			*	*	*
Read 1957							
Grigson 1959		*					
Dragon 1977					*		
Philip 1990		*			*		
Berry 1995		*	*		*		

adults. The editor of *The Children's Harp* (1850) brings us up full square with the main thesis of this chapter:

> So far as possible, we have taken our specimens from standard writers, who, with the true sublimity of genius, have often, amid their loftiest flights, poured forth simpler melodies than *meaner bards can command* when handling the lute with a *purposed view to meet the infantile capacity*.[10] [my emphasis]

Table 4   British poets writing for children and adults represented in key anthologies from 1801 to 1995

	Barbauld 1782	Blake 1789	Smith 1804	Rossetti 1872
Aikin 1801	*		x	x
Aikin 1825	*		*	x
Mylius 1820	*		*	x
Harp 1850				
Palgrave 1861	*	*		x
Patmore 1862	*	*	*	x
Easy 1864	*			x
Whittier 1874		*		
Young 1883		*	*	
Lang 1892		*		
Lucas 1897		*		*
Lucas 1907	*	*	*	
Burt 1904	*			
de la Mare 1923		*		*
de la Mare 1931		*		*
Pocock 1933		*		
Graham 1953		*		*
Smith 1953		*		
Read 1957		*		*
Grigson 1959		*		
Dragon 1977		*		*
Philip 1990		*		*
Berry 1995		*		*

Meaner bards seems to imply those who write for children.

Thus poetry written specifically for a young audience gets marginalized by influential editors and a tradition becomes established where adult poetry by the so-called 'great' poets is considered preferable to writing directed at children. And it is still happening today.

Here is Robert Hull being slightly condescending about Brian Patten's *Puffin Book of 20th Century Verse*.[11] 'Brian Patten's volume is a book of good poems for children written in the twentieth century, and that's about it.'[12] What else should it be? Or Anthea Bell discussing Prelutsky's

The Walker Book Of Poetry For Children:[13] If I am lukewarm it is because I feel that Prelutsky has been compiling down … He draws largely on specifically children's poets …'[14] Or Neil Philip in his introduction to *A New Treasury Of Poetry* 1990:

> I have also been cautious with poems written specially for children, preferring on the whole work which makes itself available to a young reader without any sense of talking or writing down. Of course, some poets have written marvellously for children …[15]

Or consider Gillian Avery's comments in her *Everyman Anthology of Poetry for Children*, 1994, where she talks of avoiding 'poems deliberately aimed at youth which – with the exception of nonsense – tend to be worthy and dull, if not arch and fey'.[16] But does it follow that poetry written for children will talk down or be dull and fey?

A tradition has developed in anthologizing for children which needs to be challenged. Traditional often means conservative, sticking with the 'tried and tested' rather than appreciating what is new, unusual, different or risky. When you combine this conservatism with nostalgia for some idealized past, often associated with adults' interest in children's poetry, then it is easy to see why anthologies for young readers fall into this pattern. There are unrecognized and unexamined historical continuities in anthologizing for children that most editors seem unaware of, and too little understanding about the poetry children actually like and choose to read. It surely is time to open up the canon particularly to show what women and poets from other parts of the world can write for children. This does not mean discarding the poetry from the past, but appreciating its value alongside new and changing voices. There is a great heritage of children's poetry in Britain and some of it is by women and working-class people and black writers, and of course, those who choose to concentrate on writing for the young.

Notes

1. Coventry Patmore, ed. *The Children's Garland*, Macmillan, London, 1862.
2. E.V. Lucas, ed. 'Some Notes on Poetry for Children', *Fortnightly Review*, Vol LX, Chapman & Hall, London, 1986, p. 391.
3. E.V. Lucas, ed. *A Book of Verses for Children*, Grant Richards, London, 1897, this edition, 1904.
4. *Mother Goose's Melody*, Marshall, London, 1760.
5. *Ibid.*
6. *Something Rich and Strange*, ed. Gina Pollinger, Kingfisher, London, 1995.
7. Iona and Peter Opie, *The Oxford Book of Children's Verse*, Oxford University Press, Oxford, 1973.
8. Lucy Aikin, *Poetry for Children*, London, 1801.

9. Andrew Lang, ed., *The Blue Poetry Book*, Longmans, Green & Co., London, 1891.
10. *The Children's Harp*, London, 1850.
11. Brian Patten, *The Puffin Book of Twentieth Century Verse*, Penguin, London, 1991.
12. Robert Hull, 'A Jostle of Poetries', *Books for Keeps*, January 1992 No. 72, London, p. 21.
13. Jack Prelutsky, ed. *The Walker Book of Poetry for Children*, Walker, London, 1984.
14. Anthea Bell, *The Signal Poetry Award*, 47, May 1985, p. 82.
15. Neil Philip, ed. *A New Treasury of Poetry*, Blackie, London, 1990, p. 15.
16. Gillian Avery, ed. *Everyman Anthology of Poetry for Children*, David Campbell Publications, London, 1994.

4

Story-telling, Stage and Screen

Introduction
Nicola J. Watson

Storytelling, stage drama and film for children have to date received remarkably little sustained critical attention. This may well change. At the turn of the twenty-first century, storytelling, first popular in 1930s Britain sponsored by the kindergarten movement and associated with the folk-tale revival, is ever more popular within schools and at literary festivals. Children's theatre has been experiencing something of a renaissance, signalled by the sell-out performances of a number of new children's pieces: Pullman's *His Dark Materials* (adapted by Nicholas Wright), *Tom's Midnight Garden* (adapted by a veteran of children's theatre, David Wood) and Michael Morpurgo's *War Horse* (adapted by Nick Stafford) amongst them. Films for children, most especially the Harry Potter series, have been making huge sums of money at the box office. Only children's television would seem presently to be wallowing in the doldrums, suffering from the combined effects of the contemporary proliferation of television channels and the impact of the internet.

Drama has nonetheless been seen as the 'Cinderella' of the academic study of children's literature, perhaps because live theatre and (by extension) film has tended to address itself to a dual 'family' audience of adults and children and therefore has not been regarded as properly 'children's' literature. Drama's low profile may in part be attributed to the field's conventional focus on British culture. Despite the fact that, overwhelmingly, theatre attendance in Britain continues to be for pantomime, children's theatre, as Carpenter and Prichard have remarked, has often been livelier outside Britain than inside it. There has been a long tradition of such theatre in

246

the USA, Canada, Australia and New Zealand, and in Russia there has been a well-developed communist youth theatre since the 1920s. Then it is the case, too, that scholars of children's literature in the West have long evinced a greater interest in fiction and picture books than in drama.

There are also problems in constructing a category of drama *for* children. Such a category comprises an indigestible and incompatible mix of material written for children to perform, children's performance of adult material, and material written for child audiences. Moreover, it is perhaps particularly true that types of drama associated with children have often been perceived as peripheral and have languished in critical obscurity. This is true of popular forms, such as pantomime, of special forms of performance, such as puppetry, and of important forms of non-professional performance associated with children as both performers and audience, ranging from masques, mummers' plays and pageants to fairy plays, nativity plays and school plays. These problems have been compounded by disciplinary fragmentation. Performance studies is specifically interested in live performance; film studies tend to stand apart from television studies; other special forms of performance and performance technology associated with children (e.g. puppet theatre) have tended to fall within theatre studies, as does the history of child performers from medieval times on. The situation has not been improved by the range of scholars potentially interested in performance for children, from theatre practitioners – directors, playwrights and educationists – through to theatre historians.

This accounts for the vast variety of perspectives on drama for children (see Further Reading). Historicist studies of educational literature have sometimes lighted on educational plays for children; practitioner educationists have been interested in it as a way of reaching and empowering children in developing countries; theatre and cultural studies have contributed some work on the history of professional child performance from the Renaissance onwards and some on stage adaptation (much of it of the 'how to' variety); and bibliophiles have done some work on cataloguing and describing nineteenth-century toy theatres, such as those put out by Pollock's. There is a body of theoretical work on political theatre for children, much of it associated with the project of the communist USSR and its aftermath. With reference specifically to screen performance, there has been some work on the history of children's cinema, and some polemical work on the conservative politics of Disney's adaptations of fairy tales. From an ethnological perspective, there has been some research carried out on children's participation in folk theatre in Africa.

Where stage and screen have been tackled from a literary point of view, it has tended to be on an occasional basis, related to the reception, adaptation, and after-lives of individually important texts. There is a body of criticism, for example, on *Peter Pan*, which began one of its lives as a stage play, and on the reception of other texts which began their lives as prose fiction but have been reincarnated on stage and screen, such as *Alice's Adventures in Wonderland*, *Little Women*, *The Wind in the Willows*, *Charlie and the Chocolate Factory* and, more recently, *Northern Lights* and *Harry Potter*. Occasionally, drama has swum into view as influencing an individual writer, one example being the attention given to the influence of toy theatres on the young Stevenson's imagination. Surprisingly, there has been virtually no work drawing on the representation of child performance in fiction, whether amateur (as in the opening chapters of *Little Women* and in *The Railway Children* and *Party Shoes*), school-based (as in Frank Cottrell Boyce's *Millions*) or professional (as in Noel Streatfeild's *Ballet Shoes* and *The Painted Garden*).

The essays

Included here, then, are three essays which together may serve as a starting-point for studying storytelling, stage drama and film for children. The first, by Joan Swann, turns its attention to the phenomenon of the recent resurgence of professionalised storytelling for children, briefly placing it in historical context, and then modelling a method of analysing such performances. It is followed by a survey of drama for children by Susanne Greenhalgh, which usefully disentangles some of the terminology used around theatre *for* children, before offering a sweeping survey of drama for children across history and around the globe, and providing along the way a guided tour through much of the relevant critical and theoretical writing in the field. The last essay included here is a discussion by Deborah Cartmell of the relation between classic texts and screen adaptations of them, considering the ways in which print texts and film versions have vied for supremacy by looking at the critical fortunes of a number of films, including *Little Women*, *The Wizard of Oz*, *Mary Poppins*, *Peter Pan*, *Charlie and the Chocolate Factory* and *Harry Potter and the Philosopher's Stone*. Those interested in adaptation as creative revision will also find Linda Hutcheon's essay, included in Part 6, valuable and thought-provoking in this context.

Further reading

Armstrong, G.S. 1985. 'Art, Folly, and the Bright Eyes of Children: The Origins of Regency Toy Theatre Re-evaluated', *Theatre Survey: The Journal of the American Society for Theatre Research*, 26 (2): 121–42.

Bazalgette, C. and Buckingham, D. 1995. *In Front of the Children: Screen Entertainment and Young Audiences*. London, British Film Institute.

Davis, T. C. 1986. 'The Employment of Children in the Victorian Theatre', *New Theatre Quarterly*, 2 (6): 116–35.

Etherton, M. 2004. 'South Asia's Child Rights Theatre for Development: The Empowerment of Children Who Are Marginalised, Disadvantaged and Excluded', in R. Boon and J. Plastow (eds) *Theatre and Empowerment: Community Drama on the World Stage*. Cambridge, Cambridge University Press.

Hollindale, P. 2009. '100 Years of *Peter Pan*', in H.K. Montgomery and N.J. Watson (eds) *Children's Literature: Classic Texts and Contemporary Trends*. Basingstoke, Palgrave Macmillan.

Levy, J. and Mahard, M. 1987. 'Preliminary Checklist of Early Printed Children's Plays in English, 1780–1855', *Performing Arts Resources*, 12: 1–97.

Mckenzie, M. L. 1982. 'The Toy Theatre, Romance, and *Treasure Island*: The Artistry of R.L.S.', *English Studies in Canada* 8 (4): 409–21.

Morton, M., Sats, N. and Krymova, N. 1979. *Through the Magic Curtain: Theatre for Children, Adolescents and Youth in the USSR: 27 Authoritative Essays*. New Orleans, Anchorage.

Munro, L. 2005. 'The Humour of Children: Performance, Gender, and the Early Modern Children's Companies', *Literature Compass*, 2 (1).

Ottenberg, S. and Binkley, D. (eds), 2006. *Playful Performers: African Children's Masquerades*. New Brunswick, NJ, Transaction.

Purinton, M. D. 2005. 'Gender, Nationalism, and Science in Hannah More's Pedagogical Plays for Children', in D. Ruwe (ed.) *Culturing the Child, 1690–1914: Essays in Memory of Mitzi Myers*. Lanham, MD, Scarecrow (with Children's Literature Association).

Speaight, G. 1971. 'The Toy Theatre', *Harvard Library Bulletin*, 19: 307–13.

Staples, T. 1996. *All Pals Together: The Story of Children's Cinema*. Edinburgh, Edinburgh University Press.

Van de Water, M. 2004. 'Russian Drama and Theatre in Education: Perestroika and Glasnost in Moscow Theatres for Children and Youth', *Research in Drama Education*, 9 (2): 161–76.

Zipes, J. 1995. 'Breaking the Disney Spell' in E. Bell, L. Haas and L. Sells (eds) *From Mouse to Mermaid: The Politics of Film, Gender, and Culture*. Bloomington, Indiana University Press.

Stories in Performance
Joan Swann

In *Written For Children*, a classic account of the history of children's literature, John Rowe Townsend refers, almost in passing, to narratives in the oral tradition: legends, romances, stories and ballads, and 'the humble folktales passed down by word of mouth from generation to generation' (Townsend, 1992: 4). For Townsend, these were not part of children's literature proper but its prehistory – an antecedent to the print texts that appeared in Britain from the eighteenth century onwards. This essay, however, is about storytelling in its own right, as a form that both precedes and runs alongside print literature. While stories for children are pervasive across a range of contemporary media – print itself, film and television, computer games – my focus here is on oral narratives. These again take a number of forms. Print, for instance, may be rendered into speech when adults read stories to and with children; story is often embedded in children's play activities in pretend play, playground rhymes and other forms of 'lore'. However, I want to look at storytelling as a distinctive performance genre that, alive and well as a contemporary practice, is also rooted in a long oral tradition. Storytelling in this sense may involve storytellers performing alone or with others, with or without musical accompaniment, with or without costumes or props. Stories may be more scripted or less. Audiences may listen quietly or may engage more actively in the performance. What unites these events is that they all involve the artful or literary performance of narrative to an audience.

In what follows I first consider the oral tradition in storytelling before turning to a recent revival of interest in storytelling for children and adults. I focus on three examples of story performances, considering both how these may be analysed as literary[1] accomplishments and what the performers have to say about the value of their work for children.

Storytelling across times and places

Researchers interested in story have documented a number of characteristics of narratives in the oral tradition: in particular, themes and story-types that recur across particular geographical locations and historical periods – the result of stories being passed from one teller to another, adapted on the way (e.g. Propp [1928] 1984; Uther 2004). The value of such work is that it shows how stories are constantly crafted and recrafted; by implication, any contemporary story bears the imprint of former tellings. A story is a retelling of events that will have been told, in one form or another, on countless occasions in the past; it is also something new, told afresh in the here and now and never to be repeated in quite this form.

Rather less has been documented on performances. Anne Pellowski (1991) identifies the earliest written references to storytelling as dating from 2000–1300BC, recorded in Egypt on papyrus. While 'children's literature' proper is said to date from the eighteenth century it is evident that, through history, children have been exposed to story and also that stories have been told specifically to children. Pellowski cites Amphitryon, a character in Euripides' play *Heracles* (c. 423BC), advising his daughter-in-law Megara on what to do while waiting for her husband's return:

> Be calm;
> dry the living springs of tears that fill
> your children's eyes. Console them with stories,
> those sweet thieves of wretched make-believe.
> cited in Pellowski, 1991: 5

And, in Aristophanes' play *Lysistrata* (*c.* 411BC), a chorus of old men refer to a story from their youth: 'I want to tell you a fable they used to relate to me when I was a little boy' (cited in Pellowski, 1991: 5).

Pellowski also provides evidence of who told stories and where they were told – from ordinary people at home and at work, to professionals such as bards, minstrels and epic performers in ancient Greek and Sanskrit traditions and across many cultures up to the present day. Looking at the relatively recent history of storytelling in Europe, from the medieval period to the present, Jack Zipes (2001) points to the diversity of contexts in which stories were told:

> there were all types of settings in which tales were told in spontaneous and organized moments: marriage, birth, and death ceremonies called for different kinds of tales. Numerous religions and ethnic groups developed particular creation stories to explain how the earth was formed and how the gods came into being. Festivals and holidays were all associated with particular stories. Soldiers recounted great heroic feats that became legends. Farming and the conditions of life in the country formed the backdrop of tales told at harvest time or around the hearth. Rumors and stories were spread about bandits, duplicitous priests, and miraculous events by merchants and travelers. Each trade, such as blacksmith, tailor, and spinner, and each profession, such as priest, peddler, sailor, had stories associated with it. Aristocrats organized court spectacles and pageants that included storytelling. Rulers sought entertainment through storytellers, and salons were formed by aristocrats and bourgeois women in which artful conversation and storytelling played important roles. Factories, churches, synagogues, temples, bathhouses, brothels, shops, prisons, schools, hospitals, saloons, and many other settings were the places that generated generic kinds of tales linked to the experiences that people had in these places. Hundreds, thousands, and millions of tales were told there and continue to be told in similar settings today. They were told to instruct, warn, satirize, amuse, parody, preach, question, illustrate, explain, and enjoy. It all depended on the teller and auditors in a given social situation. (Zipes, 2001: 133)

Here Zipes notes a range of different purposes for stories – both serious/instructional and for entertainment – a point I will come back to below in connection with contemporary story performances.

By no means all of these stories were meant specifically for children, of course, but children would be present at many storytelling events. The Scottish folklorist Alexander Carmichael provides an account of a ceilidh in the Western Isles of Scotland in the nineteenth century, in which children were squeezed in with adults, girls crouched between the knees of fathers or brothers and boys perched wherever they could climb: 'Occasionally a moment of excitement occurs when heat and sleep overpower a boy and he tumbles down among the people below, to be trounced out and sent home' (Carmichael, [1900] 1992: 23).

Historical observations, then, provide some evidence about storytelling as a practice both directed towards children and at which children formed part of the audience, or were incidental bystanders. More systematic accounts of storytelling as a form of verbal art emerged from the performance tradition in linguistic anthropology and folklore that developed in the 1960s and 1970s. One of the most influential researchers in this tradition, Richard Bauman (1986: 2), comments that, from the beginnings of the study of folklore in the eighteenth century, oral literature had been conceived of as 'stuff – collectively shaped, traditional stuff that could wander around the map, fill up collections and archives, reflect culture and so on'. This was to abstract oral literature from the context in which it had originally been performed. Bauman's interest, by contrast, was in the 'ethnography of oral performance' within particular cultural contexts. His definition of performance emphasised the importance of both performer and audience: performance is described as 'a mode of communication, a way of speaking, the essence of which resides in the assumption of responsibility to an audience for a display of communicative skill'; the performance is 'laid open to evaluation for the way it is done, for the relative skill and effectiveness of the performer's display' (1986: 3). Bauman's conception of performance underpins many contemporary studies, and I draw on these ideas below in analysing three recent storytelling performances.

Many performance-oriented studies of storytelling have focused on communities with a continuing oral tradition, such as Ruth Finnegan's well-known research on Limba stories and storytelling in Sierra Leone (1967, 2007). Finnegan comments that, in oral literature, 'the bare words can not be left to speak for themselves, for the simple reason that in the actual literary work so much else is necessarily and intimately involved' (2007: 87). Limba storytellers drew on rhetorical devices such as repetition, mimicry, gesture; they made artful use of songs, direct speech, changes in tempo, pitch and atmosphere. The audience was also crucial – they 'incited and played up to the teller through laughter, exaggerated surprise, shock, sympathy and, in stories with songs, enthusiastic singing or even occasionally dancing to the chorus' (2007: 45). Children would have been present at many performances recorded in this and similar studies – Finnegan notes that performers might omit obscenities, certain types of jokes or complex forms in the presence of children (2007: 84), and also that children learnt narrative themes and storytelling skills informally, and began telling stories amongst themselves as part of peer group enjoyment (2007: 44). However, despite the importance placed on audience in anthropological and folklore studies of performance, discussion of children's participation in storytelling events is usually fairly limited. (Pellowski (1991) provides some discussion in a chapter on 'folkstorytelling'.)

The contemporary 'revival' in storytelling

The 1970s and 1980s saw what has been termed a 'revival' of storytelling in Western/European contexts: the growth of performances, mainly by professional storytellers in a range of venues – pubs, festivals, schools and libraries. This movement has been documented in the USA by Kay Stone (1986). Stone distinguishes three contexts for storytelling: first, traditional oral narration, such as the example above from Sierra Leone. Within the USA, Stone notes that similar practices are evident in Native American communities but also in tales adapted from British traditions. People in 'tale-telling' communities in North Carolina, for instance, can trace their stories back to British ancestors from the 1700s. In this case, stories are regarded as an important literary expression, passed down from one generation to the next, and also passed between peer groups. Storytellers adapt traditional texts and create new texts based on traditional models. Stone argues that they develop a 'flexible concept of verbal creativity quite different from our perceptions of a story as a fixed text' (1986: 17).

By contrast, Stone's second context, non-traditional urban storytelling, dates from the late 1800s, with the rise of liberal and universal education. Storytelling, in this case, has clear educational associations: stories are told in schools, libraries, etc. by teachers and other professionals. Performances are scheduled – e.g. as a 'story hour' – rather than being told as and when, as in traditional communities. Storytellers tend to learn their craft from workshops or other training sessions, and stories may be memorised from books. In an apt metaphor, Stone comments: 'Nontraditional urban storytelling often resembles cooking from a recipe rather than recreating dishes learned from watching other cooks' (1986: 20).

The more recent revival in storytelling has given rise to Stone's third context, which she terms 'neo-traditional tale-telling', characterised by more dynamic performance styles. Stone argues that, in the USA, this developed from urban storytelling in the 1970s as some tellers became professionals, meeting up with and learning from others at venues such as folk festivals. While performers do not share a traditional, oral culture, they are nevertheless part of a storytelling community, and in this sense they have something in common with traditional storytellers. For Stone, they are the stepchildren of the oral tradition (1986: 28). Zipes takes a more critical view of at least some professional storytellers. For Zipes, 'genuine' storytelling should be

both magical and subversive, enabling children and others to explore themselves and the world in critical and creative ways (2001: 141). Professional
storytellers, however, need to work within market conditions, and they may
therefore seek to please their audiences and customers rather than challenging them. Zipes identifies two large camps of professional storytellers: those
who perform largely for the sake of performance and who have forgotten
any sense of cultural mission, and those who continue to reflect on their
role as storyteller and to question their own practice. In this latter case storytellers may act as animators, rather than simply as performers, using story
to empower their audiences.

In practice, contemporary storytelling performances seem to fulfil a variety
of functions. The same performer may perform on stage, with stories as an
art form demanding an aesthetic response, and use stories in workshops to
promote 'restorative justice' (e.g. the British storyteller Christine McMahon)
or to develop 'racism awareness' (the US Lakota storyteller Robert Greygrass).
Professionally performed, artful stories may also combine aesthetic pleasure
with the exploration of challenging moral dilemmas, as in a long and winding story from the British storyteller Ben Haggarty where the narrative was
broken by a debate with some seven-year-old children on whether Death was
needed in the world. It is hard in such cases to maintain a straightforward
distinction between two discrete camps of performance or performer.

Three storytellers

In this section I want to look at some examples of story performances.
The performances are by three professional storytellers who were part of
a recent revival of interest in storytelling in Britain, corresponding roughly
to the revival documented by Kay Stone in North America. Ben Haggarty,
Tuup and Jan Blake began as storytellers in London in the 1980s, and all
three currently perform both for children and adults – in schools, libraries,
pubs and storytelling cafés and at festivals.

In a series of interviews carried out for the Open University the storytellers discussed aspects of their work. As is common amongst contemporary
storytellers, they focus on stories from particular traditions. Many of Jan's
stories come from the Caribbean and West Africa: she describes this as a
cultural attraction as her parents are from the Caribbean and her ancestry is
West African. Tuup tells stories from the Caribbean for similar reasons – his
parents come from Guyana – but he also tells stories from other cultural
traditions including Native American stories. Many of Ben's stories come
from eastern Europe. They tend to be long stories with fairly complex plots,
often running to a performance of an hour or more. While all these stories

come from an oral tradition, they are usually picked up by the teller from print collections. In this case there is no record of earlier performance elements, and the stories are reanimated and reperformed at very different times and in very different places. In a continuation of earlier oral practices, even where the basic plot remains unchanged, the words of the stories are not fixed, but are adapted in performance and from one performance to the next. Ben describes a more complex stitching together of plot, in which a Romanian gypsy story, 'The Red King and the Witch', is combined with elements from another story – 'Prince Ivan, the Witch Baby and the Little Sister of the Sun' (from Arthur Ransome's *Old Peter's Russian Tales*) and various other motifs to produce a new, composite story.

The stories are meant to entertain and delight, as well as developing children's imagination. But all three storytellers comment that they have, in part, an educational function: Ben refers to 'a grain of practical advice', but his stories sometimes explore profound moral questions that go beyond the practical (I mentioned above his discussion, with seven-year-olds, of whether Death is needed in the world). Tuup refers to 'the grain of truth' which is 'sometimes the wisdom and sometimes the moral of the story'. Jan comments that stories explore the 'triumphs and failings of being a human being'. In telling stories, 'the storyteller guides the children to an arena where they can reflect'. Storytellers are, however, 'illuminators' rather than 'instructors'.

The storytellers also talk about the responsibility they have to their audience as they enter the story world. Ben comments that, in his body of stories, there are strong images that could 'terrify anybody'. Storytellers therefore have to be responsible for what they bring forward. For this process both Jan and Tuup use the metaphor of a journey in which children travel, with the storyteller, to dangerous places, maybe meeting dragons and demons or fighting in battles, and then need to be brought back safely. Jan comments: 'I'll take you up close, I'll give you the wide shots, I'll give you as much as you need to have a fully-fledged experience and then I will bring you away from that place, safe, sound and more importantly, whole.' Tuup notes similarly that when children come back out of the story 'hopefully they feel physically that they haven't journeyed, but mentally they've travelled far'.

For large parts of our interviews, we focused on a key element of storytelling – live performance. The storytellers read source materials, but do not memorise them. Certain phrases and routines are developed in performance and may recur from one performance to the next, but the stories are not scripted. How stories are performed will depend upon the place, the time available, audience response and the need to respond, on the hoof, to any other events. While some storytellers plan aspects of their performance, Jan in particular comments that she prefers spontaneity: 'I like to work with the material that is in the room, which is me, the children, the teachers and my … library of stories that I have in my mind.' She works intuitively, starting with songs or riddles to gauge the audience, and then selects stories that she feels will work.

Jan sees her own and Tuup's storytelling style as based on an African cultural tradition, though not one that she consciously learned. The unplanned nature of their work is consistent with evidence on storytelling in Africa. For instance, Roger Abrahams comments on what he terms the 'quality of immediacy in an African story' (1983: 45), and Isidore Okpewho (1992) refers to the 'maximum use of innovation and manipulation': 'In most narrative traditions across the African continent, the storyteller simply has the bare outlines of the story and is expected to make the appropriate adjustments to the details in accordance with the interests of the audience' (Okpewho, 1992: 45). Okpewho also discusses the highly visual nature of African performance styles, as storytellers dramatise the emotions and actions of their characters. This, however, is also found in the performance of other contemporary professional storytellers – I discuss examples from Ben's work below.

In live performance, storytellers need to establish a connection with their audience: Jan refers to 'a thread that gets thrown out and hooked into the audience – you know, kind of multi-threads, and we are all hooked to each other'. Tuup refers to an 'umbilical cord … between the two of you'. The audience is also involved directly in the story, for instance in call-and-response story openings (such as 'crick … crack'), questions and answers, sometimes the audience playing the part of characters, or joining in songs or rhythmic episodes. Tuup comments that audiences respond differently, depending on their familiarity with story and with storytelling traditions: African and Caribbean audiences, for instance, may be more responsive to his stories. Audiences accustomed to theatrical conventions may be quieter. It is audience and storyteller together, then, that produce a particular type of performance.

Storytellers need constantly to monitor their audience, adapting the performance in the light of audience response. Given the rapidity with which decisions need to be made, much of this must happen at a subconscious level. Ben, however, describes an element of reflexivity in managing a performance, using the image of 'a very long ear and eye, sitting out there in the audience … you need to know what you've said, you need to see how it's going down and you need to see the faces'. He refers to a 'director voice going on in your mind … arranging what's happening' as he milks something the audience is enjoying then needs to rush through another part of the story to make up time. Tuup similarly uses a metaphor from film: 'It's like … watching one of these films where … you're looking at the film, you're looking at the characters, and then the camera pans round ... you can almost see yourself in the picture and you can see everything around you.' Sometimes for Tuup, however, the audience falls away: 'it's the story that begins to move me and take me through the course of the story that I'm telling till I get to the end'.

The storytellers refer to different semiotic resources that work together to produce a performance: a combination of verbal language – the adoption of a particular language variety, accent or voice quality; poetic language such as verbal imagery, rhyme, rhythm, alliteration, metaphor, repetition of words and phrases; song, and verbal routines such as riddles; and a range of visual features such as gesture, facial expression, posture, movement, use of space, clothing, sometimes musical accompaniment, sometimes props, and particular types of backdrop. Sometimes, the use of particular semiotic resources is planned, or at least the choices made are the subject of conscious reflection – for instance, Ben refers to the importance of clothing. At the performance we recorded, Ben also wanted a 'neutral' backdrop such as a gym wall or a black cloth. In the event, he had to perform in front of bookcases, so these were covered in fabric to retain an emphasis on orality. The moment-by-moment adoption of particular performance features is, however, likely to be more intuitive: Jan comments, 'I'll use whatever I need to use, so I'll use my hands, I'll use my voice, I'll use my body, but I don't plan ... it just happens naturally, it's what the story draws out of me and I draw on the story.'

Analysing stories in performance

In the light of this evidence of how three contemporary storytellers talk about their art, I turn in this section to actual storytelling practices, and how these may be analysed. While I provide brief outlines of stories told by Ben, Tuup and Jan, my main focus here is on performance. I shall look particularly at two aspects of performance: how the storytellers represent different 'voices', whether the voice of the narrator recounting the story or the voices of different characters; and how they monitor and interact with their audiences.

The analysis here bears some resemblance to the stylistic analysis of other literary art forms such as poetry for children, but it needs to take account of features other than verbal language: as the storytellers themselves suggest, they draw on a range of semiotic resources in their work. I shall focus on the use of vocal characteristics, how the storytellers use their bodies (e.g. in gaze, facial expression, gesture and other bodily movement, body orientation) and their occasional use of musical and rhythmical accompaniment, in this case drumming and bells.

The story performances

All three performances took place in London primary schools in 2008. Ben performed to a class of 9–10-year-olds and their teachers, in a large classroom. Tuup and Jan gave consecutive performances to an audience composed of 7–8-year-old children, teachers and some family members. The performances took place in the school hall.

Ben's story

This is the long and winding narrative (lasting about 50 minutes) referred to earlier: a prince, having seen his baby sister transform herself temporarily into a ravenous witch, sets off on a quest to find the land where death can't reach him. His sister devours other family members before pursuing him.

Jan's story

Jan told a 10-minute riddling story in which a prince claims the throne from his evil father. The prince is sent off by his father to find the best and the worst things in the world to eat: if he succeeds, he will ascend to the throne; if not, he will die.

Tuup's story

Tuup's 15-minute story concerns two friends, Mr Salt and Mrs Sugar, whose natures are very different (respectively sharp-tempered and generous/forgiving) and describes an incident where they fall out and then need to be reconciled, each borrowing something of the other's character.

The representation of narrator and character voices

Note that, in all extracts, plain text shows the storyteller speaking in narrator voice; **bold** indicates where the storyteller takes on the voice of a character, using direct speech. <u>Underlining</u> indicates where the storyteller visually embodies a character.

The first extract comes from Jan's riddling story. It begins just after the prince has brought his father a piece of cooked tongue to eat, seasoned with delicious spices and presented, with garnish, on a lovely plate:

the <u>king took his royal knife and fork and he began to cut through the pink flesh that was lying on the plate in front of him. He took a mouthful.</u> **'Mmmm ...'** said the king, **'mmmm, this is, mmmm it's absolute ...'**

<u>He dispensed with the knife and fork.</u> **'Mmmmm! Mmmm! This is delicious! Mmmmm! What is it?'**

'I will answer in the form of a riddle', said the prince. **'This thing, this innocent lies between two assassins.'**

'I don't know what you mean', said the king. **'Mmmm, what is it? Mmmm!'**

In the extract, Jan begins in narrator voice then switches to take on the king's voice, the intonation and vocal intensity of the repeated 'mmmm's indicating his delight in the food. Jan's visual representation of the king, however, is more protracted and extends beyond the direct speech: in 'took his royal knife and fork' she shows him picking up his cutlery; on 'cut through' he cuts the meat, and on 'he took a mouthful' he brings his fork to his mouth; later he eats with both hands, greedily gobbling the food. In terms of language and voice quality, there is a clear distinction between the narrator and character voices, but the distinction between narrator and characters is blurred visually. In this and other stories by Jan, narrator accounts of characters and their actions are often accompanied by visual dramatisations of characters – particular facial expressions, bodily stances, movement, etc. – filling out verbal descriptions or providing additional descriptive information that is absent from the verbal text.

Storytellers vary in the extent to which they dramatise characters and their activities, but this is evident here in all three performances. A particularly striking example is Ben's depiction of the baby in his story, transformed into a witch, speeding past her brother the prince to get to the palace kitchen:

With her teeth like iron axe blades, with her fingernails like razor blades **yaahh** she flew past his head, **yaahh** she flew along the corridor, **yaahh** she flew down the stairs, **yaahh** she flew along the corridor, **yaahh** she entered the kitchen, she stood in front of that larder door and she wrestled it off its hinges and then she stared at the food **yum, yum**. And with her iron teeth she scoffed, scoffed, scoffed, scoffed, scoffed all the food and then smash, smash, smash, smash, smashed all the plates and then **yaahh** she flew out the kitchen, **yaahh** along the corridor, **yaahh** up the stairs, **yaahh** along the corridor, **yaahh** past his head, did three somersaults and turned back into ever such a sweet little baby sister.

The repetitions of 'yaahh' here (a sound that is difficult to represent in writing) are reflected in the repetition of a darting gesture, as the witch rushes screeching towards the kitchen then back to the bedroom, the 'yum, yum' is uttered in the witch's deep voice and the repeated 'scoffed' and 'smashed' are visually represented as Ben, in narrator voice, takes on the body of the large and terrifying witch. By contrast, the final 'ever such a sweet little baby sister' is uttered in a gentle and melodic tone (see Figures 12 and 13).

While I've focused here on how the storyteller may take on the voice and physical attributes of particular characters, other representational devices may be used in performance. Ben, for instance, uses a bell to represent the

Figure 12   Ben Haggerty as the witch in the kitchen: 'Yum, yum'

Figure 13   Ben Haggerty indicating the baby: 'ever such a sweet little baby sister'

'strange music' that acts as a signature for the baby/witch, heralding her appearance in the narrative.

Monitoring and interacting with the audience

All three storytellers referred, in their interviews, to the need to maintain a connection with their audience, and this represents a significant aspect of performance: storytellers need to check on audience reactions and to ensure that the audience is engaged in the narrative. There are several performance elements through which this is achieved.

First, in narrating the story, storytellers often draw on certain routines that bring an audience into the story world – the extract below shows how Tuup teaches his audience the 'crick … crack' call and response. In this case, Tuup's final extending and trilling of the 'r' sound is echoed by the children:

Tuup:	There's a call and a response. If I say to you crick, can you say to me crack and so the fire of our imagination can begin to burn bright? I say crick and you say …
Children:	Crack!
Tuup:	Crick!
Children:	Crack!
Tuup:	Crick!
Children:	Crack!
Tuup:	Crrrrrrrrrrrrick!
Children:	Crrrrrrrrrrrrack!

Storytellers also use direct questioning as a means of interacting with their audience. Questions may check on children's understanding or may encourage them to predict or speculate. More generally they are a way of securing audience participation in the narrative, and responses may be built into the storyline, as in the extract below from Tuup:

Tuup:	(*plays the bongo drum*) I'm going to share with you a story about Mr Salt and Mrs Sugar. I want someone to tell me though, what do you think is the character, the nature, the personality of Mr Salt? What do you think he is like? As a person, what do you think he is like? Salt, Mr Salt.
Child:	Bitter.
Tuup:	Bitter, bitter, bitter, bitter, bitter, bitter, bitter, bitter.
Child:	(unclear)
Tuup:	He eats! Cos when you've got salt in your mouth and you got salt in your food you've got to eat sometime. You've got to eat to take out the salt. You've got to drink, you've got to drink, you've got to drink. You've got to eat, you've got to eat. You've got to drink, you've got to drink, you've got to eat. (smiles) What else do you think about Mr Salt? What else do you think? Yes?
Child:	He's mean.
Tuup:	He could be mean. Maybe Mr Salt is a bit mean. Maybe he doesn't really think so sharply. He doesn't think about the process of words that leaves his mouth.

Tuup's repetition of 'bitter' here is accompanied by a bitter facial expression and voice quality, possibly as if eating something bitter. In 'you've got to eat … you've got to drink' Tuup embodies Mr Salt eating and drinking. The tempo built up here, along with the visual and verbal repetition, elicits laughter from the audience, and Tuup smiles. The next child's offer of 'He's mean' allows Tuup to introduce a key theme that will recur in the narrative: Mr Salt does not think about the effects of what he says.

Whereas the use of call-and-response devices, and questions, directly elicits a response from children, other narrative devices may invite participation more indirectly. In Ben's story, for instance, there are several occasions in which the prince rides (and in one case swims with his horse) for a year and a day until he reaches a new place, for example:

Ben: (*drumming on the side of his stool*)
and he rode and he rode and he rode and he rode and he rode and he rode for the whole of that day, and he rode for the whole of that night and he rode for the whole of the next day and he rode for the whole of the next night, he rode for the whole of the week, he rode for the whole of the next week, he rode for the whole of the month, he rode for the whole of the next month, he rode for a year, he rode for a year and a day.

Such sequences mark transitions between episodes, but the rhythm built up here, the repetition of 'he rode' and the repetition of similar sequences across the narrative also encourage the children to join in, echoing the storyteller's words and maintaining the rhythm.

Even when not directing particular comments or questions towards the audience, storytellers, as narrators, necessarily address the audience in recounting the story, and their gaze sometimes pans to take in different parts of the audience. This seems obvious enough when the storyteller is in narrator voice, but the situation is actually more complex. I mentioned earlier that the storyteller may embody a character's actions, even when speaking as narrator. In this case, the narrator/character may temporarily shift his/her gaze away from the audience, towards another character. But also the storyteller, in character voice, may interact with other characters while simultaneously orienting his/her gaze towards the audience. To give an example, in Tuup's story Mr Salt and Mrs Sugar kiss and make up after their quarrel, but because Mr Salt is wet after being out in the rain their lips stick and they cannot separate. In narrator voice, Tuup alternates between the representation of the protracted kiss, in profile, the fingers of his left hand gathered to a point and touching his lips, and turning to face the audience more directly, his hand still in place near his lips. After trying unsuccessfully to separate, Mrs Sugar addresses Mr Salt: 'Stop! Mr Salt, you have become wet all the way through to the bone. We have to wait until you dry off.' Although in character voice, with Mrs Sugar addressing Mr Salt, Tuup faces towards the audience, allowing him to keep half an eye on them and also to secure their involvement (see Figure 14).

Figure 14   Tuup as Mrs Sugar addresses Mr Salt

The extract below, from Jan's story, brings together different performance elements discussed earlier: Jan's adoption of narrator and character voices, and her interaction with the audience in each voice. The extract also shows a way of representing, in greater detail, how a performer may draw on a combination of verbal and visual modes to achieve these ends. In the extract, the prince has just appeared in his father's palace, and demanded that his father give him the throne. The story continues:

The king <u>looked at his fine young son, and half of him was very proud and the other half of him was filled with jealousy</u>, and he couldn't give him the throne just like that. So the king said, '**I'll give you the throne on one condition; if you can bring me the very best and the very worst thing in the world to eat I will give you the throne but if you fail, tcha! Off with your** [pause] **head.**'

I have retranscribed this extract below, including the verbal text in a left-hand column, with accompanying visual information in the form of a running commentary on the right. This representation is necessarily partial, and relies on an analytical judgement about what is relevant: different analyses would therefore include different features. The two stills from this sequence (see Figures 15 and 16) illustrate Jan's representation of the king, addressing his son. On 'give', Jan looks directly left towards the son; on 'world', Jan's gaze pans right so that while still addressing the son she is also able to take in the audience.

The king <u>looked at his fine young son,</u>	On 'looked' Jan begins to raise her left arm; arm raised then lowered, indicating son; gaze initially towards audience, then moves left as if towards son.
<u>and half of him was very proud</u>	Jan oriented slightly to left, raises both hands to left in slightly outward movement, proud expression.
<u>and the other half of him was filled with jealousy,</u>	Jan reorients to right, her hands move right, her fingers curl till almost clenched, her face twists indicating displeasure
and he couldn't give him. the throne just like that	Jan orients forwards facing audience more directly as gaze pans slightly left, then right; hands separate.
So the king said, **'I'll give you the throne on one condition;**	From beginning of direct speech, as the king addresses his son, Jan's gaze shifts to left, leans forward and to left, left hand extended in same direction.
if you can bring me the very best and the very worst thing in the world to eat I will give you the throne	From 'if', with the king still addressing his son, Jan reorients her body to face forwards then slightly right; left hand raised, slight emphatic gestures with index finger; gazing forwards then slightly right, taking in audience; on 'eat', left hand moves to mouth.
but if you fail, tcha! Off with your [pause] **head.'** (Children repeat 'head')	On 'tcha!', Jan draws left hand across throat. In pause, Jan's left hand moves to side of head, cueing audience response.

In the analysis above I have tried to show how storytelling works as a per-formance genre. All three storytellers have commented that they draw on a range of semiotic resources in their performance – verbal language, voice qual-ity and the use of the body. I have suggested that this is evident both in their construction of the story itself – as examples I focused on the representation of narrator and character voices – and in the way they monitor and interact with

Figure 15   Jan: *give* ('I'll give you the throne on one condition')

Figure 16   Jan: *world* ('the very worst thing in the world to eat')

their audience. These are not discrete performance elements; interacting with the audience is not incidental to the narrative, it is woven into the story fabric. The skill and artistry of the storyteller resides in his/her ability to orchestrate semiotic resources to construct the characters, places and events that make up the story and secure children's involvement in the story world.

Note

1   Seeing storytelling as a form of literature may be objected to by those who insist that literature necessarily involves writing. In terms of the etymology of the term this is true, but meanings don't stand still, and the phrase 'oral literature' is in wide circulation. Furthermore, even within traditional views of literature oral/written boundaries are blurred. Few would deny poetry or drama a place as literature, but even written poetry may be performed, and 'performance poetry' is not fixed but may vary from one performance to the next. Plays, similarly, may be adapted in performance and not all drama is scripted. Classical literature (e.g. Greek or Sanskrit epics) have passed from oral traditions into written form and back out again into various forms of performance.

'Literature', in its traditional sense, also refers to a culturally valued activity – to writing 'which has a claim to consideration on the ground of beauty or form or emotional effect' (*Oxford English Dictionary*). But this, similarly, may be applied to 'oral literature'. Story, in whatever form, may be moving, funny, beautiful, witty or trite. On any one occasion such judgements may be questioned, but they would not normally be restricted to one mode rather than another.

References

Abrahams, R. 1983. *African Folktales*. New York, Pantheon.

Bauman, R. 1986. *Story, Performance and Event*. Cambridge, Cambridge University Press.

Carmichael, A. [1990] 1992. *Carmina Gadelica*. Edinburgh, Floris.

Finnegan, R. 1967. *Limba Stories and Story-Telling*. Oxford, Clarendon.

Finnegan, R. 2007. *The Oral and Beyond: Doing Things with Words in Africa*. Oxford, James Curry.

Okpewho, I. 1992. *Africal Oral Literature: Backgrounds, Character and Continuity*. Bloomington, Indiana University Press.

Pellowski, A. 1991, 2nd edn. *The World of Storytelling*. New York, H. W. Wilson.

Propp, V. [1928]1958. *Morphology of the Folktale*. Bloomington, Indiana University Research Centre in Anthropology, Folklore and Linguistics.

Propp, V. [1928]1984. *Theory and History of Folklore*. Manchester, Manchester University Press.

Stone, K. 1986. 'Oral Narration in Contemporary North America', in R. Bottigheimer (ed.) *Fairy Tales and Society: Illusion, Allusion and Paradigm*. Philadelphia, University of Pennsylvania Press.

Townsend, J. R. 1992. *Written For Children: An Outline of English-Language Children's Literature*, 25th anniversary edn, 4th rev. edn. New York, HarperCollins.

Uther, H-J. 2004. *The Types of International Folktales: A Classification and Bibliography*. Parts I–III. Helsinki, Suomalainen Tiedeakatemia, Academia Scientiarum Fennica.

Zipes, J. 2001. *Sticks and Stones: The Troublesome Success of Children's Literature from Slovenly Peter to Harry Potter*. New York and London, Routledge.

Drama
Susanne Greenhalgh

In Hans Christian Andersen's story 'In the Nursery' (1865) an old man and his grand-daughter stage their own version of the romantic domestic play to which the parents have gone, building a theatre from books and old boxes and turning a broken pipe and scraps of clothing into actors. 'Is this not better than the real theatre?' asks the little girl at the end of the performance. With its interrogation of the relationship between children's play and 'real' theatre, improvisation and scripted drama, and its child's perspective of the adult patriarchal world (but mediated by an adult), this story offers a fitting prologue to the complex questions raised by drama for and by children. As Andersen's story acknowledges, scripted drama, as well as participation in theatre and other forms of performance, has been part of children's culture in virtually every society in the world at some point in their history, and yet it is still rare to find attention paid to these texts in discussion of writing for children. There are many reasons for this absence. All kinds of playtexts, not only those for children, have often been denied the status of literature, while awareness that the dramatic text constitutes only one layer of signification within the complex sign system that is theatre (where any object may stand for another), and the difficulties posed by their relationship with the intrinsic ephemerality and intangibility of actual or hypothetical performance have generated an attitude of caution towards this vast and elusive area of study. Reading a play is clearly a very different activity from reading a novel or a poem, or even listening to a story. A play's words – whether dialogue or stage directions – are always designed to produce a *performed text*, in which the verbal codes and clues are turned into characters, speech, objects, sound, space and action presented to an audience who in turn must interpret and take an attitude to what they see and hear, and whose response actively and directly shapes the nature and meaning of the experience. Furthermore, the fixing of a play as a finished text, written down and published, has been neither a priority, nor even a possibility, in many theatre cultures, which have relied instead on processes of rehearsal and memorisation (as the grandfather in Andersen's story improvises an entire short play out of his long experience as a playgoer). Even in cultures where *reading* a play has become an accepted activity in its own right, interpretation is always open to the performative *rewriting* that will accompany any new staging

Extracted from P. Hunt (ed.), *International Companion Encyclopedia of Children's Literature*, 2nd edn. (London: Routledge, 2004), pp. 599–613.

of the script. And it is through participation in performance, as actors or audience, rather than through reading, that most children experience drama.

A note on terminology for children's drama is needed. 'Creative drama', also referred to as 'creative dramatics' or 'child drama', is usually understood as an informal process-centred and expressive activity directed towards imaginative and usually improvised enactment by children (and sometimes their adult guides), without any prior script, as activities to develop the child's experience, creativity and understanding. 'Participatory drama or theatre' structures active involvement by the young audience/performers in the action (scripted, devised or improvised). Although offering itself as a more 'open' form, it can often be tacitly coercive. The term 'emancipatory theatre' has been coined for theatre with the young that genuinely allows them to choose the direction of the action. 'Children's theatre' (or 'theatre for young audiences', a term growing in popularity) involves the performance of theatrical art (scripted or devised) usually by trained professionals (which may include children) and envisaged as primarily designed for a young audience. It potentially employs all the skills and aesthetic qualities expected from 'adult theatre'. However, the term is also used of performances by children, for instance in schools. 'Children's plays' (either pre-scripted or as a documentation of a devised production) remain the staple of this form of theatre, whether performed by adults or children. 'Youth theatre' usually refers to theatre by young adolescents often intended for an audience of similar age, while 'young people's theatre' may involve this but can also include drama activities offered by professional or educational companies felt to have special relevance to the concerns of the young. Theatre in Education (TIE) combines aspects of creative drama and theatre (often involving professional theatre makers working in educational contexts) and aims at being at least participatory if not actually emancipatory. Scripts and scenarios will usually emerge out of long research preparation and sometimes from long-term engagement with projects involving the young participants in many kinds of activities, designed to encourage learning in the broadest sense. 'Reader's theatre' almost always takes place in schools and is closely linked with enhancing students' understanding and appreciation of non-dramatic forms of literature by adapting them into dramas that can be given staged readings.

Drama, has, in practice, often been inseparable from other forms of writing, including that for young audiences, as Andersen's story again illustrates. Writers of novels or poems for children, from Andersen himself to A.A. Milne, Ted Hughes and Alan Garner, have written plays as well, or even, like J.M. Barrie and his *Peter Pan* (1903–4) turned plays into children's books. From the mid-eighteenth century on, with the advent of publications addressed specifically to children, the resulting stories, rhymes, novels and poems have regularly been put into dramatic form; conversely, the global dramatic repertoire, especially Shakespeare, has been the source for countless prose narratives tailored to the supposed needs of the child reader.

Although drama has always been intrinsically intertextual with other literary forms, its primary relationship is, of course, with the actualities of theatre and performance, and thus with the material culture and ideological practices of societies. Plays, like other cultural forms, emerge from and engage with the culture that shapes them, but the ways in which they in turn also shape the culture which produces them can be viewed as more direct and visible in a mode of cultural production which is inherently and inescapably interactive and dynamic. As new dramatic conventions appear, altering the terms on which audience and playwright meet, they also create new versions of the world and its inhabitants that do not simply mirror reality but help to construct it. Drama therefore offers an especially vivid and concrete record of the ways in which childhood has been understood, perceived, imposed and contested in different periods and cultures.

It is precisely these self-reflexive, world-building aspects of performed drama that have always attracted educators and social engineers. Promising as it does possibilities both for effective instruction under the guise of entertainment and the instilling, through a public and shared mode of collective experience, of the values of an institution or a whole society, the dramatic genre is premised on *action* (as its etymological origins in the Greek word for something done suggest, and as Aristotle was the first to emphasise). Drama, more than most other genres, is acknowledged to have designs on its audience, even if only to win its applause. And these attributed powers to both educate and morally improve the young have always been proffered as a chief defence against perennial 'anti-theatrical prejudice'. Many theorists, especially in America, seek first to distinguish between the 'doing' and 'seeing' activities implied by the root meanings of the words 'drama' and 'theatre' to propose a continuum from imaginative, imitative play, regarded as natural and innate in children, to formal theatrical presentation of dramatic scripts.

The next stage on from 'natural' drama on this 'continuum' is *guided drama* involving 'child' or 'creative' drama (or 'dramatics'), which is characterised as improvisational, non-script based, emotionally expressive, developmental of personality, social and intellectual skills, language and communication, moral or social awareness, aesthetic appreciation and empathy with others, and concerned with process rather than product. This is followed by 'participation' drama, in which more 'theatrical' activities such as watching as an audience become prominent, as well as direct intervention in the unfolding dramatic action. The culmination is experience and appreciation of the arts of theatre.

Further perspectives on these questions of child agency in performance, particularly important for much contemporary drama for and with children, are offered by the materialist theories of the German philosopher Walter Benjamin. In 1928 Benjamin, as a result of his love relationship with a Russian children's theatre worker, wrote a brief but suggestive 'Proletarian Children's Theatre' programme, unpublished until the 1960s, which described a 'pre-ideological' theatre out of which a 'true' education in Marxist dialectics could emerge. Benjamin, too, emphasised play but wanted to create conditions for its 'radical release' to bring about a 'fulfilled' childhood (1928/1973: 31) through improvisation, the stimuli of other arts practices, and above all dramatic play with provided or found objects. From this engagement with the material world rather than the 'dangerous magic-realm of mere fantasy' (30) children's self-generated, rather than imposed, performance gestures would create a theatre which would be 'truly revolutionary ... a secret signal of what will come to be' (32). The ongoing debate between those who regard drama as primarily an expressive, creative form arising from universal instincts and physical/cognitive imperatives, those who prize its powers to model a world (and self) in the constant process of being constructed, and those for whom its aesthetic dimensions are most valuable and 'timeless' in turn affects what is seen as drama, and how its relation to childhood is understood.

Jack Zipes has argued that in a globalised world

> [m]ost contemporary plays for children are produced for the play's sake, not for the children's; most pander to the entertainment industry's expectations and conceal power relations ... Traditional plays show off talent while concealing any connection to the daily struggles of children or their attempt to grasp how art can play a role in their immediate lives. While many plays deal with social issues, they divert attention from those mediations that bind children into the corporate interests of the public sphere.
>
> Zipes 2003: 12

There has always been a dialectical tension between the potential of drama to create a questioning active child subject through the experience of conflict and otherness, and its use for purposes of socialisation and the encouragement of conformity with cultural norms. Here the fact that drama also concretely explores the relation between child and adult, is significant. Unlike the experience of reading, in child drama adults are almost always present, one way or another, as authors, actors, facilitators or fellow spectators. The genre always assumes, implicitly or explicitly, a dual reception, if not always appearing to offer a dual address, to both kinds of audience simultaneously. The many theories which connect theatre with the instinct to play underline the sense in which drama can be regarded as the genre, above all others, which can revive the child in its participants, whether nostalgically or provocatively.

The assumption that children constitute a specialised audience for drama, requiring plays and performances tailor made for them, is put in question by much of theatre history. In many of the cultures of the past, as is still the case in some African and Asian societies where children and adults habitually form part of the same audience, little or no distinction was made between the dramatic fare offered or performed, although children may require initiation or long apprenticeship to acquire the appropriate performance skills, as in the dance dramas of Japan, China and Indonesia. Nevertheless, it is possible to find evidence of special recognition of the young as both performers and audience at specific key points in western theatre history. The ritualised competitive displays of choral song and dance out of which Athenian drama emerged in the fourth century BC already highlighted the role of boys on the cusp of maturity, but the emergence of a new kind of 'performance culture' designed to serve the ideological needs of an evolving and highly experimental democratic *polis* accentuated the significance of the youths about to become citizens through their roles in the chorus. Here they were educated through enactment, 'playing the other' of the male free, rational and militarily active ideal citizen through impersonations of women, slaves, old men, foreigners and animals (see Zeitlin 1990), These roles for young adults also contrasted with the mute male child roles which were occasionally written into tragedy, especially by Euripides, in the form of passive victims of war or female evil, as in *The Trojan Women* or *Medea*, the first of countless adult plays to employ child figures in order to create effects of pathos and innocent suffering.

If Athenian drama can be regarded as in some ways an early form of youth theatre, other dramatic modes demonstrate more ways in which youth performance can be political. Benjamin linked children's play with the carnivalesque in its capacity to subvert and challenge the fixed structures of a culture, and seasonal periods of allowed misrule and hierarchical inversion, when boys could temporarily become priests, chiefs or kings, have been a feature of much popular festivity and ritual across the world. Children also participated in the European religious and biblical drama of the middle ages, sometimes, as in versions of the story of Abraham and Isaac, taking a central role with the emphasis again on pathos and innocence, combined with iconographic functions as emblems of the gentleness and purity of Christ or his saints and martyrs. With the revival of the traditions of classical training in rhetoric by the humanists of the Renaissance, drama became a core element in the school curriculum. The Roman plays of Terence, and to a lesser extent Seneca and Plautus, were the most favoured models for classroom declamation as well as performance, together with religious stories, either in the form of Bible or saint's tales or moral allegory, but often blended with narratives and tropes from popular oral culture.

School drama for boys, modified according to whether the institution was Catholic or Protestant, was an important influence on professional drama in continental Europe during the sixteenth and seventeenth centuries. This was particularly the case in the theatrical culture of early modern England, where, unlike much of Europe, boy actors not only took all female roles, but a distinctive professional tradition of children's companies and play repertoire developed from the court performances of choir schools, to which many of the best-known dramatists of the time, such as Lyly, Peele, Jonson, Marston, Dekker, Beaumont and Fletcher, Chapman and Middleton, contributed. These plays are far from simple, but rather fully exploit the potential for parodic, satirical and playful effect created by the presence of child performers, 'a sort of Jack-and-the-giant situation in which the audience's sympathies were clearly with the smaller characters' (Shapiro 1977: 104).

Other important sites of school drama were the educational establishments of the militant Catholic religious order, the Society of Jesus, founded by Ignatius Loyola, which for over 200 years staged often spectacular and hugely popular performances of plays written both for and by the young. Surviving examples, such as the martyr play *Vitus* written by the English recusant Joseph Simons for boys at the Jesuit college at St Omer in 1623, show they provided excellent roles for young protagonists, such as boy emperors and martyrs, and even a child Christ. This long-lasting dramatic tradition, which was also exported to the newfound Americas as part of the missionary endeavours of the order, was always a form of 'outreach' theatre, designed to attract (and if necessary convert) visiting dignitaries and natives, as well as relatives and members of the local community. It was also, as Goethe recognised when he witnessed performances in Rome, above all a theatre of the world, designed to serve the needs of the young by extending their social abilities and intellectual understanding, as well as moral virtue, and developing and staging their talents as actors and writers, through giving them the richest theatrical resources possible. It is hardly surprising therefore that Jesuit drama produced many of the most important playwrights of the time, including the Corneille brothers, Racine and Molière in France, Calderon and Lope de Vega in Spain, and Goldoni in Italy, only losing influence with the dissolution of the order in between 1750 and 1773.

All the drama discussed so far was the product of strongly gendered performance traditions, written and performed by men and boys, and often designed to produce the forms of masculinity approved by its society, though also capable of calling such certainties into question, as in the transvestite drama of Renaissance England. Even when not intended for public performance, it still offered mimetic models of, and practice in, the public skills of debate and persuasion, and was peopled by male dramatic figures equipped with nimble wits, moral awareness and will, heroic endeavour or manly endurance. However, there was a largely hidden counter-tradition, only recently excavated by feminist historians, of writing by women in the form of 'closet drama' crested for the domestic space rather than the play-house or school theatre. In convents, schools and homes this amateur female theatre offered a new kind of theatrical 'sociability', one intimately bound up with family life, and thus with children. It was necessarily intimate and small-scale, since such performance (or even reading) was only permissible within the security of close relationships, but could be interrogative, as well as imitative, of the established dramatic conventions of the male canon. The performances by children in court or noble households had also been a form of 'family' drama, but one in which the concept of 'family' was both extended and hierarchical, in which children were often equivalent in status to servants, or actually working in such roles as pages, maids or apprentices.

The impact of Enlightenment ideas about human perfectibility and the possibility of social progress through reason and scientific enquiry brought with it significant changes in ideas of childhood and family structure, influenced especially by the philosophies of Rousseau, as well as the beginnings of political feminism. The first woman to write drama specifically for these child performers and audiences was Stephanie, Comtesse de Genlis, tutor to the future king of France, Louis Philippe, whose *Théâtre a l'Usage des Jeunes Personnes*, first published in 1779–80, along with her other writings on education, was rapidly available in English.

Unlike de Genlis's plays, which aimed at gently moulding the child to socially and morally desirable ends, the plays of the Anglo-Irish writer Maria Edgeworth (1768–1849) illustrate the potential of child-focused drama to address issues of social concern and to make implicit links between the position of children as subordinated subjects and other forms of social hierarchy and oppression. Edgeworth wrote both as a member of a family circle linked with such scientific radicals as the members of the Lunar Society, and as an inhabitant of a colonised nation. The system of *Practical Education* (1798) that she and her father devised and advocated was mimetic in the sense that it was built on detailed observation and recording of children's speech and behaviour. The *Little Plays* (1827) were added to the *Parent's Assistant* anthology of educational tools for use in the domestic setting.

Despite these early stirrings of interest in drama as a vehicle for progressive education, the fact that during the nineteenth century the socialisation of the young of all classes increasingly took place in schools rather than the family meant that surviving published drama includes both school and household or other amateur drama, mainly in the form of fairy tales and folk stories, history and religious plays, sentimental comedies, improving scenarios and parodies. However, the chief forum for child-centred performance texts was becoming the professional theatre itself, more than ready to offer a more specialised product for a new category of consumer. Commercial imperatives to keep theatres open and profitable throughout the year led to the introduction of seasonal offerings for family audiences, especially at Christmas, based around appropriate parts of the existing theatrical repertoire, such as pantomime, burlesque, fairy and folk tales, and magic shows, with theatricality based more on spectacle and musical and obvious moral lessons than subtleties of plot or characterisation. Such plays were a very different form of 'family entertainment' from that which had been provided by theatre during previous centuries, and were to be the dominant mode of children's theatre in Europe and America for over a hundred years, continuing in many respects into the present. Although J.M. Barrie's *Peter Pan* attempted to break the mould by creating a more psychologically complex drama in which a child would play the child protagonist, the role would constantly be given to adults and the play turned into another version of pantomime.

Much of the subsequent development of drama for the young was also, in one way or another, a reaction to or rejection of the norms established by these commercial traditions. By the beginning of the twentieth century, such critiques were being developed from both educational and political perspectives, and to some degree these different emphases helped determine the formation of three main counter-traditions, which would influence, the emergence of different forms of children's drama in various societies. The educationally focused perspective, with creativity also a key concept, became influential in much of the English-speaking world, while, following the Russian Revolution of 1917, a more ideological view of drama for the young dominated large parts of Soviet-influenced eastern Europe, and subsequently countries of the third world, such as Cuba, China and various African and Asian states, often as part of their own revolutions. The third tendency, though still heavily influenced by socialist ideals, was more concerned with theatre as an art form or vehicle of spiritual or cultural values rather than its uses as a tool for social change. In practice, however, throughout the twentieth century these different tendencies towards education, social conditioning, creativity and aesthetic enhancement, have constantly intermingled and migrated across national borders, both through the work of individual practitioners and theorists and through international organisations and events such as festivals and theatre tours specifically designed to encourage interculturalism.

Figure 17 Pauline Chase as 'Peter Pan' in the original stage production, Duke Theatre, London, 1904. Reproduced from *Penrose's Pictorial Annual 1908–1909, An Illustrated Review of the Graphic Arts*, vol. 14, ed. William Gamble, London: A.W. Penrose, 1908–9. By kind permission of Alamy, © The Print Collector/Alamy.

Although the first state theatre for children was created in Hungary in 1919, with the support of intellectuals and artists such as Bartók, Kodály and Lukács, with similar attempts made in Germany and Czechoslovakia in 1918, it was in Russia that a national programme for children's theatre was first realised from the 1920s onwards. Theatre buildings and permanent, highly trained companies were established in all the major cities, leading to an ongoing demand for the production of new plays and the adaptation of existing writing of all genres for children and adults, as long as the state-endorsed principles of social realism and socialist idealism were incorporated. Children's theatre (generally known as TUZ) was seen as both a primary means to redress the social and economic inequalities which the revolution had been intended to overturn, by exposing the young to the cultural riches of the past and present, and also as a visible and appealing showcase for the progress made towards the promised utopia. Accordingly, the well-subsidised theatres were able to build a colourful and popular repertoire, ranging from fairy tales to versions of adult classics for different ages, and combining drama with music (as in the famous *Peter and the Wolf* commissioned from Prokofiev in 1928 by the Moscow Central Children's Theatre, led by Natalia Sats). The celebrated children's writer Samuel Marshak (1887–1975), in his role as head of the children's writers' union, was an important supporter of children's drama, and many of his stories, along with those of other well known children's authors such as Yevgeny Svarts, became a staple of the repertoire.

The seriousness of Russian theatre's engagement with both aesthetics and social goals for the young was a major and continuing influence on the rest of Europe even during the Cold War years. Although much of the drama that emerged was at the safe, traditional end of the spectrum, with the familiar reliance on fantasy and charm, in the mid-1960s, as counter-cultural political movements and reactions against them rippled through many European societies, young theatre-workers began to discover a new oppressed minority in children. They attempted to find ways to radicalise the children through reinventing the techniques of Brecht and Piscator for the new conditions; they later discovered new influences such as Augusto Boal's forum theatre and the American Living Theater, all of which introduced different ways of thinking about content, audience address and mode of presentation. Grips Theatre in Berlin, with its rediscovery of Brecht's 'fun' cabaret theatre, was to be a much-copied and enduring exemplar of the possibilities for a political children's theatre (Zipes 2003) in Europe and beyond. Countries like Poland and Czechoslovakia, with existing traditions of richly poetic, highly experimental theatrical forms, liberated children's drama into the surreal, the dreamlike and the abstract.

All over Europe, after a period of rejection of the 'cosy' fairy-tale traditions which had dominated mainstream theatre, there was a new realisation not only of the ways in which these materials could be made fresh and exciting for children, but how they could also revitalise adult theatre practices. Writing of the achievement of theatre for young audiences in Europe, Wolfgang Wöhlert celebrates it as a 'theatre of feeling and fantasy, a theatre that speaks most of all to the senses', which, in its ability to reach people from all social levels can be regarded as a 'folk theatre for all generations' that has yet never given up its specificity as a theatre for the young (Rouyer et al. 1994: 26).

In the English-speaking world generally, the development of drama for the young was driven by a combination of commercial and socio-educational imperatives in a broadly liberal humanist mode. Children's theatre in the USA can be dated to the creation of Alice Minnie Herts's Children's Educational Theater in New York in 1903, which primarily aimed to serve the 'melting-pot' requirements of the society by using drama to teach English and encourage social integration. Subsequently the production of drama for children remained dominated by similar social and pedagogic objectives, with plays performed by primarily amateur companies and written by teachers and social workers. A key figure in expanding the diet available to children from the 1920s on was Winifred Ward (1884–1975) who developed the field of 'creative dramatics' through both her writing and practice, introducing university courses on educational drama, founding the Children's Theater at Evanston and in 1944 initiating what would eventually become the Alliance for American Theater and Education (AATE). Ward advocated drama in the form both of informal educationally motivated creative drama and theatre productions, by casts of children and adults, and consequently put a new focus on encouraging innovation and quality in playwriting for children and in children's theatre companies. An early pioneer in the former field for many years was Charlotte Chorpenning (1872–1955), whose .plays for the Goodman Theater in Chicago (1925) from 1931 mostly favoured versions of 'universal' and 'familiar' fairy stories, folk tales and well-known children's books, and emphasised clear moral values. Her plays were also part of the Federal Theater Project, which introduced drama to countless deprived children across the nation during the 1930s. Although colleges and universities would remain important in developing standards and skills in playwriting through their teaching, and theatre arts programmes (many taught by faculty who themselves wrote prize-winning children's drama, like Jonathan Levy, Moses Goldberg and Suzan Zeder), the emergence of a number of regional children's theatres introduced an important new source for the patronage and encouragement of dramatic writing. Leaders in this field have been the professional children's theatre companies of Minneapolis, Seattle, Lexington and Honolulu, all of which have graduated over the years to well-equipped theatre buildings, and established close links to local schools, libraries and museums. The existence of these, and other, non-building-based companies has led to a huge increase in playwriting for children since the middle of the twentieth century. A particularly successful experimental touring company is Judith Martin's long-established Paper Bag Company (1955), which borrowed some of the practices of Russian children's theatre to offer surreal object-based scenarios combining art activities with performance in a way reminiscent of Benjamin's 'programme'.

In most of Asia, a specialised, professional children's theatre and accompanying dramatic repertoire only emerged after the Second World War, and remains undeveloped, other than in countries which were part of the USSR. In Japan, where a degree of westernisation accompanied industrialisation from the beginning of the twentieth century, theatre was influenced by both German and Soviet forms of children's theatre, and since the war a flourishing range of companies and organisations has arisen, which combine aesthetic and educational approaches and draw on the many other national performance traditions, such as puppetry and mask. Throughout Asia, and increasingly in Africa, it is possible to detect a tension between growing influence from western cultures of childhood, such as 'Disneyfied' fairy tales, transmitted globally by the media, and the desire to preserve and build on local performance traditions and narratives, and address pressing social issues through 'theatre for development'. Influences have also come through the work of western specialists in TIE and educational drama (especially in former British dominions and colonies such as Australia, New Zealand and South Africa), or the emancipatory techniques of Grips Theatre, for instance in parts of India.

In the UK, too, drama was initially influenced by developments in child-centred educational theory and practice, with some key figures emerging whose ideas would reach an international audience, such as Peter Slade, Brian Way (who founded Theatre Centre in 1953), Dorothy Heathcote and Gavin Bolton. All of these, though with different emphases, sought to place drama at the heart of the school curriculum, as a 'way of knowing' as well as teaching, and as an art form distinct from theatre. The development of professional theatre for children has reflected the importance of London as a theatre centre, with 30 per cent of productions now originating there, although as early as 1927 Scotland had had its own company founded by Bertha Waddell on the model of Soviet children's theatre. In 1947, Caryl Jenner (1917–73) founded the Unicorn Theatre which, after a difficult time in the 1990s, is now the focus for a campaign to build a specialist centre for national children's theatre practice and research. The Polka Theatre and the Oily Cart company also provide imaginative drama for the very young. Theatre in Education, which seeks to blend aspects of child drama and formal theatre, is Britain's most distinctive contribution to world drama for children, which has since been exported to former British colonies and dominions such as Australia, South Africa and Canada (whence to the USA). Despite this, many of the TIE companies which came into being in the 1960s, inspired by the new educational theories, disappeared as a result of arts and education funding cuts during the 1980s and 1990s and the creation of a National Curriculum focused on set targets for literacy achievement which has squeezed out theatre-going and creative drama activities. Dramatisations of the adult literary heritage for teaching purposes have always been an important aspect of British drama for the young. These have been augmented by stage versions of children's literature such as *Alice, Peter Pan* and *The Wind in the Willows,* which in turn eventually provided commercial and state-subsidised theatres with a popular and 'quality' alternative to the Christmas pantomime. The golden age classics have since been regularly joined by an abundance of new members of the canon, including many versions of Roald Dahl's work by the prolific and talented David Wood (who has created plays from virtually every possible kind of source, including Enid Blyton and Eric Hill's *Spot the Dog series* of picture books), *The Lion, the Witch and the Wardrobe* (Royal Shakespeare Company 1998), *Tom's Midnight Garden* (Unicorn 2002), David Almond's *Skellig* (Young Vic 2003) and an epic two-part version of Philip Pullman's *His Dark Materials* (National Theatre 2004) (see plate 20).

While adaptations of children's literature have been prevalent across the world, this genre appears particularly dominant in the UK, where it has always been a major feature of radio and television drama for children and families (Greenhalgh 1998) and where children's books and their authors have become valuable assets for the heritage and tourist industries. Following the publication of a report on education and the arts industries in 2000, the Arts Councils of England and Scotland have turned their attention to how children's theatre can be developed, through funding for more companies (in Scotland) and the encouragement of quality and diversity in writing (in England) through supporting theatre-based writing internships and sponsorship (Arts Council England 2003). Action for Children's Arts, a lobbying group made up of professionals in arts for children and chaired by David Wood, is also putting drama for children at the centre of planned conferences and 'inspiration' events, involving the Children's Laureate Michael Morpurgo (whose *When the Whales Came* is a popular adaptation) and Philip Pullman, and celebrating the centenary of *Peter Pan* in 2004.

Much remains to be done. As we move further into the twenty-first century we can celebrate decades of achievement across the world in creating spaces where children can interact imaginatively with themselves and their many worlds. The criteria used by Tony Jackson to evaluate the 'quality' of drama can help us begin to construct a full appraisal of their dramaturgy: 'Does the play matter to children? Is it something they might care about? Does it have a sense of poetry? Of flight? Does it contain a child's perspective? Is it a drama? Can it transcend and transform?' (Jackson in Arts Council England, 2003). But we should also listen to Jack Zipes when he warns that 'unless children can appropriate the scripts, all plays – Broadway plays, classical dramas, adaptations of famous novels – have minimal value for their lives' (Zipes 2003: 12). Perhaps, in the end, this is the main lesson that children's drama has to teach the adult world, to stand back and give the young room for their 'radical play'.

References

Arts Council England (2003) *The Quality of Children's Theatre: After the Birmingham Seminar*. Online. Available http://www.artscouncil.org.uk (accessed 1 December 2003).

Benjamin, W. (1928/1973) 'Program for a Proletarian Children's Theater', trans. Buck-Morss, S., *Performance* 1, 5: 28–32.

Greenhalgh, S. (1998) 'Different Worlds? Children's Books and the Media', in Reynolds, K. and Tucker, N. (eds) *Children's Book Publishing in Britain since 1945*, London: Scolar.

Rouyer, P., Nagy, P. and Rubin, D. (eds) (1994) *World Encyclopedia of Contemporary Theatre: Europe*, London and New York: Routledge.

Shapiro, M. (1977) *Children of the Revels*, New York: Columbia University Press.

Zeitlin, F.I. (1990) 'Playing the Other: Theater, Theatricality and the Feminine in Greek Drama', in Winkler, J.J. and Zeitlin, F.J. (eds) *Nothing to Do with Dionysus? Athenian Drama in Its Social Context*, Princeton, NJ: Princeton University Press, 63–96.

Zipes, J. (2003) 'Political Children's Theater in the Age of Globalization', *Theater* 33, 2: 2–25.

Screen Classics
Deborah Cartmell

Inserted in Roald Dahl's *Charlie and the Chocolate Factory* (1964) is a 'paragone,' a poetic diatribe proclaiming the inestimable superiority of literature over television and the latter's responsibility for the present intellectual degeneration of the child in which Dahl's own voice can be heard loudly and clearly:

> HIS BRAIN BECOMES AS SOFT AS CHEESE
> HIS POWERS OF THINKING RUST AND FREEZE!
> HE CANNOT THINK – HE ONLY SEES![1]

The 'paragone,' the defense of the superior claims of one discipline over another, especially in terms of the visual and the verbal, has an extensive literature, from Plato to Sir Philip Sidney, and reappears in the twentieth and twenty-first centuries in the often competing and strained relationship between literature and film, and the covert paragone detectable in both forms. The most famous of all paragones, Ben Jonson's 'Expostulation,' an attack on his all too successful collaborator, the architect, Inigo Jones, is unnervingly prophetic of the current 'he's only the author' syndrome (of Hollywood, where spectacle undeniably rules):

> O shows! Shows! Mighty shows!
> The eloquence of masques! What need of prose,
> Or verse, or sense, to express immortal you?[2]

Screen adaptation, on one level, grows out of the longstanding tradition of *ut pictura poesis*, a tradition that reflects on the mutual dependence and admiration of painting and literature. But where there is dependence and admiration, there is also incompatibility and jealousy. In the field of adaptation, the tension between the literary and the screen text is, possibly, most prominent in the area of children's texts, where concerns over film's moral influence and the threat to literacy have been prevalent since the inception of cinema. As George Bluestone observed in his pioneering work, the relationship between literature and film is simultaneously 'overtly compatible' and 'secretly hostile';[3] and, accordingly, this chapter will examine the competing, often overtly hostile relationship between film and literature by making explicit this implicit

Originally published as 'Adapting Children's Literature', in *The Cambridge Companion to Literature on Screen* (Cambridge: Cambridge University Press, 2007), pp. 167–80.

antagonism.[4] When it comes to adaptations of children's literature, the battle between film and literature seems to be at its most ferocious.

Collecting children's literary adaptations within a single work potentially reveals biases and preferences. Douglas Street's collection, *Children's Novels and the Movies* is arranged by classic children's stories and their film adaptations, thereby privileging the literary over the film text.[5] Adaptation studies tend to restrict themselves to classic literature with little or no regard for classic films – often, unbeknown to most, adaptations of little-known literary texts, or popular literature, betraying an unspoken assumption that the classic literary text is always preeminent. Consequently, this chapter considers three types of children's literary adaptations: adaptations of 'classic' children's stories, adaptations of lesser known children's texts, and adaptations of popular children's fiction.[6] Surprisingly, given the number of adaptations of children's literature to screen, the area has attracted very little critical attention. Compared to the scarcity of literature on children's adaptations[7] at the time of writing, of the top thirty US moneymaking films, twenty-three were children's films and nine of these were adaptations of children's literature.[8] Although it's difficult to pin down what exactly constitutes children's literature, it can be distinguished from other literatures insofar as it is often more loved and better known. Children, unlike adults, love to re-read their favourite stories; and, correspondingly, in adapting these texts, there will be higher demands on fidelity. Obviously, the range of children's literature is enormous, from books designed to develop reading skills to those which appeal to both adults and a younger readership. This chapter will restrict itself to literature written for the older child.

Film adaptations of children's literature are divided here into films of 'classic,' 'obscure' and 'popular' texts. A 'classic' children's book tends to inspire numerous film versions – every generation seems to have a film of *Peter Pan, Alice in Wonderland, Treasure Island,* and *Little Women,* for example. Lesser-known texts, however, tend to produce a single film and, if successful, the film becomes the ur-text in the minds of its viewers. It could be argued that *The Wizard of Oz* and *Mary Poppins* belong to this category. In this case, the film 'makes' the literary text. In addition to classics and those arguably fated to obscurity without the movie, like *Mary Poppins* (the persistence of the novels, arguably, depends on the film), there is another category – adaptations of bestselling children's writing. In recent times these would be Enid Blyton, Roald Dahl and, of course, J.K. Rowling. Significantly, the adaptations of these writers' works have been, on the whole, seen as inferior to the books. They have in no way threatened to overtake the book as the primary text in the minds of their audiences.

Classic adaptations

I have already remarked that literary texts adapted numerous times tend to have a classic status. To take one example, *Little Women* has had three major film adaptations (not to mention several television and stage adaptations, even an opera): George Cukor's 1933 film, starring Katherine Hepburn; Mervyn LeRoy's 1949 version with June Allyson as Jo and Elizabeth Taylor as Amy; and Gillian Armstrong's 1994 film, with Winona Ryder as Jo. Significantly, each deals with the Civil War (which forms a backdrop to the novel) and the tragic death of the third sister, Beth, in a manner suited to their different audiences. In LeRoy's postwar *Little Women*, closely based on Cukor's film (with the same scriptwriters), the Civil War is barely mentioned and Beth's death is not presented to us on screen; an audience recovering from the recent effects of World War II needs a different *Little Women*, one which will not re-awaken any unpleasant memories.

Although *Little Women* has not, and is not likely to have the 'Disney treatment,' undoubtedly, the Disney corporation has been the most prolific and lucrative twentieth-century adaptor of classic children's fiction, from fairytales to classic stories and novels. In most Disney films, fidelity to the text is openly flaunted; indeed, as is frequently observed, the ambition of a Disney adaptation is to usurp its source – no matter if it be a classic, obscure, or popular text – so that the film adaptation triumphs over its literary original, and, for most viewers, it is the film rather than the text that is the original.[9] Films were made for children from the beginning of cinema – five versions of Dickens's *A Christmas Carol* before 1915, an *Alice in Wonderland* in 1903,[10] but by far the greatest influence on the genre was Walt Disney whose surname has become a byword for a particularly conservative and lucrative form of children's cinema. Disney, starting with Mickey Mouse in 1928, also became involved in spin-offs, such as games, toys, and food, revolutionizing the children's cinema industry. As has been pointed out, Disney's gift wasn't for artistic impression but for the exploitation of the new technology[11] – underlying this is the 'belief' that the film will overtake the literary text. According to Richard Schickel, Disney

> could make something his own, all right, but that process nearly always robbed the work at hand of its uniqueness, of its soul, if you will. In its place he put jokes and songs and fright effects, but he always seemed to diminish what he touched. He came always as a conqueror, never as a servant. It is a trait, as many have observed that many Americans share when they venture into foreign lands hoping to do good but equipped only with know-how instead of sympathy and respect for alien traditions.[12]

Figure 18 Still from *Little Women* (George Cukor, 1933). LITTLE WOMEN © Turner Entertainment Co. A Warner Bros. Entertainment Company. All Rights Reserved. By kind permission of Warner Bros. Entertainment, Inc.

A common feature of a Disney opening is the book becoming animated or Tinker Bell sprinkling fairy dust on the words of the opening credits, cunningly signifying that the transition from book to film enhances/enlivens/ realizes and ultimately, improves the static words of the story. Clearly, Disney's visual language saturated the public and 'his' Snow White became *the* Snow White, visually anchoring the character into an instantly recognizable figure.

Disney's visual style has been identified by Steven Watts as 'sentimental modernism' in which:

- The real and unreal are combined.
- Tropes are refashioned from the Victorian period, exaggerating sentimentality and cuteness.
- Although images and experiences are broken down, rationality is always restored.
- The inanimate world is animated.
- High cultural signifiers are visually satirized.[13]

In terms of story, Disney films rely very much on the three-act classic Hollywood structure, 'build/establish/resolve,' as described by Linda Seger,[14] and contain values and themes that have been identified by Janet Wasko as:

- individualism and optimism
- escape, fantasy, magic imagination
- innocence
- romance and happiness
- good triumphing over evil.[15]

In addition to visual anchorage[16] was an ideological agenda that Disney brought to the stories, reflected in his founding role in the Motion Picture Alliance for the Preservation of American Ideals (the foundation of the Hollywood blacklist). It's no accident that the rise of Disney coincided with debates about the morality of the cinema and American values, and a very conservative view of the family is common to all these films. Disney's scant regard for his literary originals fueled debate about his influence on children – a letter by Frances Clarke Sayers to a Los Angeles newspaper articulates a growing number of concerns about Disney's threat to children's literature:

> I call him to account for his debasement of the traditional literature of childhood, in films and the books he publishes.
>
> He shows scant respect for the integrity of the original creations of authors, manipulating and vulgarizing everything to his own ends.
>
> His treatment of folklore is without regard for its anthropological, spiritual or psychological truths. Every story is sacrificed to the 'gimmick' of animation.[17]

As mentioned previously, Disney doesn't merely adapt a narrative – he virtually steals it, making it *his* story, much to the disparagement of those who seek to preserve and revere the literary original. By visually satirizing cultural signifiers, Disney films reverse the high and low culture trajectory, insinuating that low culture is better than high. There are countless examples of the uneducated, 'rough diamonds' (or versions of Rousseau's 'noble savages') outwitting the so-called 'posh' characters – the highly cultured Captain Hook versus the uneducated American Peter Pan, the British butler against the American alley cat in *The AristoCats*, the British tiger, Shere Khan, versus the American Mowgli in *The Jungle Book* are just some examples. In *Peter Pan*, the youngest Darling, Michael, is given an American accent, whereas his older siblings, John and Wendy, speak the Queen's English with the implication that the pure, natural, pre-lapsarian voice is that of an American.

Disney adaptations have been attacked for plundering and simplifying grand historical narratives, being responsible for the impoverishment of youth, and for closing the minds of their viewers through their insistence on closure – the endings of these films, repeatedly, resolve all the ambiguities and complexities of their literary sources. Finally, Disney movies often intimate to their viewers that film is better than literature. This is implied in the prefatory credits, with the book opening up into the film the point at which 'the magic begins.' Disney films can be considered as the diametrical opposite of the 'classic' or heritage film, narrowly defined as films that respect or revere the source text, producing what Andrew Higson calls 'a discourse of authenticity.'[18] Unlike the heritage movie, Disney films, as indicated above, have no regard for fidelity and, indeed, challenge their literary sources by implicitly satirizing cultural pretension, including the highmindedness of the very texts the films are based on. The most highly rated films produced by Walt Disney (not including Disney enterprises) are as follows:

Votes

15,368	*Fantasia* (1940)
14,839	*Snow White and the Seven Dwarfs* (1937)
14,470	*Mary Poppins* (1964)
9,713	*Bambi* (1942)
9,386	*The Jungle Book* (1967)
7,184	*Dumbo* (1941)
7,158	*Pinocchio* (1940)
7,157	*Lady and the Tramp* (1955)
6,201	*101 Dalmatians* (1961)
6,074	*Sleeping Beauty* (1959)
5,885	*Cinderella* (1950)
5,096	*Peter Pan* (1953)
4,924	*Alice in Wonderland* (1951)[19]

This list reveals how successful Disney adaptations are as, in a number of cases, the film overtakes the source text as the 'original' in most people's minds. Certainly this is the case of *The Lady and the Tramp, Pinocchio, Dumbo, The Jungle Book, 101 Dalmatians*, and, perhaps most notably, *Peter Pan*.

While, visually and structurally, these films have much in common, they're also strikingly similar in their ideological perspectives. On first glance, these films share common narrative ground, especially absent or neglectful fathers who must reassert themselves in some way in order for harmony to be restored. Oddly, as in Shakespeare's plays, mothers tend to be, on the whole, noticeable for their absence. The narrative is changed in ways which often promote 'family values' by upraising or reinstating the father. *Peter Pan* is changed in Disney's 1953 film, so that Mr. Darling conforms to an ideal of fatherhood, having the final word in the film after having behaved badly at the beginning. This is at odds with J.M. Barrie's novel (1911) and play (first performed in 1904) which concludes with the ageing figure of Wendy and the turn-of-the-century topical suggestion that women are changing, whereas men are stuck in the past, incapable of accepting the passage of time. The successful adaptations of 'classic' children's texts produced by Disney in the corporation's 'Golden Age' tend to 'lord' over the text, implicitly mocking the original's cultural pretentiousness by producing a popular and contemporary reading which, it is insinuated, is a preferable one. In the war between film and literature, film wins.

Adaptations of lesser read or 'obscure' texts

It is often the case that a film can breathe life into a book and serve to raise awareness of its literary worth, enabling it to move from obscurity to 'classic' status. It sometimes happens that a film, based on a little-known work, becomes itself the classic text. This is, arguably, the case with films like *The Wizard of Oz* (1939; based on L. Frank Baum's novel, 1900), *National Velvet* (1944; Enid Bagnold's novel, 1935), *Chitty Chitty Bang Bang* (1968; Ian Fleming's novel, 1964), *The Neverending Story* (1984; Michael Ende's novel, 1979), *Bambi* (1942; Felix Salten's novel, 1926) and *Mary Poppins* (1964; P.L. Travers's novels). In these films, the source text is unknown to film-goers or known, largely, due to the success of the film.

In the 1960s, after much astute diversification into television and theme parks, the Disney company moved into live action films, with the most successful of these being *Mary Poppins* in 1964. Pamela Travers completed six books in the series and the film draws mostly from the first, but uses episodes and images from the next three. The film came out of the Disney studios in 1964 and, for anyone familiar with the books, much of the story is unrecognizable, although cameo appearances of major characters are carefully inserted at the beginning of the movie, presumably to appease devoted readers of P.L. Travers. Travers herself was not entirely happy with the film, especially disliking Mr. Banks tearing up the poem, written by the children, describing their ideal nanny, which occurs at the beginning of the film:

> All had to be sweetness and light and *cruelty* in order to get the sentimental outcome of the end. I pleaded with the Disneys not to let Mr. Banks tear up the poem. No good. And they never told me Mrs. Banks was to be a suffragette. I had suggested to Disney that it be set in Edwardian times – in that way it could never be out of date – but I never guessed he would gild the lily with Women's Suffrage.[20]

The major changes the film makes are the period in which it's set (Edwardian rather than 1930s), there are two children rather than four (five later on), the father is depicted as a hard-nosed patriarch and the mother, a superficial suffragette. Another major difference is in the character of Mary. In the books, she's an ambivalent figure, not as altruistic and kindly as the one famously portrayed by Julie Andrews. Finally, the figure of Bert (a minor character in the novels), complete with phony Cockney accent, is substantially enlarged to the second billing of the film. Typical of Disney's live action movies, the film mixes animation with 'real people,' and presents us with an unrealistic view of the world (there was no attempt to make the set realistic) as is clear from the opening sequence with the view of London which is instantly recognizable to film-goers. While Travers suggested the Edwardian period to Disney to give the film a sense of timelessness, she was distressed by the outcome. In spite of the striking precision of the date (it's 1910, 'the age of men,' as Mr. Banks gleefully asserts in his song) Disney has no desire to be historically accurate. The period he creates, however, is one which seems to be obsessed with childhood, children's fashion, and toys – rocking horses, dolls' houses, teddy bears. The nursery, depicted in the film, is an image of idyllic childhood. Like the 1960s when the film was made, the period may have been chosen as it was a time of radical change, especially in relation to gender roles. The centrality of male authority is at the crux of *Mary Poppins*, the film; George Banks's first song, as Brian E. Scumsky has observed, is about the family as an image of the British nation, the father is 'Lord of the Castle.' While smugly congratulating himself on his authority over the family, ironically the suffragette mother is trying to interrupt his song to inform him that his children have disappeared.[21] Nonetheless, he is still the focus of the family and is confronted and redeemed by both Mary and Bert at significant points of the film (revealingly, Mary is never seen to speak to Mrs. Banks, reflecting the inferior role of the mother).

The central pair, Mary and Bert, become, in the film, replacement parents – the bad parents are replaced by good ones, like fairy godparents, who arouse the responsibilities of the real parents. Bert literally rescues the children from the father in the bank sequence. In the end, the bad parents are reformed through the auspices of their counterparts. The suffragette banner is sacrificed for the tail of the kite, as a better family unit has been produced, one based, arguably, on American rather than British values. Indeed American Cockney Dick Van Dyke's Bert advises the quintessentially British and hierarchically obsessed Mr. Banks as to how to behave. Bert's ability to mix with all classes and his entrepreneurialism render him the quintessential American. The view of London, as Disney himself declared, is stagy and not accurate – it is an, unashamed, American construction of London which although quaint and cozy, fundamentally is seen to be in need of Americanizing, and/or democratizing.

Travers's novels are restructured into the archetypal Christian narrative of salvation, echoing Dickens's *A Christmas Carol* and films like *It's a Wonderful Life* (1946), where a magical figure (or figures) descends on the world to save it from itself. Visually and morally, Mary Poppins is transformed from the cold and plain character of the novel. The soundtrack and songs make her almost angelic rather than the ambiguous figure she is in the book. What makes this an archetypal Hollywood adaptation of a children's text is its unashamed rewriting of the text in relation to conservative values regarding the composition of the family, coupled with its use of magic. It's easily translated into Disney's magical kingdom which subtly elevates the experience of viewing over reading, literature over film, popular culture over high culture, Americans over the British. The movement into the chalk picture, like the movement of Dorothy from black and white Kansas to the colorful world of Oz, is ultimately like moving from a 'dull' book to the more immediate and exciting world of cinema. Indeed the magical episodes, meticulously explained on the DVD featurette, including sliding up the banister, tidying the nursery with a click of a finger, and tea on the ceiling, call attention to the world of cinema, which from its inception, has been associated with magic.[22] As Dorothy discovers in *The Wizard of Oz*, the wizard's magic (whose double as fantasist is the director himself) consists entirely of the projection of an image – the magic is film itself.

The legacy of Disney's triumph over the book can be felt in popular children's literature which seems to compete with film on its own terms. Arguably, Disney's dominance ended with the production of blockbuster films, in particular, *Jaws* (1975) and *Star Wars* (1977); their huge box office success, resulting in spin-offs and sequels which capitalize on a successful formula, transformed Hollywood cinema.

Adaptations of popular children's fiction

It is hardly surprising that lesser known literary texts are normally over-shadowed and/or overtaken by their film adaptation and that in adapta-tions, such as *Mary Poppins* or *The Wizard of Oz*, the balance of power resides with the film. This trajectory, however, is reversed in adaptations of popular children's writing, where the battle between the book and the film is, it would seem, at its most ferocious.[23] In the twentieth century, Enid Blyton was replaced by Roald Dahl after his enormous success with *Charlie and the Chocolate Factory* (published in America in 1964 and in the UK in 1967), as the most popular children's writer and he has been overtaken, of course, by J.K. Rowling. While there have been a number of adaptations of Blyton's works, it's fair to say that none stand out (excluding 'Noddy'). Adaptations of *The Famous Five* (1996, 1978, 1970, 1969 and 1956) have sunk into oblivion. Although Dahl's *Charlie and the Chocolate Factory* has now two films to its name, most of Dahl's fiction has only found its way to film once and, as with the case of Blyton, the films have in no way overtaken the books in terms of popularity. This seems to be the normal fate of adap-tations of popular children's literature in which, unlike in the previous cat-egories, in the war between film and literature, the book wins hands down. Looking at Dahl's first big success, *Charlie and the Chocolate Factory*, the message is not just that the film is not as good as the book, but screen texts, on the whole, are seen to be vastly inferior to popular literature.

In the case of both Blyton and Dahl, it could be contended that the films cannot succeed because the books cater too much to a particular period, and have been regarded as 'politically incorrect.' Certainly, Dahl's writing can be seen as anti-authoritarian (attacking both adults and educational systems in novels such as *Danny the Champion of the World* [1975] or *Matilda* [1988], where school is more like a concentration camp than a nurturing refuge), anti-sentimental (the endings are sometimes cruel and seemingly unjust as in *The Witches* [1983] where the hero is turned into a mouse and left in this condition at the end of the novel), misogynistic (allegedly, women are often demonized, as in *The Witches*) and racist (the Oompa-Loompas in *Charlie and the Chocolate Factory* are virtually slaves, with Willy Wonka performing Nazi-like experiments on them).[24] Dahl's narratives are often regarded as dangerous, especially in their anti-authoritarianism, 'not good for children,' while in terms of their structure, they are often very conservative.

Although seeming not to play by the rules, Dahl's first successful novel, *Charlie and the Chocolate Factory*, comes out of the tradition that chil-dren's literature should be edifying, and teach a lesson. It is, essentially, a moral tale that 'teaches' that virtue pays off (Charlie is rewarded, the other children are punished – the punishments fit the crimes). It's structured according to biblical stories of the chosen one reaching the promised land (the Chocolate Factory), with Cinderella (rags to riches) thrown in. Perhaps the most difficult part of the book to adapt is the final punishment. After the fearful fates of Augustus Gloop, Veruca Salt and Violet Beauregarde, we have the chastisement of the unimaginatively named Mike Teavee, which in terms of order, ought to be the worst of all. In the book, it's the longest and most complex.

> *Oh, books, what books they used to know,*
> *Those children living long ago!*
> *So please, oh please, we beg, we pray*
> *Go throw your TV set away,*
> *And in its place you can install*
> *A lovely bookshelf on the wall.*[25]

Dahl's 'paragone,' arguing for the inestimable superiority of books to television takes four pages in the novel; the Oompa-Loompas work themselves into a frenzy of irritation and frustration at the condition of today's children infected by too much television, which shrinks their intellect (and Mike is literally shrunk by the experience). Dahl thematizes the conflict between literature and screen, one which I've argued is particularly present in the area of popular children's literature and film.

Unsurprisingly, this episode is toned down and reduced in the 1971 film version, directed by Mel Stuart and starring Gene Wilder, as it would not do to demean screen entertainment in a screen entertainment (especially one destined to be repeated on television), or enter into a prolonged diatribe on the dumbing down effects of spectating rather than reading. Watching the 1971 film today, Mike Teavee comes across almost positively in his detailed knowledge of television, undoubtedly a future Media Studies lecturer. Rather than endeavor to degrade viewing and reassert the value of literature, the film implicitly declares its literary value through allusions to not only Dahl, but also classic English literature. Intertextual references to high-brow literature as well as popular entertainment are inserted throughout the film. Willy Wonka is a man, living in a magical kingdom (akin to Hollywood) who is, also, a lover of literature. Literary references in the film are listed under 'trivia' in the Internet Movie Database,[26] including quotations from Shakespeare, 'Where is fancy bred,' 'So shines a good deed' (*The Merchant of Venice*), 'Sweet lovers love the spring time …' (*As You Like It*), 'Is it my soul that calls me by my name?' (*Romeo and Juliet*), Keats, 'A thing of beauty is a joy forever' (*Endymion*), and Oscar Wilde, 'the suspense is terrible, I hope it will last' (*The Importance of Being Earnest*). Apparently, Roald Dahl hated the film.[27] While the novel is 'anti-screen,' the film seems to aspire to 'literary cinema,' by rewriting Willy Wonka as a figure inspired by grand historical narratives and the great tradition of English literature. Disturbingly, Wonka played by Johnny Depp in the 2005 film, directed by Tim Burton, as reviewers were quick to note, resembles Michael Jackson as much as he does Dahl's character; Mike Teavee's intelligence is deliberately censored by Johnny Depp's Wonka (who declares Mike's mumbling is unintelligible); and the words of the Oompa-Loompas' song are barely audible, spectacularly overshadowed by a dazzling display of 'shows' (to borrow Ben Jonson's phrase) with screens upon screens. Indeed, the film is packed with films within the film, including musical and visual tributes to filmic predecessors from *The Wizard of Oz* (the first view inside the factory) to *2001: A Space Odyssey*. Wonka's repression of Mike echoes Burton's of Dahl's; the television studio sequence shamelessly contradicts and silences Dahl's attack on media visual culture.

Dahl's successor, J.K. Rowling, blends the narrative styles and devices of her predecessors, Dahl and Blyton – the adventures of the famous three in a dark but fantastic world. While *Charlie and the Chocolate Factory* is 'antiscreen,' Rowling embraces film devices in her writing, but the adaptations of her novels elicit similar responses from her fans – the films are not as good as the book, indeed, films cannot surpass the pleasure of popular writing. A reviewer for *The Washington Post* sums up the general consensus that *Harry Potter and the Sorcerer's Stone* is doomed to be only a good copy: 'the filmmakers haven't reshaped the story to suit the dramatic needs of the new medium. They didn't write a screenplay so much as cautiously string the book's chapters together like imitation pearls.'[28] In hindsight, the caption advertising the film, 'the magic begins' was ill judged as the film in no way bettered the original, as it seemed to anticipate, in the style of Disney. While the adaptations are increasingly taking more liberties with Rowling's writings, curiously, the books are regarded as both more magical and more filmic than the films.

While Mel Stuart's *Willy Wonka* can be described as 'literary cinema,' Rowling's novels are examples of what can be termed 'cinematic literature.' Rowling's popularity, I suggest, is, at least partially, down to the way the experience of reading draws from the passive experience of watching a film. The Harry Potter books seem to abide by the same conventions governing a 'classic' Hollywood film. The first of the novels, for instance, is structured, like a Hollywood blockbuster (including the promise of sequels), with action sequences inserted at regular intervals. The experience of reading is modeled on the experience of watching a movie, with Harry's prominent glasses functioning like the lens of a camera and the writing can be described as cinematic. The visit to Mr. Ollivander's shop, for instance, is structured according to a series of quick edits:

> 'Good afternoon,' said a soft voice. Harry jumped. Hagrid must have jumped too, because there was a loud crunching noise and he got quickly off the spindly chair.
>
> An old man was standing before them, his wide, pale eyes shining like moons through the gloom of the shop.
>
> 'Hello,' said Harry awkwardly.
>
> 'Ah yes,' said the man. 'Yes, yes. I thought I'd be seeing you soon. Harry Potter.' It wasn't a question. 'You have your mother's eyes.'[29]

Harry's eyes direct the gaze, with one picture being briskly replaced by another, as in a film. Rowling is constantly calling attention to 'eyes.' 'Mr. Olivander moved closer to Harry. Harry wished he could blink. Those silvery eyes were a bit creepy.'[30] In this instance, the narrative moves, like a camera, into close-up, then blurred focus, reflecting Harry's confused state. Indeed, although recalling a wide variety of other narratives, including Moses in the bulrushes and other myths of the chosen one, fairy stories, especially Cinderella, and boarding school tales, Rowling's main influence is undoubtedly the film that, arguably more than any other, changed the face of Hollywood: *Star Wars*. Harry shares a strange relationship with his nemesis, Voldemort, just like that of Luke Skywalker and Darth Vader. Harry, like Luke, discovers that he has a special ability; as Luke receives his saber from his mentor, Ben Obi-Wan Kenobi, Harry is given his wand (closely resembling the wand which 'chose' Voldemort).[31] The marketing of these novels is now almost identical to the marketing of a film – instead of lavish premieres, there are bookshop events to commemorate the release of a new installment. And while the films of these books are becoming increasingly successful as adaptations, they don't, like a Disney film, threaten to overtake the experience of reading. In the battle between the book and the film, the book is, at present, the winner.

The relationship between a literary text and its film adaptation varies according to the status of the original, but the marriages are never equal, with one partner invariably, unwittingly, or deliberately, preying upon the other. In the area of children's literature and film, there is an inclination among fans and critics to privilege one over the other, and this can be at a cost to 'classic' literature (how many children read *Alice in Wonderland* when they can see the film?) and to the benefit of contemporary children's fiction. But looking at adaptations of popular literature, the rivalry between the two can be detected in the growing tendency for children's literature to be more filmic, and film adaptations of popular literature to be more literary. The reflexivity apparent in both film and literature emphasizes both hostility and dependency, making the reading and spectating doubly complex and doubly pleasurable. As far as children's literature goes, most readers and spectators are bound to agree with Lewis Carroll's Alice who introduces the novel with what is, for her, a rhetorical question: 'what good is a book without pictures?'

Notes

1. *Charlie and the Chocolate Factory* (1964; rpt. London and New York: Penguin, 2001), p. 172.
2. *Ben Jonson: A Selection of His Finest Poems*, ed. Ian Donaldson (Oxford: Oxford University Press, 1995), pp. 1.139–41. See Judith Dundas, 'Ben Jonson and the Paragone.' *Sixteenth Century Journal* 9.4 (1978), 56–65.
3. *Novels into Film* (Los Angeles: University of California Press, 1957), p. 2. Kamilla Elliott also regards literature on film studies as evolving from earlier debates between poetry and painting and the frequent battle between words and images; see *Rethinking the Novel/Film Debate* (Cambridge: Cambridge University Press, 2003).
4. In *Literature and Film*, ed. Robert Stam and Alessandra Raengo (Malden, Massachusetts and Oxford: Blackwell, 2005), Robert Stam, in his introduction, lists eight sources of hostility to adaptation: disservice to the book; dichotomous thinking (merely assuming a rivalry exists); iconophobia; logophilia; anti-corporeality; the myth of facility; class prejudice; and parasitism. These sources are all one-sided, revealingly from the vantage of literature. Stam's book implies throughout that film needs defending when sitting beside literature and that hostility can only exist on the literary side. On the other hand, Robert Ray complains that literature and film remain in a pre-paradigmatic state as a result of their privileging the book over the film, to shore up literature's dwindling status due to the onslaught of film studies. (*How a Film Theory Got Lost and Other Mysteries in Cultural Studies* [Bloomington, Indiana: Indiana University Press, 2001], pp. 120–31).
5. *Children's Novels and the Movies* (New York: Ungar, 1983).
6. In *The Rough Guide to Kids' Movies* (New York and London: Penguin, 2004), Paul Simpson organizes children's cinema according to genre, such as 'Action and Adventure,' 'Drama,' 'Musicals' or 'Sci-fi.' I've rejected such a division here, as this would lead to a prioritizing of film over literature.
7. Douglas Street's collection, *Children's Novels and the Movies*, seems to be the only book devoted to the subject of film adaptations of children's literature.
8. http://www.imdb.com (accessed 13 July 2005).
9. This is an extreme example of what Kamilla Elliott terms 'the trumping concept of adaptation' (*Rethinking the Novel/Film Debate*, p. 174).
10. Douglas Street, *Children's Novels*, p. 10.
11. Janet Wasko, *Understanding Disney* (Oxford: Polity Press, 2001), p. 15.
12. *The Disney Version* (New York: Avon Books 1968), p. 191.
13. Steven Watts, *The Magic Kingdom: Walt Disney and the American Way of Life* (New York; Houghton Mifflin, 1997), pp. 104–5.
14. *The Art of Adaptation; Turning Fact and Fiction into Film* (New York; Henry Holt, 1992.), pp. 82–3.
15. *Understanding Disney*, pp. 117–19.

16. See Paul Wells, *The Cambridge Companion to Literature on Screen* (Cambridge: Cambridge University Press, 2007), pp. 201–2.

17. Quoted in Schickel, *The Disney Version*, p. 199. Attacks on Disney for bludgeoning children with junk and debasing literary classics were countered by those who regarded Disney as an American Institution, an upholder of morality and family values. See Steven Watts, *The Magic Kingdom: Walt Disney and the American Way of Life* (Boston and New York: Houghton Mifflin, 1997), pp. 409–10.

18. *English Heritage, English Cinema: Costume Drama since* 1980 (Oxford: Oxford University Press, 2003), p. 42.

19. As indicated on the Internet Movie Database http://www.imdb.com (accessed 13 July 2005).

20. Quoted in Brian Sibley, 'How are They Going to make *That* into a Musical?: P.L. Travers, Julie Andrews and Mary Poppins,' *A Lively Oracle*, ed. Ellen Dooling Draper and Jenny Koralek (New York: Larson Publications, 1999), pp. 51–62; p. 53.

21. ' "All That is Solid Melts into the Air": The Winds of Change and Other Analogues of Colonialism in Disney's *Mary Poppins*,' *The Lion and the Unicorn* 24 (2000) 97–109; p. 102.

22. See Robert Stam, *Literature Through Film; Realism, Magic and the Art of Adaptation* (Maiden, Massachusetts and Oxford: Blackwell, 2005), p. 13.

23. 'Popular' is defined here as literature that has been commercially but not 'academically' successful.

24. Dahl, *Charlie and the Chocolate Factory*, p. 126.

25. Ibid., pp. 173–4.

26. http://www.imdb.com (accessed 7 March 2005).

27. http://www.imdb.com (accessed 7 March 2005),

28. Rita Kempley, 'Harry Flies Off the Page: The Wizard Loses a Little of His Charm,' *Washington Post* (Friday 16 November 2001), page Co1, http://www.washingtonpost.com (accessed 7 July 2005).

29. *Harry Potter and the Philosopher's Stone* (London: Bloomsbury, 1997), p. 63.

30. Ibid., p. 63.

5

Words and Pictures

Introduction
Sharon Goodman

Much children's literature is not properly appreciable, and may even be unintelligible, without attention to its illustration. Images in children's books vary enormously in both style and function – from the primarily decorative, in what are often termed 'illustrated books', through to the fully formed visual narrative, the 'picturebook', where images and words are inextricably linked and have equally important roles in telling the story. The last twenty years or so have seen increased interest from academics and educationalists in the 'fecund, sprawling, fantastical form' of the modern picturebook (Lewis, 1996: 5), and this section focuses on some of these texts.

Illustrated children's literature has been available in Europe in various forms since the early beginnings of print technology in the fifteenth century. Some commentators and scholars date it earlier than this, and if we choose to admit other pictorial narratives as antecedents of the form, we can go back a very long way indeed. Barbara Kiefer (1995: 70), for example, notes: 'If we understand the picturebook experience as one in which participants engage both intellectual and emotional resources with a visual/verbal art form, we can trace the first picturebooks back perhaps as far as 40,000 years ago.' She means, here, the reading *experience* of visual storytelling texts, rather than the physical shape of the sort of books we now encounter, but as such one could, for example, include Aboriginal 'dreamings' (traditional indigenous Australian art, depicting aspects of the beginnings of creation) or European cave paintings as the precursors of modern written or printed storytelling. This long view meshes with a related study, Scott McCloud's *Understanding Comics* (1993), which traces the roots of *that* particular textual form back to the Bayeux Tapestry and Egyptian hiero-glyphics, among others – forms that were not specifically aimed at children, but which gave modern storytellers a wealth of textual possibilities to draw from, and re-version, for new audiences.

The earliest printed stories created specifically for children used crude woodcuts, printed in black and white and often lacking in much detail. Prior to that, children might have been familiar with illuminated manu-scripts in existence since medieval times in many countries around the world, but the slow dawn of fast, and affordable, printing technology meant that it was some time before illustrated books were widely available to children. The nineteenth century is seen by many working in the field of children's illustration as its Golden Age (Salisbury, 2004: 10), the period's technological advances bringing the advent of lithography which led, grad-ually, to full-colour reproduction. It also supplied a larger potential read-ership in the shape of a population much more widely schooled (the first Education Act was brought into force in Britain in 1870). With these two concurrent developments began the emergence of genuine marketing possi-bilities for illustrated children's books, and the extraordinarily high quality of much artwork for children in certain books from this period, such as the work of Walter Crane (1845–1915), Randolph Caldecott (1846–86) and Kate Greenaway (1846–1901) remains highly valued by historians, artists and book lovers alike.

Yet loved as picture books often are, by both children and adults, atti-tudes towards pictures in books *per se* for children are not universally positive. While many parents and educators see the images as a way of increasing the attractiveness of books to children, and thereby developing both literacy and a love of story, some feel that images distract from the verbal text (considered the primary carrier and communicator of meaning) and may impede the development of fluent and confident reading in children (Protheroe, 1992).

The essays

In different ways, the essays in this section all consider the history and development of children's book illustration. From a perspective informed by book history, Joyce Whalley provides a useful historical outline from the mid-seventeenth century to the First World War, tracing the links between improvements in colour reproduction and the increasingly widespread dis-semination of books for children. She argues that the cost of producing such texts was an important factor in these early days, as was the prevailing attitude that books for children were less valuable than those produced for adults. This meant that, at least in the seventeenth century, cheap and simplified illustration was considered by many to be adequate. Later, as the didactic and 'improving' potential of children's books became appreciated, the need for illustration was more widely accepted. Design and quality improved, and artists gained reputations in their own right, rather than being seen merely as the providers of supplementary material to the more high-minded and serious work of the author.

The next essay by William Moebius takes a chronological leap forward to the second half of the twentieth century. In strong contrast to Whalley's interest in the history of the processes and contexts of book-production, in this seminal essay Moebius focuses on the text itself. Moebius was one of the first to give serious thought to, and lay out a framework for, analysis of images in children's books. In this respect he can be seen as an important early contributor to the discipline of visual stylistics, which developed out of structuralism and semiotic analysis into what is often now called the study of multimodality – close readings of visual elements of texts in their own right, and of how the visual combines with words in texts to create meaning for readers and viewers. Moebius points out that picture books lend themselves to detailed textual analysis and reward close scrutiny – dispelling the myth that picture books are simple, or simplistic, or aimed only at children. Furthermore, he argues that images cannot – and must not – be looked at in isolation from the surrounding text; images in children's books always have a context, and a sequence, and meaning is derived at least in part from their positioning in the text overall and their interaction with the words. Indeed, every aspect of a picture book, from endpaper to endpaper, and each design element in between, can be seen as significant. As readers, our actions while reading also signify: the simple act of turning the page can be exploited by the picture-book author/illustrator to supply narrative force. Importantly, Moebius also claims that interpretation is not fixed; allusions and intertextuality may indeed be there in the text, and available for us to interpret, but a particular device may not always mean the same in symbolic terms, and generalisation is a pitfall to be resisted as we read and revisit favourite children's books.

The final essay included here, by Bette Goldstone, analyses the most recent forms of the picture book, concentrating on consciously postmodern texts such as David Wiesner's *The Three Pigs* (2001) (Plate 17). It has been recognised for some time that play is a crucial feature of picture books (Lewis, 2001) and Goldstone chooses as her focus here authors' playing with the concept of space. She argues that traditional three-dimensional space can be manipulated into five dimensions, to include that between the book and the reader and that which is the space 'beneath the physical page' – open for characters to step into. Reading itself takes on new patterns: as images and words are intertwined, the text becomes resistant to more traditional, linear and chronological practices of reading.

References

Kiefer, B.Z. 1995. *The Potential of Picturebooks: From Visual Literacy to Aesthetic Understanding*. Englewood Cliffs, NJ, Prentice-Hall.
Lewis, D. 1996. 'Pop-ups and Fingle-fangles: The History of the Picture Book', in V. Watson and M. Styles (eds) *Talking Pictures: Pictorial Texts and Young Readers*. London, Hodder & Stoughton.
Lewis, D. 2001. *Reading Contemporary Picturebooks: Picturing Text*. London, RoutledgeFalmer.
Protheroe, P. 1992. *Vexed Texts: How Children's Picture Books Promote Illiteracy*. Sussex, Book Guild.
Salisbury, M. 2004. *Illustrating Children's Books: Creating Pictures for Publication*. London, A&C Black/Quarto.

Further reading

Arizpe, E. and Styles, M. 2003. *Children Reading Pictures: Interpreting Visual Texts*. London and New York, RoutledgeFalmer.
Lewis, D. 1991. *Reading Contemporary Picturebooks: Picturing Text*. London, RoutledgeFalmer.
McCloud, S. 1993. *Understanding Comics: The Invisible Art*. New York, HarperCollins.
Nikolajeva, M. and Scott. C. 2001. *How Picturebooks Work*. London, Garland Publishing.
Nodelman, P. 1988. *Words About Pictures: The Narrative Art of Children's Picture Books*. Athens and London, University of Georgia Press.
Whalley, J.I. and Chester, T.R. 1988. *A History of Children's Book Illustration*. London, John Murray.
Wiesner, D. 2001. *The Three Pigs*. New York, Scholastic.

Texts and Pictures: A History
Joyce Irene Whalley

Children learn to read pictures before they learn to read words. Pictures also form the earliest records of man's attempts at communication: cave paintings, church murals, stained glass windows – all testify to the importance placed on pictorial representation. It is surprising therefore to realise how long it took for due significance to be placed on the illustration of children's

Extracted from 'The Development of Illustrated Texts and Picture Books', in P. Hunt (ed.), *International Companion Encyclopaedia of Children's Literature* (London: Routledge, 1996), pp. 220–30.

books. Early books for the young were not without pictures, but they were not illustrated books.

What is the difference? A good illustrated book is one where the accompanying pictures enhance or add depth to the text. A bad illustrated book is one where the pictures lack relevance to the text, or are ill placed and poorly drawn or reproduced – these are books with pictures rather than illustrated books. In this outline study of illustrated children's books we shall trace the rise of the importance of pictures and the improvement in standards of illustration, until on occasions the pictures assume greater significance than the text – or even replace it.

The emphasis in this study is on books for children's leisure reading, not text books. Nevertheless, the first illustrated book of any significance for children was in fact a Latin text book. This was *Orbis Sensualium Pictus*, by Johann Amos Comenius, published in 1658. There had been many Latin text books before this, but Comenius, an educationalist from Moravia, was among the first to realise that children best remember things they have *seen* rather than merely read about. His book was translated into English by Charles Hoole in 1659. It consisted of a picture at the top of every page, with the name of each object depicted in it listed below in Latin and then in English. The crude little woodcut illustrations covered a great variety of topics, both familiar and unfamiliar, and so provided the widest range of pictures for the young then available. The book was popular throughout Europe and remained in use in schools for many years. A popular imitation in English was James Greenwood's *The London Vocabulary*, which by 1771 had reached its sixteenth edition.

But the point about all these books, to our eyes at least, is that the illustrations were so crude. This was not because good illustration was impossible in the seventeenth and eighteenth centuries, but the models for children's book illustration were taken from the lower end of the market, from chapbooks and broadsheets, selling to a partially literate readership at a fraction of the cost of the better class adult book. This fact is in itself indicative of the attitude at that time to children's books, their production and illustration.

It is appropriate here to consider the methods available in the seventeenth and eighteenth centuries for the actual reproduction of illustrations, which were of course largely manual processes. For children's books in particular, the most important method of reproducing illustration was by woodcut – a process that goes back to the late fifteenth century. In this method, everything that was not required to print was cut away on the block so that the resulting illustration was one of mass rather than line. Such illustrations lacked subtlety, especially in the small size common in children's books. But the method was cheap and the blocks could go through the press at the same time as the type, so that in an illustrated book text and pictures could be printed together. Children's books have always been required to be cheaper than adult books, and in a society where such books were little regarded, this form of simplified – or crude – illustration was considered quite suitable. It was also the method used in the production of chapbooks and broadsheets, which themselves lay at the cheaper end of the market.

A superior form of illustration, and one used in technical books and the more expensive eighteenth-century adult works, was engraving. This is an intaglio process, by which the line of the drawing is engraved onto a copper plate, which is subsequently inked for printing. To reproduce this incised inked line, the plate has to be put under great pressure in a printing press, and cannot therefore go through at the same time as the type, which is raised. As a result, any book using engraving as a means of illustration either had to go twice through the press, or else it had its illustrations and text printed separately (this was the more common method). Engraving was certainly used in children's books, especially in the more expensive ones produced towards the end of the eighteenth century. It was also used by John Harris and William Darton in the mainly didactic works produced by them in the early decades of the nineteenth century. Engraved illustration permitted the reproduction of far greater detail in a picture, and a good engraver could produce very fine effects of line as well as of mass, giving much greater variety to the illustrations.

But the use of this more expensive process of illustration indicates that a change had taken place in the course of the eighteenth century in the whole attitude to children and their books. This change was initiated to a large extent by one man, John Newbery, who in 1744 set up his shop in St Paul's Churchyard, London, where he produced a wide range of children's books. He was not the first to do this – Thomas Boreman had preceded him in this new approach to children's books. But Newbery was the first to appreciate, and to exploit commercially, the market in illustrated children's books. He realised that his new product had to be reasonably cheap and so his books were small – no disadvantage in young eyes – and certainly illustrated, but by the cheapest method, namely the woodcut. Few names of the artists employed by Newbery are known, and many of the pictures he published were used again and again, in his own or other publishers' books. This was made possible by the general nature of the pictures: two children in a garden, a coach and horses, a lady and a child in a room. Such basic pictures could easily have stories written round them, though of course there were even at that date illustrations specially commissioned for specific books.

By the end of the eighteenth century the idea of illustrated books for children had become established and some of their authors had become well

THE

CHILDREN

IN

THE WOOD.

Embellished with 7 Wood Cuts.

YORK:

Printed and Sold by R. Burdekin,
Price One Halfpenny.

Figure 19   Front cover, *The Children in the Wood. Embellished with 7 Wood Cuts*, chapbook. Printed and sold by R. Burdekin, English (York); possibly *c.*1820. By kind permission of V&A Images, Victoria and Albert Museum. Image no: 2007BM3039.

known – although others still preferred to hide behind such phrases as 'by the author of ...' or 'by a lady'. These books tended to emphasise religious and moral matters (not good illustrative material), or social behaviour which was seen as the key to prosperity. By contrast, the early nineteenth century turned towards more factual themes. Children's books were of course written by adults and for the most part bought by adults for their children. It is surprising, therefore, that such poor quality material was for so long allowed to circulate among the young by people who would not have tolerated similar standards in their own books. Moreover it was the most scorned type of reading – the chapbook – which in the end effected the revolution in children's books.

The chapbook was a small, crudely illustrated booklet of about 2½ × 4 inches, which could be easily carried in the chapman or pedlar's pack as he traversed the countryside selling ribbons, pins, ballads and other small items to villages and farmsteads. The middle-class child probably only obtained sight of these cheap booklets through the servants' hall, but whether the child saw them or not, they certainly flourished among the poorer and semi-literate members of the population. Their content was varied: folktales, nursery rhymes, ballads, riddles, short entertaining or moral tales. All these continued to flourish as a substratum of literature, ready to surface when the time was right and a change had taken place in children's reading, when fairy tales, folktales and nursery rhymes were once again permitted in the nursery.

But while the crude woodcut illustration continued to prevail in the cheaper productions for children, certain improvements were taking place. By the early nineteenth century the rationalism so much in favour for children's literature was being supplemented by an appreciation of new discoveries of all kinds. The publishers William Darton and John Harris caught the public mood admirably in the books they produced over the next few decades. Nearly always didactic in content, these books sought to bring to children an awareness of the wider world beyond the British Isles, as well as to explore in depth the wonders of their own country. The titles of such works are themselves revealing. John Harris produced a number of travel books specifically for 'Little Tarry-at-Home Travellers', while there were also such works as *Scenes of British Wealth* (1823), *Rural Employments* (1820) and *City Scenes; or A Peep into London for Children* (1828). Publications of this sort demanded, and got, plenty of illustration. But since detail was essential in these pictures, engraving was the method most frequently employed to reproduce them. This often meant that the books contained texts which were separated from the pictures. These were usually grouped together, two or three to a plate, for the technical reasons described earlier.

This was not a very satisfactory arrangement for the young child. Neverthe-less, these books, often with the pictures hand coloured, were a popular if rather expensive contribution to children's reading.

By the 1830s there were various methods of illustration in use in chil-dren's books, which were now being produced in considerable quantity. The didactic books still led the field, but there were also religious and moral tales, now often by named authors, and it was certainly accepted that for the most part children's books should be illustrated.

The 1840s saw great developments in the field of children's books, in content and in production. Edward Lear's *Book of Nonsense*, and the first translations of Hans Andersen's *Fairy Tales* both appeared in 1846. The *Fairy Tales* of the Brothers Grimm had appeared with Cruikshank's illus-trations as early as 1823–6, although their circulation was probably not widespread until later. But equally important for the acceptance of non-sense and fairy tale in the nursery, was the advent of Henry Cole and Joseph Cundall. Henry Cole was a man who had a finger in many pies baked in the mid-nineteenth century, including such outstanding events as the Great Exhibition of 1851. But he was also a father, and as such was appalled at the state of children's books when he came to provide them for his own family. Under the pseudonym 'Felix Summerly' he instituted the Home Treasury series. In this he published fairy tales and nursery rhymes, com-missioning well known artists of the day, many of whom he knew person-ally, to illustrate them. He also commissioned special covers for his books. Joseph Cundall, with his interest in producing well-designed books, was the right man to work with Henry Cole. Such productions should have been outstanding, but it must be confessed that to modern eyes the Home Treas-ury series often appears somewhat dull. The cover designs were based on various traditional arabesque patterns, taken from older bindings, and were usually printed in gold on coloured paper, but they were not eye-catching, especially for children. The illustrations were of good quality, relevant and attractive – but (no doubt because of the cost) very few in number. These booklets were certainly very tasteful productions, but left to themselves children do not necessarily exhibit good taste, preferring a brightly coloured cover to a well-designed one. Nevertheless, a precedent had been set by which all aspects of a book designed for children should be given the same degree of attention previously allocated to adult books.

By the middle of the 19th century, entertainment was much more to the fore, and nonsense, folk and fairy tales, as well as longer stories, were now provided for children's reading. Other more subtle trends are noticeable in the illustrations of the period. Following the popularity of Heinrich Hoffmann's *Struwwelpeter* in 1844 (see Plate 1), there was a fashion for a more primitive or archaicising style, which would certainly amuse the young, and a tendency to facetiousness. We can also see the beginning of the cult of childhood, as the illustrators start to depict coy, quaint or sentimental children – something almost unthinkable at the beginning of the century. Obviously didactic, religious and moral books continued to be published – after all, even today children's books still have an underlying moral tone, even if it is scarcely noticeable.

Colour became much more widely used from the 1850s onward, especially in the popular 'toy books'. The toy book had nothing to do with toys, but was basically a publishers' description of a paper-covered picture book. In its earliest manifestations it consisted of about eight pages, with a minimum of text and a picture on each page, which was usually blank on the back.

As we move into the 1860s we reach the peak period of British book illustration for children and adults alike, since by now the illustrators worked equally for both the juvenile and the adult market, boldly putting their names with those of the authors on the title page.

Not only did Britain now produce black-and-white illustrators of very high calibre, but these also had the satisfaction of being much in demand, so that security further encouraged them to work to the highest standards. The spread of popular illustrated papers continued, while the increase in the actual reading public, and a middle class with more leisure, all encouraged the production of books of all kinds. This was the era of Dickens, Wilkie Collins and Trollope, and also of the gift book (the Victorian equivalent of the 'coffee-table' book) – and all these works were lavishly illustrated, providing plenty of work for the book artist.

Although colour was now more prevalent and improving in quality, it is interesting to note that the best illustrators of the period still preferred to work in black and white, in the method of wood engraving derived from Thomas Bewick. But we should always remember that in the production of these illustrations two sets of hands were at work – the artist who drew the original art work, and the engraver who engraved it on the block ready for printing. But here too in Britain at this period a good school of engravers had developed, the best-known often working for the firm of the Dalziel Brothers. Richard (Dicky) Doyle, C.H. Bennett, and 'Crowquill', all produced outstanding children's books during this decade. There were new names, too, at least as far as children's books were concerned, who were often already artists in their own right. One of these was John Millais, with his illustrations for books such as *Little Songs for Me to Sing* (1865), or Arthur Hughes, who produced the evocative drawings for George Macdonald's *At the Back of the North Wind* (1869), as well as other similar high quality illustrations, all usually set spaciously on the page.

Figure 20 'Here is Christopher Robin', from A.A. Milne, *Stories of Winnie-the-Pooh*, illus. E.H. Shepard (1926), London: Methuen, 1989. Copyright © The Estate of E.H. Shepard reproduced with permission of Curtis Brown Group Ltd, London.

The book was now considered as a work of art in itself, and layout and cover were, in the best instances, receiving as much care as the text and illustrations. Illustration could also be much more sophisticated too, as we see in the often dramatic work of Ernest Griset. Griset was for long a rather neglected artist, though much appreciated in his own time. His illustrations to a work like *The Purgatory of Peter the Cruel* (1868), in which the incidents are sometimes shown from an unusual view point, such as that of a fly or a frog, and his melodramatic designs for Aesop's *Fables* or Defoe's *Robinson Crusoe* (reminiscent of Gustav Doré), put him high on the list of mid-century illustrators.

But surely dominating the mid-1860s and early 1870s we must consider the two Alice books by Lewis Carroll. Here we have perhaps for the first time an artist and a writer working together to produce a definitive form of an illustrated story. Others have since tried to interpret Carroll's *Wonderland* creatures, but surely no one has portrayed them so memorably as their first illustrator, Sir John Tenniel (see Plate 3). Subsequent artists have also given permanent form to a writer's imagination (Shepard's illustrations for A.A. Milne's Winnie-the-Pooh books spring to mind; see Figure 20), but here in a book for children was the first complete interpretation of a fantasy world, which has survived more than a century of change in children's books.

Would the Alice books have survived to the same degree if they had been unillustrated? It is an interesting speculation, since it can also be applied to other books where text and pictures complement each other so perfectly – in Beatrix Potter's work for example. Certainly Lewis Carroll depicted his creatures verbally with great care, but readers would have been left to imagine the exact form of the *Wonderland* creatures without Tenniel's guide. This is perhaps the great mark of a good book illustrator, in that the visual forms they give to the text linger in the mind, whereas those of lesser illustrators (and there have been many of Alice alone) do not.

In the last quarter of the nineteenth century, technical developments were increasing in all fields of book production and helped to satisfy the immense growth in children's reading. This increase in readership was brought about by the various Education Acts, starting with that of 1870. With the expansion of literacy went also the further development of the illustrated journal, widening in scope and reaching lower down the social scale – with the consequent need for ever cheaper productions.

At the end of the century there was a conscious effort to reduce costs, which led to the employment once again of hack artists – often unnamed as in the past – together with poor quality paper and type, as we can see from those journals and cheap books which have survived. In colour printing, especially the three-colour process, there was both good and bad, and on the whole, the good was much more expensive. Fortunately the 'toy book', in the hands of publishers such as Darton, Routledge and Warne, ensured that the standard was largely maintained, aided by the arrival on the scene in the last quarter of the nineteenth century of a great triumvirate of illustrators, Walter Crane, Randolph Caldecott and Kate Greenaway, together with the remarkably competent colour printer, Edmund Evans.

Of the three artists mentioned, Randolph Caldecott was probably most truly a book illustrator. Walter Crane was certainly more prolific, but his other work in the decorative arts tended to spill over into his books, making him more of a book decorator than an illustrator. This is particularly evident in his 'toy books', where contemporary motifs – the fan, the sunflower, the general air of japonaiserie – manifest themselves on nearly every page. If we look at Crane's *Sleeping Beauty,* for example (see Plate 5), we find the whole of the centre page spread covered in illustration and design, and looking more like a decorative tile than a book picture. The same is equally true of his illustrations to *Goody Two-Shoes* and *Aladdin*.

By contrast, Randolph Caldecott made great use of space in his illustrations, allowing his line to speak for itself, and his pictures to enhance the (often traditional) texts he chose to illustrate. In *The Queen of Hearts* for example (see Plate 4), the simple basic nursery rhyme is 'expanded' by the pictorial comment of the cat who has seen the knave steal the tarts – no text is used, or indeed needed. The same is equally true of his other 'toy books', such as *The House that Jack Built* or *The Three Jovial Huntsmen*.

Kate Greenaway, however, was to some extent in a category of her own, and for the most part she chose to write and illustrate her own poems – *Under the Window* (see Plate 12) and *Marigold Garden* are perhaps her best known books. She 'invented' a style of dress and a 'never-never' period of her own, in which she placed her elegantly clad and immaculately clean children. Her work was highly stylised and very popular – although not very well drawn (her figures tend to have no bodies under their clothes) – and this popularity has remained firm to the present day. These books were not cheap, with their fine colour printing and high-quality illustrations, but they formed a small if influential section of the children's book market.

In the early years of the twentieth century this highly sophisticated type of work was carried to extremes by the productions of several artists whose books lie on the border line between those for children and those for adults. Kate Greenaway's books had been intended for children, with their simple rhymes and games, but illustrators like the Frenchman Edmund Dulac, Kay Nielson from Denmark, and Arthur Rackham offered a fantasy world which was scarcely that of the child. Of the quality of their illustrations to well known works like *Cinderella,* Hans Andersen and others, there can be no doubt, and the lavishness of production ensured that the books were duly treasured, but they stand to one side of the general production of children's books.

Although the names of Rackham, Neilson and Dulac may be linked together as indicating a particular type of lavish book for children, their styles were very different. Of the three, Rackham was possibly the most significant because of the stories he chose to illustrate, and also because his very personal style invited imitation. Even today it is possible to describe a woodland scene as 'Rackhamesque', and the picture which arises in the mind's eye is revealing. For Rackham made good use of line as well as colour, at the same time using both to convey a twilight fairy world, based on the factual (trees, flowers, buildings), but to which his art added an air of fantasy, sometimes even of the grotesque and the eerie. Although a frisson of fear does not come amiss to some children, as Charles Lamb pointed out in his essay 'Witches and other night fears' (*Essays of Elia*, 1823) the more sensitive child may be greatly alarmed by illustrations, even in so-called children's books. Both Nielson and Dulac relied more on a subtle use of colour rather than line, and both made use of oriental and other exotic touches to conjure up the romance in the children's books they illustrated.

Almost contemporary with these illustrators, and with a stronger touch of the real world, was Beatrix Potter. This writer, like Charles Henry Bennett, was also her own illustrator, and as a result her artistic creations have a homogeneous quality with her text. Beatrix Potter based her art on the real world – she made many detailed studies of animals, flowers and scenes before she began to illustrate each story. Her tales are of course fantastic – but in quite a different way from those artists whom we have just been considering. There it is the trappings of their art that give rise to the fantasy – it lies in the colour, the line, the mystery. But Beatrix Potter takes identifiable places and animals, and, without comment, gives them lives and speech which make them live and move in a world which is both ours and theirs. It is probably this mixture, together with the concern for the physical make up of the little books, that has kept her work among the foremost of the twentieth-century illustrated books.

But the first two decades of the twentieth century saw a great outpouring of books of all kinds for children in Britain. The Education Acts of the previous century and the provision of a public library service all ensured a good reading public – though not necessarily a public for good books. There was much 'run of the mill' illustration in weekly comics and in the popular Christmas annuals and 'bumper books'. But a lot of good work was also being provided for children, often in black-and-white to ensure relative cheapness.

There were many prolific and competent artists working for the children's market in the decades before the First World War, besides those who catered more for the luxury trade. Interestingly, most of their work was done in black and white, though their range within this limitation was quite remarkable. Among such artists was H.J. Ford, who provided the illustrations for Andrew Lang's widely read twelve colour fairy books, which began with *The Blue Fairy Book* in 1889 and ended with *The Lilac Fairy Book* in 1910. Norman Ault and the Brock brothers were also working in the early decades of the century along similar lines, while an artist of rather greater stature and imagination was Leslie Brooke, whose *Johnny Crow's Garden*, published in 1903, was deservedly popular. Having noticed at the beginning of this chapter an instance of the influence of continental artists on British book making, it is interesting to note at this period some examples of influences working in the opposite direction. This was especially true of Maurice Boutet de Monval, whose books were influenced by Greenaway, although his colours are more subtle, and he has a charming sense of humour. He in turn greatly influenced the work of Henriette Willebeek Le Mair, a Dutch artist, with her flat pastel colours and rather flat ornamental pictures. Her work was very popular in the first decades of the twentieth century, especially accompanied by nursery rhymes, and several of her books have been recently reprinted.

In the late nineteenth century and the early years of the twentieth century there were almost as many women illustrators as men; notable were the Scot Jessie M. King, Anne Anderson, Jessie Wilcox Smith and Mabel Lucie Attwell. But the immediate future lay with what was almost a throwback to an earlier style. The work of William Nicholson, Cecil Aldin and John Hassall carried with it overtones of the chapbook style of the 1890s. Simple masses and flat colours, set on a spacious page, were quite striking when they first appeared, as we can see in such work as Nicholson's *An Alphabet* (1898) and Aldin and Hassall's *Two Well-worn Shoe Stories* (1899). It was to some extent this simpler style which was to appeal to the book makers of the 1920s and 1930s, though all too often these lacked the courage to allow the use of blank spaces which had contributed so much to the success of the earlier artists' work. But the 1914–1918 war made a break which though not immediately apparent in the children's books of the 1920s, soon asserted itself, and a new era of children's book illustration began to develop.

Further reading

Alderson, B. (1986) *Sing a Song for Sixpence: the English Illustrative Tradition and Randolph Caldecott*, Cambridge: Cambridge University Press in association with the British Library.
Barr, J. (1986) *Illustrated Children's Books*, London: British Library.
McLean, R. (1972) *Victorian Book Design and Colour Printing*, 2nd edn, London: Faber.
Muir, P. (1985) *English Children's Books 1600–1900*, 4th imp., London: Batsford.
Whalley, J.I. (1975) *'Cobwebs to Catch Flies': Illustrated Books for the Nursery and Schoolroom, 1700–1900*, London: Elek.
—— and Chester, T.R. (1988) *A History of Children's Book Illustration*, London: John Murray, with the Victoria and Albert Museum.

Picturebook Codes
William Moebius

It is easy to be captivated by the lovable and endearing creatures that inhabit the modern picturebook. Whether our taste for picturebooks was formed by the work of Beatrix Potter or by that of her distinguished successors, we know, even if we often disavow it, this infatuation with the image of her Mrs Tiggy-Winkle (a hedgehog), Mary Chalmers' Harry (a cat) or Cyndy Szekeres' Pippa Mouse, Ernest Shepard's or William Pene du Bois' bears, Clement Hurd's rabbits, or Bernard Waber's Lyle (a crocodile) and Arthur (an anteater). Disarmed, entangled in a net of affection, we are almost ready to eat, as it were, out of the handling of the illustrator.

The story 'behind' the image, a story often supplied by the illustrator, may lead us to form our attachment to such images; is it possible that the sweetness of Raphael's Madonna is made sweeter by the story of Jesus, or the poignancy of Rembrandt's self-portraits by the story of Rembrandt's own life? The story in the child's picturebook may have no such scriptural or historical pre-existence; it unfolds for us just now, a variety-show of images and texts. We anticipate the next while looking at the one before, we laugh now that we see what we had not noticed or expected before, we let our eyes wander off a familiar character's face to a puzzling word on the page and back again. Unlike the framed settings of a Biblical text of a Raphael or Rembrandt, the pictures in a picturebook cannot hang by themselves; picturebook texts do not fare well when they are extracted and anthologized in various bibles of children's literature. Each works with the other in a bound sequence of images/text, inseparable in our reading experience one from the other.

Each page affords what Barbara Bader, the pioneer historian of the genre in its American development, has called an 'opening'; implied, of course, is a closing, a deliberate shutting out of what came before, and a constant withholding of what is to come. Unlike a published reproduction of a mural or a frieze, upon which the eye can wander, scanning a wide field for pattern, for signs of unity, the picturebook opening allows only limited exposures. Each page, if read at the speed of a slow reader, has only a minute or less to impress itself on our attention, to earn a place in our memory, as the story compels us forward, in what Bader, borrowing from Rémy Charlip, calls 'the drama of the turning of the page'.

Extracted from W. Moebius, 'Introduction to picturebook codes', in *Word and Image*, 2: 2 (1986), pp. 141–58.

We can pour emotion and affection into these pages, if we choose, under the license of our second childhood; or, as I wish to do here, we can watch more closely, looking past the lovable expression on the monkey's or ant-eater's face, and attend to elements of design and expression that comprise what we might call 'codes'.

Some historical considerations first. Readers of either of two lavishly illustrated histories of the picturebook or its parent, the illustrated book for children, will recall the attention given by both Susan Meyer and Barbara Bader to developments in media and printing techniques; out of each technical advancement, certain picturebook artists found a personal style. But more to our point, both historians also give rather detailed accounts of how, from Edmund Evans on, the making of the picturebook was seen more and more to require an integral relationship between picture and word, a 'total design'. Rather than being an album of pictures, or a text with some 'tipped-in' illustrations, the picturebook was, after Edmund Evans, conceived of as a whole 'product'. Text was 'script' or libretto (sometimes, as we shall see, better seen as footnote, or even as decorative flourish). Cover, endpapers, title-page design, all were carefully chosen elements of a whole, an experience wrapped, not without conscious intention, as a gift. Yet, as Bader's treatment of the subject reveals, distinctions were still to be made, almost 100 years after Evans' first publishing efforts, between 'illustration-as-communication' and 'illustration-as-art'.

No approach to the picturebook can overlook the importance of medium and design as a part of the reader's experience. Nor can we pretend to be unaffected by pictures we encounter in picturebooks that could be cut out, framed and placed over the fireplace. Yet I believe that in the picturebook what matters is something more than the artist's mastery of materials and technique, or the felicity of the book's design. These may prove attractive features to some readers, and may even foster an appreciation of 'good' books, of 'objects of beauty' in younger readers. By focusing attention on codes in the picturebook, we are no less concerned with dignifying the artist's creation. We are, as it were, making soundings in the harbour of 'design-as-communication', marking the deeper channels of a modern art-form.

Such soundings must begin simply enough with the *world* as it is depicted in the picturebook, of what has been called the 'presented world'. By using the word 'depict' I mean to include verbal as well as pictorial elements. What is presented in the text usually obeys certain conventions of recognizability and continuity. We depend on a number of stable visual cues, so that we can say 'There goes Curious George again', or ask 'Isn't he there behind that bush'? Whenever we ask 'Who's that'? of a picturebook character, we expect the answer to hold for that image during the entire story, unless we are alerted to a metamorphosis. We expect George to keep looking like George, and not like any monkey or anthropomorph, unless we are led to believe that George will now simulate such another. To remain recognizable, a character need only reveal a few signal traits such as curly hair (Ira), a proboscis (Arthur) a striped tail (Frances) or a blue jacket (Peter Rabbit). These metonyms of personality, species, gender, character type constitute elements of a semic code, but may also play a role in action, as the main character undergoes an identity crisis related to the presence or absence of a primary feature.

Characters remain recognizable despite the omission of particular features, lips, eyebrows, etc., we know they would possess if they were to step out of the book. And the world they inhabit remains imaginable even though it is sometimes not depicted at all at a given opening. What we refer to as the 'blank face' of the picturebook character might as well also apply to the carefully managed '*blanchissage*' of the world in certain illustrations.

Between text and picture, or among pictures themselves, we may experience a sort of semic slippage, where word and image seem to send conflicting, perhaps contradictory messages about the 'who' or the 'what' of the story. Here is a kind of 'plate tectonics' of the picturebook, where word and image constitute separate plates sliding and scraping along against each other. Let's look, for an example, at the cover and title page of *Where the Wild Things Are*. The front cover features the title of the book like a headline across the top; reading down the page into the picture, our eye falls on a seated animal-like creature who is dozing off in the foreground at one corner of the page. Behind this creature runs a stream and a fringe of palm-like trees. The expression 'Wild Things' in the headline is generic, almost too abstract. What is a wild thing? In no bestiary will we encounter quite the specimen of 'wildness' shown here, bull's head and human feet, sporting a one-piece blue fur suit, sitting like a Manet gentleman in *Le déjeuner sur l'herbe*. Perhaps we will be reminded of a Seurat or a Douanier Rousseau. Stillness and quiet prevail. We turn to the title-spread. Here, not quite so high, is the same expression 'Wild Things'. But now, in addition to two others of the original furry breed, pictured on the left, comes a new figure dancing onto the page from the right. Is this too a wild thing? It looks like a boy in some sort of wolf suit ... Suddenly the title has acquired the status of a banner above a rogue's gallery. The images on both the cover and title page each angle for our respect under the firm, immutable authority of the inscription *Where the Wild Things Are*. But between these images lies a buffer zone, an undefined 'wilderness'. What Roland Barthes has called the 'reference code' is probably also active here, as we attempt to cross this buffer zone. Only later may we discover that Max has earned the appellation 'wild thing' from his mother, thanks to his 'mischief of one kind/ or another'; the benign creature with the horns is 'wild' only in appearance, and is easily tamed by Max, 'the wildest thing of all'. In order to make this distinction of kind, we must first have had some acquaintance with the different connotations of the word 'wild' outside the text. The cover and title-page have hardly told us everything necessary to sort out the meaning of the 'wild thing'. The unresolved question of 'What is a wild thing?' coupled with the hint that not all 'wild things' think or act alike, prompts us to read on, to turn up or over new evidence, to become the loyal subjects of the hermeneutic code.

The best picturebooks can and do portray the intangible and invisible, ideas and concepts such as love, responsibility, a truth beyond the individual, ideas that escape easy definition in pictures or words. With her lens as historian, Bader sees 'a new non-imitative way of working generally, a way of expressing intangibles, communicating emotion, sensation – one which invited the viewer, too, to see things in a new way'. After Max has enjoyed his fling with the wild things, and exercised his enormous power over them, he falls into a reverie of a world that neither he nor the reader can see, a world 'where someone loved him best of all'. Max's mother never does appear in *Where the Wild Things Are*, except as represented by her tokens, shown in the final illustration, a three-layer cake, a glass of milk, a bowl of something steaming. On the final page, without a picture, the text tells us 'And it was still hot'. Here the 'it' emerges as unspeakable and unseeeable motherlove.

That so many picturebook characters come, in the end, to recognize or to experience the value of the intangible over the tangible, of what is 'loved best of all' over what is closest at hand, the unseen over the seen, deserves an essay of its own. Here I would offer just two observations in passing. The first is that such a pattern of story (and pattern of reader response, from dependence on the plain and literal to the development of a sense of independence in the face of individually discovered yet intangible meanings) accords with a pattern of cognitive development described by Piaget in terms of the passage from preoperational and concrete operational thought to formal operations, from the various 'realisms' to the recognition of symbol. Second, I would point out that the frequent depiction in picturebooks of gates, doors, windows and stairs, of roads and waterways, and the changing representation of light, artificial and natural, to accord with different degrees of character understanding, are not accidental or fortuitous phenomena, but downright basic to the symbolic force of the story. A character who looks out the window or stands in the door, as Max does in *Where the Wild Things Are*, is implicated in the unspoken meanings of thresholds. Whether stairs, steps or extended ramp, the incline may provide a measure

This is George.
He lived in Africa.
He was a good little monkey
and always very curious.

Figure 21 Illustration and text from H.A. Rey, *Curious George*, Boston: Houghton Mifflin Co. Copyright © 1941, and renewed 1969 by Margret E. Rey. Curious George is a registered trademark of Houghton Mifflin Harcourt Publishing Company. By kind permission of Houghton Mifflin Harcourt Publishing Company. All rights reserved.

of the character's stature or of progress towards a depth or height of understanding or confusion. There is nothing doctrinaire about such pronouncements. Nothing should tie interpretation of stairways or doorways and such in picturebooks to a single intention or effect. Such pieces of the symbolic code work differently in different stories, and will lend themselves to different interpretations. But they should not be overlooked.

'The presented word' may also bear the marks of 'presented worlds' in other texts. For example, Sendak plays with the familiar image of 'The Thinker' or, more subtly, alludes to Rodin's Adam in the final illustration of *Where the Wild Things Are*, which shows Max, hand on forehead, striding into his room, still wearing his wolf-suit, but clearly emerging as a young man. The phenomenon of intertextuality is more common in the picturebook than might appear.

The picturebook also asks us 'How much do you see'? To help us in this respect, it is likely to contain figures who represent points of view other than those of the main character. It may do this by editorializing in the text, or by depicting tacit witnesses on the fringes or in the foreground or background of the picture.

As specific onlookers in the text tease us with their inside view, with what they see, we may ask ourselves, again, what indeed do we see? As Gombrich once pointed out, '… we are all inclined to judge pictures by what we *know* rather than by what we *see*'. It is here that we may sketch out for further study the operation of certain graphic codes. These serve not so much to indicate the artist's command of the medium, or to demonstrate the artist's grasp of an ineffable beauty, as to enhance the reader's feeling comprehension of events and emotions. Graphic codes do not depend on the relation of objects to each other in a world outside the text; these we would call 'iconographic'. The images of a child looking out of a window or of a boat winding its way down a watercourse belong to such iconographic codes. To be able to read a graphic code we must consider the disposition of objects on the page, the handling of line and colour, we must examine the 'presentational process'. It would be misleading and destructive of the possibility of an 'open text' to say that within the graphic codes, this particular gesture means one thing or another, regardless of the specific text. We must speak of 'dominances' and 'probabilities', to borrow from the language of de Beaugrande. My intention in the following discussion is to toss out some leads, and to let each reader conduct research according to the demands of specific texts. I will offer a brief description of each code.

The codes of position, size and diminishing returns

The position of the subject on the page constitutes a code. It often matters whether the main character is depicted high or low on the page, in the centre or on the fringe, on the lefthand side or the right. Height on the page may be an indication of an ecstatic condition (as in *Curious George*) or dream-vision (as in Daugherty's *Andy and the Lion*) or a mark of social status or power, or of a positive self-image. Being low on the page is often by contrast a signal of low spirits or of unfavourable social status. These figures may be strengthened or weakened depending on whether the character is centred or in the margin, large ('close-up') or small ('distanced') (we here introduce the code of size), or presented in one or in more than one scene on the same page (the code of 'diminishing returns'). The more frequently the same character is depicted on the same page, the less likely that character is to be in control of a situation, even if in the centre. Whenever Curious George is shown in a succession of vignettes on the same page or facing pages, he is probably having fun and about to lose his freedom. In such a succession of vignettes, those at the top of the page may signal a more competent character than those at the bottom. A character that is on the margin, 'distanced' or reduced in size on the page, and near the bottom will generally be understood to possess fewer advantages than the one that is large and centred. Large size alone is not a sufficient criterion for the reading of advantage; it may be a figure of an overblown ego.

As with the stage, it matters whether the actors are shown on the left or the right. A character shown on the left page is *likely* to be in a more secure, albeit potentially confined space than one shown on the right, who is likely to be moving into a situation of risk or adventure. The left-hand page will complete a thought, let us know that we can go on, that the thinking of the previous page is complete. In the *Story about Ping*, the duck family moves across the page to the right as they leave the safety of the boat in the morning, and boards the boat from right to left in the evening. When Ping finally returns from his wanderings, he moves up the plank to the right, not the left, as the boat has now become an adventure unto itself, a wise-eyed boat worth inhabiting, and no longer quite to be taken for granted.

Codes of perspective

Supplementing the codes of position, size and diminishing returns are those of perspective, in which we follow the presence or absence of horizon or horizontals, vanishing points, and contrasts between façades and depths. Where it has been present earlier, the sudden absence of a horizon, of a clear demarcation between 'above' and 'below' is likely to spell danger or trouble.

A character located within a two-dimensional façade is likely to be less 'open-minded', less able to give imaginative scope to desire than one pictured within a three-dimensional 'depth'. In *Where the Wild Things Are*, the frustrated feelings of Max begin to find an outlet with the appearance of a window at the back; there is even a crescent moon, for more depth.

The codes of the frame and of the right and round

The code of the frame enables the reader to identify with a world inside and outside the story. Framed, the illustration provides a limited glimpse 'into' a world. Unframed, the illustration constitutes a total experience, the view from 'within'. *Where the Wild Things Are* demonstrates this point with considerable force, as Max's universe expands from the small, framed picture of himself in a room to the unframed doublespread of himself in the place where the wild things live. As the frame usually marks a limit beyond which text cannot go, or from which image cannot escape, we may associate a sense of violation or of the forbidden or of the miraculous with the breaking of the frame, as when the ocean-side tree spreads over the text as Max 'sailed off through night and day'.

I find it useful to relate the code of the frame to the code of round vs. rectilinear shapes. A character framed in a series of circular enclosures is more likely to be secure and content than one framed in a series of utterly rectangular objects. Often, an emphasis on rectangular shapes is coupled with a problem, or with an encounter with the disadvantages of discipline or civilized life. In the *Story About Ping*, Ping is held captive in an inverted basket, which appears on the page in broad bands at right-angles to one another.

One other aspect of the frame must be mentioned. The picturebook provides a temporal as well a a spatial frame. It has an opening and a closing page, a cover with two sides. What the front and back pages say is often mutually complementary, symmetrical even, as in *Curious George*, who begins and ends his story in a tree. And given the presence of the outer frame or covering, the 'heart' or 'core' of the book lies somewhere in its middle, in the wild things' wordless dance, or in the proliferation of verbal signs (Waber).

The codes of line and capillarity

The intensity of a character's experience may be represented by the thickness or thinness of lines, by their smoothness or jaggedness, by their sheer number or profusion or by their spareness, and by whether they run parallel to each other or at sharp angles. Thin, spare lines may suggest mobility and speed, thick, blurred or puffy lines, paralysis or a comfortable stasis. Jagged lines and those that run at sharp or odd angles to each other usually accompany troubled emotions or an endangered life, as when Ping fights for freedom from his captor in the water, or Bear Mouse eludes the diving hawk. Smooth and parallel lines, such as those of the junk Ping calls home, or of Bear Mouse's burrow suggest a settled, orderly world. What I call the code of capillarity refers to the presence or absence of capillary-like squiggles or bundles; an abundance of such marks often signals vitality or even a surfeit of energy, rendering the scene crowded, nervous, busy, as if each line were a living organism, part of a giant audience. Swabs of plain colour provide relief from such jungles of line. It is interesting to watch the gradual progress towards a simple, painted backdrop in *Where the Wild Things Are*. Max begins his story in a room, the back wall of which is represented by myriad fine cross-hatchings. Draped over a line of tied handkerchiefs, a segmented or interrupted line, is a bedspread with a pattern of pink flowers. The cross-hatchings of the wall-covering, the knotted handkerchiefs, the pattern on the bedspread contribute to a high degree of capillarity, of nervous energy, as, of course, does the anger on Max's face. Once Max is shut up in his room three pages later, the cross-hatchings seem less complicated, and the top of the pink bedspread and the blue sky visible through the window show few traces of such capillarity. At the point a few pages on where Max has begun his moondance, the cross-hatched backdrop has disappeared, to be replaced by a smooth, yet white, speckled sky. Max has moved into a calm state from an anxious one, into a position of command from one of frustration.

The code of colour

While we may attribute colour-coding to factors outside the text, we should not overlook what colour can say inside the text. Apart from the traditional associations of certain colours with certain moods or feelings, and apart from the association of bright colours with exhilaration and discovery, and of dark colours with disappointment and confusion, we need to be sensitive to colour as a linkage among different objects. In the *Story About Ping*, for example, the Yangtze and the uniforms of the Chinese fishermen are blue, the duck and the sunlight, yellow. Plunging into the depths of blue leads Ping into the clutches of the men in blue. Disobedience is associated with a blue captivity, freedom with yellow and white.

The graphic codes as we have outlined them above are interactive, simultaneous, though not always congruous with the codes of the verbal text, or of the presented world. At a glorious moment in *Curious George* in which George is depicted as central on the page, of medium size, associated with a round shapes (the balloon) and contained within one, all indications of positive feelings fraught with uncertainty (it is the righthand page), the text tells us that George was 'afraid' and indeed George does hover high above the ground in that 'presented world'. But George is smiling broadly, confirming the message of the graphic code, unperturbed by the narrator's alarmism.

Primary sources

Betty Boegehold/illustrations by Cyndy Szekeres, *Here's Pippa Again* (New York: Dell, 1975).

Margaret Wise Brown/illustrations by Clement Hurd, *Good Night Moon* (New York: Harper & Row, 1947).

Mary Chalmers, *Throw a Kiss, Harry* (New York: Harper & Row, 1958).

James Daugherty, *Andy and the Lion* (New York: Viking, 1938).

Marjorie Flack/illustrations by Kurt Wiese, *The Story About Ping* (New York: Viking, 1933).

Russell Hoban/illustrations by Garth Williams, *Bedtime for Frances* (New York: Harper & Row, 1960).

A.A. Milne/illustrations by Ernest H. Shepard, *Winnie-the-Pooh* (New York: E.P. Dutton, 1926).

William Pene du Bois, *Bear Circus* (New York: Viking, 1971).

Beatrix Potter, *Mrs Tiggy-Winkle* (London: Frederick Warne, 1905).

H.A. Rey, *Curious George* (Boston: Houghton Mifflin, 1941).

Maurice Sendak, *Where the Wild Things Are* (New York: Harper & Row, 1963).

Bernard Waber, *Lyle and the Birthday Party* (Boston: Houghton Mifflin, 1966).

Bernard Waber, *An Anteater Named Arthur* (Boston: Houghton Mifflin, 1967).

Bernard Waber, *Ira Sleeps Over* (Boston: Houghton Mifflin, 1972).

Bernard Waber, *Lyle Finds His Mother* (Boston: Houghton Mifflin, 1974).

References

Barbara Bader, *American Picturebooks: From Noah's Ark to the Beast Within* (New York: Macmillan, 1976).

R. de Beaugrande and W. Dressler, *Introduction to Text Linguistics* (London: Longman, 1981).

E.H. Gombrich, *The Story of Art* (Oxford: Phaidon, 1996).

Susan E. Meyer, *A Treasury of Great Children's Book Illustrators* (New York: Abrams, 1983).

Postmodern Experiments
Bette Goldstone

It is in the nature of picturebooks to be cultural artifacts reflecting societal mores, values, and beliefs. It is also in the nature of picturebooks to demonstrate extraordinary flexibility, openness, and inventiveness due to their brevity and the interplay of two artistic forms – narratives and illustrations (Nodelman). In a world that is changing at an almost unfathomable speed, if is not surprising that this highly dynamic and culturally reflective artistic form

Extracted from 'The Paradox of Space in Postmodern Picturebooks', in L. Sipe and S. Pantaleo, *Postmodern Picturebooks: Play, Parody and Self-referentiality* (London: Routledge, 2008), pp. 117–29.

is evolving at an accelerated rate. In the last three decades, picturebooks have become 'increasingly experimental, with thematic complexities and sophisticated artistry that have entirely changed their look' (Mikkelsen 31). These changes have been so dramatic that a new subgenre has evolved – the postmodern picturebook (Goldstone).

Equally true, it is in the nature of postmodern picturebooks to continue to experiment: break boundaries, question the status quo, challenge the reader/viewer, reflect technological advances, and appeal to the young who are at least as comfortable (if not more so) playing on the computer screen than they are on a jungle gym (Pantaleo). Postmodernism, whether reflected in picturebooks for children or in art and literature targeted for adult audiences, demonstrates a profound shift in societal perception and behavior. Rather than trying to interpret and represent a stable reality with clear parameters and mores, postmodern artists reflect upon a world – complex and confusing, a world which questions its purpose and function and has unstable and quixotically changing boundaries. In a quest to untangle this quagmire, postmodern illustrators and authors infuse their books with playfulness, parody, self-referentiality, nonlinearity, multiple perspectives, and irony (Nikola-Lisa). But more importantly, in their desire to better comprehend our existence and convey these insights to the young reader/viewer, artists present a new visual world, a new way of seeing.

One significant reason for this unique visual interpretation is the reconceptualization of space both in terms of illustration and text. Postmodern picturebook artists transform book space in ways which simultaneously are inventive while reflecting concepts and ideals from fine arts, technology, and scientific theory. Artists, and thus viewers, conceptualize traditional illustrative space as having three hypothetical planes of spaces. The illustration/painting/photograph may exist on all three planes giving the illusion of depth. To better understand this, picture in your mind's eye – a TV screen. The glass front is impermeable. Characters and props are located in three general spatial areas: The spot very close to the screen (foreground), another further back (mid-ground), and one removed to the far distance (background). Characters move and objects are placed within this carefully constructed and circumscribed space. Traditionally, picture-books compress the space even further, creating a relatively narrow stage for the story to visually unfold, with much of the action occurring in and on the space of the mid-ground. Also in this traditional form, the text is neatly placed most often at the bottom of the page, existing often in its own space separate from the actual illustration. In *Where the Wild Things Are*, Max, for most of the book, hangs out in the mid-ground. The creatures and Max come close to the picture surface only when their wildness gets out of control – as if the foreground were not the most comfortable place to be. The background is used sparingly with some scattered greenery; the text goes from left to right along the bottom of the pages. In Leo Lionni's *Frederick*, the protagonist of the same name and his mouse community live in a narrow band of space, with our poet-at-large and the busy animals moving in between fore- and mid-grounds. Peter, in *The Snowy Day*, has the most freedom. As Peter wakes up in the morning, he is seen – close to the viewer – on his bed in the foreground. When he plays outside, he moves almost exclusively between the middle and backgrounds. After he returns home, he settles in once again more closely to the viewer, moving between fore- and mid-grounds. Again in both *Frederick* and *The Snowy Day*, the story line runs along the bottom of the page, describing and amplifying the images but not part of them.

Postmodern picturebook creators continue to utilize these three traditional spatial dimensions, but now have expanded useable story space in three ways:

1. Space has been redefined, reconnoitered, and manipulated into five dimensions. The fourth dimension is the space shared between the physical book and the reading/viewing audience. Characters and objects can leave the standard three planes of space and move into space traditionally reserved for the audience. The fifth dimension is a spatial area that lies beneath the physical page. Characters now step off the page surface into spaces hidden underneath the flat rectangular page area. There the characters engage in newly formed story lines.
2. The picture surface is now porous and dynamic. This permeability allows characters and audience to move back and forth from the illusionary world of the story into 'real' space and then back again. Book characters and story elements spill out of the book into the audience space, while audience members enter the story world. This dynamic page surface allows room for alternative realities to lie beneath the page. The page surface now has an atmospheric quality; it is translucent and mobile.
3. These additional two dimensions and the porous surface plane allow new possibilities for location and function of the text. The text is now not necessarily segregated from the pictorial space but is woven around characters, objects, and settings. Words can now be placed literally all over the pages, can be manipulated by the characters in the story, and can become props within the space. Although text still can be seen as a separate component, there now are new ways for narration to be integrated within the whole.

These three conceptual innovations allow for movement and interactions not before seen in picturebooks. Children's picturebooks have always been magical in their creative offerings, but postmodern picturebooks present startling new ways to read and view a page. Picturebook pages, text, and illustrations can evaporate, multiply, pile up on top of one another, be peeled back, be constructed into things other than picturebook parts, and are far more versatile than Gutenberg could have ever imagined. These changes create a tableau for ingenious and out of the ordinary fictional and artistic representations.

To further define this new fourth dimension, characters now have the ability to see the audience, to speak with the audience, and move toward and into the audience's space. The reader/viewer becomes an 'insider,' lost in text and image at that moment in time (Benton). In David Wiesner's quintessential postmodern picturebook, *The Three Pigs*, the wolf not only first huffs and puffs and blows the house down but also blows the pig out of the story (see Figure 22). The audience, pig, and wolf are equally perplexed

Figure 22   'The Wolf blows the pigs out of the story', from David Wiesner, *The Three Pigs*, New York: Clarion Books, 2001. Copyright © 2001 by David Wiesner. By kind permission of Clarion Books, an imprint of Houghton Mifflin Harcourt Publishing Company. All rights reserved.

and astonished. Midway through the story, another pig breaks through the picture plane. Nose to nose, eyeball to eyeball with the audience, the pig ponders, 'I think ... someone's out there' (see Plate 17).

Just as book characters are no longer confined to page space, members of the audience are no longer relegated to an out-of-book experience. We can (and do metaphorically) move directly into the book. Human hands – life size and realistic – enter *Bad Day at Riverbend* and *Black and White*, manipulating the pages and story. In *Bad Day at Riverbend*, 'shiny, greasy slime' begins to cover the town in mysterious irregular lines (Van Allsburg). At the story's end, the audience sees a human hand armed with a crayon. Evidently, some little person has been happily scribbling away in a coloring book of the old west. In *Black and White*, four distinct stories mingle with each other creating astonishing connections (see Plate 16). Just as the reader/viewer believes he/she understands the story, a human hand reaches into the last page, picking up one of the important story components – a train station – as if it was a toy in a Lionel train set.

Although this blurring of real and fiction could create mayhem, it does not. Rather a very clear invitation is delivered, 'Come on in!' These postmodern elements engage the reader/viewer powerfully. The reader/viewer has a clear mandate; think about this story, relate this story to other reading experiences, manipulate the story so it makes sense. Do not be shy, be a coauthor. Feel free to play with story, add to it and alter it!

The postmodern illustrated fifth dimension is the space designated underneath the physical page. Characters can peel back, fly through, see around, gnaw through the physical white page and find an expanded universe; their world is not confined by a rectangular page space. Again in Wiesner's 2002 Caldecott winner, the three pigs explore the world around the physical pages (see Figure 23). By pushing, shoving, and folding pages of their story, they discover new worlds with alternative realities and a freedom to go beyond their intended destiny. But these pigs, like others before them, eventually realize that there is no place like home. Empowered with new-found knowledge and friends, they rebuild their original story-land, making it a better place to live. In *The Story of a Little Mouse Trapped in a Book*, the title tells it all. A mouse is stuck in a book. Determined to find freedom, the ingenious protagonist nibbles the perimeters of the white page, and carefully lifts the sheet away revealing a green pastoral landscape. Undaunted, the creature now makes an airplane out of the paper and flies down to a new bucolic existence. Max, Frederick, and Peter explore, play in and comprehend one universe; that which is the standard, stable, thirty-two white-paper pages found in traditional picturebooks. It is outside their comfort zone to go beyond the relative safety of the page space.

Figure 23 'Let's explore this place', from David Wiesner, *The Three Pigs*, New York: Clarion Books, 2001. Copyright © 2001 by David Wiesner. By kind permission of Clarion Books, an imprint of Houghton Mifflin Harcourt Publishing Company. All rights reserved.

This new spatial arena – worlds hidden beyond the physical pages – is also the underlying premise of *Zoom, Re-Zoom,* and *The Red Book*. All three of these books fold into themselves. As the reader/viewer looks intently at an illustration, an insight develops: 'This is not an illustration in the book I am holding, but an image of another place – a space that exists underneath the pages – beyond the book.' This new space has its own potential story awaiting. In *Zoom,* this wordless picturebook opens with an image the viewer cannot quite identify. On subsequent pages the image recedes and we learn it is the face of a wristwatch. As each page turns over, a new understanding of the story takes place. On the next page we see the watch is on the arm of an archeologist tracing hieroglyphs in an ancient Egyptian room. We cognitively shift the story's meaning and predict a new possible scenario. On the next page the illustration shows us that the archeologist is working in an obelisk in a square in modern Paris. The story does not stop here. The story's space and plot changes and expands. The story is built on layer upon layer of realities which turn into imaginary spaces over and over again. Existing in this book (as well as *Re-Zoom* and *The Red*

Book – both similarly designed) are complex and highly imaginative worlds hidden beneath the picture planes. These books convey very clearly to the young reader/viewer that hidden within the mundane and obvious are exciting possibilities that await discovery. The books urge the reader/viewer to actively search out the extraordinary and inquire about the unlikely.

These two new spatial planes can occur only because the picture surface is porous and permeable. The TV set we imagined has a glass surface that is impenetrable. It contains all the action behind it. In postmodern picturebooks, the page now is a dynamic, interactive surface that permits movement. Obviously the fourth spatial dimension, with characters, objects, and viewers sharing common space, could not exist without this feature. Likewise, the fifth dimension of multiple spatial planes existing behind the page could not occur if the page was static and inert. This porous surface truly broadens the possibilities for artistic interpretations.

Another innovative use of space is the placement and function of the alphabetic text on the page surface. The function of the text has expanded to go beyond the job of narration to now entering into the illustration's spatial domain. This allows characters to manipulate the words. In *Arlene Sardine* the letters in the words vary in thickness and their angles have been softened. These letters now appear to be sea creatures swimming alongside the school of brislings. In *Zin! Zin! Zin! A Violin* the words swirl across the space to the tempo of the violin's music. In *Mysterious Thelonious* the words are placed on a grid background in patterns akin to notes on a staff. In *Black and White* the words on the title page slip off the page, just as the burglar has slipped out of his prison cell. In *The Three Pigs* the letters get knocked about quite a bit (see Figure 24). At the end of the story, the characters pick up letters from the alphabetic mess on the floor, and write a new ending. This integration of text within the actual image space allows for the illustrator to remind the reader/viewer of the artificiality of text, allows the reader/viewer to witness the construction of the story, and permits a nonlinear reading of the text. In texts such as these, the words are 'read' in the same process as we 'read' pictures. When viewing an image we are attracted to colors, forms, lines, and compositional elements which may be located anywhere in the picture. In traditional picturebook formats, text is sequential and linear, linked to time. Images on the other hand are linked to space – nonsequential, spontaneous, and not bound by temporal restraints (Kress). For example, the sequence of words read, what is printed (and thus viewed) first, second, and third is of consequence. When reading pictures, it does not really matter what we look at first, second, and third. What is of significance is where objects and characters are located, how they are positioned to one another, and in what spatial plane they lie.

Figure 24 'The pigs fall down the chimney', from David Wiesner, *The Three Pigs*, New York: Clarion Books, 2001. Copyright © 2001 by David Wiesner. By kind permission of Clarion Books, an imprint of Houghton Mifflin Harcourt Publishing Company. All rights reserved.

This represents a significant change. In postmodern picturebooks, the text loses, at times, its temporal quality. Text and image are always inextricably intertwined in picturebooks. This is a crucial element. Readers/viewers/listeners are pulled between image and text – wanting to linger over the pictures, but also needing to move quickly ahead to learn what will happen next (Nodelman). When text takes on this dual role of telling the story and being part of the illustration, the act of reading slows down – the tension between word and picture diminishes. Where the words and letters are situated, how they relate to the characters in position and form become as important as what they say. We are witnessing a change in the reading process. Postmodern picturebook artists make the synergy of words and images more apparent. The former boundary between words and pictures has been broken. This characterizes a change in text function as moving from describing the world to showing it. Writing is now display oriented (Kress).

The illustrations described, although quite different, are all brilliant in their inventiveness and ingenuity. They all use space in unique ways. These books contain images that interrupt the flow of linear, three-dimensional traditional picturebook patterns, establishing new ways to visually interpret and read, play with the artifice of fiction, and make book production visible. But it also needs to be recognized that postmodern picturebook artists incorporate visual techniques and styles used before. As mentioned previously, children's literature does not emerge from a vacuum, but rather from a deeply embedded and complex multicultural heritage that artists and authors then interpret. In any picturebook, the illustrations, the presentation format, underlying themes, portrayal of character and setting reflect cultural knowledge, belief systems, mores, literary conventions, and artistic styles. This does not diminish what postmodern picturebook creators do. Their innovation and excellence lie in the fact that they experiment with and manipulate these previously used visual concepts by placing them in a new milieu – the picturebook.

References

Benton, Michael. 'The Self-Conscious Spectator.' *The Centre of Language in Education, University of Southampton, Occasional Papers* 30 (1994): 1–22.

Goldstone, Bette. 'The Postmodern Picture Book: A New Subgenre.' *Language Arts* 81.3 (2004): 196–204.

Kress, Gunther. *Literacy in the New Media Age.* London: Routledge, 2003.

———, and Theo Van Leeuwen. *Reading Images: The Grammar of Visual Design.* London: Routledge, 1998.

Mikkelsen, Nina. *Words and Pictures: Lessons in Children's Literature and Literacies.* Boston: McGraw, 2000.

Nikola-Lisa, W. 'Play, Panache, Pastiche: Postmodern Impulses in Contemporary Picturebooks.' *Children's Literature Association Quarterly* 19.3 (1994): 35–40.

Nodelman, Perry. *Words about Pictures: The Narrative Art of Picturebooks.* Athens, GA: University of Georgia Press, 1988.

Pantaleo, Sylvia. 'Grade 1 Students Meet David Wiesner's Three Pigs.' *Journal of Children's Literature* 28.2 (2002): 72–84.

Children's literature cited

Banyai, Istvan. *Re-Zoom*, New York: Penguin, 1998.

———. *Zoom.* New York: Viking, 1995.

Felix, Monique. *The Story of a Little Mouse Trapped in a Book.* La Jolla, CA: Green Tiger, 1988.

Keats, Ezra Jack. *The Snowy Day.* New York: Scholastic, 1962.

Lehman, Barbara. *The Red Book.* Boston: Houghton Mifflin, 2004.

Lionni, Leo. *Frederick.* New York: Knopf, 1967.

Macaulay, David. *Black and White*. Boston: Houghton Mifflin, 1990.

Moss, Lloyd. *Zin! Zin! Zin! A Violin*. New York: Scholastic, 1995.

———. *Arlene Sardine*. New York: Orchard, 1998.

Raschka, Chris. *Mysterious Thelonious*. New York: Orchard, 1997.

Sendak, Maurice. *Where the Wild Things Are*. New York: Harpers Collins, 1963.

Van Allsburg, Chris, *Bad Day at Riverbend*. Boston: Houghton Mifflin, 1995.

Wiesner, David. *The Three Pigs*. New York: Scholastic, 2001.

6

Contemporary Transformations

Introduction
Ann Hewings

> Books hold our personal histories; our bookshelves are the record of
> our lives. Our childish loves, our adolescent passions, our sudden crazy
> obsessions, are all up there in our room, to remind us ... Digital books
> will have their place. An electronic work of reference is useful, if not
> exactly beautiful. But ... [j]ust as online games have not stopped people
> wanting to experience the whack of leather on willow, or the thrilling
> shuffle of a deck of cards, so online reading will never replace the physi-
> cal and emotive delight of a lovely fat papery book.

Kindersley, 2007

It is of course ironic that this remark rejecting the latest 'death of the book'
story was posted on a blog site. While its cutting-edge locale and virtual
form highlights the potential for new developments in reading that the
internet has created, its voice nostalgically affirms the writer's strong physical affinity with the printed book. But will that affinity with books be as
strong for today's children growing up in the digital age? Indeed, is the literary landscape at the beginning of the twenty-first century changing so dramatically that children's reading and children's literature itself are in danger
of becoming irrelevant?

Arguably, at the turn of the millennium children's literature is thriving despite the changes in lifestyle and leisure habits of many children, but
equally its forms are changing and becoming more fluid under the combined pressures of new media, globalisation, and changing concepts of the

boundaries between childhood and adulthood. This section accordingly takes as its subject the future of the book and of the consumption of children's literature in the digital era and within a global marketplace, and aims to be representative of new work in the field on the direction of travel of children's literature.

The essays

The first essay included here, by Linda Hutcheon, takes up the question of the adaptation of children's literature. Historically, there have been many examples of different versions and adaptations of children's literature across different media. The changes between the serialised magazine version and the book of Stevenson's *Treasure Island* come to mind, as does the proliferation of print variants, stage versions, statues and screen realisations of *Peter Pan*. What is distinctive about the early twenty-first century is that this process has accelerated and proliferated: texts may now be reincarnated in a bewildering variety of modes – audio, stage, television, film, abridgements, pop-up books, t-shirts, jigsaws, computer games, lunch-boxes. Hutcheon argues forcefully that such adaptations of stories to different media should not be regarded as second-rate or derivative. They should instead be regarded as the creative means of preserving or reinvigorating tales for a new generation.

Suman Gupta, in his essay 'Harry Potter Goes to China', is also interested in the creative mutation of texts, but takes translation and its relation to globalisation as his focus. He explores the cross-cultural adaptation of the Harry Potter books, a series which has its roots in traditional British school and adventure fiction. From the buying of uniform and books to the house system and prefects, the books draw on what would seem a highly specific British cultural and literary history, yet they have successfully crossed both linguistic and cultural boundaries. Gupta enquires into the popularity of these books in China, pursuing possible explanations for this success in the changing construction of childhood in China at the beginning of the twenty-first century. He concludes that it has as much to do with China's opening up to the world beyond its borders as it has to do with the texts themselves.

Rosie Flewitt's essay considers the impact on children's literature of digital technology, arguing that scholars of children's literature can no longer concentrate solely on print literacy, but need to acknowledge the other forms of engaging with literature that modern children experience, particularly through interactive media, from electronic toys to e-books. Flewitt illustrates how reading practices surrounding literature are changing alongside the technology, so that children, before they can 'read' conventional books, can navigate around interactive story sites, making choices about what to focus on, listen to or play with. Such skills are likely to prepare them to participate in the more open, postmodern fiction opportunities provided by hyper-media. The profundity of this change is stressed by Peter Hunt (2006: 237) when he writes: 'Electronic media are not simply changing the way we tell stories: they are changing the very nature of story, of what we understand (or do not understand) to be narratives.'

If literature and reading are both arguably undergoing radical change, so too is the readership for children's literature. Changes to who engages with literature, and how, are explored by Rachel Falconer in her essay 'Cross-reading and Crossover Books'. In looking at literature that challenges the boundaries of what is considered suitable for children and simultaneously looking at adults reading what has been categorised as *children's* fiction she identifies major shifts in contemporary culture. She argues that child-hood, like gender, should be viewed as a matter of performance rather than biology and that the boundaries between childhood and adulthood are con-sequently permeable both ways. The rise in the cultural value accorded to the fresh perspective of youth, particularly to the supposedly less-fettered childlike imagination, both draws children and young people into 'adult' arenas and simultaneously invites/entices adults into participating in the 'lightness' found in a variety of types of children's literature. This is not, Falconer stresses, at the expense of the exploration of issues which have influenced literature across age groups and down the ages – birth, adoles-cence, death. Rather, contemporary crossover fiction is one way of explor-ing these issues in both fantasy and contemporary worlds.

References

Hunt, P. 2006. 'Futures for Children's Literature: Evolution or Radical Break?', in P. Hunt (ed.) *Children's Literature: Critical Concepts in Literary and Cultural Studies, Volume 1*, London, Routledge: 237–45. (Originally published in *Cambridge Journal of Education*, 30(1) 2000: 111–19.)

Kindersley, T. 2007. 'The Death of the Book, Again'. theblog books www.blogs.guardian.co.uk/books/2007/04/the_death_of_the_book_again.html, accessed 22 May 2008.

Further reading

Buckingham, D. 2000. *After the Death of Childhood: Growing up in the Age of Electronic Media*. Cambridge, Polity.

Burn, A. 2004. 'Multi-text Magic: Harry Potter in Book, Film and Videogame', in F.M. Collins and J. Ridgman (eds) *Turning the Page*. Oxford, Peter Lang: 227–49.

Mackey, M. 2002. *Literacies across Media: Playing the Text*. London, Routledge.

Mallan, K. '"Just a Boy in a Dress": Performing Gender in Male-to-Female Cross-Dressing Narratives', in F.M. Collins and J. Ridgman (eds) *Turning the Page*. Oxford, Peter Lang: 251–67.

In Praise of Adaptation
Linda Hutcheon

[A]daptation can be described as the following:

- An acknowledged transposition of a recognizable other work or works
- A creative *and* an interpretive act of appropriation/salvaging
- An extended intertextual engagement with the adapted work

Therefore, an adaptation is a derivation that is not derivative – a work that is second without being secondary' (*TA*: 8–9).

An adaptation is not vampiric: it does not draw the life-blood from its source and leave it dying or dead, nor is it paler than the adapted work. It may, on the contrary, keep that prior work alive, giving it an afterlife it would never have had otherwise ... We retell – and show again and interact anew with – stories over and over; in the process, they change with each repetition, and yet they are recognisably the same. What they are not is necessarily inferior or second-rate – or they would not have survived. Temporal precedence does not mean anything more than temporal priority. Sometimes we are willing to accept this fact, such as when it is Shakespeare who adapts Arthur Brooke's versification of Matteo Bandello's adaptation of Luigi da Porto's version of Masuccio Salernitano's story of two very young, star-crossed Italian lovers (who changed their names and place of birth along the way). That awkwardly long lineage points not only to the instability of narrative identity but also to the simple but significant fact that there are precious few stories around that have not been 'lovingly ripped off' from others. In the workings of the human imagination, adaptation is the norm, not the exception (*TA*, pp. 176–7).

It's no secret that more children's books are borrowed and sold after an adaptation has appeared – and that this continues over the years, since DVD and video sales keep the story alive. But financial advantage isn't the only motivating factor for adapting children's literature to other media. If we remember that one of the earliest literary adaptations to film was Cyril Hepworth's 1903 eight-minute silent film of *Alice's Adventures in Wonderland*, we might agree with those who claim that children's literature as a cultural form has a historically long and perhaps even a special relationship with adaptation, which may explain why it is so frequently 'mediated

---

This is an edited version of extracts from L. Hutcheon, *A Theory of Adaptation* (New York and London: Routledge, 2006) (referred to as *TA*) and 'Harry Potter and the novice's confession', in *The Lion and the Unicorn*, 32 (2008), pp. 169–79.

and recontextualized through film, theatre, television, radio and other more recent technologies such as the audio cassette, computer games and CD-ROM' (Collins and Ridgman, 2006: 9). It is argued that 'the rules of the game in children's literature and the carnivalesque endlessness of its imaginative possibilities put it in close touch with the popular media' (Collins and Ridgman, 2006: 10). But adult literature had been adapted into children's literature too, and that dimension should not be lost in our focus on adaptation across media.

But *what* gets adapted (and *why*) when children's literature moves from one page to another or from the page to the stage or screen (movie, TV or video screen)? Sometimes it's familiar *stories* that get adapted – not only because they *are* familiar, but because they *should be* familiar. Priscilla Galloway once explained to me that one of her motives for writing the 'Tales of Ancient Lands' series she created was 'salvaging' – someone had to save these stories before children (who became adults) forgot about them forever. So her 1997 illustrated book (with Normand Cousineau) called *Daedalus and the Minotaur* both retells the tale we know from Apollodorus, Ovid and Pausanius and makes some changes, changes that teach children about toleration, love, and disability. As she puts it in the epilogue, 'My recreation shows events and people from the old story in new guises, and puts flesh on old bones, though I like to believe myself true to the ancient tale' (1997: 103).

But the didactic urge to 'salvage' isn't always the only motivating factor for adapters. Sometimes, as we have seen, in adapting, Galloway (1995) changes the point of view of a familiar story, telling us the tale of 'Jack and the Beanstalk' from the perspective of the giant's devoted wife in order to show us something the 'old story' might not have considered. Philip Pullman (2000) obviously likes to do this too: in *I Was a Rat* we get the Cinderella story and its sequel through the eyes of a rat magically transformed into one of the heroine's attendants – who was *not* restored at midnight to his true form. In these cases, we clearly need to know and recognise the adapted work in order to 'get' the adaptation or at least get the point of it *as* an adaptation. We can always read these new versions without knowing the adapted work, but we would read them differently. There is a whole other, extra dimension that comes with knowing the adapted work, a dimension that makes the experience of reading a richly 'palimpsestuous' one, as we oscillate between the version of the story we already know and the one we are reading now.

But it isn't always a specific *narrative* or its particles that get adapted; sometimes it's a whole imaginative *world*, a 'heterocosm' (literally, another cosmos) ... Lyra Belacqua's Oxford is arguably an adaptation of our own. Stories and worlds get adapted, but so, in a sense, do entire works of literature: their stories, worlds, characters, themes – the whole thing. I call these *adaptations* rather than simply *intertexts* or allusions because of the fact that they are changed as well as replicated. In biology, that is what adaptation is: replication with variation. Much has been written about Philip Pullman's rewriting in *His Dark Materials* of Heinrich von Kleist's 'On the Marionette Theatre', and even more has been ventured about his adaptation of Genesis, of Milton's *Paradise Lost* and of Blake's interpretation of that text (as well as of Blake's own *Songs of Innocence and Experience)* (see Reynolds, 2006; Walsh, 2007). Adapting from innocence to experience is the positive life challenge faced by the adolescent Lyra and Will; and their (young) daemons, with their constantly changing shapes, are perfect metaphors for adaptation of all kinds, and not only (most obviously) of Jung's theory of our opposite sex animus or anima. Children's literature is, in a way, all about adaptation, about change, just like Ovid's *Metamorphoses*.

Not surprisingly, Pullman's *His Dark Materials* has been adapted for the stage, in two three-hour plays done by the National Theatre in London, adapted by Nicholas Wright and directed by Nicholas Hytner. BBC Radio 4 did a radio drama version, now available on CD, and RTE (Irish Public Radio) did a version of *Northern Lights*. The film adaptation of *The Golden Compass*, directed by Chris Weitz, premiered in December 2007. Whether or not this adaptation's audiences know that Pullman himself has also adapted the theory of the Oxford quantum physicist David Deutsch about multiple parallel worlds that can be inferred (if not seen) from scientific experiment, they experience the adapters' visualisation of that adapted theory in the film. They just experience it differently, with no palimpsest.

It has been argued that Pullman's intertextual allusions (what I'm calling his multiple adaptations) are part of his address to a specifically adult (and middle-class) readership (Reynolds, 2006: 191). But Pullman himself has reminded us that the ancient story-telling traditions always had a mixed audience (Pullman, 1998: 45). And, if I understand the theory of children's literature correctly, it has always been what Sandra Beckett calls 'crossover' literature – aimed at a double audience of both child and adult, the adult experiencing with the child or the adult the child becomes. This is true for their adaptations as well. As one children's film critic puts it: 'To watch again children's films in adulthood lets us travel self-consciously to somewhere now closed off from us, because the audience has changed, because we have changed' (Newton, 2006: 18). But, in a way, the double address remains nonetheless. Many of these adapters admit to writing deliberately on two or more levels, hailing their audience thereby not only separately, as child and as adult, but through various conflations: 'the child within the adult and the adult within the child' (Collins and Ridgman, 2006: 13). And then there is the child in the process of *becoming* the adult, whose expanding consciousness is being shaped by his or her experience of reading these stories. As Pullman has taught us, innocence is not a state of stasis to be nostalgically preserved; nor is experience only loss. Readers literally go from innocence to experience over the course of a narrative, and certainly in moving from an adapted text to an adaptation, they become 'knowing' readers, no longer presumed innocent.

It has become a truism of adaptation theory lately that adult literary adaptations are held to the criterion of 'fidelity' to the adapted text much more than children's book adaptations are: the loosely based retellings of stories like *The Little Mermaid* by Walt Disney are usually cited as examples (Reynolds, 2006: 195). But I don't think director Christopher Columbus was in jest when he said he was terrified that the young readers of the first Harry Potter novel would be furious with him if he were not faithful to the text they loved so much (cited in Whipp, 2002).

J.K. Rowling is herself, of course, a mighty adapter – of everything from the Dungeons and Dragons games to Wagner's music drama, *Siegfried*. Add in other ingredients like 'Cinderella', the Victorian boarding school novel, Enid Blyton, folktales about magic mirrors (see Tucker, 1999), and even the orphan *Bildungsroman* like *Great Expectations* or *Jane Eyre* (Burn, 2006: 233), stir, and you have a recipe for that successful adaptive concoction we know as Harry Potter. And Harry himself has been 'remediated', to use the term coined by Bolter and Grusin (2000). We not only have the films, but there is the video game too, where you can 'be' Harry (or at least be right behind him) as he faces new dangers and adventures – and new Quidditch challenges.

With this latest digital remediation, we move from *telling* stories (as Rowling does) and from *showing* them (as the film directors do), to *interacting with* them. This increases our level or even kind – and certainly intensity – of immersion in the narrative and its world: through our bodily connection, our physical as well as cognitive and imaginative energies are expended. There are aural (music, sound effects), visual and kinesthetic provocations to response to active game-playing. We know that adult books have been adapted for children for centuries – think of *Robinson Crusoe*'s many abridgements and illustrated versions. But the transfer of that story to CD-ROM by Romain Victor-Pujebet in 2000 offered not only a different mode of engagement for readers but arguably also a different mode of accessing the narrative. First of all, our visual engagement changes, from reading black marks on white pages (or looking at two-dimensional illustrations) to involve a new kind of spatial negotiation through what is called '360°

Navigation'. This is a first-person game, where the player has to survive the Island of Despair and find a way to get off. What I find most interesting about this CD-ROM version is how it is in constant dialogue with the novel: Crusoe's journal is accessible at all times to the gamer to help us figure out what to do and even how to do it. Defoe's Crusoe was precise and explicit, so his journal acts as a kind of 'narrative manual' that we can use, but in a non-linear way (see Sainsbury, 2006: 220). But however we use it – to solve problems or to follow the narrative (and we do both) – our engagement with the story it tells changes with the addition of the physical immersion into the action of the represented world of the story.

Theme parks do the same thing, of course: children can meet at Disney World all the cartoon characters they see on screen. Not surprisingly, theme park rides are often adapted from films – Mr. Toad's Wild Ride at Disneyland (until 1998) evidently came from the 1949 film, *The Adventures of Ichabod and Mr Toad*, an adaptation of A. A. Milne's 1929 stage play, *Toad of Toad Hall*, itself an adaptation of Kenneth Grahame's *The Wind in the Willows* (see Ridgman, 2006: 43–44). And I won't even go into *Pirates of the Caribbean* – but it went in the other direction, from Disney amusement ride to film(s) and back to simulated interactive virtual-reality theme-park game at Disney World (see Hutcheon, 2006: 138–39). Can museums and buildings associated with a work of children's literature offer the same or similar interactive immersion? I'm thinking of Green Gables and other buildings associated with Lucy Maud Montgomery on Prince Edward Island, where children and adults (especially, I'm told, Japanese tourists) can walk through the environment they know from the books (or recognise from the film and television sets) (see Mackey, 2006: 63–64). Commercialisation? Adaptation? Today, they go together. But so too do canonisation and adaptation. If a children's book is adapted to the stage or screen, that testifies to its 'classic' status. It also, of course, helps to confer that very status in the first place (Collins and Ridgman, 2006: 11).

References

Beckett, S.L. 1999. *Transcending Boundaries: Writing for a Dual Audience of Children and Adults*. New York and London, Garland.

Bolter, J. and Grusin, R. 2000. *Remediation: Understanding New Media*. Cambridge, MA, MIT Press.

Burn, A. 2006. 'Multi-Text Magic: Harry Potter in Book, Film and Videogame', in F.M. Collins and J. Ridgman (eds) *Turning the Page: Children's Literature in Performance and the Media*. Bern, Peter Lang: 227–49.

Collins, F.M. and Ridgman, J. (eds) 2006. *Turning the Page: Children's Literature in Performance and the Media*. Bern, Peter Lang.

Galloway, P. 1995. *Atalanta: The Fastest Runner in the World*. Toronto, Annick Press.

Galloway, P. 1995. *Truly Grim Tales*. Toronto, Stoddart.

Galloway, P. 1997. *Daedalus and the Minotaur*. Toronto, Annick Press.

Hutcheon, L. 2006. *A Theory of Adaptation*. London and New York, Routledge.

Hutcheon, L. 2008. 'Harry Potter and the Novice's Confession', *The Lion and the Unicorn*, 32: 169–79.

Mackey, M. 2006. 'Inhabiting *Anne*'s World: The Performance of a Story Space', in F.M. Collins and J. Ridgman (eds) *Turning the Page: Children's Literature in Performance and the Media*. Bern, Peter Lang: 61–82.

Newton, M. 2006. ''Til I'm Grown: Reading Children's Films; Reading Walt Disney's *The Jungle Book*', in F.M. Collins and J. Ridgman (eds) *Turning the Page: Children's Literature in Performance and the Media*. Bern, Peter Lang: 17–38.

Pullman, P. 2000. *I Was a Rat*. New York, Knopf.

Pullman, P. 1995. *Northern Lights*. London, Scholastic.

Pullman, P. 1998. 'Let's Write It in Red: The Patrick Hardy Lecture.' *Signal*, 85 (January 1998): 44–62.

Reimer, M. 2007. *Home Words: Discourses of Children's Literature in Canada*. Waterloo, ON, Wilfrid Laurier University Press.

Reynolds, K. 2006. '*His Dark Materials* in Performance: Finding a Balance between Heritage and Mass Media', in F.M. Collins and J. Ridgman (eds) *Turning the Page: Children's Literature in Performance and the Media*. Bern, Peter Lang: 185–206.

Ridgman, J. 2006. 'From River Bank to South Bank: *The Wind in the Willows* and the Staging of National Identity', in F.M. Collins and J. Ridgman (eds) *Turning the Page: Children's Literature in Performance and the Media*. Bern, Peter Lang: 39–60.

Sainsbury, L. 2006. 'Rousseau's Raft: The Remediation of Narrative in Romain Victor-Pujebet's CD-ROM Version of *Robinson Crusoe*', in F.M. Collins and J. Ridgman (eds) *Turning the Page: Children's Literature in Performance and the Media*. Bern, Peter Lang: 207–26.

Tucker, N. 1999. 'The Rise and Rise of Harry Potter', *Children's Literature in Education*, 30, 4: 221–34.

Walsh, C. 2007. 'From "Capping" to Intercision: Metaphors/Metonyms of Mind Control in the Young Adult Fiction of John Christopher and Philip Pullman', *Language and Literature*, 112.3: 233–51. www.lal.sagepub.com/cgi/reprint/12/13/233, accessed 18 July 2007.

Whipp, G. 2002. 'Director Remains Faithful to Harry', *Toronto Star*, 21 September, H4.

Harry Potter goes to China
Suman Gupta, with assistance from Cheng Xiao

The fluid text

To try to come to grips with the Harry Potter phenomenon in China it is necessary to foreground a concept of textual fluidity rather than depend on the conventional notion of a definitive text. The definitive text here is the English Harry Potter text – the seven volumes in the series penned by Rowling, published by Bloomsbury/Scholastic. It is difficult to establish a set of linear relations from this definitive text to the Chinese context for reasons which I go into below. However, if we think of the Harry Potter phenomenon in China as having to do with a fluid text we have a tractable path before us, which is as revealing of the Chinese context as of other contexts in a globalised world. The idea of textual fluidity was formulated succinctly by John Bryant as follows:

> The textual condition – encompassing processes of creation, editing, printing, and adaptation – is fundamentally fluid not because specific words lend themselves to different meanings or that different minds will interpret the words fixed on the page in different ways, but because writers, editors, publishers, translators, digesters, and adapters change those words materially. Moreover, these material revisions can attest not simply to localized fine tunings but to new conceptualizations of the entire work. Thus, a literary work invariably evolves, by the collaborative forces of individuals and the culture, from one version to another. If we want to know the textual condition, we must get to the versions of a text, and there we will also find an even deeper condition of creativity within a culture.[1]

Bryant's 'fluid text' stretches both before and after what is usually regarded as a definitive text, and has as much to do with the process of textual production as with reception and adaptation. By emphasising these processes, Bryant dilutes the presumption of textual unity, of the stability of originals and definitive editions, which we usually take for granted. The receptive side of the fluid text is germane here. When Rowling's seven books appeared in the market as definitive editions of the Harry Potter text they entered an extraordinarily widely dispersed receptive field. They were translated into more than sixty languages, produced as audio books, adapted into films; they generated an enormous mass of fan sites and 'fan fiction', computer games, a vast range of Harry Potter-branded commodities (picture books, postcards, posters, playing cards, cups, t-shirts, etc.); textbooks and curricula at various levels excavated the books; an immense amount of mass media and academic writing was devoted to them. All these are part of the Harry Potter fluid text. The seven English editions are but flickering points in this fluid text, constantly modified by and relocated within the contours of fluidity, but also constantly there as points of return and reference. The fluid Harry Potter text bubbles out and beyond the definitive text and continuously undermines its definitive status.[2]

I have observed that it is difficult to trace linear relations from the definitive Harry Potter text to the Chinese context. To some extent this is because there are distinct slippages between these, which arise less from the absence of China in the definitive text than from a very low-key registering of China which is more problematic than absence. Insofar as a geopolitical location can be discerned *within* the definitive text China is quietly but indicatively placed beyond the pale.

There is a much-discussed sense of location that Harry Potter readers are likely to be aware of. According to Andrew Blake, the books successfully branded a contemporary multicultural Labour-governed Britain.[3] The Muggle and magic worlds mark their English locations and play out their Englishness in obvious ways: the naming of places and persons, the use of idioms and colloquialisms, rituals of social discourse (in the news, shops, schools, offices, etc.), manifestations of tacit class-consciousness. Alongside those a limited sense of an extrinsic world is indicated: the Quidditch World Cup has Bulgarian and Irish teams; there are magic schools abroad; there are stereotypical French and Bulgarian characters. There is also a careful accounting of the multicultural world *contained* in Britain, especially through the attribution of recognisably non-English names and ethnicities to characters. At both the axes of alluding to a world outside Britain and taking into account the heterogeneous world inside Britain, the definitive Harry Potter text presents the merest trace of gestures towards China, but gestures which slip at both axes. So, at the axis of registering the world outside the Chinese Fireball dragon appears briefly in the *Goblet of Fire*. The origin of different families of dragons is one of the ways in which the extrinsic world is gestured towards '"This is a Hungarian Horntail," said Charlie. "There's a Common Welsh Green over there, the smaller one – a Swedish Short-Snout, that blue grey – and a Chinese Fireball, that's the red"' (*Goblet of Fire*: 287).[4] Now the dragon (and also the phoenix) is more central to Chinese mythology and iconography than anywhere else in the world, so much so that numerous Western texts metaphorically refer to China itself as the 'dragon'. Those who are aware of Chinese iconography know that the Chinese dragon is not red (not unless political hues are being united with the metaphor of the nation as dragon), and is associated with water and not fire (thus quite different in all its associations from the Western dragon). The red Chinese Fireball dragon therefore makes concrete in the Harry Potter magic world a Western misreading and misrepresentation of Chinese mythology and iconography. At the other axis of registering the world within multicultural Britain there's also the merest gesture towards a possibly Chinese association. Amidst the names indicative of different ethnic origins appears that of Cho Chang (Harry's first love interest), which sounds East Asian, possibly Chinese. There is nothing in the original books to give that association substance – no information about Cho Chang is available to clarify an East Asian connection – but in the films she is embodied as distinctly racially East Asian, Chinese. So there's only the name to go by. But even here things are murkier than the English reader might think. The other names of ethnically 'other' characters are unambiguously identifiable: Angelina Johnson is described as black; Anthony Goldstein is of German origin and probably an Ashkenazi Jew; Padma and Parvati Patil are very plausible Indian names, with probably Marathi Hindu origins. To the Chinese reader Cho

Chang poses a problem in that it doesn't recall clearly any common Chinese name. The nearest sound equivalents to Cho each have disagreeable meanings, unsuitable for names. In the Chinese translations of the Harry Potter books, the nearest sound equivalent which makes sense is chosen, 秋张 or Qiu Zhang (meaning Autumn), which actually sounds rather different. Both Cho and Chang could be Korean family names rendered in English, but are unlikely first names. At both axes, the Chinese trace in the definitive text is so uncertain and self-effacing that it serves more effectively to exclude consideration of China than to bring it into awareness.

Nevertheless the Harry Potter phenomenon in China has been particularly noteworthy. That has to do more with the fluid Harry Potter text – which incorporates various levels of translation and receptive adjustment – than with the definitive text in itself.

Translations

Harry Potter surfaced in a noticeable fashion in China with the simultaneous publication of Chinese translations from the first three books in the series by the People's Literature Publishing House in October 2000. Even then it was a remarkably confident entry: where children's books in China usually have a print run of 10,000, the first three Harry Potter translations had first print runs of 200,000 each. The enormous success of Harry Potter in China is marked by the increasing figures of first print runs for subsequent books in translation: the fourth (*Goblet of Fire*) had a first print run of 400,000, the fifth and sixth (*Order of the Phoenix* and *Half-Blood Prince*) of 800,000,[5] and the final book of 1 million.[6] The fluid Harry Potter text in China is to do pre-eminently with the translated versions. Despite a strong drive to make English the second language in China, consumption of the English editions there has been relatively negligible. There is, however, a similar kind of quantitative increase to be noted there too: about two hundred English editions of the first book were taken to China for sale, by the sixth (*Half-Blood Prince*) the figure was above ten thousand.[7]

Translating the Harry Potter English text into any language presents a set of problems which need to be carefully negotiated. Reporting on translations of the Harry Potter books into a range of languages, Gillian Lathey points particularly to the following: markers of what is perceived as Britishness, such as tone and humour; proper names (in the Harry Potter books these often work by aural assonance and verbal association); and the use of dialect and register, especially to indicate social status (as for Hagrid and the house elves) or foreignness (for Fleur Delacoeur, for instance).[8] Translating from English to Chinese puts particular pressure on some of these.

The written English alphabet consists of letters which roughly represent a phoneme or sound, while written Chinese characters are each a word, morpheme or semantic unit and represent a meaning as well as a speech syllable. So in written Chinese phonetic variations in speech are less easy to convey (written Chinese is less malleable to represent non-standard speech), and whatever is written represents a sound and concurrently has a meaning (though that meaning may be pragmatically disregarded). Thus, translating Western proper nouns into Chinese usually involves finding characters which convey the nearest sound equivalent, and either the meanings of those characters are disregarded or, sometimes, characters are carefully selected to convey also some quality of the thing/person/place in question (even if that is not contained in the Western proper noun). It is easily comprehended that insofar as, say, social status or foreignness is suggested in English writing by the sounds of words enunciated, this is impossible to represent in written Chinese translation, and that translating Western proper nouns into Chinese involves complex cultural negotiations. The translation of Harry Potter names into Chinese is a good index of one of the levels of cultural negotiation and textual fluidity involved here.

I have already mentioned the cultural slippages and negotiations that attach to translating the name of the possibly Chinese Cho Chang into Chinese. Perhaps these slippages account to some degree for the remarkably little interest that Chinese readers evince in Cho Chang in fan sites and fan fiction in China. The name Cho Chang is so redolent of ambiguity and ignorance from a Chinese point of view that it is difficult to embrace without unease. Other fascinating cultural negotiations between the English original and the Chinese translation of names can be seen in the differences that are found in the *two* available Chinese translations of the books – produced in Taiwan and in the People's Republic of China mentioned above. A telling example here appears with regard to the translation of the name 'Voldemort'. In the Taiwanese edition this was represented by the characters 佛地魔 (fo di mo) and in the Chinese by the characters 伏地魔 (fu di mo). The character 'di' means 'earth' and 'mo' means 'devil', the character 'fo' means 'buddha' and 'fu' means 'crouching'. To read 'Voldemort' as 'devil crouching in the ground' makes good sense in terms of the person it refers to; any association of 'buddha' with Voldemort is desperately misplaced. None of this has any bearing on the name 'Voldemort', which to European ears may suggest something like 'desire of death'.

The business of translating names is but a small thing, but it spins out into a mass of cross-cultural negotiations made in translating from the English to the Chinese. Without presuming a knowledge of Chinese, this can be conveyed to some extent by conducting exercises in back-translating. The idea is to have someone who is fluent in both Chinese and English translate back into English from the Chinese translations without reference to the originals and then to compare the back-translated text with the originals. This can be a revealing exercise, making it possible to see in the back-translation to what extent extra linguistic information has been conveyed. This is illustrated in the following extracts. The passage is from *Philosopher's Stone* and describes the moment when Harry steps into Diagon Alley and the magic world for the first time:

> The sun shone brightly on a stack of cauldrons outside the nearest shop. *Cauldrons – All Sizes – Copper, Brass, Pewter, Silver – Self-Stirring – Collapsible* said a sign hanging over them [...] A plump woman outside an apothecary's was shaking her head as they passed, saying, 'Dragon liver, seventeen Sickles an ounce, they're mad.' [...] A low, soft hooting came from a dark shop with a sign saying *Eeylops Owl Emporium – Tawny, Screech, Barn, Brown and Snowy*. Several boys of about Harry's age had their noses pressed against a window with broomsticks in it. 'Look,' Harry heard one of them say, 'the new Nimbus Two Thousand – fastest ever –'
>
> *Philosopher's Stone*: 36

The back-translation from the Chinese reads:

> Bright sunlight flashed on a pile of pots outside the door of the nearest shop. Above the pots hung a board with the words: 'big pots made of brass, tin, silver – all types – automatic-stirring, collapsible' [...] A fat woman stood outside a medicine shop. As they passed her, she shook her head and said, 'Dragon liver, seventeen sickles per ounce, they are mad.' [...] From a dark shop came a low and soft woo-oo sound, the shop sign on the door said, 'Yila Owl Shop – grey forest owls, horn-sounding [like the French horn] owls, brown owls, snow owls'. Several boys of Harry's age had their noses pressed on the glass of a shop window. Inside the window there were flying brooms. 'Look,' Harry heard a boy say, 'that's the newest type of Halo 2000 – highest speed –'.

The original English passage performs, by the use of language, something that is seminal not just for Harry's but also the reader's entry into and continuing engagement with the magic world. It mixes together two registers: 1. a set of words that are immediately associated for English readers with something old-fashioned (often archaic words) and sometimes specifically with witchcraft (through fairy tales and folklore, through popular cultural forms), such as 'cauldron', 'apothecary', 'broom', 'sickle' (associated with harvests and druidic rituals), 'pewter'; 2. the linguistic strategies of modern advertising, snappily referring to innovations for convenience ('self-stirring – collapsible'), listing types of products ('Copper, Brass, Pewter,

Silver', 'Tawny, Screech, Barn, Brown and Snowy'), giving the catchy brand-name ('Nimbus Two Thousand'). The manner in which the two registers are seamlessly mixed together both brings alive in a contemporary sense and updates the associations of a magic world. In the back-translation the second register (of advertising) is conveyed clearly enough, but the first is conveyed only to a limited extent – 'pot' and 'brooms' don't have the specific witchcraft associations of 'cauldron' and 'broomstick', 'medicine shop' doesn't have the air of quaintness of 'apothecary', the 'sickle' in Chinese is a pure sound translation and meaningless in itself. And yet, the limited sense of old-fashioned fantasy of the first register is given a particular turn in the Chinese version, in that the whole passage comes with a stronger sense of the exotic – strange happenings and things are made stranger by the unmistakable foreignness (from the Chinese point of view) of this environment. This sense of foreignness can be discerned in the slightly more laboured manner in which the back-translation reads compared to the original: it is a bit more carefully precise, a bit more particular about positioning and explaining the relation of people and things in Diagon Alley.

These illustrations of the text-based negotiations that occur within the fluid text of Harry Potter as it disperses in China – the level of interlingual translation: that is, the translation between the two languages – are only one aspect of the many levels of translation involved. The most important point to grasp here is that the interlingual translation of the English editions into the Chinese is a planned and relatively small part of a larger process of translation. What actually happened here was that the entire Harry Potter phenomenon, at all levels – as an advertising and marketing phenomenon, as a reading phenomenon, as a media phenomenon, as a phenomenon registered as such by academics and educationists, as a sociocultural phenomenon – was systematically translated into China on an industrial scale. This is discernible even in the manner in which the interlingual translation of the books was conducted. The Chinese translations of the first three books were completed within three months: translators were commissioned in June 2000 and the translations were in the market by October 2000. All subsequent translations were also produced within three months of the appearance of the English editions. The translation process was overseen by the publishers in a functional fashion for quick turnover and consistency, and with little opportunity for mulling over translators' equivocations. The most revealing overview of this grand translation project has been given by the Director of the People's Literature Publishing House, Ye Zhenning. In a 2002 speech[9] he laid out the overall structure of the project to translate the Harry Potter phenomenon into China. It was based on the perception that, despite its success in the West, the series might not do well in China. The prevailing expectations of children's literature in China seemed to be different. The record of foreign bestsellers wasn't encouraging, and the Harry Potter books seemed at that stage not to have done well in the nearest comparable Eastern market, Japan. The plan for bringing Harry Potter to China therefore became a considerably larger one than simply translating the books and making them available. The shape of the book itself – as a physical object – was designed carefully to stand out in the Chinese context. The size of the books, the page layout, the colour of the paper (chosen to discourage piracy), and the print quality were all carefully considered. Chinese illustrators were invited to work on the covers, but were rejected in favour of the American design (with the covers embossed). Beyond the physical appearance of the books, distribution and retailing was meticulously organised. An extensive media campaign was orchestrated before publication – through websites, and broadcast and print media. Posters were printed informing readers of the international acclaim of the series. The first three books were released simultaneously nationwide on 6 October 2000 at 10 a.m., with performances by Chinese actors in bookstores. Media awareness was maintained thereafter in a programmatic fashion. Harry Potter-branded gifts and postcards were produced. Favourable scholarly articles and statements from scholars were engineered. Within a short period of time the entire externally established apparatus for marketing and reception was translated and transplanted into China in 2000, adjusted and modified for the Chinese social context, and maintained thereafter. In some sense, it thereby transformed literary production and reception in China. The interlingual translation of the texts was a crucial but small part of this project.

The critical reception of Harry Potter that resulted in China was determined by this vast translation project. But critical reception necessarily and almost always manages to escape any engineering, and has its own dynamics.

Constructing childhood

In April 2008 I was fortunate in being given the opportunity to initiate and participate in a workshop on 'Harry Potter in China' at the Institute of World Literature, Peking University.[10] Here brief presentations were made by representatives of the People's Literature Publishing House (which published the Chinese translations) and the China Youth Publishing House (which has published a series of Harry Potter fan fiction by Chinese authors), followed by discussions between students and academics there. The issues covered here represent most of the strands of discussion of the Harry Potter phenomenon in China. There were three main thrusts to the discussions. First, it was asserted that the Harry Potter text is exemplary in various ways, and should be emulated by Chinese authors and sought within China by publishers. The representative of the People's Literature Publishing House, Wang Xiaoya, observed that the experience of publishing Harry Potter had, in effect, opened up the Chinese market to global literary and cultural circulation. In both presentations and discussions it was agreed that the text answers to the media-savvy globalised sensibility of children in contemporary China as elsewhere in the world, in a way that literature produced for children within China is failing to. Secondly, it was observed that the particular success of Harry Potter in China had to do with the specific sociocultural conditions that prevail there – especially in relation to a fraught generation gap between those born in or after the 1980s (post-1980s and post-1990s generations include those who had grown up with the Harry Potter phenomenon in China), and those before (who are now parents and teachers). This point was made emphatically by the editor of the China Youth Publishing House, Zhiang Yong, who characterised the young generation as the 'I-generation' (which expects social good to be achieved through individual fulfilment). They regard as fake the current establishment values of their parents and teachers, members of the earlier 'we-generation' (which feels that children should be socialised to comply with communal concepts of social good). Zhiang suggested that this generational difference is evidenced in a 'deficit of love' resulting in part from parenting and education becoming forcefully aspirational and children growing reactively self-centred. In the heated discussion that followed, some, who identified themselves as of the post-1980s generation, dismissed the 'deficit of love' idea as generalising nonsense. Both sides agreed that the Harry Potter books, with their unstinting ability to face up to human nature in a realistic rather than an idealistic fashion (including depictions of cruelty, cowardice, betrayal, loneliness, death) while both presenting a strong concept of love and a powerful sense of individual ability as collective good, have served to stem the sense of alienation that the new generation in China feels. Thirdly, it was generally agreed that the Harry Potter phenomenon in China was an aspect of China's emerging place in the world stage as an economic and political and cultural force. It was observed that the phenomenon was both impelled by and has generated a greater sense of connectedness with the world, and a widely shared feeling that China has an active global role to undertake in the future.

It seems to me that what was revealed in the discussions of these three strands, and entirely consistently with wider scholarly and media debates about the Harry Potter phenomenon there, is a prevailing anxiety about how contemporary Chinese childhood should or could be understood.

Some elaboration of these arguments in terms of the wider context of China clarifies this.

The above arguments are pre-eminently addressed to the Chinese context that surrounds and receives the Harry Potter books, and do not really engage the text itself. This is consistent with pretty much all Chinese media coverage of and scholarly work on the Harry Potter text and phenomenon thus far. Just by being a success, by selling well, by being popular, by sustaining a phenomenon, the Harry Potter text is taken as *a priori* 'good' or 'worthy' (moral connotations intact). So Chinese critical reception of the Harry Potter text very rarely expresses the kind of scepticism about the text itself available in, for instance, the writings of Jack Zipes, Andrew Blake or Suman Gupta,[11] and thereafter. The acceptance of the 'good' or 'worthy' view of the Harry Potter text does, however, involve constant restatement of the content of the text. Thus, at different times it is the exotic Western roots, the plotting, style and character development, the representation of some value (love, heroism, individual achievement, realistic portrayal of human nature, etc.) that is highlighted as that which makes the text 'worthy' or 'good'. But in every instance the text's 'goodness' or 'worthiness' is taken as a foregone conclusion. Thus, an academic paper by Li Nishan maintains that the text arouses feelings of happiness and freedom full of 'Western magic-colour' ['xifang mohuan secai'], encourages role-playing and childhood development, and 'moistens and lifts the soul'.[12] Another academic paper by Huang and Liang examining the text's double-world narrative finds that it stimulates the 'creative force, and helps the spirit fly',[13] and yet another by Zhang and Kong on Harry Potter in the context of contemporary children's literature is largely a eulogy.[14] The argument typically goes as follows: the Harry Potter text is 'good' and 'worthy' – its success in China has done 'good' in China – the reason it has done 'good' in China is because there are such-and-such lacks, such-and-such unfulfilled desires and aspirations, in the social, cultural and political formation of China – the 'good' and 'worthy' impact of the text provides an opportunity to put those deficiencies into perspective and to correct them. There is an unmistakable and pervasive prescriptive strain of self-criticism, self-improvement and self-development in the Chinese reception of Harry Potter.

Along with that, the workshop discussions – also in keeping with published criticism – assume that the Harry Potter text and phenomenon are pretty much exclusively to do with children (in the broad sense of including early teenagers). This is actually not in keeping with available data: according to a 2007 survey, the majority of Harry Potter readers in China are between 14 and 24.[15] But it is largely taken for granted that Harry Potter readers are children and that the books are clearly addressed to children.

With these preconceptions in view, the Chinese critical response typically makes two linked moves: first, use Harry Potter to characterise – and thus effectively construct – childhood in contemporary (2000 onwards) China; secondly, discern how Harry Potter departs from, and may be used to modify, the provision of reading material and education for Chinese children.

The characterisation of childhood in the workshop deliberations interestingly revolves around decadal generational divides, such as post-1960s, post-1980s, post-1990s. This terminology is widely prevalent in mass media and academic discourse in China at present. On the one hand, the artificiality and neatness of decadal generational distinctions seems to be at odds with what is obviously a flowing and continuous social process and experience. It is evidently used as a mode of imposing structure on an amorphous area, with arbitrary chronological markers to pin down a slippery process (much as historiography generally does in terms of decades or centuries). The decadal terminology also suggests that such an imposed structure is not ideologically led and has at least the appearance of neutrality. As Shao Yanjun observes in relation to the manner in which authors are now grouped in China:

> These purely chronological terms [decadal generational designations] are different from earlier characterizations of literary groups in China, such as 'rightist writers', 'educated youth writers', 'root-finding writers', 'avant-garde writers', etc. Since the 1990s the tendency in China has been to demarcate writer groups not according to their experience and stylistic or ideological tendencies, but only according to the period they were born in. Through 'post-sixties', 'post-seventies', 'post-eighties', to the nascent 'post-nineties' writers, this method of chronological division has continued, demonstrating that Chinese literature has entered a phase in which there is no dominant theme and no mainstream.[16]

On the other hand, the device of decadal generational divides has caught on because it seems to make sense in China. This has something to do with the pace of social change in China, which is seen as being so rapid that each decadal generation could be meaningfully *assumed* to have significantly different formative experiences – especially in the first decade of childhood. Thus, the post-1950s generation would be the first to be entirely formed under the post-1949 socialist system; the post-1960s generation would have their formative years marked by the Cultural Revolution; the post-1970s generation would be the first to have grown in the post-Cultural Revolution and post-Mao (who died in 1976) period; the post-1980s and post-1990s generations would be the first to consciously assimilate to a 1990-onwards market-socialist transformation, and also the first to be composed almost entirely of only-children (following the adoption of the one-child policy in

1979). Not uninterestingly, the Harry Potter phenomenon also appears in China at the significant decadal (indeed millennial) moment of 2000.

So, unsurprisingly, a structuring device that is assumed as a convenience (like a grid) for locating social processes begins, once assumed, to gather a life of its own. The characterisation of the post-1980s and post-1990s generations – the Harry Potter generations – as such seems immediately to construct them in analytically preconceived ways. Children become personified, as a whole, as individualistic or materialistic or media-savvy in an environment of market-socialism; contemporary childhood generally comes to be assessed in terms of children as single progeny (and therefore spoilt, self-centred and dependent on friendships and extrinsic relationships). With such a construction of childhood in place, understanding the Harry Potter phenomenon in China involves fitting the phenomenon to the construction. This is seen in the workshop discussions and is also evidenced in a range of mass-media features and scholarly publications in China. The argument goes further to maintain that the Harry Potter text and phenomenon *fit* this decadal characterisation of contemporary Chinese childhood in a way that children's literature produced in China and educational provision available in China do not. This has been a constant refrain in the area: for instance, Zhang and Kong castigate Chinese children's writing for lacking originality, being 'adultized', having a lecturing tone, being too didactic in contrast to Harry Potter;[17] Li Nishan argues that the Chinese educational system curtails thinking and enjoins responsibility in a soul-destroying fashion, from which Harry Potter has provided welcome relief.[18] Using Harry Potter as an example, Xu Yurong wonders why Chinese children's literature puts children off while British children's literature gives children pleasure,[19] and so on.

The Harry Potter phenomenon is thus placed amidst a perceived slippage between the construction of contemporary childhood and the texts and systems for children that are produced and available in China. Harry Potter is seen as repairing that slippage, constructing a bridge, and also thereby highlighting the slippage. And, in doing so, Harry Potter reveals another, so to say, turn of the screw within the construction of contemporary Chinese childhood: *the perception of the slippage and consequent reception of Harry Potter are symptoms of a deep-seated anxiety about constructing childhood itself in China.* The idea is that Chinese educational systems and children's literature have in the past constructed, and continue to construct, childhood in a way that has rendered children unhealthily passive. Children were constructed in terms of some idea of the 'greater good', some idea of a rigid top-down social and moral order along socialist or, for that matter, Confucian lines. Children were constructed to absorb this order passively through education and books. The anxiety now is that for the children of the post-1980s generations this placement in passivity is no longer possible. Children from the post-1980s generation onwards have become active agents who are, at least tendentiously, outside the control of such determination and socialisation. They are spilling outside the confines of whatever is perceived as Chinese (very materially through new media), refusing to subscribe to former notions of social and moral order that have been in place, and are interrogating the prerogatives of adults (parents). The flow of Harry Potter into China, and its resounding success, is therefore signified in the workshop, in mass-media reports and in scholarly writing as symbolic of this coming to life of the child's agency in China.

It is difficult to say whether, and to what extent, this mode of thinking about Harry Potter in China stands up to historical experience and evidence. In the workshop and in all the published sources cited above, the argument is made impressionistically with little reference to empirical and analytical research.[20] These arguments appear to be based on few facts about contemporary and past childhood in China, present and past educational systems and about literature for children. In terms of the latter, it is debatable whether such Chinese texts as were available to children during, say, the Cultural Revolution,[21] that most extreme pole of 'other' times, would have given them a social or political world-view that is radically different from the Harry Potter text. The children of the Cultural Revolution, for instance, had access to 'revolutionary martyr stories' in textbooks (such as stories about Liu Wenxue, Dong Cunrui, Huang JiGuang, Qin Shao Yun) which were redolent with violence, death and heroism. These would have conveyed to them a clearly morally divided universe of good and evil. The moral division could be mapped on to the 'good' or 'just' revolutionary social order inside China as opposed to the imperialist capitalist reactionary Western powers outside. The moral division could also be contained within China, insofar as a 'reactionary' or 'bourgeois' tendency could be revealed among the Chinese people themselves, and even within the Party. Perhaps the difference is primarily that the Harry Potter books are unambiguously categorised in the genre of fantasy (and can therefore be taken light-heartedly), while those 'revolutionary martyr stories' were reality in their time (and therefore grimly serious), or perhaps the fantastic nature of the latter was not wholly unperceived even at the time, though it was expedient not to acknowledge any such thought. And further back, the rich tradition of Chinese fantasy writing with Confucian overtones, and their contemporary renovations in the form of historical romances and martial arts fantasies, also calls for a complex accounting in this context. There are many inconclusively engaged questions and uncertainties here, and the prevailing reception of Harry Potter in China outlined above is, ultimately, far too schematic and impressionistic. Ironically, this overly schematic reception arguably reiterates, through its uncritical acceptance of the Harry Potter text and phenomenon as 'good' and 'worthy', through its unanalytical approach to these, something of the penchant for rigid ordering that such reception ostensibly seeks to counter.

But these uncertainties and ambiguities are part of something larger within China, something that exceeds the singularity of the Harry Potter text and phenomenon in China. The latter are a minuscule bubble in a much larger effervescence in the social, cultural and political formation of contemporary China. This is the effervescence of a prevailing sense of being in transition, of a ubiquitous sense of 'opening up' and 'catching up with the West', of a vaunted sense of assuming a significant place in the processes of globalisation – all clearly expressed in the workshop deliberations outlined above, and in numerous mass-media and scholarly works. This sense causes a particular sort of anxiety within contemporary China, just as recognition of such a 'rise of China' causes another sort of anxiety – a sort of fear – in the anglophone West where Harry Potter comes from.

Notes and references

1 John Bryant, 2002. *The Fluid Text: A Theory of Revision and Editing for Book and Screen.* Ann Arbor, University of Michigan Press: 4.
2 In approaching the Harry Potter phenomenon in China, the mass media has focused primarily on copyright infringements. This has been a concern as much in China – e.g. Li Li, 2000. 'Copyright? What Copyright?' *Beijing Review*, 26 July: 22–3 – as elsewhere – e.g. Howard W. French, 2007. 'China Market Awash in Fake Potter Books', *New York Times*, 1 August.
3 Andrew Blake, 2002. *The Irresistible Rise of* Harry Potter: *Kid-Lit in a Globalised World.* London, Verso.
4 All quotations from the Harry Potter English text are from the Bloomsbury, London, volumes and are identified by the latter part of the title.
5 Jiang Wandi, 2007. 'Wild About Harry', *Beijing Review*, 7 June: 19.
6 Wang Shanshan, 2007. 'Latest Potter Book Now in Chinese, Officially', *China Daily*, 29 October: 3. www.chinadaily.com.cn/cndy/2007-10/29/content_6212029.htm, accessed 1 May 2008.
7 Ma Jianguo, 2005. 'The Sixth Volume of Harry Potter is about to be launched, the English Edition has Arrived in Beijing', www.XINHUANET.com, accessed 15 July.
8 Gillian Lathey, 2005. 'The Travels of Harry: International Marketing and the Translation of J.K. Rowling's Harry Potter Books', *The Lion and the Unicorn*, 29, 2: 141–51.
9 Ye Zhenning, 2002. 'The Development and Marketing of Harry Potter in China' ['hali bote de zhengti kaifa he yingxiao'], *China Bookmerchant's Newspaper* [*zhongguo tushu shangbao*], August. www.sinobook.com.cn/press/newsdetail.cfm?iCntno=284, accessed 1 June 2008.
10 I am very grateful to Zhao Baisheng, Director of the Institute of World Literature, Peking University, for organising this. Thanks are due to Wang Jiake and Wei Liping for helping me to follow the discussions, and to Zhang Chunguang for making a full recording of the workshop for me.
11 Jack Zipes, 2000. *Sticks and Stones: The Troublesome Success of Children's Literature from Slovenly Peter to Harry Potter.* New York, Routledge; Andrew Blake, see note 3; Suman Gupta, 2003. *Re-Reading Harry Potter.* Basingstoke, Palgrave.

12 Li Nishan, 2005. 'Expedition of the Soul in the Game-Spirit of Harry Potter' ['xinling de tanxian'], *Journal of Fujian Educational College* [*Fujian jiaoyu xueyuan xuebao*], October: 79–83.

13 Huang Yunting and Liang Hongyan, 'On the Art of the Double-World Narrative in Fantasy Novels' ['lu muohuan xiaoshuo zhongde shuangchong shijie'], *Journal of the South China University of Technology* [*huanan ligong duxue xuebao*], 9, 6, December: 63–67.

14 Zhang Ying and Kong Dan, 2002. 'Harry Potter and the Characteristics of Contemporary Children's Literature' ['hali bote yu xinshiqi ertong wenxue de tedian'], *Journal of the North East University: Philosophy and Social Science* [*dongbei shida xuebao*], 5: 95–97.

15 Jing Xiaolei, 2007. 'Universal Potter', *Beijing Review*, 7 June. The survey was conducted by Douban.com.

16 Shao Yanjun, 2008. 'A Study of the Phenomenon of Pretty Women's Writing: Weihui, Mianmian, Chunshu', *Wasafiri (China Special Issue)*, 55.

17 Zhang and Kong, see note 14.

18 Li Nishan, see note 12.

19 Xu Yurong, 2006. 'Children's Literature Should be Happy Literature: On the Revelations Available from Harry Potter' ['ertong wenxue ying chengwei kuile wenxue'], *Journal of Social Sciences* [*chengdu daxue xuebao*], 4: 127–8.

20 In English: Anne Behnke Kinney, 1995. *Chinese Views of Childhood*. Honolulu, University of Hawaii Press; Mary Ann Farquhar, 1999. *Children's Literature in China: From Lu Xun to Mao Zedong*. Armak, NY, M.E. Sharpe.

21 Cultural Revolution texts could be expected to be, and generally are, about as ideologically reductive and propagandist as possible – as in the case of the 'revolutionary martyr's stories'. However, children's writing of this period presents complexities that are worth noting. Of Hao Ran Cultural Revolution children's stories Farquhar (note 20) observes: 'despite all the rhetoric, the model writer of fictions for all audiences in China of this period ignored overt preaching, revolutionary propaganda, and model heroes in writing his children's stories' (290).

Reading Transformations
Rosie Flewitt

> Oh, books, what books they used to know,
> Those children living long ago!
> So please, oh please, we beg, we pray
> Go throw your TV set away,
> And in its place you can install
> A lovely bookshelf on the wall

Dahl, 1964

In Roald Dahl's *Charlie and the Chocolate Factory* (1964), just after the young television addict Mike Teavee has jumped into a TV set and shrunk to the size of 'a midget', the Oompa-Loompas launch into a three-page diatribe against the evils of children watching too much television, which will, in their view, make their 'powers of thinking rust and freeze'. Here, Dahl reflected the concerns of many for whom the written word represented the most highly valued form of literary expression, and for whom engaging with new media was by definition an intellectually inferior activity to book reading. Thirty years later, Margaret Mackey warned that 'to talk about children's literature, in the normal restricted sense of children's novels, poems and picture-books, is to ignore the multi-media expertise of our children' (Mackey, 1994: 17). As a new generation of readers now grows up in the dawn of the twenty-first century, this chapter explores the forms of literature that they are encountering in a range of media, whether their experiences of literature are substantially different from those of older generations and what 'reading stories' means in today's multimedia world. Consideration is given particularly to the literary landscapes of children aged 3–11 in different social settings, both in and out of school, and to the different ways they experience a range of literary texts, focusing on print, interactive and electronic forms of literature, and transformations of literary originals in new media.

A brief history of literature in our time

The historical development of literature for children reflects changing attitudes towards childhood and changing practices around literature. The contemporary children's author Elizabeth Laird talks about the influence on her writing of growing up in a deeply religious family, where stories were considered to have an inherent truth imbued with profound, moral meanings that readers would muse over.[1] This sharing of *literature as scripture* for discussing morality has to some extent been superseded in the Western world by the broader notion of *literature as education*, where others' insights are used to introduce children to a diversity of social and cultural worlds. Alongside a continuing emphasis on *reading for pleasure*,[2] the concept of *literature as entertainment* has emerged as stories have wandered from the printed page into new media, such as film, television and online environments. Many traditional tales have endured these transformations, but some newer versions remain contentious. What, we might wonder, would the Oompa-Loompas make of the versions of traditional tales and nursery rhymes now available in online children's games and animated narrations?

Twenty-first century children's literature

The prevalence of multimedia as part of daily life in technologically developed countries means that many children today encounter a wide range of static and interactive texts, in print form and on electronic handheld devices, computer, film and TV screens. A large-scale study of children's interests in new media found through surveys and interviews of over 1,500 6–17-year-olds that 'books are widely seen as old-fashioned, boring, frustrating, and on their way out' (Livingstone and Bovill, 1999: 19). What might be the implications of such findings for the future of children's literature? New technologies offer new horizons for literature, both for the transformation and representation of traditional printed books, and for the emergence of new literary forms of expression, such as digital narratives in electronic games, online hyperfiction and e-poetry. New media are 'not simply changing the way we tell stories: they are changing the very nature of story, of what we understand (or do not understand) to be narratives' (Hunt, 2000: 111). They are blurring the boundaries between author and reader, and stretching the already highly contentious boundaries of what literature is.

This chapter therefore adopts an exploratory and potentially controversial definition of literature, and considers examples of a broad and inclusive range of genres of fiction, rhymes and poetry encountered by children in diverse media, which go beyond the familiar modes of printed words and illustrations that are typical of the traditional printed page.

Multimedia literature and multimodality

Before continuing, it will be useful to clarify what is meant by the terms 'medium/media', 'mode', 'multimodal' and the related term 'affordances'. 'Medium' refers here to the way that literature is disseminated, whether through handwriting on paper, a printed book, the radio, audio recording, television, film or computer. The forms that media take and how they are used in daily life are dependent both on technological invention and on the economic prosperity and cultural values in a given society.

The term 'mode' derives from social semiotics (Halliday, 1978) and refers to the way that meaning is represented, for example through speech, writing, image, body movement, gesture or gaze. Modes of communication are shaped over generations by the ways that people use them in their social and cultural lives. Different modes offer different potentials, or *affordances*, for the expression of ideas. In a written text, what can be expressed is shaped to a large extent by the established rules of grammar and lexis, whereas an illustration may afford more potential to convey the precise shape of an object. Modes also have dimensional affordances: the modes of speech and writing are governed by a linear logic of sequence, with one element following or preceding another. By contrast, still images (e.g. photographs, paintings, line drawings) are governed by a non-linear logic of space and simultaneity, and relationships between the elements are communicated through positioning (near or far away, central or peripheral, etc.). Moving images are governed by the logics of both spatiality and sequence. Kress (2003) suggests that 'the world told' is very different to 'the world shown', and proposes that the increasing prevalence of communications technologies is engineering a profound shift in the ways in which we engage with texts, both receptively and productively.

The term 'multimodality' takes into account how the range and combinations of modes used in any act of expression all contribute to an 'orchestration' of meaning (Kress, Jewitt, Ogborn and Tsatsarelis, 2001), where the overall meaning is more than the sum of its different modes. For example, the medium of printed books has historically conveyed literary meanings primarily through the modes of printed words and page layout, sometimes supplemented by illustrations. More recently, interactive books have combined these with the additional modes of spoken language and sound.

As an example of how these terms can be applied, Example 1 (p. 356) illustrates how literary meanings are orchestrated through multiple modes in digital literary texts.

As previously mentioned, media and modes are located in and shaped by social contexts and 'new' media connect with the conventions of 'old' media (Manovich, 2002). Unsurprisingly, therefore, we can see in Example 1 that although the computer screen is a comparatively new medium for literature, there are many characteristics of the story sequence that mirror the performance of reading a traditional book. The falling blossom between the scenes is an on-screen equivalent of turning a page, as a new scene appears when the blossom clears. The narrator asks questions as a parent or carer might do, or as the *Listen with Mother* and *Watch with Mother* radio and television programmes did for decades. If Jamie were sharing a traditional storybook with an adult, he might be expected to respond to a question, but in this instance he does not – here his response is embodied in the physical action of clicking the mouse over an icon, rather than in words. Jamie watches with keen interest when his favourite character, Igglepiggle, prepares his possessions ready for a journey. The artefacts that Igglepiggle chooses are familiar, such as his much-loved and ever-present blanket, and each carries the resonance of a story in its own right, making intertextual reference to stories that Jamie has encountered on other occasions. The narrated story is therefore being told at many different levels at once, evoking narratives from Jamie's prior experience and knowledge and enriching the simple tale as it unfolds.

Unlike a story book however, which usually begins at the first page and follows a predetermined sequence until the end of the book, this on-screen narrative experience offers Jamie a sequence of choices about what he views and in what order, and the links between the screens mean that each 'reading' can be different. Although his options are limited by the potentials of

EXAMPLE 1:   MULTIPLE MODES IN ON-SCREEN NARRATIVE

Jamie is four years old, and enjoys playing with a computer adaptation of the popular young children's television programme In the Night Garden. *This could be described as an online interpretation of a traditional illustrated story book, featuring a group of characters who live in a woodland glade. The characters are stylised, each a different shape and size. Their images are sometimes superimposed on film of a real wood, and sometimes set against drawn images of a wood. The wood has different seasons, and night and day. The characters 'talk' in an unintelligible language which has pitch and rhythm but no identifiable words. Each has its own unique characteristics, its own 'tune', and symbolic possessions that reflect its interests and pastimes (see www.inthenightgarden.co.uk).*

It is late in the afternoon. Jamie is tired after his preschool session and is now at home exploring the already familiar In the Night Garden *site alone while his mother is preparing tea. On the home page, Jamie can choose between the gently shifting icons of 'Sleep time activities' (represented by words and a flower icon), or 'Awake time activities' (represented by words and the outline of a character). He hesitates, and while he is choosing, a squeaky, highly decorated Zeppelin (Pinky Ponk) flies slowly across the top of the screen. He clicks on the 'Sleep time activities' icon for a story, and a new screen appears with four icons to choose from, set in an illustrated background: 'See the characters go to sleep', 'Bedtime story pdf', 'Animated storytime book' and 'Bedroom door sign printable'. He clicks on the latter, looks at the static image that appears, clicks to close it, then selects the icon for an animated story. The screen changes to an image of a carousel set in a cartoon wood. A 'Start' icon appears in red, and wavers in the bottom right corner. Jamie clicks on it. Petals fall and the screen changes again to a close up of the carousel, with a shifting icon 'Spin the gazebo'.*

Jamie's mother comes back into the room: 'Which story would you like?', she asks. Jamie glances up to his mother momentarily, clicks on the 'Stop' icon as the carousel shows his favourite character, Igglepiggle – a cuddly, shy, bouncy, blue teddy. Two more icons appear: 'Watch story' and 'Spin again'. Jamie hesitates and studies the screen. Silently, his mother points to 'Watch story', and he clicks on this icon.

The story takes a few seconds to load, then opens with an image of Igglepiggle sitting on the ground, with flowers spinning around him. Jamie's mother begins to read aloud the instruction that appears in a speech bubble 'Click on the spinning flowers to hear the characters', but Jamie clicks before she reaches the end of the sentence – he already knows its meaning. A narrator's voice begins to tell the story, and each narrated sentence appears in printed writing at the base of the image. Sounds and musical jingles accompany the narrator's voice, and the on-screen characters perform the actions that are being narrated. Once the narrator has finished, petals fall, filling the screen, then the screen clears and a new scene appears. Jamie clicks on each new screen to make the narration continue, telling a story of a little journey Igglepiggle makes with some of his possessions. Jamie's mother goes back to the kitchen to set the table while Jamie watches, listens to and navigates his way through the story, seeming particularly animated at times, and leaning forwards as though to touch some items as they appear on screen. The narrator sometimes asks questions: 'Whose house is that?'; 'Are they in or are they out?' Jamie does not respond, but is prompted by these questions to click on the symbol for the story to continue.

When the story is over after a few minutes, his mother, who has been able to hear the progress of the story from the adjoining room, calls Jamie through for his tea.

the program, Jamie is able to make independent choices in his selection, but accessing these options requires a relatively high level of literacy in reading and interpreting on-screen icons and layouts, and physical dexterity. Less confident/less experienced users might need the support of a more experienced peer or adult in order to negotiate their way through the myriad of hyperlink choices available without becoming frustrated.

This does not appear to be an issue for Jamie, though. When 'reading' these on-screen narratives, he uses a combination of modes, including whole-body movements to position himself in relation to the screen, hand and finger movements to manipulate the mouse and click on icons, and arm and hand movements when he moves to touch items on the screen. To access the narrative, Jamie must either understand the meaning of seemingly obtuse symbols, or 'read' the words (either by reading, which he does not seem to do, or by recognising word shapes and sequence). A non-familiar reader of *In the Night Garden* might wonder why a flower icon is used to symbolise a 'bedtime story', but for Jamie these are well-known icons which make intertextual reference to the television series. He occasionally (although rarely) talks to the on-screen characters, and imitates the characters' activities by moving his body in time with theirs. Similarly, the on-screen story exploits multiple modes; the narrative is built up through combinations of the characters' actions, their lilting if unintelligible 'talk', comic sounds, some jingles between scenes, voice-over narration, changes in screen layout and changes of colour and scene. At the age of four, Jamie is already adept in his manipulation of the keyboard and mouse and in his reading of the screen, so he is able to become immersed in the multi-sensory combinations of symbols, sounds, language, images and animations.

Literature and multimedia literacy practices

Example 1 highlights how literature is experienced as part of everyday, social practice: Jamie is exploring a narrative, mostly on his own, towards the end of the day while his mother is preparing a meal. Viewing literacy as social practice takes into account how literary experiences occur in different social and cultural contexts and for different purposes (Street, 1984; Barton and Hamilton, 1998). A common practice around literature that has occurred regularly in many children's lives is that of adults reading or telling 'bedtime stories'. Alongside their literary encounters at home, children also engage with literature in a variety of social practices in school, and their experiences of literature travel with them to and from home and school.

In Example 1, Jamie is enjoying a story as part of a relatively new social practice of using computers for leisure, in a technological world where increasingly the same digital tools are used for work and leisure. The purpose of the particular event described appears to be partly educational – he is learning about the themes of the narratives, such as friendship and planning, about how to access stories on a computer, and he is developing complex skills that are essential for computer literacy. At the same time, he is experiencing the stories for entertainment – the activity is enjoyable and is keeping him occupied, safe and happy for a short time while his mother cannot give him her full attention. The narratives of *In the Night Garden* are also present amongst his peer group in preschool, where his knowledge of the story lines and characters acts as a tool for social networking, allowing him to be included in other children's activities as they incorporate elements of the familiar narratives, songs, rhymes and characters in their make-believe play.

Multimedia exploration of traditional literature

Given that many children now have access to a range of media during their leisure time, and that there is strong evidence suggesting a decline in 'reading for pleasure' at home (Livingstone and Bovill, 1999), educational settings can be a prime site for children's literary encounters. More enlightened educators have begun to explore how new media and popular culture can be combined to engage children's motivation and enjoyment of literature. For example, one multi-ethnic East London primary school in England has developed a programme of work for 9-, 10- and 11-year-olds that explores traditional print literature through different media (Woodberry Down Primary School, 2007). Here, children have followed 5–6 week explorations of Beverley Naidoo's *The Other Side of Truth* (2000), and Benjamin Zephaniah's *Refugee Boy* (2002) as cross-curricular multimedia projects. These explorations include the creation of online blogs about the narratives and themes in the books, recording mock radio interviews with the characters, and exploring cultural references within the narratives that overlap with the children's out-of-school interests, such as making their own musical productions and recordings of Nigerian, Ethiopian and Eritrean music. By drawing on both new media and popular culture to explore literature, the educators have pulled the children's out-of-school interests and skills into the classroom, weaving together the disparate strands of their lives to promote their enjoyment of literature and to provide what Marsh (2005) refers to as a coherent and affirming framework for learning.

Less inventive yet contentious approaches have been adopted commercially to promote classical literature through children's online and DVD book resources, where literature already published in book form can be experienced on screen. Often, readers can select the font type and size, and can choose from options of accompanying sounds/music and/or a narrator to read the story aloud. Some of these representations lack the kinds of creative interpretations of literature through new media discussed above, and they make scant use of the affordances of the multiple modes potentially available. For example, a digital version of *Alice's Adventures in Wonderland* consists of the original, written text presented with some illustrations in the margins, and accompanied by short and rather tinny excerpts of classical music played as each chapter opens.[3] By contrast, the BBC television channel *CBeebies* has an online web resource of a range of new and classic children's stories, including a cartoon version of excerpts from Shakespeare's *A Midsummer Night's Dream* with sections of speech which reproduce the original sixteenth-century written text. In the *CBeebies* adaptation, the on-screen presentation is dominated by still and moving visual images, with the written text appearing at the base of the screen, changing colour as the narrating voices read the words.[4]

Illustrated and interactive children's literature

> Alice was beginning to get very tired of sitting on the bank, and of having nothing to do: once or twice she had peeped into the book her sister was reading, but it had no pictures or conversations in it, and where is the use of a book, thought Alice, without pictures or conversations?
>
> Carroll, 1865

Illustrated story books have long been and continue to be popular presentations of literature for young children, where authors and illustrators draw on the affordances of pictures to motivate children's interest, adding to or contradicting the written narrative, or portraying multiple narrative voices. In John Burningham's books about *Shirley* (Burningham, 1992; 1994), words and images tell the story of a typical family visit to the beach, or of Shirley taking a bath, while further images with no words show Shirley's imagined, exciting adventures, swashbuckling with pirates and riding bareback with knights in shining armour.

Publishers as early as the eighteenth century realised the interactive potential of illustrations by making flaps to lift and tabs to pull, creating the illusion of movement (see Reynolds, 2007). Once luxury items, 'pop-up' books enjoyed a resurgence in the late 1970s and 1980s, when interactive, illustrated stories became widely available and affordable, as in the case of Eric Hill's 'Spot the Dog' series, where children find and lift flaps to reveal characters mentioned in the words, requiring young readers' bodily involvement to animate aspects of the narrative. More recent creations include Robert Sabuda's pop-up *Alice in Wonderland* (2003) (see Plate 19).

In these examples of illustrated books, images dominate the page space, and are co-dependent with words for developing the sequential narrative. More recent forms of interactive illustrated books exploit the potentials of microchip technology, incorporating sounds and actions in the story-telling, as described in Example 2, where a 3-year-old boy is sharing an interactive Bob the Builder book with his mother at home. Bob is a familiar character he has encountered across diverse media in popular TV culture, in comics and in books.

In the brief exchange shown in Example 2, the mother conveys the relationship between the different elements in the task of 'reading' this book by using a combination of words, gaze and pointing gestures. The complexity of

EXAMPLE 2:   ENJOYING AN INTERACTIVE PICTURE BOOK

Michael is 3 years old and has just finished eating dinner with his family. He leaves the table to fetch an illustrated Bob the Builder *book and his Bob the Builder doll. He settles back at the table next to his mother and asks her if she will read the book with him. This is a precious time of day for both of them in a single-parent family, when the working mother dedicates time to her youngest child to play a game or read together while Michael's four older siblings do their homework. The book on its own can be read as a story about Bob's day at work, which includes number-counting, or it can become interactive through the doll. Here, 'reading' involves finding number symbols in the book and corresponding numbers on the doll, then pressing buttons that activate audio chips on the doll, Bob, who narrates a page of the story as each button is pressed.*

Michael presses a button at random on Bob, and Bob begins to speak. The mother watches her son, then turns her gaze from Michael, opens the first page in the book and glances back to Bob as she explains: 'Look, first you've got to find number 1: which is number 1?' Michael follows her gaze direction from the number 1 in the book, to Bob and back to the book, studies the book page and then points to the number 1 on Bob's shirt. His mother confirms his actions are correct: 'Right, number 1, this is number 1' and presses hard on the corresponding button on Bob. Bob speaks:'Hello. I'm Bob the Builder. I'm wearing my hard hat and tool belt full of tools ready for work'. Michael places his finger on the number 1 button, but before he has time to press it, his mother instructs him: 'That's it, now turn the page.' Michael hesitates, and the mother gently turns the page: 'Now you have to find that one', she says, as she points to the number 2 on the second page. Michael asserts his right to control the activity as he turns his gaze from the book to his mother:'Let me do it.' He studies the book for a few seconds, then turns his gaze to Bob. 'This one', his mother encourages, pointing towards a number 2 on Bob. Michael presses, there is the sound of a telephone ringing and Bob answers:'Hello, Bob the Builder's yard' he begins, and he goes on to name all the tools he will need to fix the job he is being called about. Michael's mother points to the illustrations of the items as they are named. When Bob has finished speaking, she says:'Right, now we find number 3.' They continue the reading, enjoying the book together as Michael becomes increasingly confident with the procedure of finding number symbols on the page and then on Bob, pressing them and listening to the next instalment of the story.

identifying and manipulating the different components in the task means that Michael needs varying degrees of support, sometimes to recognise numbers and relationships between components, sometimes to press the stiff buttons. The mother uses gaze to gauge the help he needs on a second-by-second basis, fine-tuning her responses to her interpretations of his needs, and respecting his plea for independence to complete the tasks himself. They continue the activity until they have finished the book, both evidently enjoying the 'reading'. Following his mother's talk, gaze direction and actions enables Michael to complete some aspects of the task, but the complexity of the many components means his enjoyment of this 'reading' is dependent on his cognitive ability to recognise and match number symbols, on his negotiation of the different artefacts of book and doll and on his physical dexterity at pressing the buttons. This reading therefore is highly interactive and has several purposes: for education closely matched to a school numeracy agenda; for pleasure, as a highly valued time for mother–son affection and closeness; for entertainment and the thrill of identifying with a familiar television story character and listening to an unfolding narrative told in the familiar voice of that character.

Interactive e-books and hyper-literature[5]

The comparatively sudden rise of computers, electronic games and the internet as part of everyday life for many children has opened up new digital environments for experimenting with literary representations and narrative structures. Traditionally, narratives for children have tended to respect established generic traditions, to follow a logical and often linear sequence that begins, has a middle and then ends. In the late 1970s and the 1980s, under the dual influence of postmodernist trends and the rise in popularity of video games, a publishing craze of adventure gamebooks began to change this trend and to reflect children's popular culture interests, merging the genres of literary fiction and games. Mostly written with boys in mind, gamebooks offered readers choices about which story lines to follow, sometimes by rolling a die to be directed to a numbered paragraph or page in an illustrated, printed text. In Rose Estes's gamebook series *Endless Quest* (1982—), the main character is referred to as 'you' in the text, but has a name, gender and personal history, creating narratives that resemble miniature novels with many different possible endings.

Digital media offer more varied potential for the ways in which stories are constructed, further stretching understandings of what narrative is. The traditional notion of a (single) creative literary author producing great works of literature dissolves when technology allows 'readers' to take on an authoring role by interacting with and redesigning texts, either working alone or collaboratively with other 'readers'. *In the Night Garden*, shown in Example 1, offers very young children an element of choice in the creation of their own short stories from a range of options about familiar events in the lives of their favourite characters, making each reading an active and intensely personal experience. Multi-user versions of story-making are also available on the popular *CBeebies* website, where young children can work together to select text to put in speech bubbles within linear cartoon stories. The site allows text to be inserted in any order, so readers are free to follow a logical order, or they can subvert the order, and create comical versions.

Sites such as these are simple digital adaptations of traditional print activities that allow readers to contribute to the creative act by selecting narrative options. For more original literary creations, software tools are readily available for authors to explore hypertext writing. *Storyspace*[6] allows multiple narrative threads to be developed, where 'participatory readers' can interact with a myriad of options in a random order. This level of interactivity often creates spiralling rather than sequential storylines, where the author can retain control of the story variables, with a finite number of potential story resolutions, but because the structure is non-linear and complex, each reading can be unique. *Storyspace* is being used in a variety of settings, including primary, secondary and tertiary classrooms in the USA, to help children explore new hypertext literary environments. Multi-user domains (MUDs)[7] permit multiple authors to contribute to story construction, offering large numbers of choices for readers, and a fundamentally different reading experience to traditional notions of solitary reading for pleasure.

A range of e-narratives for older children have begun to explore the multimodal affordances of words, images, movement and sounds to enhance the story experience. R.L. Stine's 'The Nightmare Room' series[8] is an online interpretation for young readers of a classic horror story. The site opens with a voice-over introduction by the author, against chilling, repetitive, muffled tones, reminiscent of entering a funfair ride on a ghost train:

> Welcome, I'm R. L. Stine
> You have left the world you know behind
> You are now entering a chilling shadow world
> Where you will live your darkest fears
> Go ahead and scream no-one can hear you and there's no escape[9]

With the spooky background sounds ever present, the reader can use the cursor to navigate around a series of photographic images, and can select whether to read the short story, explore other stories, capture images, link to a gaming site, download screen savers or, for educators, download a free writing toolkit to help children create their own digital stories. In this e-narrative, the story pages are offered in numerical sequence, but they can be accessed in any order (see Plate 18).

Hyper-media narratives make further use of the affordances of online media to offer narrative options through hyperlinks. Guyer and Joyce's *Lasting Image*,[10] set in post-Second-World-War Japan, presents images alongside words in a traditional, illustrated-story format, but with some parts of the illustrations blurred and some clear. By placing the cursor over the clear illustrations, the 'reader' can click on hyperlinks to different story elements, with further hyperlinks hidden behind the onscreen written narrative. Readers can therefore opt to follow a linear story by clicking on the forward arrows at the base of each screen, or they can choose a non-sequential order, accessing different storylines through the hyperlinks concealed in the images and words. While to some extent, this flexibility resembles the choices that have always been available to readers by flicking through a book or reading the end first, the multimodal experiencing of sounds, colour changes, images and words combine to create a fundamentally new kind of literary experience.

Interactive narratives such as these foreshadow the future development of cyberspace literature for children. However, the extent of the choices available is limited by the imagination and skill of authors and software writers, and on their perceptions of readers' likely capabilities. One imaginative and visually witty venture into the affordances of online modes that readers of this chapter might enjoy is Peter Howard's online *Sub-atomic and Particle Poetry*,[11] which considers the relationship between poetry and particle physics. Howard's combinations of written and spoken words, visual innuendo and movement are best viewed, rather than explained.

The future for children's literature?

Contemporary authors of children's literature are beginning to respond to the affordances of new writing technologies, but their full potential has not yet been wholly tapped into. Reynolds (2007) suggests this reticence to experiment with new narrative forms for children links not only to aesthetics, but also to current cultural perceptions of childhood as a time where literary conventions should be learnt, and where reassuring stability is needed to maintain social coherence.

This chapter has considered how the diversification and multimodal affordances of new media are influencing the kinds of literary texts that children experience, and are creating ways of engaging with texts that go beyond traditional understandings of what 'reading' and 'narrative' are. Inevitably, new themes are emerging in traditional, printed fiction that reflect multimedia popular culture and new forms of e-social networking. New media are also introducing new social contexts for literature, and are changing the social practices that young children experience around literary texts. Communication technologies are bringing about a convergence of what previously have been considered distinct social realms, such as home/school, entertainment/information, education/leisure. Rather than reading by torchlight under the covers alone in their room at night, many children in the twenty-first century are sitting in front of a webcam, talking online, constructing multi-authored narratives with their school friends, and in school are metamorphosing classic book stories in new media representations.

So what will the future hold for children's literature? Interactive digital texts offer the potential fundamentally to change the ways in which narratives are structured, blurring the boundaries between 'author' and 'reader', as 'readers' can be selective in the structuring of a range of narrative options, and MUDs open a new door for multiple authorship. Hyper-narratives can be non-linear, they need not be predominantly text- or graphics-based and can incorporate diverse modes and media. E-literature readers can choose which media they experience a story in; single or multiple users can have the power to control how a story unfolds. However, all such developments are limited by the imagination, skill and expectations of their creators, and many current digital narratives lack the kinds of integrity and aesthetic pleasure that older generations associate with reading. While at the beginning of the twenty-first century we are witnessing the development of radically new narrative potentials, we remain constrained by cultural expectations of what narrative is and by the affordances of technological invention. In the near future, hand-held, voice-receptive mobile devices may begin to tell us local stories through satellite navigation devices as we walk or drive around a city. It seems inevitable that future generations of readers born into a digitally negotiated twenty-first-century world will develop an intuitive understanding of digital narratives, and will begin to tell new stories in new ways that neither we nor the Oompa-Loompas can even begin to imagine.

Notes

1 Paper presented to UK Literacy Association Children's Literature and Creative Curriculum Conference, the British Library, London, www.ukla.org/site/conferences/event/childrens_literature_conference
2 www.literacytrust.org.uk/vitallink/readingforpleasure.html
3 www.antelope-books.com/childrens/info.html
4 www.bbc.co.uk/cbeebies/fullscreen/stories/dream.shtml
5 These terms overlap, but 'interactive e-books' here describes electronic texts that offer 'readers' choices in which linear storylines they pursue, whereas 'hyper-literature' refers to non-linear texts which can be constructed variously through series of hyperlinks.
6 www.eastgate.com/storyspace/index.html
7 'Multi-user domain' is a term used to describe multi-player computer games on the internet, where multiple players meet to play a game or construct an online narrative in a virtual world.
8 www.thenightmareroom.com
9 Each new line represents a new screen shot, with dark background, and white, ghostly lettering appearing as the narrator reads.
10 www.eastgate.com/LastingImage/Welcome.html
11 www.wordcircuits.com/gallery/subatomic/index.html

References

Barton, D. and Hamilton, S. 1998. *Local Literacies: Reading and Writing in One Community*. London, Routledge.
Burningham, J. 1992. (new edn) *Come away from the Water, Shirley*. London, Red Fox.
Burningham, J. 1994. (new edn) *Time to Get out of the Bath, Shirley*. London, Red Fox.
Carroll, L. 1865. *Alice's Adventures in Wonderland*. Macmillan.
Dahl, R. 1964. *Charlie and the Chocolate Factory*. New York, Alfred A. Knopf.
Halliday, M.A.K. 1978. *Language as Social Semiotic*. London, Arnold.
Hunt, P. 2000. 'Futures for Children's Literature: Evolution or Radical Break?', *Cambridge Journal of Education*, 30 (1): 111–19.
Kress, G. 2003. *Literacy in the New Media Age*. London, Routledge.
Kress, G., Jewitt, C., Ogborn J. and Tsatsarelis, C. 2001. *Multimodal Teaching and Learning: The Rhetorics of the Science Classroom*. London, Continuum Books.
Livingstone, S. and Bovill, M. 1999. *Young People, New Media*. London, London School of Economics.
Mackey, M. 1994. 'The New Basics: Learning to Read in a Multimedia World', *English in Education*, 28 (1), 9–19.
Manovich, L. 2002. *The Language of New Media*. Cambridge, MA: MIT Press.

Marsh, J. 2005. 'Ritual, Performance and Identity Construction: Young Children's Engagement with Popular Cultural and Media Texts', in J. Marsh (ed.) *Popular Culture, New Media and Digital Literacy in Early Childhood*. London, Routledge/Falmer: 28–50.

Naidoo, B. 2000. *The Other Side of Truth*. London, Puffin/Penguin.

Sabuda, R. 2003. *Alice in Wonderland: Pop-up Book*. New York, Simon & Schuster.

Street, B.V. 1984. *Literacy in Theory and Practice*. Cambridge, Cambridge University Press.

Reynolds, K. 2007. *Radical Children's Literature: Future Visions and Aesthetic Transformations in Juvenile Fiction*. Basingstoke, Palgrave Macmillan.

Woodberry Down Primary School. 2007 www.woodberrydown.moonfruit.com/#/tosothome/4518214001, accessed 3 July 2008.

Zephaniah, B. 2002. *Refugee Boy*. London, Bloomsbury.

Cross-reading and Crossover Books
Rachel Falconer

With the phenomenal success of J. K. Rowling's *Harry Potter* septology, first published between 1997 and 2007, children's literature has begun to attract an adult readership on a mass scale never witnessed before in the UK. In recent years, the term 'crossover literature' has emerged as a way of referring to this category of fiction, aimed at a primary audience of child readers, but also engaging substantial numbers of adult readers. 'Crossover' can, of course, flow in more than one direction. Child readers have always read and still do read adult literature, in adaptations, abridgements, or simply straight off the 'adult' shelf. And indeed, many other borders are routinely crossed in one's choice of reading, borders of gender, class, race, nation, ethnicity, religion, and so on. As Jennifer Donnelly says, books are not gated communities.[1] But the term 'crossover literature' has been used over the last decade by publishers and reviewers to refer to the specific, recent phenomenon of large numbers of adults reading children's literature.

Historical roots

Although the scale of cross-reading in the present day is unprecedented, there is, nevertheless, a long and rich tradition of adult readers engaging with children's literature. Many classic children's authors, for example, J.M. Barrie, Kenneth Grahame, Edward Lear and Beatrix Potter, to name but a few, have long attracted a substantial adult readership. Robert Louis Stevenson's *Treasure Island* (1883) was written as entertainment for his twelve-year-old stepson, in the genre of 'an adventure story for boys.'[2] When it was published as a novel, however, it proved to be an instant success with adult reviewers and general readers (Cordingley xiii). Rider Haggard's *King*

Solomon's Mines (1885), one of the many Victorian adventure novels now being re-published in crossover editions, was originally dedicated 'to all the big and little boys who read it.'[3] Lewis Carroll's *Alice's Adventures in Wonderland* (1865) was famously written for a real child, Alice Liddell, but some of the earliest reviewers of *Alice's Adventures* recognised its crossover appeal. In *The London Review* in 1865, it was praised as 'a delightful book for children – or, for the matter of that, for grown-up people, provided they have wisdom and sympathy enough to enjoy a piece of downright hearty drollery and fanciful humour.'[4] In the United States, Louisa May Alcott wrote *Little Women* as a 'story for girls,' at the suggestion of an editor, Thomas Niles, who had correctly identified a gap in the market for this age and gender of reader.[5] By 1895, *Little Women* had become a national institution, read not only by young girls but by many adults, both male and female (Alderson, xxi).

Closer to our own era, there have been children's books which achieved cult status amongst adult readers. Tolkien's *The Lord of the Rings* (1954–55) began in the 1940s as a sequel to *The Hobbit* (1937), which was written for young readers. And *The Lord of the Rings* itself gave rise to a new wave of high fantasy writing, which from its inception was a crossover genre. Richard Adams's *Watership Down* (1972) also originated from stories told to children, but grew into a richly allusive epic work, read also by adults. The novel is said to have influenced George Lucas's creation of *Star Wars*, a crossover film that has had at least as much influence on popular Western culture as Rowling's *Harry Potter* has had more recently.[6] And many realist and dystopian novels, such as George Orwell's *Animal Farm* (1945) and J.D. Salinger's *The Catcher in the Rye* (1951), have been read by adults as well as children for decades, something which calls into question the common assumption that only fantasy can easily cross age groups.

Difficulties of defining 'crossover' as a literary genre

Despite this rich historical precedence, I would maintain that 'crossover' became recognised as a distinct category of fiction only very recently. And even now, to identify crossover fiction as a 'genre' is anomalous (in the same way that the label 'children's literature' is anomalous), in that it defines a set of books by its readership rather than by any internal formal characteristics. When one considers the diversity of books that have crossed from child to adult readers, it is impossible to identify a stable set of themes, styles or modes of address shared by all these works. Maria Nikolajeva suggests that contemporary children's fiction appeals to adult readers because it is more sophisticated than classic children's fiction.[7] But in most cases, the reverse seems to be true. Often, adult readers would appear to be turning to children's fiction to escape what Pullman describes as 'the tricksiness and games-playing of modern and post-modern literary fiction.'[8] This rejection of postmodern narrative may in part explain the penchant for re-reading children's classics, such as Lewis's *The Chronicles of Narnia*, re-issued in new, edgy-looking dust-jackets. Moreover, while many writers and publishers have been keen to claim that a crossover book is one that has a 'universal' appeal, I would argue that many crossover readers are conscious of crossing a boundary, and reading books that are not explicitly aimed at their age group. Some children's books acquire an aura of universality over time, but others remain very much addressed to a younger audience, and yet adult readers take pleasure in these fictions too.

Since there is no possibility of defining crossover literature as a genre according to what it *is*, formally, it seems to me more productive to define crossover by what it *does*. It appeals to a dual-aged readership, as we have already noted; and in my view, a text can only be described as a 'crossover' if this fact is demonstrably proven in the history of its reception. But from here, one can begin to ask the more interesting and specific questions: in what ways does it cross over? What does the text do to a reader when it 'crosses over' that is distinct from other text-reader relationships? What does the reader do to the text when s/he 'crosses over'? If the crossover text is contemporary, and new to the adult reader, is memory of other childhood reading nevertheless a component in the reader's cross-reading experience? Do adults seek comfort and security in cross-reading children's literature? Or, conversely, do adults read children's literature to expose themselves to new risks?

Engaging with some children's fiction, whether familiar or new, presents challenges to an adult's core sense of identity, founded on memories of childhood. And since much children's fiction sets up a child's world in opposition to an adult's, for an adult to enter that world requires a willingness to question his or her own entrenched values. To invoke the two categories of reading proposed by Victor Nell, some cross-reading might dull one's consciousness of the world, while other cross-reading might increase consciousness of the world, and awareness of one's reading self.[9] The latter form of cross-reading, to increase self-awareness, is well illustrated by Francis Spufford's memoir, *The Child That Books Built*.[10] In re-reading his favourite books from childhood, Spufford discovers the threads leading to his present identity, since 'the stories that mean most to us join the process by which we come to be securely our own' (Spufford, 21). Retrospectively, Spufford comes to realise how they had fused powerfully 'with the accelerated coming-to-be we do in childhood,' exerting a shaping force over his future life (Spufford, 9).

The questions raised above, and those explored in Spufford's memoir, touch on just some of the issues that might be explored in relation to specific crossover texts. From an academic standpoint, one of the most useful things that crossover fiction does is to call into question many of the traditional definitions of children's literature, which often consist of prescribing what the latter should or should not exclude.[11] More generally, engaging with such fiction can increase an adult reader's awareness of the differences between child- and adulthood as distinct states of being and becoming. Raising such questions, we can become more aware of the ways in which our culture is developing and moving towards new concepts of self, of childhood, of aging and dying.

The question of dual address

If crossover literature has to have a dual audience to be classed as such, perhaps it can also be identified formally by its use of the dual address? In *The Narrator's Voice*, Barbara Wall usefully distinguishes three modes of address in children's fiction: 'single address' to a child reader alone; 'double address' to a child and to an adult reading 'over the child's head'; and, finally but (in her view) rarely, 'dual address' to child and adult as equal, but distinctly different readers.[12] Drawing on these distinctions, one might argue that in recent years, the instances of 'dual-address' in children's fiction had risen sharply, which would explain why so many more adult readers are finding themselves engaged by children's books (though one would still have to explain why dual address had become so widespread). Working from Wall's thesis, a critic might suggest that a novel like Pullman's *Northern Lights* was dual addressed, with a simple level of adventure plot aimed at child readers, and a morally challenging level for older readers where, for example, religious faith could be questioned and criticised. But judging from the reviews posted by children on Internet discussion boards, young readers are equally if not more interested than adults in the book's questioning of religion and other issues, such as the ethics of scientific discovery and exploitation of the natural world.[13] There may be differences between child and adult responses to the novel, but these are not as easy to codify into different levels of address as we might suppose.

More fundamentally, the concept of dual address does not even begin to account for our changing attitudes to age and identity, which have become extremely fluid and complex in the twenty-first century. What exactly does it mean to read 'as a child' or 'as an adult'? How could these different experiences ever be distinctly separated, since one's reading identity cannot be frozen into distinct units of time? As David Rudd writes of children's literature, 'there is always difference [from adult literature], but it is never complete; it is always in process, for notions of children change across time, gender, race and class. Also, each child changes over time, playing at adult-hood in various guises.'[14] So too does an adult change over time, playing at, and with, and against all the phases of childhood and adolescence. To con-clude on the question of definition, then, if there is any formally identifiable feature of this 'genre' of literature, it must be that its boundaries are essen-tially unfixed. Not only are the texts themselves often generically hybrid, but readers are hybridising different readerly identities when they 'cross over' to reading a book that was intended, at least ostensibly, for someone other and elsewhere. Cross-reading is another of the ways in which we may become, in Kristeva's phrase, 'strangers to ourselves.'[15]

Watersheds in the development of crossover fiction

Undoubtedly, what kick-started the crossover phenomenon of the millen-nial decade was the unforeseen popularity of J.K. Rowling's *Harry Potter* series amongst adult readers. In Britain, the seven novels were published by Bloomsbury, as children's books, but recognising how many adults had enjoyed *Harry Potter*, Bloomsbury took the unprecedented step of issuing the first 'adult edition,' that is, the same text, but with a different dust-jacket, in 1998. This experiment proved so popular that by 2004, child and adult editions of subsequent volumes were being released simultaneously. It has been much debated whether the success of *Harry Potter* had a stimulat-ing effect on the children's publishing industry or the reverse.[16] The answer is probably mixed, but what is certain is that the nature of the industry changed during this period, with publishers offering huge advances to a few, potentially best-selling authors.

Despite Rowling's unlooked-for success in the late 1990s, however, it was not until the new millennium that the crossover novel received national, crit-ical recognition as a legitimate and serious genre of literary fiction. In 2001, Philip Pullman's *The Amber Spyglass* won the Children's Book category of the Whitbread (now Costa) Award, then went on to win the overall prize of Book of the Year. This feat was repeated in 2003, but with a crossover book that was entered in the 'Novel' category (rather than Children's Book) category: this was Mark Haddon's *The Curious Incident of the Dog in the Night-time*. Not only was Haddon's novel, about a boy with Asperger's Syndrome, *not* a work of fantasy; it had also been published, from the first, in dual editions, by a children's publisher (David Fickling) and an acclaimed publisher of adult literary fiction (Faber). 2003 might be described as cross-over's *annus mirabilis*, since this was also the year that the Carnegie Medal judges chose to showcase 'writing that is as enjoyable for adults as it is for children and young people,' selecting Jennifer Donnelly's *A Gathering Light* as exemplary of this dual-aged appeal.[17] As they moved up the ranks culturally, crossover novels also gained ground on the popular front by being featured on national television book clubs, such as the BBC's 'Page Turners' and Channel 4's 'Richard and Judy Book Club'. In addition, the BBC ran a TV campaign in 2003, entitled 'The Big Read' which invited viewers to cast votes for the 'nation's best-loved book.' Unsurprisingly, J.R.R. Tolkien's *The Lord of the Rings* won, but more revealing was that, of the top 100 books listed, over half could be described as children's and young adult fiction, including a mixture of classic and contemporary texts.

Crossover literature in context

The growth of crossover audiences, in both fiction and film industries, reflected a more pervasive hybridisation of child and adult cultures taking place across many Western countries over the millennial decade. In Britain, there was a major shift of political climate from Thatcherite conservatism to youth-conscious New Labour. The promotion of youth culture under Tony Blair's reign as Prime Minister can have done nothing to damage the popularity of children's authors. And beyond the politics, a cult of 'the inner child' or the 'kiddult' was permeating adult cultural life on many levels in the late 1990s. First coined by Peter Martin in 1985, the term 'kidult' or 'kiddult' was applied to any adult who retained an active interest in children's culture generally, though not necessarily children's literature.[18] Writing in *The Observer* in 2000, Ben Summerskill described the typical kiddult as being a single, professional male in his thirties; 'he wears Caterpillar boots and Levis. He rides a motor scooter, with a pavement model for warm weather. When he gets home, he watches *It's a Knockout* before turning on his Sony PlayStation.'[19] The oddness of this cultural trend is perhaps best exemplified by Mandy Patinkin's CD, *Kidults*, released in 2001, which bizarrely mixed children's Broadway musical songs with sentimental songs about childhood, for adult listeners.

Reasons for this marked trend towards youth culture, and with it the expansion of children's fiction into mainstream adult markets, must be understood in the broader context of Western developments in science, technology and economics. Scientists are much more able to intervene in the processes of reproduction and aging than they have been in previous generations. Prolonged youth has become an achievable aspiration for the wealthy, given advances in cosmetic surgery, and late parenthood has also become more feasible, due to advances in fertility treatment for older women.

In an article in *The Economist*, entitled 'Bright Young Things,' Chris Anderson argues that rapidly evolving technology is the 'defining event' of the current generation of young people.[20] The Internet, mobile phones and personal stereo systems have transformed the lives of teenagers in Western, developed nations, and left some adults struggling to keep pace with the waves of technological change. Anderson argues that since the restructurings of Western business corporations in the 1980–90s, the work-place has been tailored for young or 'youthful' employees who are rewarded not, as previously, for length of service but for meeting short-term goals and challenges (Anderson 5). The value that society, particularly in the late nineties and early 2000s placed on youth and youth culture, on so-called 'childliness' with the emphasis on creativity and adapatability, can be explained, as part of a general shift from a 'hard' to a 'soft' capitalist ideology. Thus Costea, Crump and Holm argue that in the decade before 1990, a Protestant work ethic of 'salvation through self-abnegation' gave way to a new, 'soft' capitalist ethic of 'self-work'.[21] In soft capitalist corporations, the employee moves fluidly between work and leisure, using both as arenas in which to cultivate and express an 'authentic self'.

The emergence of children's literature into the cultural mainstream must be assessed in the light of these broader socio-economic changes, not all of which have necessarily been positive. But contemporary children's and young adult fiction does not merely reflect this emergent, soft capitalist ethic of self-discovery. Indeed it is in children's and crossover fiction – particularly fiction which addresses the theme of adolescent crossing from childhood to adulthood, that we can discover the most careful and sustained scrutiny of these new capitalist myths of limitless youth and self-expression.

Adult themes for young readers

Once one takes into account this broader shift in cultural attitudes to what is perceived as the virtues of 'childliness' *per se*, it is hardly surprising to find crossover occurring across a broad range of literary genres, both highbrow and popular, and from all the age ranges of children's fiction, from picture books to young adult and teen fiction. While crossover fantasy and science fiction continue to dominate the best-seller lists, there are also many examples of historical romance and adventure, reworked fairy tales, gothic mystery, mythic primitivism and urban realism crossing from child to adult audiences. More notably, many hybrid works, incorporating two or more traditional genres, drew the attention of adult readers. For example, Malorie Blackman's *Noughts and Crosses*, hybridizing realism and dystopia, was successfully adapted for national theatre, and attracted a mass adult audience. Realist novels such as Lionel Shriver's *We Need to Talk About Kevin* not only attracted young adult readers, but also became the focal points for discussion about poverty, child violence and other issues on national radio, newspapers and television.

Genres combining text and graphics, such as picture books, cartoons (notably Matt Groening's *The Simpsons* and Nick Park's *Wallace and Gromit*), graphic novels and children's or 'family' films, have a particularly strong following amongst adult audiences.[22] Graphic novels, such as *Ghostworld* and *From Hell*, have been reinvented as feature films, and iconic American 1950s comic book heroes, such as Batman and Superman, are re-emerging as darker, more morally ambivalent protagonists in mainstream, Hollywood films. Even films ostensibly pitched at much younger audiences, such as *Shrek* and *Monsters, Inc.*, gained critical recognition amongst adult viewers, and beat mainstream adult films to win Oscars and Baftas.

The crossover appeal of contemporary picture books is a particularly interesting case, since these books have traditionally been marketed for the youngest readerships. Some picture books deal with surprisingly weighty themes and issues, such as war or genocide.[23] Judith Kerr's *The Tiger Who Came to Tea* (1968) touches obliquely on the darker material of her autobiographical novel about Nazism, *When Hitler Stole Pink Rabbit* (1971). And Raymond Briggs's *The Tin-Pot Foreign General and the Old Iron Woman* (1984) satirizes Margaret Thatcher's role in the Falklands War. Such crossover picture books have garnered critical praise from adult readers, in part due to the subtlety of their presentation of serious, dark content in a lighter, pictorial frame.

Children's books such as these may be described as crossover in the sense that their thematic content stretches the boundaries of what has been considered by the previous generation to be appropriate reading matter for young readers. Fiction for teenagers, as well as for readers aged eight to twelve, now freely treats of subjects such as underage sex, drug abuse, depression, mental illness, torture and genocide. This fiction still causes controversy amongst adult critics and reviewers, as it is feared that this over-sophisticated material will contribute to the 'tweenager' phenomenon (very young children acting like teenagers). The prolific author Jacqueline Wilson, who has been dubbed 'the voice of the "tweenage" generation', writes ever more explicitly about divorce, abandonment and mental disorders. Wilson's novels did not, however (at least until recently), appeal to adult readers; these were books with crossover *content*, that 'children like, but that makes adults uncomfortable', as one reviewer put it.[24] But such responses may be due to adults' lack of awareness about the changing conditions of contemporary childhood. In the twenty-first century, through television, advertising and the Internet, children from a very young age have access to a much wider range of adult-oriented material than would have been available to earlier generations. Many Western children are feeling the pressure of growing up very quickly as they become more thoroughly absorbed into the networked global economy than ever before.

For 'tweenagers' there are positive and negative aspects to participating in the economy on a par with adults. On the one hand, children's voices are more often heard alongside adults' in public debates about politics, education and the environment. And they are also increasingly taking leading roles in the arts, from acting to writing and directing their own work. Christopher Paolini became a best-selling *New York Times* author by the age of nineteen, first with *Eragon* and then later books in the *Inheritance* fantasy cycle. Paolini provides a success story of a teenager engaging positively in a global, kiddult-oriented economy. But there are negative sides to this economy that must also be considered. There is evidence to suggest that children and young adults are more, and more frequently, exposed to commercial interests than young people of any previous generation. According to a British Government report, also endorsed by the Archbishop of Canterbury, the child-oriented market in the UK was said to be worth about £30 billion in the early 2000s.[25] In 2001, a BBC documentary, 'Little Women: A Day In The Life Of A Tweenager,' documented the lives of a group of 7 to 12 year old girls from southern England who shopped at Harrods, watched wrestling on Sky Sports, discussed rape, and dressed like their favourite pop idols. The 'Commercialization' report, quoting the National Consumer Council, noted that many children, aged ten or younger, had 'internalised 300 to 400 brands – perhaps twenty times the number of birds in the wild that they could name' (6), and concluded that British children were among the most materialistic in the world, ahead of American children. Jack Zipes too argues that children are dangerously exposed to financial exploitation, and that we are 'turning [children] into commodities'.[26]

The transition to adulthood is particularly stressful for contemporary teenagers, according to diverse research studies. John Coleman, Director of the Trust for the Study of Adolescence, believes that 'the transition to adulthood in Western societies has become problematic during the last few decades'.[27] In his view, getting into the labour market is much more difficult now than it was during the latter half of the twentieth century (Coleman 59). Government reports have also shown that young people, especially those growing up in 'high deprivation' areas, are increasingly involved in crime, either as victims or offenders. The film *Kidulthood* (where in a rare usage, 'kidult' is applied to teenagers) depicts the young adult experience of violence on city estates. As this film (and its sequel, *Adulthood*) illustrates, the actual, lived experience of adolescence in the twenty-first century may be nothing like the beautiful youth to which middle-aged kiddults so eagerly aspire.

In an era in which many young people grow up surrounded by violence and crime, it is important that the books and films they read and watch should address the reality of their lives. Since these books implicitly challenge dominant cultural myths of the innocence of childhood, they are likely to continue to provoke controversy amongst adult readers. But social realist fiction aimed at a primary audience of young adult readers may also speak powerfully to adults for the very reason that it exposes these myths as anachronistic. Melvin Burgess's *Junk* is an example of one such text. Written empathetically from a number of different perspectives, ranging from young teenager to middle-aged adult, the novel explores the devastating effects of heroin addiction on a young couple. *Junk* neither glamorises nor demonises drug addiction; rather, it compassionately shows the aspiration, longing, and grief that can lead to addiction of different types, and at any age.

Childish books for adult readers

It is worth remembering that the crossover phenomenon is multi-faceted, and needs to be considered from a range of different angles. The psychic appeal of violent fantasy, mediated through an adolescent's viewpoint, cannot explain why lighter works for younger children, such as Lemony Snicket's *A Series of Unfortunate Events*, are also becoming best-sellers amongst adult readers, and often being adapted into feature films. Ironically, while young adult fiction causes public controversy for being 'too mature' for its readers, adult readers are also roundly criticised for being 'infantalised', engaging with books that are 'too immature' for their age.[28] Typical of the hostile media response to adults reading young children's fiction was David Aaronovitch's attack on 'kiddults' in *The Independent*: 'I don't like to see grown-ups reading Harry Potter books when they haven't managed Nabokov, and men on shiny scooters should be walking or cycling.'[29]

In one sense, these criticisms appear to be justified. Many adults *are* acting more like children, just as more children are acting like adults, in the twenty-first century. The divisions between age groups are becoming increasingly porous and flexible, and the crossover of fiction across previously well-defined boundaries is an important sign of this general cultural shift in the West. In contrast to previous concepts of a series of distinct stages of biological development, many psychologists today regard aging as a more complex, fluid and cyclical series of movements.[30] The defining feature of contemporary coming of age would appear to be that it can happen at any age of life because age, like gender, is being treated as a conscious ideological construction rather than a biological fact.

Many of the children's novels that have crossed to adult readerships reflect this increasingly fluid sense of age and maturity. Thus many child protagonists are represented as being of uncertain mental or virtual age. For example, in Philip Pullman's *His Dark Materials* trilogy, Lyra and Will are twelve, biologically speaking, but they can act on occasion like mature adults. When Will first meets Lyra, he notices that 'her expression was a mixture of the very young – and a kind of deep sad wariness' (*The Subtle Knife*, 25). In Garth Nix's *Sabriel*, the eponymous heroine tells an adult soldier, 'I am only eighteen years old on the outside ... But I first walked in Death when I was twelve ... I don't feel young any more' (Sabriel 46). And these novels go beyond merely reflecting the uncertainties of aging in contemporary culture. They also question and challenge the idea of structureless psychic development, and define new boundaries for the present age. Thus it becomes Sabriel's task to restore the crumbling wall that is meant to separate the worlds of the dead and the living. And Lyra and Will have to counteract ecological disasters caused by too much traffic between worlds (Cittàgazze in *The Subtle Knife*, and Lyra and Will's own worlds, in *The Amber Spyglass*). Together they work to repair this damage, and they also restore the 'natural' aging process, whereby children lose their innocence and acquire adult experience. Adult readers engaging with such fiction are not so much becoming 'infantilised', then, as being made more keenly aware, as well as critical, of the sliding temporalities involved in growing up, and down, in Western culture today.

By simply dismissing adult reading of children's books as 'infantilising', cultural critics have also failed to recognise the broader historical and socio-economic significance of this crossover phenomenon. Within the foreshortened time-spaces of contemporary Western societies, the qualities of lightness and agility, heretofore associated with childhood, have come to be greatly valued in the adult world.[31] At the same time, while flexible capitalism puts a premium on lightness and mobility, in other respects, these are the very qualities which capitalism itself tends to inhibit. Increasingly, we live in crowded, noisy, hectic places, and the Internet, while liberating, can also contribute to a massive sense of information-overload. In *Six Memos for the Next Millennium*, Calvino argues that reading certain kinds of literature can develop mental qualities or capabilities that are essential to combating the 'weight, inertia and opacity' of contemporary life. The qualities he enumerated were lightness, quickness, exactitude, visibility, multiplicity and consistency, and these qualities, he argues, can be strengthened and sharpened by reading certain kinds of narrative (Calvino 7). Children's literature has a long history of celebrating lightness and mental agility, as Jerry Griswold's study, *Feeling Like a Kid*, demonstrates.[32] Peter Pan, Mary Poppins, Superman, and the flying boy-wizard, Harry Potter himself, are examples he cites of protagonists in children's literature who overcome evil by out-flying or out-floating it (Griswold 75–102). But for Griswold, as for Calvino, 'lightness' does not imply 'light-weight'. Rather, it is a serious, agonistic force to be deployed against a range of petrifying or dispiriting forces that may inhibit a child or adult's development. If Western culture places a premium on lightness, yet also paradoxically inhibits the exercise of mental agility, imagination and flexibility, then there may indeed be a pressing social and psychological need for adults, especially, to engage with the kind of literature that preserves and develops these habits of mind.

J.K. Rowling's skill in producing a buoyant, effervescent narrative reflects, in part, the influences of a postmodern society that values playfulness, flexibility and spontaneous creativity. Her *Harry Potter* septology is both a product of this contemporary preference for lightness, and a revisionary response to it. The idea of life as magic metamorphoses, a marketing ideal which is often reproduced uncritically in the first three *Harry Potter* books, eventually yields to a different vision later in the series. This is not to imply that the early books are false in their reflection of contemporary life; no less than Rowling's young magicians', our 'real' lives are saturated with the promise of effortless transformations. Indeed it is less a sense of magic possibility than the weight of cultural expectation which now presses us to overhaul our existing identities (bodies, wardrobes, houses, gardens, souls, Internet connections, etc.). In this sense, the early *Potter* books are simply reflecting the pressure to metamorphose that consumers feel in a capitalist culture. But the lightness celebrated in the first three books of the *Harry Potter* series is tested against progressively more serious opponents and counter-themes; and what emerges in the last four books is an overwhelming emphasis on the importance of friendship, social connectivity, and humanistic forms of redemption to set against the fear of death. Considering the range of magic fantasies being published for younger children, and read by adults, one might argue more generally that these novels often strive to represent deeper and more meaningful forms of metamorphosis than are expressed in the illusion-and-bang! universe of advertising.

Conclusion

By the twenty-first century, children's literature had come to be accepted by a great many adult readers in Britain as fiction that engaged seriously with the major issues of our time: the war of religions, the conflicting demands of the individual and of society, the relativity of good and evil, the limits of natural resources, and the ethical dilemmas posed by advancements in science and technology. Philip Pullman, one of the most outspoken apologists for children's literature in recent years, has polemically declared that 'there are some themes, some subjects, too large for adult fiction; they can only be dealt with adequately in a children's book'.[33] If this is true, or more importantly, if large numbers of adult readers are coming to share this view, then crossover fiction looks likely to expand exponentially in the years to come. No doubt cross-reading will continue to provoke public debate, on the one hand raising concerns over the exposure of young children to adult culture, and on the other hand, prompting criticism of adults being 'dumbed down' by engagement in youth culture.

But the tendency to provoke cultural debate is one of crossover literature's most significant and positive attributes. Through such debates, we will come to examine and reflect on the changing attitudes to childhood, adulthood, transition and development, in the beginning of the twenty-first century.

Notes and references

1 J. Donnelly, 'Carnegie Winner Offers Message for Teens', *The Bookseller* (16 July 2004), p. 30.
2 David Cordingly, 'Introduction', *Treasure Island* (New York: The Modern Library, 2001), p. xii.
3 F.J. Harvey Darton and Brian Alderson, *Children's Books in England: Five Centuries of Social Life* (London: British Library & Oak Knoll Press, 1999, 3rd edition), p. 296.
4 Lewis Carroll, *Alice's Adventures in Wonderland*, ed. Richard Kelly (Letchworth, Hertfordshire: Broadview Press, 2000), p. 275.
5 Valerie Alderson, Introduction, Louisa May Alcott, *Little Women* (Oxford: Oxford University Press, 1994), pp. vii–viii.
6 S.F. Said, 'The Godfather of Harry Potter', *Daily Telegraph* (15 October 2002).
7 Maria Nikolajeva, *Children's Literature Comes of Age: Toward a New Aesthetic* (London: Garland Publishing, 1996).
8 Philip Pullman, 'Writing Fantasy Realistically', Sea of Faith National Conference (2002). See: http://sofn.org.uk/conferences/pullman2002.html, accessed 1 December 2007.
9 Victor Nell, *Lost in a Book: The Psychology of Reading for Pleasure* (New Haven, NJ: Yale University Press, 1988), p. 231.
10 Francis Spufford, *The Child That Books Built* (London: Faber & Faber, 2002).
11 See, for example, Myles McDowell, 'Fiction for Children and Adults: Some Essential Differences', in *Writers, Critics and Children*, ed. Geoff Fox and Graham Hammond (London: Heinemann Educational, 1976).
12 Barbara Wall, *The Narrator's Voice: the Dilemma of Children's Fiction* (Basingstoke: Macmillan, 1991), pp. 20–36.
13 See for example http://bridgetothestars.net/forum/, accessed 7 November 2007.
14 David Rudd, 'Shirley, the Bathwater, and Definitions of Children's Literature', *Papers: Explorations into Children's Literature* 5: 2–3 (1994), pp. 88–103 (93).
15 Julia Kristeva, *Strangers to Ourselves*, trans. Leon S. Roudiez (London: Harvester Wheatsheaf, 1991).

16 See, for example, Simon Taylor, ed., *Keynote Market Assessment Children's Publishing* (Hampton, 2005).

17 Brabazon, press release, quoted on the Carnegie Greenway Medal website. http://www.cilip. org.uk/aboutcilip/newsandpressreleases/archive2004/news040430.htm, accessed 19 October 2007.

18 Peter Martin, 'Coming Soon: TV's New Boy Network', *New York Times* (11 August 1985). See: http://www.nationmaster.com/encyclopedia/Kidult, accessed 10 Nov 2008.

19 Ben Summerskill, 'Playtime as Kidults Grow Up at Last', *Observer* (23 July 2000), p. 20.

20 Chris Anderson, 'A Survey of the Young: Bright Young Things', *Economist* (23 December 2000), p. 7.

21 Bogdan Costea, Norman Crump and John Holm, 'Dionysus at Work? The Ethos of Play and the Ethos of Management', *Culture and Organization* 11:2 (June 2005): 139–51 (140).

22 On the history of children's film, see Ian Wojcik-Andrews, *Children's Films: History, Ideology, Pedagogy, Theory* (London: Garland, 2002). On recent changes in children's television programming in Britain, see D. Buckingham, H. Davies, K. Jones and P. Kelley, 'Public Service Goes to Market: British Children's Television in Transition' (London: Institute of Education, 1998). See http://www.ccsonline.org.uk/mediacentre/Research_projects/cmc, accessed 11 November 2002.

23 See Barbara Harrison, 'How Like Wolves', in *Children's Literature* 15 (1987): 67–90.

24 *Ibid.*

25 The Commercialisation of Childhood', Compass Report, 2006, endorsed by Archbishop Rowan Williams. Available at www.compassonline.org.uk/publications, accessed 7 July 2007.

26 Jack Zipes, *Sticks and Stones: the Troublesome Success of Children's Literature from Slovenly Peter to Harry Potter* (London: Routledge, 2002), p. xi.

27 John Coleman, 'Into Adulthood', in *The Seven Ages of Life*, pp. 57–80 (76).

28 See Steven Barfield, 'Of Young Magicians and Growing Up: J.K. Rowling, Her Critics, and the "Cultural Infantilism" Debate', in Cynthia Whitney Hallett, ed., *Scholarly Studies in Harry Potter* (Lampeter: Edwin Mellen Press, 2005), pp. 175–98.

29 David Aaronovitch, 'What's So Smart about Being Childish?' *Independent* (6 June 2001).

30 See, for example, Klaus Riegel, 'Adult Life Crises: A Dialectical Interpretation of Development', in *Life-Span Developmental Psychology: Normative Life Crises*, ed. Nancy Datan and Leon H. Gindberg (New York: Academic Press, 1975), p. 76.

31 See Ursula Heise, *Chronoschisms: Time, Narrative and Postmodernism* (Cambridge: Cambridge University Press, 1997), p. 6.

32 Jerry Griswold, *Feeling Like a Kid: Childhood and Children's Literature* (Baltimore: Johns Hopkins University Press, 2006).

33 Philip Pullman, Carnegie Medal speech (1996), quoted by Angelique Chrisafis, 'Fiction Becoming Trivial and Worthless, Says Top Author,' *Guardian* (12 August 2002).

Index

Note: Definite and indefinite articles are ignored in the alphabetical sequence, but are not inverted. For example, *The Bad Boys' Paper* is filed under 'B'. Page numbers in italic refer to illustrations.